Śrī Prema-sampuṭa

The Treasure Chest of Pure, Transcendental Love

For further information, free download of titles, and more,
please visit:
www.purebhakti.com

śrī śrī guru-gaurāṅgau jayataḥ

Śrīla Viśvanātha Cakravartī Ṭhākura's

Śrī Prema-sampuṭa

The Treasure Chest of Pure, Transcendental Love

translated from the Hindi edition of

Śrī Śrīmad Bhaktivedānta Nārāyaṇa Gosvāmī Mahārāja

VṚNDĀVANA • NEW DELHI • SAN FRANCISCO

Artwork on the front cover and front flap © Śyāmarāṇī dāsī. Used with permission.

Śrī Prema-sampuṭa, 2nd Edition

First Edition: 2000 copied, February 2008
Second Edition: 2000 copies, September 2011
    Printed at Rakmo Press Pvt. Ltd.
    C-59, Okhla Industrial Area, Phase-1, New Delhi (India)

ISBN 978-1-935428-10-7
Library of Congress Control Number 2011937525

British Library Cataloguing in Publication Data. A catalogue record for this book is available from the British Library.

Cataloging in Publication Data--DK
    Courtesy: D.K. Agencies (P) Ltd. <docinfo@dkagencies.com>

    Viśvanātha Cakravartin.
[Premasampuṭa. English & Sanskrit]
    Śrīla Viśvanātha Cakravartī Ṭhākura's Śrī Prema-sampuṭa = The treasure chest of pure, transcendental love / translated from the Hindi edition of Bhaktivedānta Nārāyaṇa Gosvāmī Mahārāja. -- 2nd ed.
    p.   cm.
In Sanskrit (roman); translation and foreword in English.
ISBN 9781935428107

    1. Krishna (Hindu deity)--Poetry. 2. Rādhā (Hindu deity)--Poetry. 3. Love poetry, Sanskrit. 4. Love poetry, Sanskrit--Translations into English.   I. Bhaktivedānta Nārāyaṇa, 1921- II. Title. III. Title: Treasure chest of pure, transcendental love.

DDC 891.21   23

Dedicated to my Holy Master

*śrī gauḍīya-vedānta-ācārya-kesarī nitya-līlā-praviṣṭa
oṁ viṣṇupāda aṣṭottara-śata śrī*

Śrīmad Bhakti Prajñāna Keśava Gosvāmī Mahārāja

*the best amongst the tenth generation
of descendants in the bhāgavata-paramparā
from Śrī Kṛṣṇa Caitanya Mahāprabhu,
and the founder of the Śrī Gauḍīya Vedānta Samiti
and its branches throughout the world*

Acknowledgements
to the English edition

Translation:
Śānti dāsī , Vraja-sundarī dāsī

Translation Consultation:
Śrīpāda B. V. Mādhava Mahārāja, Amala-kṛṣṇa dāsa, Mādhava-priya dāsa, Vijaya-kṛṣṇa dāsa, Śrīmatī Umā Dīdī, Pūrṇimā dāsī

Hindi Translation Check:
Mukunda-datta dāsa

Editing:
Śrīpāda B. V. Nemi Mahārāja, Vaijayantī-mālā dāsī, Viṣṇu-priyā dāsī

Editing Input:
Mañjarī dāsī, Jaya-gopāla dāsa, Sundara-gopāla dāsa, Śyāmarāṇī dāsī

Sanskrit Proofreading:
Śrīpāda B. V. Bhāgavata Mahārāja

English Proofreading:
Jānakī dāsī, Kantā dāsī, Kṛṣṇa-vallabhā dāsī, Ratikalā-devī dāsī, Sulatā dāsī

Layout and Cover Design:
Kṛṣṇa-kāruṇya dāsa

Front Cover Artwork:
Śyāmarāṇī dāsī

We are grateful to those who financially contributed to this edition, especially Kṛṣṇa-līlā dāsī (Fiji). www.mygvp.com

Foreword
(translated from the Hindi edition)

Today I am most joyful to be able to present this Hindi edition of Śrī Prema-samputa to the faithful reader. Śrīla Viśvanātha Cakravartī Ṭhākura, the highly exalted preceptor and crown jewel of Śrī Gauḍīya Vaiṣṇava ācāryas, has masterfully crafted this incomparable narrative poem in language that is simple, yet replete with deep meaning.

Once, Śrī Kṛṣṇa, disguised in the attire of a heavenly damsel, came to Śrīmatī Rādhikā and stood before Her completely silent. The sight of this incredibly beautiful celestial damsel filled Śrīmatī Rādhikā with bliss and She became most eager to befriend Her. Śrīmatī Rādhikā asked Her several questions, but the girl offered no reply.

Śrīmatī Rādhikā thought the beautiful sakhī might not be well, and that this was the reason for the damsel not speaking to Her. Nonetheless, Rādhikā persisted in Her attempts to communicate with Her, and finally the maiden spoke. She said, "I heard of Your glories in the heavenly planets and have come to this Earth to meet You. When I arrived, I saw Śrī Kṛṣṇa's rāsa-līlā being performed at Vaṁśīvaṭa in Vṛndāvana. For some reason You left the dance to go into the forest, and Śrī Kṛṣṇa abandoned all the other gopīs to follow You. After spending some time with You, He disappeared. When He also left You, You began to cry bitterly. I saw Your pitiful condition and became enraged with Śrī Kṛṣṇa. It is for this reason that I have now come to You." The disguised Śrī Kṛṣṇa then proceeded to describe Kṛṣṇa's many faults.

The heavenly damsel said, "It is true that Śrī Kṛṣṇa has all good qualities, but He has one bad quality that destroys all the good ones. You, Śrī Rādhā, have left everything – Your father, mother, brother, friends, husband, society, modesty and the orders of Your elders – all so that You can love Kṛṣṇa. Yet He treats You so cruelly that He even abandons You and disappears. I cannot fathom this. In My opinion, You should not love Him, for if You do, Your future will be full of suffering."

These words prompted Śrīmatī Rādhikā to explain to the damsel the very nature of *prema*. This explanation is the subject of *Śrī Prema-samputa*.

Samputa means "that place where precious jewels and other valuable stones are carefully hidden from the vision of people". Śrīla Viśvanātha Cakravartī Ṭhākura has revealed the *unnata-ujjvala prema* in Śrī Rādhā's heart, which is likened to a treasure chest, and protected it in a box in the form of this book. Therefore, the name of this book is *Śrī Prema-samputa*. Śrī Rādhā describes Her *prema* in the following two verses (Verses 108 and 109):

ekātmaniha rasa-pūrṇatame 'tyagādhe
   ekā susaṅgrathitam eva tanu-dvayaṁ nau
kasyiṁścid eka-sarasīva cakāsad eka-
   nālottham abja-yugalaṁ khalu nīla-pītam

yat sneha-pūra-bhṛta-bhājana-rājitaika-
   vartty agravartty amala-dīpa-yugaṁ cakāsti
tac cet are taratamo 'panudat parokṣa-
   mānandayed akhila-pārśva-gatāḥ sadālīḥ

Śrī Rādhā's body and Śrī Kṛṣṇa's body are separate, yet there is no difference in Their nature (*svarūpa*). Śrī Kṛṣṇa is by nature blissful (*ānanda*) and Śrī Rādhā is by nature joyful (*hlādinī*). The truth according to the Vedas is that the potency (*śakti*) and the holder of potency (*śaktimān*) are non-different: *śakti-śaktimatorabhedaḥ*. Although there is no difference between the personality (*svarūpa*) and the personality's potency (*śakti*), when these transcendental pastimes are savoured, it becomes apparent that each has unique specialities and therefore, they differ in some ways.

ॐ   ॐ   ॐ

nitya-līlā-praviṣṭa oṁ viṣṇupāda

Śrī Śrīmad
Bhaktivedānta Nārāyaṇa Gosvāmī Mahārāja

nitya-līlā-praviṣṭa oṁ viṣṇupāda

Śrī Śrīmad
Bhaktivedānta Vāmana Gosvāmī Mahārāja

nitya-līlā-praviṣṭa oṁ viṣṇupāda

Śrī Śrīmad
Bhaktivedānta Svāmī Mahārāja

nitya-līlā-praviṣṭa oṁ viṣṇupāda

Śrī Śrīmad
Bhakti Prajñāna Keśava Gosvāmī Mahārāja

The Life History of Śrīla Viśvanātha Cakravartī Ṭhākura

Śrīla Viśvanātha Cakravartī Ṭhākura appeared in a family of *brāhmaṇas* from the Rāḍhīya community of the Nadiyā district in West Bengal. He was celebrated by the name Hari-vallabha, and he had two older brothers, Rāmabhadra and Raghunātha. During his childhood, he completed his study of grammar in Devagrāma village. He then studied devotional scripture at the home of his spiritual master in the Śaiyadābāda village of the Murśidābād district. While living in Śaiyadābāda, he wrote *Bhakti-rasāmṛta-sindhu-bindu*, *Ujjvala-nīlamaṇi-kiraṇa* and *Bhāgavatāmṛta-kaṇā*. Soon after, he renounced household life and went to Vṛndāvana, where he wrote many other books and commentaries.

After the disappearance of Śrī Caitanya Mahāprabhu and the six Gosvāmīs of Vraja, the current of unalloyed devotion (*śuddha-bhakti*) continued to flow through the influence of three great personalities: Śrī Narottama dāsa Ṭhākura, Śrīnivāsa Ācārya and Śrī Śyāmānanda Prabhu. Śrīla Viśvanātha Cakravartī Ṭhākura is fourth in the line of disciplic succession coming from Śrīla Narottama dāsa Ṭhākura.

Śrīla Narottama dāsa Ṭhākura's disciple, Śrīla Gaṅgā-nārāyaṇa Cakravartī Mahāśaya, lived in Bālūcara Gambhilā in the Murśidābād district. He had a daughter named Viṣṇupriyā but no sons, so he adopted the devotee Śrī Kṛṣṇa-caraṇa. Kṛṣṇa-caraṇa was the youngest son of another disciple of Śrīla Narottama dāsa Ṭhākura named Rāmakṛṣṇa Bhaṭṭācārya, who was from the *brāhmaṇa* community of Vārendra. Śrī Kṛṣṇa-caraṇa's disciple was Śrī Rādhā-ramaṇa Cakravartī, the spiritual master of Śrīla Viśvanātha Cakravartī Ṭhākura.

In *Sārārtha-darśinī*, Śrīla Viśvanātha Cakravartī Ṭhākura's commentary on *Śrīmad-Bhāgavatam*, he has written the following verse at the beginning of the five chapters describing Śrī Kṛṣṇa's *rāsa* dance (*Śrī Rāsa-pañcādhyāyī*):

> *śrī-rāma-kṛṣṇa-gaṅgā-caraṇānnatvā gurūnuru-premnaḥ*
> *śrīla-narottama-nātha śrī-gaurāṅga-prabhuṁ naumi*

Here, the name "Śrī Rāma" refers to Śrīla Viśvanātha Cakravartī
Ṭhākura's spiritual master, Śrī Rādhā-ramaṇa; "Kṛṣṇa" refers to his
grand spiritual master, Śrī Kṛṣṇa-caraṇa; "Gaṅgā-caraṇa" refers to his
great grand spiritual master, Śrī Gaṅgā-caraṇa; "Narottama" refers to
his great-great grand spiritual master, Śrīla Narottama dāsa Ṭhākura;
and the word *nātha* refers to Śrīla Narottama Ṭhākura's spiritual
master, Śrī Lokanātha Gosvāmī. In this way, he offers obeisances to
all those in his disciplic succession up to Śrīman Mahāprabhu.

Refuting the opinions of the atibāḍī[1] Rūpa Kavirāja

Hemalatā Ṭhākurāṇī was the learned Vaiṣṇavī daughter of Śrīnivāsa
Ācārya. Once, an estranged disciple of hers named Rūpa Kavirāja
concocted his own doctrine which opposed the philosophical
conclusions of Gauḍīya Vaiṣṇavism. He taught that the position
of *ācārya* could only be occupied by one in the renounced order –
never by a householder. Rūpa Kavirāja disregarded the necessity of
following *vidhi-mārga* (the path of regulated devotional practice) and
propagated a so called *rāga-mārga* (doctrine of spontaneous attraction)
that was undisciplined and disorderly. His new doctrine stated that
one could abandon the practices of hearing and chanting and practise
rāgānuga-bhakti by remembrance alone. For this, Hemalatā Ṭhākurāṇī
ensured that Rūpa Kavirāja was expelled from the Gauḍīya Vaiṣṇava
community. Since that time, Gauḍīya Vaiṣṇavas have known him as
an *atibāḍī*.

Fortunately, Śrīla Cakravartī Ṭhākura was present at this time,
and he refuted Rūpa Kavirāja's false conclusions in his *Sārārtha-darśinī*
commentary on *Śrīmad-Bhāgavatam's* Third Canto. Śrīla Cakravartī
proved unequivocally that qualified householder descendants of an
ācārya may act as *ācārya*. He said that it is unlawful and contrary to
the statements of scripture for unfit descendants of *ācārya* families to
adopt the title "Gosvāmī" out of greed for disciples and wealth.

Householder disciples in the line of Śrī Nityānanda Prabhu's son,
Vīrabhadra, and descendants of the rejected sons of Śrī Advaita

---

[1] A member of one of the eleven unauthorised *sahajiyā* communities who concoct
their own methods of devotional service.

Ācārya award and accept the title "Gosvāmī", an action considered improper by Vaiṣṇava *ācāryas*. Although Śrīla Cakravartī Ṭhākura acted as an *ācārya*, he personally never used the title "Gosvāmī", in order to instruct the foolish and unfit descendants of *ācārya* families of modern times.

Protecting the honour of the Gauḍīya Vaiṣṇava sampradāya through Śrīla Baladeva Vidyābhūṣaṇa

In his old age, Śrīla Viśvanātha Cakravartī Ṭhākura spent most of his time in a semi-conscious or internal state, deeply absorbed in *bhajana*. During that time, a debate broke out in Jaipur between the Gauḍīya Vaiṣṇavas and Vaiṣṇavas who supported the doctrine of *svakīyā*, or the Lord's pastimes of wedded love.

The Vaiṣṇavas from the antagonistic camp [of the Śrī Rāmānuja line] had led King Jaya Singh II of Jaipur to believe that the worship of Śrīmatī Rādhikā with Śrī Govindadeva is not supported by the scriptures. Their contention was that Śrīmatī Rādhikā's name is neither mentioned in the *Śrīmad-Bhāgavatam* nor in the *Viṣṇu Purāṇa*, and that She was never married to Śrī Kṛṣṇa according to Vedic ritual.

The antagonistic Vaiṣṇavas further objected that the Gauḍīya Vaiṣṇavas did not belong to a recognised *sampradāya*, or line of disciplic succession. From time immemorial, there have been four Vaiṣṇava *sampradāyas*: the Śrī *sampradāya*, the Brahma *sampradāya*, the Rudra *sampradāya* and the Sanaka (Kumāra) *sampradāya*. In this age of Kali, the principal *ācāryas* of these four *sampradāyas* are, respectively, Śrī Rāmānuja, Śrī Madhva, Śrī Viṣṇusvāmī and Śrī Nimbāditya. The Rāmānuja Vaiṣṇavas said that Gauḍīya Vaiṣṇavas were outside these four *sampradāyas* and therefore without pure lineage. Further, they argued that because Gauḍīya Vaiṣṇavas did not have their own commentary on *Brahma-sūtra* (also known as *Vedānta-sūtra*), they could not be following a genuine Vaiṣṇava disciplic succession.

Mahārāja Jaya Singh knew that the prominent Gauḍīya Vaiṣṇava *ācāryas* of Vṛndāvana were followers of Śrīla Rūpa Gosvāmī, and he summoned them to Jaipur to take up the challenge of the Śrī

Rāmānuja Vaiṣṇavas. The elderly Śrīla Cakravartī Ṭhākura was fully absorbed in the transcendental bliss of *bhajana*, so he sent his student Śrīla Baladeva Vidyābhūṣaṇa to address the Jaipur assembly. Gauḍīya Vaiṣṇava *vedānta-ācārya* Śrī Baladeva Vidyābhūṣaṇa, the crown of the assembly of learned scholars and the greatest among exalted teachers of Vedānta, left for Jaipur accompanied by Śrīla Cakravartī Ṭhākura's disciple Śrī Kṛṣṇadeva.

The caste *gosvāmīs* had forgotten their own connection with the Madhva *sampradāya* and disrespected the Gauḍīya Vaiṣṇavas' doctrinal view, saying it has no connection with Vedānta. This caused considerable disturbance to the true Gauḍīya Vaiṣṇavas. But Śrīla Baladeva Vidyābhūṣaṇa used irrefutable logic combined with powerful scriptural evidence to prove the Gauḍīya *sampradāya* to be a pure Vaiṣṇava *sampradāya*, called the Śrī Brahma-Madhva-Gauḍīya-Vaiṣṇava *sampradāya*, coming in the line of Śrī Madhvācārya. Śrīla Jīva Gosvāmī, Śrīla Kavi Karṇapūra and other previous *ācāryas* also accepted this as fact. The Gauḍīya Vaiṣṇavas accept *Śrīmad-Bhāgavatam* as the genuine commentary on *Vedānta-sūtra*. For this reason, no one in the Gauḍīya Vaiṣṇava *sampradāya* had written a separate commentary on *Vedānta-sūtra*.

The name of Śrīmatī Rādhikā, the personification of the pleasure-giving potency (*hlādinī-śakti*) and the eternal beloved of Śrī Kṛṣṇa, is mentioned in various Purāṇas. Throughout *Śrīmad-Bhāgavatam*, particularly the Tenth Canto in connection with the description of the Lord's pastimes in Vṛndāvana, Śrīmatī Rādhikā is referred to indirectly and discreetly. Only *rasika* and *bhāvuka* devotees conversant with the conclusions of scriptures can understand this confidential mystery.

In the learned assembly in Jaipur, Śrīla Baladeva Vidyābhūṣaṇa refuted the arguments and doubts of the opposing party, and they were silenced by his presentation. He established that the Gauḍīya Vaiṣṇavas are in the disciplic succession from Śrī Madhvācārya. Despite his victory, however, the contesting party did not accept the Gauḍīya *sampradāya* to be of pure Vaiṣṇava lineage because

the Gaudīyas had no commentary on *Vedānta-sūtra*. Śrīla Baladeva
Vidyābhūṣaṇa therefore composed the famous Gaudīya commentary,
Śrī Govinda-bhāṣya. Once again the worship of Śrī Śrī Rādhā-Govinda
commenced in the temple of Śrī Govindadeva, and the validity of the
Śrī Brahma-Madhva-Gaudīya *sampradāya* was firmly established.

It was only on the authority of Śrīla Viśvanātha Cakravartī
Ṭhākura that Śrī Baladeva Vidyābhūṣaṇa was able to write *Śrī
Govinda-bhāṣya* and prove the connection of Gaudīya Vaiṣṇavas with
the Madhva *sampradāya*. There should be no doubt in this regard.
This accomplishment of Śrīla Viśvanātha Cakravartī Ṭhākura,
performed on behalf of the *sampradāya*, will be recorded in golden
script in the history of Gaudīya Vaiṣṇavism.

Attainment of the meaning of the kāma-gāyatrī by the mercy of Śrīmatī Rādhikā

In his *Mantrārtha-dīpikā*, Śrīla Viśvanātha Cakravartī Ṭhākura
describes a special event. Once, while reading *Śrī Caitanya-caritāmṛta*,
he came upon a verse (*Madhya-līlā* 21.125) describing the meaning of
the *kāma-gāyatrī-mantra*:

> *kāma-gāyatrī-mantra-rūpa,   haya kṛṣṇera svarūpa,*
> *sārdha-cabbiśa akṣara tāra haya*
> *se akṣara 'candra' haya,   kṛṣṇe kari' udaya,*
> *tri-jagat kailā kāmamaya*

The *kāma-gāyatrī* is identical with Śrī Kṛṣṇa. In this king of *mantras*,
there are twenty-four-and-a-half syllables, and each syllable is a full
moon. This aggregate of moons has caused the moon of Śrī Kṛṣṇa to
rise and fill the three worlds with *prema*.

This verse establishes that the *kāma-gāyatrī* is composed of twenty-
four-and-a-half syllables, but despite deep deliberation Śrīla
Viśvanātha Cakravartī Ṭhākura could not ascertain which syllable
in the *mantra* was the half-syllable. He scrutinised grammar books,
Purāṇas, Tantras, scriptures dealing with drama and rhetoric, and
other great texts. Among the vowel and consonant groups in *Śrī*

Harināmāmṛta-vyākaraṇa, the grammar methodology of Śrī Jīva Gosvāmī, he found mention of only fifty letters. He studied the arrangement of letters in texts such as *Mātṛkānyāsa*, and in the *Rādhikā-sahasra-nāma-stotra* of *Bṛhan-nāradīya Purāṇa* he found that Vṛndāvaneśvarī Śrīmatī Rādhikā is also named Pañcāśad-varṇa-rūpiṇī, one whose form is composed of fifty syllables. In all the literatures he studied, however, he found mention of only fifty vowels and consonants. There was no mention of any half-syllable.

Śrīla Viśvanātha Cakravartī Ṭhākura's doubt increased. He wondered whether Śrīla Kṛṣṇadāsa Kavirāja Gosvāmī may have made a mistake in his writing. Of course this could not have been possible because Śrīla Kavirāja is omniscient and therefore free from material defects such as falling into illusion or error.

If the fragmented letter "t" (the final letter of the *kāma-gāyatrī*) were taken as the half-syllable, then Śrīla Kṛṣṇadāsa Kavirāja Gosvāmī would be guilty of the fault of disorder, for in *Śrī Caitanya-caritāmṛta* (*Madhya-līlā* 21.126–8) he has given the following description:

> *sakhi he! kṛṣṇa-mukha—dvija-rāja-rāja*
> *kṛṣṇa-vapu-siṁhāsane, vasi' rājya-śāsane,*
> *kare saṅge candrera samāja*

> *dui gaṇḍa sucikkaṇa, jini' maṇi-sudarpaṇa,*
> *sei dui pūrṇa-candra jāni*
> *lalāṭe aṣṭamī-indu, tāhāte candana-bindu,*
> *sei eka pūrṇa-candra māni*

> *kara-nakha-cāndera ṭhāṭa, vaṁśī-upara kare nāṭa,*
> *tāra gīta muralīra tāna*
> *pada-nakha-candra-gaṇa, tale kare nartana,*
> *nūpurera dhvani yāra gāna*

In these lines, Śrīla Kṛṣṇadāsa Kavirāja Gosvāmī describes Śrī Kṛṣṇa's face as the first full moon, His cheeks are two further full moons, the dot of sandalwood on the upper portion of His forehead is the fourth full moon, and just below this is the moon of the eighth day (*aṣṭamī*), in other words, a half-moon. According to this description, the fifth syllable is a half-syllable. Yet if the fragmented "t", the final letter of the *kāma-gāyatrī-mantra*, is seen to be a half-syllable, then the fifth syllable cannot be seen as such.

Śrīla Viśvanātha Cakravartī Ṭhākura was in a profound dilemma because he could not decipher the mysterious half-syllable. He concluded that if the syllables would not reveal themselves, he would be unable to behold the worshipful deity of the *mantra*. He decided that if he could not obtain the audience of the deity of the *mantra*, it would be better to die. Thinking this way, he set out at night to the banks of Śrī Rādhā-kuṇḍa to give up his life.

After the second division of the night had passed, Śrī Cakravartī Ṭhākura fell into light sleep when the daughter of Vṛṣabhānu Mahārāja, Śrīmatī Rādhikā, appeared before him. "O Viśvanātha, O Hari-vallabha," She said affectionately, "do not lament. What Śrīla Kṛṣṇadāsa Kavirāja has written is the absolute truth. By My grace, he knows all the inner sentiments of My heart. Have no doubt about his statements. The *kāma-gāyatrī* is a *mantra* to worship My dearly beloved and Me, and We become revealed to the devotees through the syllables of this *mantra*. No one can know Us without My kindness. The half-syllable is described in the book *Varṇāgama-bhāsvat*. It was after consulting this text that Śrī Kṛṣṇadāsa Kavirāja determined the actual identity of the *kāma-gāyatrī*. Study this book and broadcast its meaning for the benefit of all faithful people."

When he heard this instruction from Vṛṣabhānu-nandinī Śrīmatī Rādhikā Herself, Śrīla Cakravartī Ṭhākura arose, calling out in great lamentation, "O Rādhā, O Rādhā!" When he regained composure, he proceeded to carry out Śrīmatī Rādhikā's order.

According to Śrīmatī Rādhikā's indication, the letter "ya" preceding "vi" in the *mantra* is considered a half-syllable, and all the other syllables are full syllables, or full moons.

Thus, by Śrīmatī Rādhikā's mercy, Śrīla Viśvanātha Cakravartī Ṭhākura became acquainted with the deep meaning of the *mantra*. He attained the direct audience of his worshipful deity, and in his internal, perfected spiritual body (*siddha-deha*), he was able to participate in the Lord's eternal pastimes as His loving associate. He established the deity of Śrī Gokulānanda on the bank of Śrī Rādhā-kuṇḍa, and while residing there, he experienced the sweetness (*mādhurya*) of the eternal pastimes of Śrī Vṛndāvana. It was at this time that he wrote his *Sukha-varttinī* commentary on Śrīla Kavi Karṇapūra's *Ānanda-vṛndāvana-campūḥ* and stated therein:

> *rādhā-parastīra-kuṭīra-vartinaḥ*
> *prāptavya-vṛndāvana-cakravartinaḥ*
> *ānanda-campū-vivṛti-pravartinaḥ*
> *sānto-gatir me sumahā-nivartinaḥ*

Completely leaving aside all other things I, Cakravartī, only desire to attain Śrī Vṛndāvana. Residing in a simple hut on the bank of Śrī Rādhā-kuṇḍa, the topmost place of Śrī Rādhā's pastimes, I write this commentary on *Ānanda-vṛndāvana-campūḥ*.

In his old age, Śrīla Cakravartī Ṭhākura spent most of his time in a fully internal state or in a semi-conscious state, deeply absorbed in *bhajana*. His principal disciple, Śrī Baladeva Vidyābhūṣaṇa, took over the responsibility of teaching the scriptures.

Re-establishing the doctrine of parakīyā

When a slight decline in the influence of the six Gosvāmīs took place in Śrī Vṛndāvana, a controversy arose around the doctrines of wedded love (*svakīyāvāda*) versus paramour love (*parakīyāvāda*). To dispel misconceptions regarding *svakīyāvāda*, Śrīla Cakravartī Ṭhākura wrote *Rāga-vartma-candrikā* and *Gopī-premāmṛta*, both of which are replete with scriptural philosophical conclusions. Thereafter, in his *Ānanda-candrikā* commentary on the verse *laghutvam atra yat proktam*, of Śrī Ujjvala-nīlamaṇi (1.21), he showed that the theory of *svakīyā* was fallacious, and he established the conception of *parakīyā* with scriptural evidence and irrefutable arguments. Further, in his *Sārārtha-darśinī* commentary on *Śrīmad-Bhāgavatam*, he gave strong support to *parakīyā-bhāva*.

Certain scholars opposed the conclusions of Śrīla Cakravartī Ṭhākura on worship in the mood of *parakīyā*. When he defeated them with superior erudition and sound reasoning they resolved out of envy to kill him. They knew that Śrī Cakravartī Ṭhākura used to circumambulate Śrī Vṛndāvana early each morning, so they hid in a dark, dense grove and waited for him to walk by. As his adversaries watched him approach, he suddenly disappeared, and in his place, a beautiful young girl of Vraja appeared, picking flowers with some of her friends.

The scholars asked the girl, "Dear child, just a moment ago a great devotee was coming this way. Did you see where he went?" The girl replied that she had seen him, but that she did not know where he had gone. Her astonishing beauty, gentle smile, graceful manner and sidelong glances captivated the scholars. Their hearts melted, and all the impurities in their minds were vanquished. They asked the girl who she was, and she replied, "I am a maidservant of Śrīmatī Rādhikā. She is presently at Her in-laws' house at Yāvaṭa, and She sent me here to pick flowers." Having spoken thus, the girl disappeared, and in her place the scholars saw Śrīla Cakravartī Ṭhākura once again. They fell at his feet and prayed for forgiveness, and he forgave them all. There are many such astonishing occurrences in the life of Śrīla Cakravartī Ṭhākura.

In this way, Śrīla Cakravartī Ṭhākura refuted the theory of *svakīyā* and established the truth of pure *parakīyā* – an achievement of great import for the Gauḍīya Vaiṣṇavas.

Śrīla Viśvanātha Cakravartī Ṭhākura not only protected the integrity of the Śrī Gauḍīya Vaiṣṇava *dharma*, but he also re-established its influence in Śrī Vṛndāvana. Anyone who evaluates this accomplishment will be struck with wonder at his uncommon genius. Gauḍīya Vaiṣṇava *ācāryas* have composed the following verse in praise of his extraordinary work:

> *viśvasya nātharūpo 'sau bhakti-vartma-pradarśanāt*
> *bhakta-cakre vartitatvāt cakravarty ākhyayābhavat*

He is known by the name Viśvanātha, lord of the universe, because he indicates the path of *bhakti*; and he is known as Cakravartī, or he around whom the circle or assembly turns, because he always remains within the assembly (*cakra*) of pure devotees. Therefore, his name is Viśvanātha Cakravartī.

In about 1754, on the fifth day of the light phase of the moon in the month of Māgha (January–February), when Śrīla Viśvanātha Cakravartī Ṭhākura was around a hundred years old, he left this material world in Vṛndāvana, deeply absorbed in internal consciousness. Today his *samādhi* stands next to the temple of Śrī Śrī Rādhā-Gokulānanda in Śrī Dhāma Vṛndāvana.

The glories and legacy of Śrīla Viśvanātha Cakravartī Ṭhākura

Following in the footsteps of Śrīla Rūpa Gosvāmī, Śrīla Cakravartī Ṭhākura composed an abundance of transcendental literature on *bhakti*, thereby establishing in this world the innermost desire of Śrīman Mahāprabhu's heart. He also refuted faulty conclusions opposed to the genuine following of Śrī Rūpa Gosvāmī (*rūpānuga*) and is thus revered in the Gaudīya Vaiṣṇava society as an illustrious *ācārya* and an authoritative, self-realised soul. He is renowned as a great transcendental philosopher and poet, and a *rasika* devotee.

A Vaiṣṇava poet, Kṛṣṇa dāsa, has written the following lines at the conclusion of his translation of Śrīla Cakravartī Ṭhākura's *Mādhurya-kādambinī*:

> *mādhurya-kādambinī-grantha jagata kaila dhanya*
> *cakravartī-mukhe vaktā āpani śrī-kṛṣṇa-caitanya*

Śrīla Viśvanātha Cakravartī Ṭhākura has blessed the whole world by writing *Mādhurya-kādambinī*. In reality, Śrī Kṛṣṇa Caitanya Mahāprabhu has spoken this work through the mouth of Śrīla Cakravartī Ṭhākura.

> *keha kahena-cakravartī śrī-rūpera avatāra*
> *kaṭhina ye tattva sarala karite pracāra*

Some say that Śrīla Cakravartī Ṭhākura is an incarnation of Śrīla Rūpa Gosvāmī. He is expert in the art of describing complex truths in a way that is easy to understand.

> *ohe guṇa-nidhi śrī-viśvanātha cakravartī*
> *ki jāniba tomāra guṇa muñi mūḍha-mati*

O ocean of mercy, Śrīla Viśvanātha Cakravartī Ṭhākura. I am a foolish person, so how can I understand your qualities? (Therefore, kindly reveal your transcendental qualities within my heart. This is my prayer at your lotus feet.)

Few Gauḍīya Vaiṣṇava *ācāryas* have written as many books as Śrīla Cakravartī Ṭhākura. The following proverb regarding three of his books is quoted among Vaiṣṇavas to this day: "*kiraṇa-bindu-kaṇā, ei tina niye vaiṣṇavapanā* – Having attained a proper understanding of these three books, *Ujjvala-nīlamaṇi-kiraṇa, Bhakti-rasāmṛta-sindhu-bindu* and *Bhāgavatāmṛta-kaṇā*, one can claim to be a Vaiṣṇava."

Below is a list of his books, commentaries and prayers, which comprise a storehouse of incomparable wealth of Gauḍīya Vaiṣṇava devotional literature:

(1) *Vraja-rīti-cintāmaṇi*

(2) *Śrī Camatkāra-candrikā*

(3) *Śrī Prema-sampuṭa* (*khaṇḍa-kāvyam*)

(4) *Gītāvalī*

(5) *Subodhinī* (commentary on *Alaṅkāra-kaustubha*)

(6) *Ānanda-candrikā* (commentary on *Śrī Ujjvala-nīlamaṇi*)

(7) *Commmentary on Śrī Gopāla-tāpanī*

(8) *Stavāmṛta-laharī*, which includes:

    (a) *Śrī Guru-tattvāṣṭakam*

    (b) *Mantra-dātṛ-gurorāṣṭakam*

    (c) *Parama-gurorāṣṭakam*

    (d) *Parātpara-gurorāṣṭakam*

    (e) *Parama-parātpara-gurorāṣṭakam*

    (f) *Śrī Lokanāthāṣṭakam*

(g) *Śrī Sacīnandanāṣṭakam*

(h) *Śrī Svarūpa-caritāmṛtam*

(i) *Śrī Svapna-vilāsāmṛtam*

(j) *Śrī Gopāladevāṣṭakam*

(k) *Śrī Madana-mohanāṣṭakam*

(l) *Śrī Govindāṣṭakam*

(m) *Śrī Gopināthāṣṭakam*

(n) *Śrī Gokulānandāṣṭakam*

(o) *Svayam-bhagavattāṣṭakam*

(p) *Śrī Rādhā-kuṇḍāṣṭakam*

(q) *Jaganmohanāṣṭakam*

(r) *Anurāgavallī*

(s) *Śrī Vṛndādevyāṣṭakam*

(t) *Śrī Rādhikā-dhyānāmṛtam*

(u) *Śrī Rūpa-cintāmaṇiḥ*

(v) *Śrī Nandīśvarāṣṭakam*

(w) *Śrī Vṛndāvanāṣṭakam*

(x) *Śrī Govardhanāṣṭakam*

(y) *Śrī Saṅkalpa-kalpadrumaḥ*

(z) *Śrī Nikuñja-keli-virudāvalī (virutkāvya)*

(aa) *Surata-kathāmṛtam (āryaśatakam)*

(bb) *Śrī Śyāma-kuṇḍāṣṭakam*

(9) *Śrī Kṛṣṇa-bhāvanāmṛtam Mahākāvyam*

(10) *Bhāgavatāmṛta-kaṇā*

(11) *Ujjvala-nīlamaṇi-kiraṇa*

(12) *Bhakti-rasāmṛta-sindhu-bindu*

(13) *Rāga-vartma-candrikā*

(14) *Aiśvarya-kādambinī* (unavailable)

(15) *Mādhurya-kādambinī*

(16) Commentary on *Bhakti-rasāmṛta-sindhu*

(17) Commentary on *Ānanda-vṛndāvana-campū*

(18) Commentary on *Dāna-keli-kaumudī*

(19) Commentary on *Śrī Lalita-mādhava-nāṭaka*

(20) Commentary on *Śrī Caitanya-caritāmṛta* (incomplete)

(21) Commentary on *Śrī Brahma-saṁhitā*

(22) *Sārārtha-varṣiṇī* commentary on *Śrīmad Bhagavad-gītā*

(23) *Sārārtha-darśinī* commentary on *Śrīmad-Bhāgavatam*

ॐ ॐ ॐ

My most revered Śrī Gurudeva, *ācārya-keśarī aṣṭottara-śata* Śrī Śrīmad Bhakti Prajñāna Keśava Gosvāmī Mahārāja, guardian of the Śrī Gauḍīya *sampradāya* and founding *ācārya* of Śrī Gauḍīya Vedānta Samiti and the Gauḍīya *maṭhas* established under its auspices, republished the books of Śrīla Bhaktivinoda Ṭhākura and other previous *ācāryas* in the Bengali language, along with publishing his own works. Today, by his heartfelt desire, enthusiastic blessings and causeless mercy, books such as the following have been printed in Hindi, the national language of India: *Jaiva-dharma, Śrī Caitanya-śikṣāmṛta, Śrī Caitanya Mahāprabhu kī Śikṣā, Śrī Śikṣāṣṭaka, Bhakti-rasāmṛta-sindhu-bindu, Ujjvala-nīlamaṇi-kiraṇa, Bhāgavatāmṛta-kaṇā, Śrī Gīta-govinda, Śrī Bhajana-rahasya, Śrī Gauḍīya-gīti-guccha, Śrīmad Bhagavad-gītā, Śrī Veṇu-gīta, Bhakti-tattva-viveka, Vaiṣṇava-siddhānta-mālā, Śrī Brahma-saṁhitā, Rāga-vartma-candrikā, Śrī Bṛhad-bhāgavatāmṛtam, Gauḍīya-kaṇṭhahāra* and *Śrī Camatkāra-candrikā.* Gradually, other books are being published as well.

Śrīla Viśvanātha Cakravartī Ṭhākura composed *Śrī Prema-sampuṭa* in Sanskrit, and many editions have since been published in Bengali. Among them, that of Śrī Hari-bhakta dāsa of Śrī Dhāma Vṛndāvana is particularly full of transcendental moods, and its language is also easy to understand. This Hindi translation is based on that edition.

I have full faith that *rasika* and *bhāvuka sādhakas*, and *sādhakas* on the path of *rāgānuga-bhakti* eager to attain *vraja-rasa* will hold this book in great veneration. Faithful people who study it will be able to enter Śrī Caitanya Mahāprabhu's *prema-dharma*, the eternal religion of pure, transcendental loving service to Śrī Kṛṣṇa.

May my most worshipful Śrīla Gurupādapadma, who is the embodiment of the Supreme Lord's compassion, shower his abundant mercy upon me. In that way, I may attain ever-increasing qualification to fulfil his innermost desire through my service. This is my humble prayer at his lotus feet, which can bestow *prema*.

This first edition was produced with great speed, so there may be minor faults: we request the faithful readers to inform us of them so we can correct these faults for future editions.

An aspirant for a particle of mercy from Śrī Hari, Guru and the Vaiṣṇavas,

Humble and insignificant,
Tridaṇḍibhikṣu Śrī Bhaktivedānta Nārāyaṇa

Śrī Utthāna Ekādaśī
12 November 2005

Śrī Prema-sampuṭa

The Treasure Chest of Pure, Transcendental Love

prātaḥ kadācid urarī-kṛta cāru-rāmā-
veśo hariḥ priyatamā-bhavana-praghāne
gatvāruṇāṁśuka-taṭena pidhāya vaktraṁ
nīcī na locana-yugaḥ sahasāvatasthe (1)

*L*oving attachment has a particular nature that is extra-ordinary. Within the heart of the lover, a yearning may spontaneously arise to hear from his beloved's mouth about the excellence of her love for him and the inferiority of his love for her.

Early one morning, under the control of such love, Vrajendra-nandana Śrī Śyāmasundara, the unrestricted, carefree enjoyer of *rasa*, disguised Himself as a young woman of heart-stealing beauty, and went to the courtyard of Śrīmatī Rādhikā, the dear, darling daughter of Vṛṣabhānu Mahārāja. Covering His lotus-like face with a crimson veil, He appeared before Śrīmatī Rādhikā, His eyes bashfully lowered.

ॐ ॐ ॐ

Previously, on the night of the *rāsa* dance on the banks of the river Kālindī, Śrī Śyāmasundara had accepted defeat in the midst of the *gopīs*. At that time He had told them, "*na pāraye 'ham niravadya saṁyujām...* – I am not able to repay My debt to you all." Now He was absorbed in the same mood of loving attachment

He had conveyed with those words. Thus desiring to hear His beloved Śrī Rādhā speak proudly and unhesitatingly while in Her affectionate sulky mood (praṇaya-māna), He disguised Himself as a lovely young lady. These are the moods of the lover (nāyaka) and beloved (nāyikā) that are specifically described in Śrī Prema-samputa.

ārād-vilokya tam atho vṛṣabhānu-putrī
provāca hanta lalite! sakhi! paśya keyam
svasyāṁśubhir hari-maṇīmayatāṁ nināya
mat-sadma padma-vadanādbhuta-bhūṣaṇāḍhyā (2)

When Vṛṣabhānu-nandinī Śrīmatī Rādhikā saw this charming young woman in the distance, She addressed Her dear friend, Śrī Lalitā. "O *sakhī* Lalitā, look, just look! Who is this beautiful young woman adorned with astonishing ornaments? The glow of Her lotus-like face rebukes the lustre of lotus flowers, and the radiance of Her *śyāma*-complexioned body illuminates our courtyard. Our whole house appears to be decorated with sapphires."

śrutvā sakhī-giram atho lalitā viśākhe
taṁ procatur drutam avāpya tadābhimukhyam
kā tvaṁ kṛśodari! kutaḥ kim u vātha kṛtyaṁ
brūhīty asau prativacas tu dadau na kiñcit (3)

On hearing Śrīmatī Rādhikā's words, Lalitā and Viśākhā quickly approached the young maiden and inquired, "O slender-waisted girl, who are You? Where have You come from and why have You come here? Please remove our curiosity by answering these questions." But that young girl did not reply.

śrī-rādhikāpy atha vitarka-puraḥsaraṁ tam
papraccha kautuka-vaśād upagamya samyak
kā tvaṁ svarūpa-mahasaiva manoharantī
devāṅganāsi kim aho suṣameva mūrttā (4)

When She did not answer, Śrī Rādhikā became even more curious. After careful thought, She came before the disguised Śrī Kṛṣṇa and inquired, "O beautiful one, who are You? The lustre of Your limbs has stolen our minds. Are You a divine maiden? Upon beholding You, it seems that You have appeared before us embodying the entirety of the world's beauty."

> *tūṣṇīṁ sthitaṁ tad api taṁ punar āha bhāvi-*
> *nyātmānam āśu kathayātra yadi tvam āgāḥ*
> *jānīhi nas tava sakhīḥ paramāntaraṅgāḥ*
> *kiṁ śaṅkase nata-mukhiḥ! trapase 'tha kiṁvā* (5)

Still, the pretty young maiden did not reply. "O Bhāvinī (beautiful woman)," Śrī Rādhikā said, "it is You who have come here to us, so please introduce Yourself at once and remove our curiosity. O shy one, in our company, there is no reason to be timid or reserved. Please understand that we consider You to be our intimate friend."

> *niśvasya kañcana viṣādam ivābhinīya*
> *vaktraṁ vivṛtya tam akhaṇḍita-mauna-mudram*
> *sā prāha hanta rujam āvahasīti satyaṁ*
> *jñātaṁ na tām ṛta ihedṛśatā tava syāt* (6)

When the young maiden – Śrī Kṛṣṇa – heard Śrīmatī Rādhikā's words, She sighed deeply. Actually, mere words cannot describe Her response. She turned Her face away and continued to remain silent. Upon seeing the girl's condition, Śrī Rādhā asked, "O beautiful one, I understand that Your heart is certainly in pain, otherwise You would not act like this.

> *taṁ brūhi kañja-mukhi! viśvasihi prakāmaṁ*
> *mayy eva tat pratikṛtau ca yathā yateya*
> *udgīrṇa eva suhṛd-antika eti śāntiṁ*
> *yan-mānasa-vraṇa-vipākaja-tīvra-dāḥ* (7)

"O lotus-faced one, with full trust in us, please openly and clearly tell us about Your pain. I will try My best to nullify the cause of Your anguish. When, within the heart, a deep wound of despair opens, the unbearable anguish one suffers can be mitigated by revealing it to intimate friends.

> *kāntena kiṁ tvam asi samprati viprayuktā*
> *tasyaiva vā viguṇatodayath prataptā*
> *kiṁ svāgasas tad avisahyatayā vibhesi*
> *tat kiṁ nu kalpitam aho piśunair na satyam* (8)

"Are You now suffering separation from Your beloved? Or have You become exceedingly perturbed upon discovering some shortcoming in him? Or have You committed some great offence that has shattered the affection of Your beloved? Is that why You are fearful? Perhaps, in order to destroy the love and affection that Your beloved has for You, some wicked person has falsely accused You of a misdeed, although You have actually done no wrong. Is that why You are unhappy?

> *kimvā vivodhari manaḥ sa ghṛnaṁ tavābhū-*
> *nmande ratam kvacana pumsi-vare dūrāpe*
> *tattvam kaṭūkti paṭunā yata mādṛśīva*
> *santarjjyase guru-janena tato 'si dūnā* (9)

"Is it that You have realized that the one You have wed is dull and unlucky? Is it that You would never have married him if You had known before, and now that You do know, You are disinclined toward him? Or has Your heart become attached to a most wonderful person who is unattainable? Alas, alas, do You feel dejected because, like Me, You are subject to the constant harsh reproach of scornful elders?"

> *kaccin nu tanvi! khara-vāk-śara-viddha-marmā*
> *saubhāgya-leśa-madirāndha-dhiyaḥ sapatnyāḥ*

sambhāvyate tvayi na caitad aho parā kā
tvatto vahatv atula saubhaga-cāru-carccām (10)

The continued silence of the beautiful young damsel only served to increase Śrī Rādhā's apprehension. "O comely one," She said, "has Your co-wife become proud, intoxicated by her tiny drop of good fortune? Has her intelligence become corrupt and as a result, has she pierced Your heart with the arrows of her sharp words? No, surely this could not happen to You. I cannot believe there is a young woman in the entire universe more fortunate than You. You could not possibly have a co-wife. Why would a man who is married to a wife endowed with all good qualities ever abandon her to marry another?

tvaṁ mohinī śrutacarī kim u mohanārthaṁ
śambhor ivendu-mukhi! kasya haṭhād udeṣi
kiñ cekṣate yadi haris tad-apāṅga-viddha-
stvāṁ kautukaṁ bhavati tad-vyatimohanākhyam (11)

"O moon-faced one, we have heard from Bhagavatī Paurṇamāsī-devī that there was once an incarnation of the Supreme Lord named Mohinī, who was so extraordinarily lovely that She could enchant the great Śrī Mahādeva (Lord Śiva). Are You that Mohinī? Tell Me, who is it that You hope to infatuate with Your fascinating beauty by coming here unexpectedly? It is true that Śrī Mahādeva was captivated by You, and that You were not in the least attracted to him, but if Your side-long glance were to pierce Śrī Hari, and if He were to shoot a side-long glance back at You, You would surely become utterly bewildered. There is nothing to compare with Your beauty nor with the beauty of our Śrī Kṛṣṇa, that crown jewel of the kings of gallants. If You saw one another, You would both become so enamoured by each other's beauty that You would violate the boundaries of self-composure, and an exceptional and amazing *rasa* would appear from Your mutual attraction."

śrutvottarīya-pariyantrita-sarva-gātraṁ
romāñcitaṁ tam upalabhya jagāda rādhā
hā kiṁ sakhi! tvam asi daihika-duḥkha-dūnā
vakṣo 'tha pṛṣṭham athavā vyathate śiras te (12)

As Śrī Kṛṣṇa disguised as a celestial damsel continuously drank the nectarean words flowing from the lotus mouth of inquisitive Śrī Rādhikā, He felt a transcendental rapture well up in His heart, and the hairs of His body stood up in ecstasy. In order to hide this, He covered His limbs with His veil.

When Śrī Rādhikā saw this, She imagined that the damsel must have some kind of bodily ailment. "O *sakhī*," She asked, "are You experiencing some discomfort in Your body? Are You feeling some pain in Your chest, Your back or Your head?"

vātsalyataḥ pitṛ-padair bahu-mūlyam eva
prasthāpitaṁ yad-akhilāmaya-śātanākhyam
tailaṁ tad asti bhavanāntarato viśākhe!
śīghraṁ samānaya tad āpaya sārthakatvam (13)

In this way, Śrī Rādhikā guessed about the young maiden's illness. "O friend Viśākhā," She said, "My honourable father fondly sent Me a precious medicinal oil that is a sure remedy for all kinds of ailments. Please quickly bring it from the house. The nature of love and affection is such that if an article dear to oneself is used for one who is near and dear, its very existence becomes meaningful.

tailena tena kila mūrttimatā madīya-
snehena subhruvam imāṁ svayam eva sāham
abhyañjayāmy akhila-gātram apāsta-todaṁ
naipuṇyataḥ sakhi! śiro mṛdu mardayāmi (14)

"O *sakhī* Viśākhā, I feel a deep affection for this *sakhī* who has just arrived. This oil, which removes all diseases, is a manifestation of My father's love for Me; hence, I will use it to massage this beautiful girl's entire body with My own hands. I will also skilfully massage Her head, then all Her suffering will be relieved.

nairujya-kāri-vara-saurabha-vastu-vṛnda-
prakṣepa-cārutara-koṣṇa-payobhir enām
saṁsnāpayāmi vigatāruṣam āsya padma-
mullāsayāmy atha girāpi virājayāmi (15)

"And listen, bring some warm water mixed with the finest healing ingredients for Me to bathe Her in. I will alleviate Her suffering and then Her lotus-like face will appear happy. Perhaps then She will speak with Me.

vācā mayā mṛdulayātihita-pravṛttyā
snehena cānupādhinā paramādṛtāpi
no vakti kiñcid adhunaiva kaṭūkṛtāsyā
tiṣṭhed iyaṁ kapaṭinī yadi hanta sakhyaḥ (16)

"O *sakhīs*, I have spoken sweet and gentle words to this girl, and I am ready to personally give Her an oil-massage and other beneficial treatments. With an open heart, I have honoured Her and shown Her sincere affection. Still, I have not heard a single word from Her lips. She is being deceptive about the nature of Her ailment and just sits here with a doleful face.

asyā rujas tad-aparāṁ karavai cikitsāṁ
yām prāpya tanva-sumano-nikhilendriyāṇām
vyādhiḥ praśāmyati bhaved atipuṣṭir eṣāṁ
dhanvantari-prahita-divya-rasair ivāddhā (17)

"Now I shall administer a new treatment for this lovely girl's disease. Just as the divine nectar-tonic given to Me by Dhanvantari cures any disease, this remedy will remove, within a second, all the diseases of Her body, life force, mind and senses. It will especially serve to nourish Her body.

*kuñjādhirāja-kara-kañja-talābhimarṣa-
masyā urasy atitarāṁ yadi kārayāmi
seyaṁ hasiṣyati vadiṣyati sītkariṣya-
tyasmāṁś ca hāsayitum eṣyati kāñcid ābhām* (18)

"Listen, and I will tell you more about this new treatment. Until now, this *sakhī* has been sitting here, overcome by some incurable disease and incapable of uttering a single word. However, if Her whole chest were touched by the lotus-like palms of the Lord of our *kuñja*, She would soon start to talk, giggle and sob. Having experienced the indescribable pleasure of the touch of *rasika-śekhara* Śrī Kṛṣṇa's hand, She would murmur indistinct sounds. What more can I say? She would assume such a radiance that we would all laugh without end. Her body would manifest all the signs of having met with Śrī Kṛṣṇa, and by His touch, all kinds of exceptional symptoms would manifest. This would make us happy."

*śrutvā giraṁ sa pihita-smita-hāsya-padma-
munnīya ramyatara-savya-karāṅgulībhiḥ
utsārya kiñcid alakā-nava-guṇṭhanañ ca
nyañcattaraṁ kiyad udañcayati sa mūrddhnaḥ* (19)

When Śrī Kṛṣṇa, who was disguised as a heavenly damsel, heard Śrīmatī Rādhikā speak in this way, a gentle smile appeared on His face. He concealed His smile, and then slightly raised His lowered lotus-like face. With the charming fingers of His left hand, He gently brushed a stray curl from His forehead, and pulled His veil down over His head a little further.

*kiñcij jagāda ramaṇī ramaṇīya-kaṇṭha-
sausvaryam eva racayan vacanaṁ yad eṣaḥ*

sā tac cakora-lalaneva papau cirāya
kāñcic camatkṛtim avāpa ca sālipāliḥ (20)

The disguised Śrī Kṛṣṇa assumed the sweet voice of a young lady and showered alluring words as sweet as nectar upon all those present. Like *cakorī* birds, Śrī Rādhā and Her *sakhīs* drank every word with eager hearts. In this way, they experienced supreme bliss and felt such astonishment that mere words cannot describe. Upon hearing the sweet talk of the beautiful new girl, they revelled in a bliss equalled only by the rapture they felt upon hearing the talk of Śrī Kṛṣṇa Himself.

devy asmi nāka-vasatiḥ śṛṇu yasya heto-
stām agamaṁ su-vadane vidhurī-kṛtātmā
kutrāpi me vividiṣāsti vivakṣite 'rthe
sampādayiṣyati parā tvad ṛte kutas tām (21)

The new *sakhī* said, "O beautiful Śrī Rādhā, I am a damsel from the heavenly planets. Please hear why I have come to You with such an agitated heart. I have a desire to know something about a particular matter, and who but You can fulfil My desire?"

naivābhyadhās tvam anṛtaṁ yad udeṣi devī-
tyasmābhir ittham adhunaiva hi paryaceṣṭhāḥ
yan-mānuṣīṣu katamāsti bhavat-sadṛkṣā
kāntyānayān upamayā tvam ivekṣase tvam (22)

Upon hearing these words, Śrī Rādhikā said, "O lovely one, You have introduced Yourself as a heavenly damsel. This is surely not false. In fact, I had guessed as much even before You spoke, because no woman of this mortal world can rival You in beauty. Your beauty is incomparable and unprecedented; indeed, You are in a class of Your own.

yat tvayy ahaṁ sarala-dhīr vitathaṁ vitarka-
vaividhyam apy akaravaṁ śarad-ambujāsye
tat paryahāsi-ṣamito 'stu na me 'parādha-
stvaṁ snihyasīha mayi yady abhavaṁ tvadīyā (23)

"O You whose face resembles an autumnal lotus, I have considered many possible reasons for Your sadness, such as feeling separation from Your husband, and I have told You of them, but actually, I was joking. Please do not take offence to My words. Now You have become affectionate toward Me, and I have become Yours."

kiṁ saṅkucasy ayi sakhī tvam abhūs tvadīyo
devījano 'py aham abhūvam iti pratīhi
tvaṁ prema-rūpa-guṇa-sindhu-kaṇānubhūter
dāsī bhavāmy aham apīti sadābhimanye (24)

The celestial damsel said, "Rādhā, You are My *sakhī*. Why are You so reserved? Although I am a heavenly damsel, I have become Your subordinate. Do not doubt it. I constantly yearn to be Your maidservant so that I may experience one drop of the ocean of Your love, beauty and qualities.

yad vacy ahaṁ tad avadhehi yato viṣādo
durvāra eṣa tam apākuru saṁśayaṁ me
naivādhunāpi virarāma darāpi hṛd-bhu-
tāpas tvadīya-lapanāmṛta-sekato 'pi (25)

"Please listen carefully while I tell You why My heart feels such anguish, and then dispel the doubt that causes Me this despair. Your nectar-sweet words have fallen like soft rain upon My heart, but they have not even slightly soothed the distress within it.

vṛndāvane dhvanati yaḥ sakhi! kṛṣṇa-veṇu-
stad-vikramaḥ sura-pure prabalatvam eti

sādhvī-tater api manaḥ sa-ghṛṇaṁ yato 'bhūt
kaṇṭhopakaṇṭha-milana smaraṇe 'pi patyuḥ (26)

"O *sakhī*, the flute-song that is heard in Śrī Vṛndāvana has also entered our heavenly abode. Its power is such that the chaste ladies there no longer wish to embrace their husbands. In fact, the mere thought of doing so disgusts them. When the Lord of the universe, Śrī Kṛṣṇa, attracts their minds and hearts, their thoughts no longer run toward their mortal husbands. Anything connected with Śrī Kṛṣṇa has this power. The slightest connection with Him completely removes the desire to enjoy anything material.

śliṣṭveva muñcati suraḥ sa-vitarkam ātma-
kāntāṁ drutaṁ jvalad-alāta-nibhāṅga-yaṣṭim
hālāhalaṁ muralikā-ninadāmṛtaṁ yat
pītvaiva sātanu-mahājvara-mūrcchitābhūt (27)

"This flute sound is as sweet as nectar, but it is mixed with deadly poison. Anyone who hears it feels an unprecedented joy as if they are tasting nectar; but afterwards, when they have not attained Śrī Kṛṣṇa, they suffer sharp pains as if they have been poisoned. The moment that sound enters the ears of the heavenly damsels, they desire to enjoy with Śrī Kṛṣṇa in every way. Bewildered by the high fever of amorous love, their bodies blaze like fiery coals. Their husbands embrace their burning bodies but quickly release them. 'What sudden ailment is causing her high temperature?' they wonder. As soon as anyone hears the sound of Śrī Kṛṣṇa's flute, the desire to meet with Him manifests in their heart, making them restless. This is the power of Śrī Kṛṣṇa's flute-song.

asmat-pure 'sti na hi kāpi jaraty ataḥ kā-
starjantu kā nu nikhilā api tulya-dharmāḥ

kā vā haseyur aparā yad imāḥ satītvaṁ
viplāvayan muralikā ninado vyajeṣṭa (28)

"One of the names of our heavenly city is Tridaśālaya, meaning a place where the inhabitants experience only three stages of life: childhood, adolescence and youth. They never grow old. Since none of the women ever age, they all feel attracted to the sound of the flute. Who, then, is in a position to rebuke others or joke at their expense? The sound of the flute destroys the heavenly damsels' chastity and defeats each and every one of them.

evaṁ yadi pravavṛte prativāsaraṁ sa
veṇu-dhvaniḥ prabhavituṁ vibudhāṅganāsu
tarhy ekadā hṛdi mayaiva vicāritaṁ hā
ko 'yaṁ kutaś carati vādayitāsya ko vā (29)

"In this way, the influence of the flute-song spread day by day among the heavenly damsels. Then one day, filled with wonder, I thought to Myself, 'From where does this sweet sound come? Who is playing that flute?'

itthaṁ divaḥ samavatīryya bhuvīha sādhu
vaṁśīvaṭe 'vasam ahaṁ katicid dināni
dṛṣṭo harer anupamo vividho vilāsaḥ
kāntā-gaṇaḥ priya-sakhāly api paryyacāyi (30)

"After due consideration, I was able to trace the sound of the flute from the heavenly planets, and in that way I came down to this Earth. I happily stayed at Vaṁśīvaṭa for some days. There I witnessed the unequalled pastimes performed by You and Śrī Kṛṣṇa, and I became acquainted with His dear, beloved *sakhīs*."

rādhā sa-narma-madhurākṣaram āha dhanye!
tvaṁ gaṇyase sura-pure vara-cāturī-bhāk

anyā punar balavad-utkalikā kṛpāṇī
kṛttendriyaiva sumanastvam apādapārtham (31)

After hearing the words of the heavenly damsel, Śrī Rādhā spoke sweetly and jokingly. "O most fortunate one, I consider You the most clever of all heavenly damsels in the celestial realm, because only You, Your mind cut asunder by the sword of Your strong eagerness to meet the flute-player, are trying to find out the source of the flute-song. The other damsels are not trying to trace this source. For this reason, only You can really be called Sumanā, for only You have an undisturbed mind. (In other words, You are Sumanā because like Me, You have become attached to *para-puruṣa*[1] Śrī Kṛṣṇa.)"

ॐ   ॐ   ॐ

The purport is that the demigoddesses are so intensely eager to attain Śrī Kṛṣṇa that their minds cannot remain steady, and they are suffering all kinds of severe pains because they always want to enjoy sensual pleasures. Therefore, they cannot think of any solution to suspend their eagerness [to attain Śrī Kṛṣṇa]. For them to be called Sumanā, "one with a beautiful mind", is not applicable. This heavenly damsel on the other hand, not only became eager to meet with the flute-player, but She decided to come here and suspend this eagerness by meeting Him. Therefore, only She is blessed and only She can appropriately be called Sumanā.

manda-bhramad-bhru madhura-smita-kānti-dhārā-
dhaute vidhāya radana-cchadane sa cāha
rādhe! parāṁ sva-sadṛśīṁ na hi viddhi kiṁ bhoḥ
śakye 'valokitum apīha pareṇa puṁsā (32)

When the celestial damsel heard Śrī Rādhā's delightful joking words, a sweet and effulgent smile came upon Her lips, and Her eyebrows danced slightly. "Rādhā," She said, "do not consider

---

[1] The husband of another woman.

other women to be like You. Do not think that My attachment to Your lover Śrī Kṛṣṇa is like Yours. Now that I am here, will Your lover, Śrī Kṛṣṇa, be able to control Me in the same way He controls You?"

kimvā pareṇa puruṣeṇa harer vilāsa-
mevānvabhū rahasi sādhu yad-artham āgāḥ
tad brūhi kiṁ tava vivakṣitam atra madhye
narmātanomi yadi mām akaroḥ sakhīṁ svām (33)

Śrī Rādhikā replied, "I do not know Your reason for coming here, but in any case, while You are here, please try to experience Śrī Kṛṣṇa's confidential, loving pastimes. What is the need of a relationship with any other man? Anyway, what was it that You wanted to ask Me? Until now I have just been joking and playing with You, because You have accepted Me as Your friend."

narmātanudhva sakhi! narmaṇi kā jayet tvām
prāṇās tv abhūs tvam ayi me kiyad eva sakhyam
tvaṁ mānuṣī bhavasi kintv amarāṅganās tā
mūrddhnaiva te guṇa-kathā punatīr namanti (34)

The heavenly damsel replied, "O *sakhī*, please continue to joke. Who can defeat You in this art? O Rādhā, You are more than just a friend to Me; You are as dear to Me as My very life-air. It is true that You are only a human being, but nonetheless, the young heavenly damsels bow their heads when they hear about Your purifying qualities."

ॐ ॐ ॐ

The meaning here is that although Śrī Rādhikā manifests a human-like form, desiring to relish the mellows of different pastimes, She is not an ordinary person. In fact, She is the embodiment of the complete potency of the Supreme Lord Śrī Kṛṣṇa, who is the source of all incarnations. It is therefore not surprising that the young heavenly damsels bow down when they hear the narrations of Her qualities.

Śrīla Śukadeva Gosvāmī's description of the advent of Śrī Kṛṣṇa in Śrīmad-Bhāgavatam (10.1.17–23) is written in the same mood as the above verse (34): Once, when Mother Earth was distressed because of the atrocities of deceitful demons who were dressed like kings, she took the form of a cow and approached Śrī Brahmā. She cried pitifully as she revealed her misfortune to Brahmā. Hearing her narration full of sorrow, Brahmā took her and the other demigods to the shore of the Milk Ocean. There the Supreme Person Kṣīrodakaśāyī Viṣṇu told Śrī Brahmā, who was absorbed in meditation: "*tat-priyārtham sambhavantu sura-striyaḥ* ... – the wives of the demigods should take birth in Vraja for the pleasure of Śrī Kṛṣṇa and His beloveds" (Śrīmad-Bhāgavatam 10.1.23). Therefore, it is not inappropriate for the heavenly damsels, who are fit to be maidservants, to bow down.

**neyam stutis tava na cāpi taṭa-sthatā me
nāpi hriyam bhaja vadāmy anṛtaṁ na kiñcit
sindhoḥ sutāpi girijāpi na te tulāyāṁ
saundarya-saubhaga-guṇair adhirodhum īṣṭe (35)**

The heavenly damsel then said, "*Sakhī*, I will never lie to You, so please do not be embarrassed by My praise. My ornamented language was not spoken just to flatter You, and I am not joking out of indifference to You. Really, Your beauty, fortune and other qualities cannot be equalled even by Pārvatī, nor by Śrī Lakṣmī, the daughter of the ocean."

ॐ ॐ ॐ

A similar sentiment is expressed in Śrī Caitanya-caritāmṛta (Madhya-līlā 8.182-4) wherein Śrī Rāya Rāmānanda answers Śrī Gaurāṅga-sundara's questions:

*yāhāra saubhāgya-guṇa vāñche satyabhāmā
yāṅra ṭhāñi kalā-vilāsa śikhe vraja-rāmā*

*yāṅra saundaryādi-guṇa vāñche lakṣmī-pārvatī
yāṅra pativratā-dharma vāñche arundhatī*

> *yāṅra sadguṇa-gaṇane kṛṣṇa nā pāya pāra*
> *tāṅra guṇa gaṇibe kemane jīva chāra*

In these verses he explains that even Pārvatī and Śrī Lakṣmī pray to attain Śrī Rādhā's beauty and other qualities. Śrīla Rūpa Gosvāmī also writes in *Śrī Ujjvala-nīlamaṇi* (*Śrī Hari-priyā-prakaraṇam*, 3.18):

> *rāgollāsa-vilaṅghatārya-padavī-viśrāntayo 'py uddhura-*
> *śraddhā-rajyad-arundhatī-mukha-satī-vṛndena vandyehitāḥ*
> *āraṇyāpi mādhurī-parimalavyākṣipta-lakṣmī-śriya-*
> *stās trailokya-vilakṣaṇā dadatu vaḥ kṛṣṇasya sakhyaḥ sukham*

Arundhatī and other eminent, chaste women reverentially praise the *vraja-gopīs'* behaviour, even though the beautiful young girls of Vraja stray from the path of chastity due to being overpowered by their love for Śrī Kṛṣṇa. The *gopīs* are country girls who dwell in the forest, but their sweetness defeats the beauty of Śrī Lakṣmī, the queen of Vaikuṇṭha. Within the three worlds, the beloveds of Śrī Kṛṣṇa are most extraordinary. May they bestow happiness upon you.

In this verse it is mentioned that because Śrī Rādhā is the foremost of Śrī Kṛṣṇa's beloveds, Her *mādhurya* and other qualities surpass the qualities of Śrī Lakṣmī. Śrī Kṛṣṇa has unlimited potencies, of which three are prominent: His internal spiritual potency (*cit-śakti*), His external potency (*māyā-śakti*) and His marginal potency (*jīva-śakti*). Of these three, the internal potency, which is also known as *svarūpa-śakti*, is most prominent. *Sac-cid-ānanda* Śrī Kṛṣṇa's internal potency has three divisions: transcendental bliss (*ānanda*), also called *hlādinī*; transcendental, eternal existence (*sat*), also called *sandhinī*; and transcendental knowledge (*cit*), also called *saṁvid*.

The essence of *hlādinī-śakti* gives bliss to Śrī Kṛṣṇa and to His devotees, and it is called *prema*. The highest essence of *prema* is *mahābhāva*, of which Śrī Rādhikā is the embodiment.

Śrīmatī Rādhikā is foremost among Śrī Kṛṣṇa's beloveds, and just as Śrī Kṛṣṇa is the source of all incarnations of the Supreme Lord, so Śrī Rādhā is the source of all the expansions of Śrī Kṛṣṇa's beloveds, which include the *vraja-gopīs*, the queens of Dvārakā and Mathurā, and all the goddesses of fortune in each of His abodes.

In *Śrī Caitanya-caritāmṛta* (*Ādi-līlā* 4.83) Śrīla Kavirāja Gosvāmī quotes *Bṛhad-gautamīya-tantra*:

> *devī kṛṣṇa-mayī proktā rādhikā para-devatā*
> *sarva-lakṣmī-mayī sarva-kāntiḥ sammohinī parā*

She who shines brilliantly and who is non-different from Śrī Kṛṣṇa is called Śrīmatī Rādhikā. She is most worshipful and presides over all goddesses of fortune. She possesses all splendour and completely bewilders Śrī Kṛṣṇa. She is the supreme internal potency of the Lord.

Śrī Caitanya-caritāmṛta (*Ādi-līlā* 4.90, 92) explains this verse (*devī kṛṣṇa-mayī ...*) as follows:

> *sarva-lakṣmī-gaṇera tiṅho hana adhiṣṭhāna*
>
> *sarva-saundarya-kānti vaisaye yāṅhāte*
>
> *sarva-lakṣmī-gaṇera śobhā haya yāṅhā haite*

She is the abode of all goddesses of fortune. ... All beauty and splendour rest in Her. All the goddesses of fortune derive their beauty from Her.

These scriptural evidences establish that the qualities and fortune of Śrī Pārvatī-devī or Śrī Lakṣmī cannot equal those of Śrīmatī Rādhikā.

> ***premnā punas tri-jagad-ūrddhva-pade 'pi kācit***
> ***tat-sāmya-sāhasa-dhuraṁ manasāpi voḍhum***
> ***śaknoti nety akhilam eva mayā śrutaṁ tat***
> ***kailāsa-śṛṅgam anu haimavatī-sabhāyām (36)***

The heavenly damsel continued, "Listen, and I will tell You more. Is any woman as courageous as You in loving affairs, even in the Vaikuṇṭhā planets far beyond the three material worlds? Is there a woman who can even imagine that she is Your equal? These words of praise do not come from My imagination; I have heard Your glories in the assembly of Pārvatī-devī atop of Mount Kailāśa.

śrutvā mahān ajani me manaso 'bhilāṣa-
stad-darśanāya samapūri sa cāpi kintu
tāpa-tad-antar iha yo rabhasād adīpi
tenāsphuṭan na kaṭhino hi mamāntarātmā (37)

"When I heard of Your qualities, I developed an intense desire to meet with You. It is true that seeing You has fulfilled My desire, but still My heart is burning with distress. The only reason My heart has not shattered in its fire is because it is so hard."

ko 'sau tam āśu kathayeti muhus tayokto
vaktuṁ śaśāka na sa bāṣpa-niruddha-kaṇṭhaḥ
aśru-plutekṣaṇa-mathāsya mukhaṁ svayaṁ sā
svenāñcalena mṛdulena mamārjja rādhā (38)

Śrī Rādhikā, who is most loving, heard the heavenly damsel's words, which were full of unbearable agony, and asked, "My friend, what has caused Your intense and intolerable suffering? Please tell Me straightaway."

Tears flowed incessantly from the damsel's eyes, Her throat choked up and She was unable to speak. Śrī Rādhikā gently wiped the damsel's face and eyes with Her own, soft veil.

ॐ ॐ ॐ

The intention behind Śrī Kṛṣṇa's display of deep, inner grief was to make a convincing show that His grief was genuine.

sthitvā kṣaṇaṁ dhṛtim adhād atha tām uvāca
premā tavāyam atulo 'nupadhir valīyān
kṛṣṇe 'tikāmini babhūva kathaṁ dunoti
svāṁ svāṁś ca viśvasiti yo 'tyapade 'py abhijñaḥ (39)

The heavenly damsel remained in that mood for a moment, and then calmly and patiently replied, "O innocent one, Śrī Kṛṣṇa is a licentious debauchee. How could You fall in love with such a lusty person? In this world, Your *prema* is unequalled. Because it is causeless, it is indestructable, and because it is so powerful, nothing can check it. Yet those who knowingly make something that is unworthy the object of their loyalty only cause distress to themselves and their dear ones.

saundarya-śaurya-vara-saubhaga-kīrtti-lakṣmī
pūrṇo 'pi sarva-guṇa-ratna-vibhūṣito 'pi
premāviveca-katamatvam asau vibhartti
kāmitva-hetukam asau śrayitum na yogyaḥ (40)

"Let Me tell You something more. It is true that Śrī Kṛṣṇa is complete with sweet beauty, bravery, matchless fortune, fame and other opulences, and that He is adorned with all jewel-like qualities; nevertheless, He has one fault that nullifies all these opulences: He is quite unable to discriminate in matters of *prema*, because He has so many amorous desires. It is never appropriate to find refuge in such a person.

tasmin dine bahu-vilasya muhuḥ prakāśya
premā tvayā sarabhasam rajanau tu kuñje
saṅketa-gāmṛju-dhiyam bhavatīm vidhāya
kāñcit parām sa ramayan kapaṭī jahau tvām (41)

"Just listen. On that day, Śrī Kṛṣṇa played with You in various ways. With eagerness, He repeatedly displayed an articifical love for You. But later, O simple-hearted woman, that falsehearted cheat abandoned You to enjoy with another young woman, even though He had arranged to meet with You that night in a *kuñja*.

yat tvam tadā vyalapa eva sakhīs tudantī
vallīḥ patatri vitatīr api rodayantī
sarvam tadāli! nibhṛtam maya-kānya-bhāli
vamśīvaṭa-sthitatayā valitā ruṣaiva (42)

"Your *sakhīs* were distressed when they heard You lamenting, and even the creepers, animals and birds of the forest cried in pain. At that time, I also became filled with mental anguish, for I was hiding at Vaṁśīvaṭa, watching."

ॐ ॐ ॐ

When Śrīmatī Rādhikā experiences separation from Śrī Kṛṣṇa, *mohanākhya-mahābhāva* arises within Her. In *Śrī Ujjvala-nīlamaṇi* (*Sthāyī-bhāva-prakaraṇam*) it is stated that *mohanākhya-mahābhāva* causes such an agitation within the universe that even the non-human species cry. That is why Śrī Kṛṣṇa is saying here (Verse 42) that the trees, creepers and birds also cried.

In *Śrī Caitanya-caritāmṛta* (*Madhya-līlā* 2.43) it is stated:

> akaitava kṛṣṇa-prema,   yena jāmbunada-hema,
> sei premā nṛloke nā haya
> yadi haya tāra yoga,   nā haya tabe viyoga,
> viraha haile keha nā jīyaya

Unalloyed *kṛṣṇa-prema*, like pure gold from the Jāmbu River, does not exist in this world of man. If it manifested in this realm, there would be no separation; if separation occured, one's life would cease to exist.

> *rāse tathaiva viharann aparā vihāya*
> *prema tvayaiva sahasā prakaṭī cakāra*
> *sthitvā kṣaṇaṁ sa bhavatīm amucad vanānta-*
> *rekākinīṁ rati-bhara-śrama-khinna-gātrīm* (43)

The heavenly damsel then said, "On the night of the *rāsa*, Śrī Kṛṣṇa abandoned all the other *vraja-sundarīs* to take You with Him, to sport with You, and to show You profuse affection. However, after a short while, when You became tired from Your amorous, loving sports, He suddenly left You all alone in the forest.

> *tarhi plutaṁ vilapitaṁ gahanā ca mūrcchā*
> *ceṣṭāpy atibhrama-mayī tava yad yad āsīt*

vyāpyaiva hā bahu-janūṁsi hṛdi sthitaṁ me
tat kaṣṭam aṣṭa-vidhayaiva tanoḥ prakṛtyā (44)

"At that time You displayed various conditions of Your body and heart – You lamented loudly and fainted over and over again. Your movements showed that You were confused; they were not natural. Alas, seeing You in that condition was so painful I will never forget it. Even in future births, as I pass through the eight stages of life, such as birth, old age and death, Your anguish will ceaselessly pierce My heart like a sharp iron spear.

devī-jano 'smi hṛdi me kva nu kaṣṭam āsīd
daivād yaśasvini! babhūva bhavad-didṛkṣā
mām āgamayya bata sākṛta kīla-viddhāṁ
yasyāsti naiva sakhi! nirgamane 'py upāyaḥ (45)

"O glorious one, is it possible for pain to remain in My heart? After all, I am a damsel from the heavenly planets. But alas, at an inauspicious moment, a yearning to see You suddenly manifested. It was that desire alone that brought Me here, and now, O *sakhī*, it is piercing My heart like a sharp iron spear. Indeed, I cannot see how to remove it at all."

❧ ❧ ❧

Śrī Kṛṣṇa condemned Himself in order to gauge the depth of Śrī Rādhikā's love for Him. He knew that the super-excellence of Rādhikā's love would be established in this world if Her love neither faltered nor decreased slightly after She heard this criticism of Him. Śrī Kṛṣṇa spoke in this way in order to relish the nectar-like words scented with *prema* that flowed from the earnest and solemn heart of Śrī Rādhikā, the crown jewel of His beloveds.

sandānitaṁ tvayi mano na divaṁ prayātuṁ
sthātuñ ca nātra tila-mātram apīttham iṣṭe
udghūrṇate pratipadaṁ na padaṁ labheta
adyābhavaṁ tvayi cirāt-prakaṭī kṛtātmā (46)

"*Sakhī*," continued the heavenly damsel, "My heart has become so bound to Yours that when I see You suffer, I become powerless to return to the heavenly planets. At the same time, I cannot remain here bearing such heavy grief in My heart. Since I cannot find peace, I have come to see You to express the feelings aroused by what is revolving in My mind.

kṛṣṇāt punar bahu vibhemi na dharma-loka-
lajje dayā-dhvani kadāpi na pāntha tāsya
bālye striyās taruṇimany acirād vṛṣasya
vatsasya madyam anu yo vyadhitaiva himsām (47)

"What is more, I am very afraid of Śrī Kṛṣṇa, because He has no sense of religion, or moral principles, nor does He fear public opinion. He is so hard-hearted that He has never stepped foot on the path of mercy. When He was just a little baby, He killed a woman, the *rākṣasī* Pūtanā. In His youth He killed the bull Vṛṣāsura, and in His boyhood He killed the calf Vatsāsura. So, as You can see, from His very childhood He has engaged in violent, irreligious acts."

gāndharvikāha subhage! tvayi kāpi śakti-
rākarṣiṇī kila harāv iva santatāsti
yan nindasi priyatamam tad api prakāmam
mac-cittam ātmani karoṣy anuraktam eva (48)

When Śrī Rādhikā heard the heavenly damsel speak such words of criticism about Kṛṣṇa, She said, "O most fortunate one, Śrī Kṛṣṇa is the beloved of My life. His potency to attract My heart is unparalleled. Although He has hurt Me time and again, I am unable to sever My heart's attachment to Him.

"Often I decide to stop talking to Him because of His improper behaviour, but the moment I see Him again, I forget everything. I see a power in You similar to the power I see in Him, because even though You are criticizing Śrī Vrajarāja-kumāra (the son of the king of Vraja), who is more dear to Me than millions of My own lives, You still attract My heart, making Me attached to You. Surely it is unnatural to feel affection for someone who criticizes a loved one, unless one comes under the control of some supernatural power; then, maybe it could happen. The nature of unconditional love is such that once it manifests it is not easily destroyed. This love is so firm and so vast that it never wavers, nor can it ever be annihilated even after hearing criticism of the loved one."

🙦 🙦 🙦

In *Śrī Caitanya-caritāmṛta* this is explained with the verse *akaitava kṛṣṇa-prema, yena jāmbunada-hema, sei premā nṛloke nā haya / yadi haya tāra yoga, nā haya tabe viyoga, viyoga haile keha nā jīyaya.* The translation of this verse was given earlier, in Verse 42.

> **tvaṁ me sakhī bhavasi cen na divaṁ prayāsi**
> **nitya-sthitiṁ vraja-bhuvīha mayā karoṣi**
> **tat-prema-ratna-vara-sampuṭam udghaṭaya**
> **tvāṁ darśayāmi tad-ṛte na samādadhāmi (49)**

Śrīmatī Rādhikā continued, "O Sundarī, if You really consider Yourself My *sakhī*, do not return to the heavenly planets. Stay with Me in this land of Vraja for all time, and then I will be able to open My treasure chest to show You the amazing jewel of *prema*. It is not possible to understand the *prema* that Śrī Kṛṣṇa and I have for each other just by talking about it. It is only possible to understand by observing it. If You and I do not live together, how will I ever make You understand this *prema*, and how will I be able to remove Your doubt? Stay with Me, and I will be able to make You understand clearly why I cannot become indifferent toward Śrī Kṛṣṇa, even though I suffer so greatly because of Him."

hantādhunāpi na hi viśvasiṣi prasīda
dāsī bhavāmi kim u māṁ nu sakhīṁ karoṣi
tvaṁ sādhi sādhu dhin u vā tuda vā gatir me
rādhe! tvam eva śapathaṁ karavāṇi viṣṇoh (50)

When the disguised Śrī Kṛṣṇa heard the words of Śrī Rādhikā, He said, "Alas, alas, You still lack faith in Me, even though We now know each other. Rādhā, You want Me to be Your *sakhī*, but that is something for the distant future. At the moment, I am just Your maidservant. Please be happy with Me, and control Me in every way. O Rādhā, I swear by Śrī Viṣṇu that You are My one and only shelter, whether You punish Me or show Me mercy."

ॐ ॐ ॐ

Śrī Kṛṣṇa's words here are completely true. This is because without *mādanākhya-mahābhāva* it is impossible to fulfil the boundless desire to enjoy of *śṛṅgāra-rasa-rāja*[2] Śrī Kṛṣṇa.

vaktuṁ tadā pravavṛte vṛṣabhānu-nandi-
nyākarṇya tāṁ vividiṣām iha ced dadhāsi
premeya-devam idam eva na cedam etat
yo veda veda-vidasāv api naiva veda (51)

When Vṛṣabhānu-nandinī Śrī Rādhikā heard this, She said, "O My friend, if You desire to hear about My *prema*, then listen: Anyone who says, 'This is the extent of *prema*', 'this is *prema*', 'this is the nature of *prema*' or 'this is not the nature of *prema*' knows nothing about *prema*, even if they have studied the Vedas and all other scriptures.

ॐ ॐ ॐ

The nature of *prema* cannot be explained in words. Indeed, *prema* will not manifest in one's heart as long as one has a mind with which to deliberate upon it. One who deliberates upon the nature of *prema* remains unqualified for it, even if that is his sole subject of deliberation.

---

2 "The king of the transcendental mellow of amorous love"

Prema is completely beyond all else. It is *sva-samvedya*, meaning it can only be experienced by itself. *Prema* will not manifest if one's heart has any inclination other than to make the beloved completely happy. *Prema* is nothing other than being fully absorbed in meditating on what makes the beloved happy – "Will my beloved become happy by my doing this?" In such a condition, no other consideration can be present. One who merely deliberates upon *prema* cannot realize it, and upon attaining *prema*, nothing else is perceived. All scriptures may be realized through deliberation, but not *prema*.

> **yo vedayed vividiṣuṁ sakhi! vedanaṁ yat**
> **yo vedanā tad akhilaṁ khalu vedanaiva**
> **premā hi ko 'pi para eva vivecane sa-**
> **tyantardadhāty alam asāv avivecane 'pi (52)**

"O *sakhī*, suppose someone wants to grasp the nature of *prema* and tries to explain it to another, even though he has no realization of it himself. In that case, he who tries to explain it is cheating, and any realization resulting from those words is simply a fraud. *Prema* is the most excellent of topics, and it cannot be described in words. It disappears upon being analysed and becomes even more concealed when it is not.

༅ ༅ ༅

Prema is incomparable, and it can only be experienced by itself. Language cannot illuminate it, and it cannot be understood by hearing about it from one in whose heart it has not manifest. It is simply fruitless labour to try to understand or explain *prema*, because understanding it is purely dependent upon experiencing it.

Prema disappears when it is analysed – this was discussed in the explanation of the previous verse. It cannot manifest in a heart that is intent on analysing it. And if the intelligence to analyse it appears after it has awakened in the heart, *prema* cannot remain there.

One may not have the slightest tendency to analyse *prema*, but still, unless one meditates on whether or not one's actions are pleasing to Śrī Kṛṣṇa, it will not manifest in one's heart. Now, even though the slightest tendency to analyse *prema* may be absent, it still will not manifest in one's heart unless one meditates on whether or not one's actions are pleasing to Śrī Kṛṣṇa. This is because *prema* is found only in a person whose natural tendency deep in his heart is to act entirely for Śrī Kṛṣṇa's pleasure. Unless one meditates on whether or not one's actions are pleasing to Kṛṣṇa, the tendency to act solely for His happiness will not arise in the heart. In that case, only the tendency to perform activities to fulfil the desire for one's own happiness will appear, and then *prema* cannot arise.

dvābhyāṁ yadā rahitam eva manaḥ svabhāva-
siṁhāsanopari virājati rāgi-śuddham
tac-ceṣṭitaiḥ priya-sukhe sati yat-sukhaṁ syāt
tac ca svabhāvam adhirūḍham avekṣayet tam **(53)**

"When the heart is filled with *rāga* – attachment to Kṛṣṇa with affection – a mood naturally reigns in which there is no other desire than to give happiness to one's beloved. And when one makes the beloved happy, even though one's tendency of heart is neither to deliberate on how to do so nor to neglect it, happiness naturally arises. At this time, *prema* becomes visible in one's innate activities.

కా   కా   కా

When *prema* arises, specific conditions of the heart manifest, such as it becoming filled with *rāga*. The symptom of *rāga* is described in *Śrī Ujjvala-nīlamaṇi* (14.126) as follows:

duḥkham apy adhikaṁ citte sukhatvenaiva vyajyate
yatas tu praṇayotkarṣāt sa rāga iti kīrttyate

Due to the excellence of *praṇaya* (strong loving attachment), the heart's condition becomes such that it experiences supreme bliss even in extremely distressful situations, all because of the possibility that one will attain one's beloved. Without that possibility, even the condition of complete happiness is distressful. This state of heart is called *rāga*.

When *prema* arises, other conditions of the heart also arise. At that time the heart becomes purified, and no desires appear there other than to give pleasure to the beloved. Furthermore, one neither neglects the beloved nor meditates on serving him. This is because service to him will manifest naturally. At that time there is no tendency in the heart to gain knowledge about *prema*.

These conditions of heart must occur naturally. *Prema* cannot be created artificially. Its presence can be perceived when *anubhāvas* or *sāttvika-bhāvas* manifest naturally. There is no other way to perceive *prema*. The following symptom reveals that *prema* has appeared in a person's heart: upon seeing the happiness of one's beloved, a happiness naturally arises in one's own heart. That happiness causes *anubhāvas* and other transcendental sentiments to manifest.

> *loka-dvayāt sva-janataḥ parataḥ svato vā*
> *prāṇa-priyād api sumeru-samā yadi syuḥ*
> *kleśās tad apy atibalī sahasā vijitya*
> *premaiva tān harir ibhān iva puṣṭim eti (54)*

"Just as a lion defeats elephants and nourishes itself by eating them, similarly this extremely powerful *prema* nourishes itself by conquering the unlimited and difficult miseries caused by conditions in this world, by other planets, by family members, by enemies, by one's own body or by matters related to the body, and even by troubles caused by one's beloved that are as insurmountable as Mount Sumeru.

ॐ ॐ ॐ

Śrī Rādhikā is explaining that *prema* is inherently free from obstacles. Once it has manifested, not even hundreds of thousands of obstacles can obstruct it. In such *prema* there is no place for concern about worldly comforts, religious duties, the attainment of residence in heaven, and so forth. Reproaches by family members and abuse by enemies cannot enter the ears, and one even forgets to protect one's own body. *Prema* has absolutely no obstacle. Even the lover's own attempts to break it by neglecting his beloved's love do not act as an obstacle to *prema*. The symptom of *prema* is given in Śrī Ujjvala-nilamaṇi (Sthāyi-bhāva-prakaraṇam, 14.63) as follows:

sarvathā dhvaṁsa-rahitaṁ saty api dhvaṁsa-kāraṇe
yad-bhāva-bandhanaṁ yūnoḥ sa premā parikīrttitaḥ

When the deep emotion that binds a young couple does not break, despite many reasons for it to do so, it is called *prema*.

In fact, multitudes of difficulties nourish *prema* rather than obstruct it. If the current of a quickly flowing river is obstructed, the water will overcome the obstruction and flow with redoubled force. Similarly, attraction for the beloved increases in proportion to the obstacles encountered. As a result, the force of that *prema* increases a hundredfold.

The great sage Bharata Muni, who is the original *guru* of the scriptures on *rasa*, has explained this phenomenon as follows (as quoted in Śrī Ujjvala-nīlamaṇi, 1.20):

bahu vāryate yataḥ khalu yatra pracchanna-kāmukatvaṁ ca
yā ca mitho durlabhatā sā manmathasya paramā ratiḥ

The *prema* that is strongly objected to by society and religion, in which the lover (*nāyaka*) and beloved (*nāyikā*) must hide their amorous desires, and in which loving union is difficult to attain, is called *manmatha-sambandhita paramā prīti*, the supreme passionate affection.

Therefore, it is seen that a multitude of obstacles nourishes *prema* rather than inhibits it.

snigdhāṅga-kāntir atha garva-dharo 'tyabhīto
viśrambhavān svapiti kiṁ gaṇayed asau tān
kaṇṭhī-ravaḥ śuna ivābhibhavan sarāga-
steṣv eva rājatitamāṁ tamasīva dīpaḥ (55)

"The proud, confident and graceful lion sleeps fearlessly without disturbance. Similarly, that *prema* which brims with affection, exhibits pride due to the rise of *māna* and reaches the stage of *praṇaya*, can never be destroyed. In that *prema*, the pride of possessiveness – 'he is mine; he is exclusively my beloved' -- is firmly situated within the heart of the lover.

"Just as a lion considers a dog to be insignificant, so *prema* does not recognize insignificant, dog-like obstacles. Just as a lamp's glow becomes brighter in the darkness, so the glory of *prema* becomes more lustrous in the face of obstacles. With those obstacles conquered, *prema* becomes more radiant than before. Thus situated, it never diminishes.

> *lāmpaṭy ato nava-navaṁ viṣayaṁ prakurva-*
> *nāsvādayann atimadoddhuratāṁ dadhānaḥ*
> *āhlādayann amṛta-raśmir iva tri-lokīṁ*
> *santāpayan pralaya-sūrya ivāvabhāti* (56)

"*Sakhī*, through lascivious desire, this *prema* makes one continually relish the beloved in new and fresh ways. Like the moon, it pleases the three worlds with excessive intoxication, and it also burns like the sun at the time of universal devastation.

৵ ৵ ৵

The meaning here is that the lover (*nāyaka*) has such deep love and affectionate attachment to many beloveds (*nāyikās*) that he develops a longing for more and more *nāyikās*. Tasting such new moods greatly delights the *nāyaka*. This love and affection causes the beloved to experience separation from the lover when he goes to another *nāyikā*. The beloved dreams about the happiness of past and future meetings with the lover, and thus she becomes submerged in an ocean of unprecedented enjoyment. As the moon's rays cool the three worlds, the *prema* that exists when the *nāyaka* and *nāyikā* meet creates an enjoyment that cannot be described in words. At that time, the lover and beloved perceive the three worlds to be filled with happiness. Yet, in a state of separation from each other such *prema* gives more pain than millions of forest fires, and it seems that everything is burning.

enaṁ vibhartti sakhi! kaḥ khalu gopa-rāja-
sūnuṁ vinā tri-bhuvane tad-upary-adho 'pi
premāṇam enam alam eṇa-dṛśo 'nvavinda-
nnatraiva goṣṭha-bhuvi kāścana tāratamyāt (57)

"My dear *sakhī*, in the entire universe, in the upper planetary systems such as Maharloka, and in the lower planetary systems such as Rasātala, is anyone worthy of receiving this *prema* other than Vrajendra-nandana Śrī Kṛṣṇa? It is only in this land of Vraja that some doe-eyed girls taste this *prema*, according to their various individual *bhāvas*.

ॐ   ॐ   ॐ

Prema can only be attained when one is completely independent and free from care, and when one can completely relinquish the pride born of one's occupational duty. No ordinary human being can possess *prema*, for such a person is always controlled by time, fruitive activities, illusion, the senses and so forth. Consequently, he cannot peacefully feel affection for anyone.

All forms of Bhagavān, starting with the *guṇa-avatāras* and *puruṣa-avatāras* up to Śrī Nārāyaṇa, the Lord of the spiritual sky, are supremely independent, but they engage in activities such as creating material universes, delivering devotees and establishing religion, and they all carry the identity of being the Supreme Lord. They are not able to simply love someone because they cannot be free from the anxiety of these responsibilities, even for a moment, nor can they give up their opulence. Śrī Kṛṣṇa's manifestations, such as Śrī Mathurānātha and Śrī Dvārakānātha, are also unable to show genuine love and affection. However, Vrajendra-nandana Śrī Kṛṣṇa is not a king, but the son of a king, a prince, and thus He is completely carefree. When He falls in love with someone He forgets everything, even that He is Bhagavān. Only He has the capacity to truly love someone.

Furthermore, no one can be a true *premikā* if her heart harbours a trace of desire or slight consideration for her own personal happiness. This kind of mood can be found only in the *gopīs* of Vraja, because they have given up everything, including their social duties and obligations, the religious principles prescribed in the Vedas, their shame, patience and bodily comforts, and their spiritual happiness, solely to serve Śrī Kṛṣṇa for His pleasure. They have also given up their relationships with friends, relatives and family members, despite being scolded and reproached by them. Therefore, only the *vraja-sundarīs* can love Śrī Kṛṣṇa purely.

premā hi kāma iva bhāti bahiḥ kadācit
tenāmitaṁ priyatamaḥ sukham eva vindet
premeva kutracid avekṣyata eva kāmaḥ
kṛṣṇastu taṁ paricinoti balāt kalāvān (58)

"Sometimes *prema* manifests externally as *kāma*, or transcendental lust, from which the beloved, Śrī Kṛṣṇa, obtains unlimited happiness. And sometimes mere lust is portrayed as *prema*. Only the crown jewel of clever personalities and the abode of all arts, Śrī Kṛṣṇa, is able to understand its true nature."

🙐   🙐   🙐

The desire to gratify one's own senses is called lust, or *kāma*. In *prema* there is no trace of desire for one's own sense enjoyment, and one only endeavours to arrange for Śrī Kṛṣṇa's satisfaction. In the world of *prema*, the love of the *vraja-sundarīs* is situated on the topmost stage and is called *adhirūḍha-mahābhāva*. Śrī Caitanya-caritāmṛta (Ādi-līlā 4.171–2) states:

ataeva kāma-preme bahuta antara
kāma—andha-tamaḥ, prema—nirmala bhāskara

ataeva gopī-gaṇera nāhi kāma-gandha
kṛṣṇa-sukha lāgi mātra, kṛṣṇa se sambandha

There is a great difference between *kāma* and *prema*. *Kāma* is dense darkness, and *prema* is like the pure sun. There is not the slightest trace of *kāma* in the *gopīs*. Their relationship with Śrī Kṛṣṇa is solely based on giving Him pleasure.

Some acts, such as embracing and kissing, are common to both *kāma* and *prema*, so externally they appear to be similar, yet their true natures are in fact opposite. In *Bhakti-rasāmṛta-sindhu* (1.2.283–4) it is also said:

> *premaiva gopa-rāmāṇāṁ kāma ity agamam prathām*
> *ity uddhavādayo 'py etaṁ vañchanti bhagavat-priyāḥ*

The *prema* of the *vraja-sundarīs* manifests in such a way that it appears to be *kāma*. Śrī Uddhava and other dear devotees of the Lord pray to attain this *kāmarūpā-bhakti*.

The *vraja-sundarīs' prema*, which seems to be *kāma*, is supremely pleasurable to Śrī Kṛṣṇa, who is topmost of those who relish transcendental mellows. This is because the nature of love is that one who loves always longs to see the beloved happy. If this mood is not manifest, then love cannot remain. Because the *vraja-sundarīs* have no desire for their own happiness, waves of bliss manifest in their limbs when they give joy to Śrī Kṛṣṇa. They clean their bodies and decorate them with beautiful clothes and ornaments with the sole purpose of giving satisfaction to Śrī Kṛṣṇa. In *Ādi Purāṇa* it is stated:

> *nijāṅgam api yā gopyo mameti samupāsate*
> *tābhyaḥ param na me pārtha nigūḍha-prema-bhājanam*

O son of Pṛthā, the *gopīs* decorate their bodies because they consider them to be Mine. No one is a greater repository of deep *prema* than they.

In *Śrī Caitanya-caritāmṛta* (*Ādi-līlā* 4.191–2, 195) it is also said:

> *āmāra darśane kṛṣṇa pāila eta sukha*
> *ei sukhe gopīra praphulla aṅga-mukha*
> *gopī-śobhā dekhi' kṛṣṇera śobhā bāḍe yata*
> *kṛṣṇa-śobhā dekhi' gopīra śobhā bāḍe tata*
> *ataeva sei sukha kṛṣṇa-sukha poṣe*
> *ei hetu gopī-preme nāhi kāma-doṣe*

[The *gopīs* think,] "Śrī Kṛṣṇa has obtained so much pleasure from seeing us," and thus their faces and bodies blossom. Śrī Kṛṣṇa's beauty increases when He sees the beauty of the *gopīs*, and the *gopīs'* beauty increases, the more they see Kṛṣṇa's beauty. ... The happiness of the *gopīs* nourishes Kṛṣṇa's happiness because their *prema* is completely free from the fault of *kāma*.

Śrī Kṛṣṇa is not satisfied by one who flaunts their *kāma* as *prema*, and He is not controlled by it. Śrī Kṛṣṇa also does not find happiness in *prema* contained with *kāma*. The *prema* of the queens of Dvārakā could not control Śrī Kṛṣṇa when mixed with the desire to satisfy their own senses. This is also explained in *Śrīmad-Bhāgavatam* (10.61.4):

> smāyāvaloka-lava-darśita-bhāva-hāri
> bhrū-maṇḍala-prahita-saurata-mantra-śauṇḍaiḥ
> patnyas tu ṣoḍaśa-sahasram ananga-bāṇair
> yasyendriyaṁ vimathituṁ karaṇair na śekuḥ

The sixteen thousand queens of Śrī Kṛṣṇa were unable to allure His senses even by their smiling sidelong glances and the dancing of their captivating eyebrows, which, like Cupid's arrows, are expert in amorous messages.

> **kṛṣṇāntikaṁ sakhi! nayāśu nikāma-taptāṁ**
> **mām ity udāharati kintu tad-ātmajena**
> **kāmena tat-sukhaparaṁ dadhatī sva-bhāvā-**
> **deva sva-cittamayam atra na kāminī syāt (59)**

Śrī Rādhikā continued, "*Sakhī*, when a young woman says, 'I am burning in the fire of lust; please take me quickly to the lord of my life,' she cannot be called lusty, because at that time, the nature of her heart is firmly fixed in giving pleasure to her beloved. The passionate mood that manifests to give happiness to her beloved cannot be called mere lust (*kāma*); rather, it is true love, or *prema*.

> **premāmbudhir guṇa-maṇī-khanir asya śāṭhya-**
> **cāpalya-jaihmyam akhilaṁ ramaṇīyam eva**
> **premāṇam eva kila kāmam ivānganāsu**
> **sandarśayan svam udakarṣayad eva yas tāḥ (60)**

"*Sakhī*, Śrī Vrajendra-nandana is both an ocean of *prema* and a mine of jewel-like qualities. His deceitfulness, fickleness, crookedness and other such qualities are extremely charming. He devises how to increase women's love for Him by presenting His *prema* – in the semblance of lust – before them all."

ॐ ॐ ॐ

Vrajendra-nandana Śrī Kṛṣṇa's form consists of pure sweetness. His mood of heart-stealing sweetness appears even when opulence (*aiśvarya*) is manifest in His pastimes of killing the demons. Therefore, Kṛṣṇa's moods of fickleness, crookedness and so forth are sweet. Śrī Govinda's form is filled with *rasa*, and the movements of all His limbs cause waves of bliss to arise. He increases the love of His beloved *gopīs* through His crookedness, fickleness and other qualities. If Śrī Kṛṣṇa did not display qualities, such as crookedness, the *gopīs'* love would not manifest the waves of *vyabhicārī-bhāvas* and other transcendental moods of ecstasy, as well as the stages of *khaṇḍita* and so forth. And thus the greatness of their love would not be revealed to the world. Śrī Kṛṣṇa shows His yearning to meet with His *gopī* beloveds and thus gives unlimited bliss to their hearts. When they desire to make Him happy by offering all that they have to Him, Śrī Kṛṣṇa shows His eagerness to enjoy that offering in every way. Śrī Govinda is the personification of unalloyed goodness, and desires are spontaneously born within Him to reciprocate with the love of His devotees. Without this, love cannot increase.

> *kā vāṅganāḥ śata-sahasram amuṣya kāma-*
> *paryāptaye mada-kalāḥ prabhavantu yat tāḥ*
> *premā tad atra ramaṇīṣv anupādhir eva*
> *premaika-vaśyatamatā ca mayānvabhāvi (61)*

Are hundreds and thousands of beautiful girls, intoxicated by youthful lust, able to satisfy, by their various kinds of endeavours, Śrī Kṛṣṇa's desire for an amorous meeting? Śrī Kṛṣṇa is self-satisfied (*ātmārāma*) and free from material desires (*āptakāma*), so no one can enchant Him by their lust. He is only controlled by pure *prema*. Therefore, Śrīmatī Rādhikā says, "*Sakhī*, stay in Śrī Vṛndāvana. Experience for Yourself how the *vraja-ramaṇīs' prema* for Śrī Kṛṣṇa is free from any desire for personal happiness, and how Śrī Kṛṣṇa is controlled only by such *prema*.

tatrāpi mayy atitarām anurajyatīti
loka-pratītir api na hy anṛtā kadāpi
yat prema merum iva me manute parāsāṁ
no sarṣapais tri-caturair api tulyam eṣaḥ (62)

"Although the *prema* of all the beautiful young girls of Vraja is unconditional, everyone knows that Śrī Kṛṣṇa is much more attracted to Me than to all others. Indeed, this is true, because Śrī Kṛṣṇa feels My *prema* to be as boundless as Mount Sumeru, and the *prema* of the other girls like a few mustard seeds.

৵ ৵ ৵

Pure and genuine *prema* is only seen in Vraja; nowhere else. Sometimes the *prema* of the queens of Dvārakā is mixed with *kāma*, but the *vraja-sundarīs' prema* is always free from duplicity and any personal desire. For this reason, only the *vraja-sundarīs' prema* reaches the level of *mahābhāva*. This is described in *Śrī Ujjvala-nīlamaṇi* (*Sthāyī-bhāva-prakaraṇam*, 14.156):

> *mukunda-mahiṣī-vṛndair apy asāv atidurlabhaḥ*
> *vraja-devy eka-saṁvedyo mahābhāvākhyayocyate*

Modanākhya-mahābhāva is only possible for the *gopīs* of Śrīmatī Rādhikā's group, such as Śrī Lalitā. It is not possible in other *gopīs*. This is explained in *Śrī Ujjvala-nīlamaṇi* (*Sthāyī-bhāva-prakaraṇam*, 14.176): *rādhikā-yūtha evāsau modano na tu sarvataḥ*.

Mādanākhya-mahābhāva is only present in Śrī Rādhikā. It does not arise in anyone else. This is stated in *Śrī Ujjvala-nīlamaṇi* (*Sthāyī-bhāva-prakaraṇam*, 14.219):

> *sarva-bhāvodgamollāsī mādano 'yaṁ parāt paraḥ*
> *rājate hlādinī-sāro rādhāyām eva yaḥ sadā*

Hence, by deliberation upon the true nature of *prema*, one can conclude that Śrī Rādhikā's *prema* is topmost.

premānurūpamayi rajyati yat parāsu
rāgānurūpam iha dīvyati nāparādhyet
daivād vyatikramam upaiti kadācid asmāt
nāsau sukhī bhavati tena ca māṁ dunoti (63)

"O friend, Śrī Kṛṣṇa is attracted toward other *nāyikās* and can sport with them according to the extent of their *prema* for Him. This is not a fault of Śrī Kṛṣṇa. If this principle were ever to be transgressed by a *gopī*, then Śrī Kṛṣṇa would not become satisfied, and I also would feel distress.

৯ ৯ ৯

Śrī Kṛṣṇa would not be happy if He were to show more affection to a *gopī*, or sport with her more than her affection for Him warranted, because such a beloved (*nāyikā*) would not be able to satisfy His expectation. He would thus become unhappy. And when He feels sad, Śrīmatī Rādhikā also feels sad.

saṅketa-gām api vidhāya mad-eka-tāno
māṁ nājagāma yad ihābhavad antarāyaḥ
ruddhaḥ kayācid anurodha-vaśāt sa reme
mad-duḥkha-cintana-davārddita eva rātrim (64)

"When Śrī Kṛṣṇa indicates that I should meet with Him, I go to Our assigned meeting place. But if He does not arrive there, it is only due to some obstacle. Although He is completely enchanted by Me, He still may sport with another beautiful girl, being bound by her request. But in doing so He feels no pleasure, because all night long the forest fire of remembering My suffering causes Him distress.

৯ ৯ ৯

The suffering that Śrīmatī Rādhikā feels in separation from Śrī Kṛṣṇa drowns the entire universe in an ocean of distress. When Śrī

Kṛṣṇa is directly embraced by any other *nāyikā*, He remembers Śrī Rādhikā's distress in separation from Him and faints. This is described in *Śrī Ujjvala-nīlamaṇi* (*Sthāyī-bhāva-prakaraṇam*, 14.181): *atrānubhāvā govinde kāntāśliṣṭe 'pi mūrcchanā.* That is why Śrī Rādhikā says, "When Śrī Kṛṣṇa goes to other *nāyikās*, He cannot be peaceful because He thinks of My unhappiness."

tenaiva me hṛdi mahā-davathur babhūva
mad-veśa-bhūṣaṇa-vilāsa-paricchadādi
tan-moda-kṛd viphalatām agamat kim adye-
tyākranditaṁ yad api tarhi tad anvabhūs tvam (65)

"*Sakhī*, while He sports with other young girls of Vraja, He thinks about My suffering, and because of this My mind becomes afflicted by His unhappiness. When that happens, I lament, 'Everything – My dress, My ornaments, My coquetry and My beautiful appearance are all useless. Alas, alas, they cannot give pleasure to Śrī Kṛṣṇa.'

"You have heard Me weeping at such a time.

prātas tam atyanunayan tam atarjayaṁ bho-
statraiva gaccha sukham āpnuhi tat punaś ca
roṣaḥ sa tat-sukha-paraḥ priyatottha eve-
tyālocaya vraja-bhuvo 'py anurāga-caryām (66)

"When Śrī Kṛṣṇa came the next morning and beseeched Me to forgive Him, I chastised Him angrily, saying, 'Go back to that beloved mistress of Yours and enjoy with her some more!' This anger was actually for Śrī Kṛṣṇa's happiness. Internally, I was asking Myself why He would go to a place where He finds no pleasure. My anger was only due to *prema*, which consists wholly and solely of the endeavour to give Śrī Kṛṣṇa pleasure. Reflect upon the loving affairs in Śrī Vṛndāvana in the light of this consideration. These affairs are transcendental and most astonishing.

adyotayaṁ muhur ahaṁ nija-kāmam eva
kiṁ māṁ vihāya ramayasy aparāṁ śaṭheti
vācā sa cāpi rati-cihna-juṣā sva-mūrttyā
vyajyaiva kāmam atha mantum urī cakāra (67)

"'You rogue, why did You leave Me so You could go and sport with other women?' With such language I repeatedly expressed My own desire for enjoying. His lusty activities were evident by the love-marks on His transcendental body, so He had to admit His fault.

premā dvayo rasikayor ayi dīpa eva
hṛd-veśma bhāsayati niścala eva bhāti
dvārād ayaṁ vadanatas tu bahiṣkṛtaś cet
nirvāti śīghram athavā laghutām upaiti (68)

"O my friend, *prema* is like a lamp. The hearts of both the *rasika nāyaka* and *nāyikā* are like a chamber, and the mouth is like a door. As long as the lamp of *prema* illuminates only the chamber, it will remain steady, but if its light is allowed to shine out through the door, the lamp will quickly become fainter or even go out.

ॐ ॐ ॐ

Prema cannot remain strong if it is expressed with words such as, "I love you dearly"; on the contrary, it will decrease.

antaḥ-sthitasya khalu tasya ruci-cchaṭākṣi-
vātāyanād adhara-gaṇḍa-lalāṭa-vakṣaḥ
cāru pradīpya tad-abhijña-janaṁ sva-bhāso
vjñāpayed api vilakṣaṇatām upetāḥ (69)

"The splendour of the lamp of *prema* in the pavilions of the lover's and beloved's hearts shines through the lattice of their window-like eyes. It illuminates their lips, cheeks, foreheads and breasts in a most wondrous way, and reveals its unique and

inexpressible beauty to one who is experienced in regard to the
nature of *prema*.

ॐ ॐ ॐ

It is inappropriate to express *prema* in words, for they cause its
intensity to diminish. But even if one does not express one's *prema* in
words, it cannot be concealed when facing the object of one's *prema*.
When *prema* appears in the heart, then the eyes, cheeks, lips and
forehead blossom, and an unprecedented, radiant mood appears.

> *kāntena kintu bahu-vallabhatā juṣā syāt*
> *niṣkrāmito 'pi sa muhur na hi yāti śāntim*
> *mithyaika-bhāṣana-paṭutvam ayī prathāsya*
> *kāmaṁ diśed yavanikeva pidhāya taṁ drāk* (70)

"The following words, however, would issue from the mouth
of Śrī Kṛṣṇa, the lover of so many young damsels: 'My beloved,
I love You so much; You alone are My very life.' In this way, He
would continuously express His love, yet still, His love would not
diminish. This is because it is Śrī Kṛṣṇa's habit to only speak very
clever words of falsity. This habit immediately veils His *prema* like
a curtain and makes it appear as lust. In other words, all of Śrī
Kṛṣṇa's declarations, which are to be taken as false, actually cover
His *prema* to make it appear merely as lust.

> *tvayy eva me priyatame 'nupamo 'nurāgaḥ*
> *svapne 'pi vastum aparā kim u hṛdya-piṣṭe*
> *itthaṁ harir vadati mānavatīḥ sadānyā*
> *māṁ khaṇḍitān tu rati-cihna-bhṛd eva vakti* (71)

"When one of Śrī Kṛṣṇa's beloveds starts to sulk, He tells
her, 'O My beloved, I love you alone. Could any other young
girl attain a place in My heart?' And when I become jealous
(*khaṇḍitā*) on seeing the marks made by another *nāyikā* on His
body, He pacifies Me with words of a similar nature.

mad-vaktra-netra-suṣamā sama-mādhurīka-
saundaryya-varṇana-balad-vijihīrṣa eva
prāṇās tvam eva hi mameti vadan vyanakti
na prema tat sad api kintv iha kāmam eva (72)

"In this situation, Śrī Kṛṣṇa glorifies the beauty, matchless grace and sweetness of My face and eyes, and in His intense eagerness to sport with Me, He speaks words such as, 'You alone are My life.' With such talk He covers His *prema* for Me, and instead shows lust.

santapyate yadi punar virahāgni-puñjai-
rutkaṇṭhayā culukitaḥ sva-gabhīrimābdhiḥ
prema vyanakti dayitāpi girā yathaiva
yat te sujāta-caraṇāmburuheti padye (73)

"O *sakhī*, despite all this, if a beloved *gopī* is burning in the fire of separation from Śrī Kṛṣṇa, and if her eagerness has evaporated the ocean of her gravity to a palmful of water, she will reveal her *prema* through words.

ॐ ॐ ॐ

Evidence of this is found in verses such as the following:

yat te sujāta-caraṇāmbaruhaṁ staneṣu
bhītāḥ śanaiḥ priya dadhīmahi karkaśeṣu
tenāṭavīm aṭasi tad vyathate na kiṁ svit
kūrpādibhir bhramati dhīr bhavad āyuṣāṁ naḥ

Śrīmad-Bhāgavatam (10.31.19)

Dearly beloved, we are afraid of causing pain to Your very soft lotus feet, and we therefore place them gently on our hard breasts. Do Your soft feet not suffer when You step on sharp stones and pebbles as You roam through the forests? Our minds are reeling with anxiety for You, who are our very soul.

tasmin mahā-virasatātitam asya pāre
na prāṇa-vāyur api sañcarituṁ śaśāka

prema-pradīpa-vara ety ati-dīptim eva
sneho nu yat pracuratāṁ ciram ācikāya (74)

"Although the movement of the life-air is checked when one is in the darkness of the suffering of separation, the lamp of profound *prema* shines long and bright with the oil of abundant affection.

      ॐ   ॐ   ॐ

The *vraja-sundarīs'* life-air cannot remain in their bodies when they are suffering in separation from Śrī Kṛṣṇa; yet at the same time it does not leave, because their immense affection causes their *prema* to increase.

rāse mayaiva vijahāra vihāya sarvā-
statrāpi māṁ yad amūcat śṛṇu tasya tattvam
premāmbudher vraja-purandara-nandanasya
mām eva mantur adhikāṁ na kadāpi mantuḥ (75)

"During the *rāsa* dance, Śrī Kṛṣṇa gave up the company of all the other *gopīs* and sported with Me alone, but after that He left Me as well, and I will tell You why. There is no fault in Vrajendra-nandana Śrī Kṛṣṇa, who is the ocean of *prema*. He accepts Me alone as His most beloved.

adhyāsya mām atula-saubhaga-divya-ratna-
siṁhāsanaṁ bahu-vilāsa-bharair vibhūṣya
gacchan vanād vanam arīramad eva kāntā-
manyāṁ punaḥ smṛti-pathe 'pi nināya nāyam (76)

"The basis of this statement is that Śrī Kṛṣṇa seated Me on a divine jewelled throne of matchless fortune, decorated Me with the ornaments of various playful pastimes, and enjoyed with Me as We roamed from forest to forest. At that time, He did not remember His other beloveds.

kiñcin mayaiva manasaiva vicāritaṁ ta-
rhyetaṁ mahotsava-sudhāmbudhim aty-apāram
naivānvabhūn mama sakhī-tatir āvayoḥ sā
viśleṣa-saṅgara-dhutā kva nu kiṁ karoti (77)

"Then, I began to think, 'Alas, My *sakhīs* are not able to experience this vast and fathomless ocean of ecstatic nectar. They are burning in the fever of separation from Me, and I do not know where they are wandering in their search for Me.

atrāsvahe yadi punaḥ katicit kṣaṇās tā
ālyo milanti rabhasād abhito bhramantyaḥ
ity abhyadhāṁ priyatamātha na pāraye 'ham
gantuṁ muhūrttam iha viśramaṇaṁ bhajeva (78)

"'My *sakhīs* are roaming about here and there, and if We sit here for just a moment, they will soon reach this spot and find Us.' Thinking in this way, I said, 'O My beloved, I cannot walk any more. Let Us rest here for a while.'

tan me manogatam idaṁ sahasaiva sādhu
sarvaṁ viveda sa vidagdha-śiromaṇitvāt
cāturya-sampad-atulo rasikāgra-gaṇyaḥ
kiñcit sapady atha hṛdaiva parām amarśa (79)

"Śrī Kṛṣṇa fully understood My inner mood at that time, because He is *vidagdha-śiromaṇi*, the crest jewel of clever personalities. Being extremely cunning, and matchless in His ability to relish divine mellows, He thought to Himself,

etāṁ nayann upavane yadi bambhramīmi
sambhāvitāly atirujā puru-viddha-cittām
kiṁ syāt sukhaṁ yadi dadhe sthitim atra gopyaḥ
sarvā mileyur api tāḥ kuṭila-bhruvo mām (80)

enāṁ punaś ciram anekam upālabheran
bhaṅgaś ca sāmpratika-keli-rasasya bhāvī
sampatsyate 'dya na hi rāsa-vinoda-nṛtyaṁ
tāsu krudhā nija-nijaṁ sadanaṁ gatāsu (81)

"'If Śrī Rādhikā and I roam in the groves alone, She will not feel the slightest happiness. Rather, Her heart will be full of pain because She will be aware of the possible distress of the *sakhīs*. As long as She bears such pain in Her heart, there can be no pleasure in Our union. However, if I do stop here for a short while, the *sakhīs* will be jealous of the fact that We are together. They will look at Me with crooked eyebrows and reproach Śrī Rādhikā, thus interrupting the loving exchange between Us. Then they will all go home angrily, and we will not be able to delight in the *rāsa* dance tonight.'

yat prārthitaṁ sva-kutukena purānayaiva
śaknoṣi kiṁ nu kulajārbuda-lakṣa-koṭīh
āliṅgituṁ priyatama! kṣaṇam ekam anvi-
tyāste didṛkṣitam idaṁ mama pūrayeti (82)

tasmād imām api jahat-pala-mātram eva
nirdūṣaṇāṁ vinayinīṁ prathamaṁ vidhāya
mantuṁ sva-mūrddhny akhilam eva dadhāmy ṛṇī syāṁ
tāḥ snehayāni nikhilā api sarvathā syām (83)

"O *sakhī*, Śrī Kṛṣṇa then thought further: 'Previously Śrī Rādhikā made this request: "O beloved, I desire to see how You embrace innumerable virtuous *gopīs* at the same time. Kindly satisfy My curiosity." If the *rāsa* dance with the *gopīs* does not take place, Śrī Rādhikā's desire will not be fulfilled. Now, if I leave Rādhikā for a moment, that will remove Her pride born of good fortune. It will make Her humble and free from blame in the eyes of the other *gopīs*. I will accept all the blame. I will show the other young ladies of Vraja that the fault is all Mine, and not Śrī Rādhikā's. But if I leave Rādhikā, I will not be able to serve Her and thereby reciprocate with Her affection for Me. As a result I will become indebted to Her, and all the *gopīs* will become affectionate toward Her.

vaiśleṣika-jvaram apāram atulyam asyāḥ
sandarśya vismaya-mahābdhiṣu majjitānām
sva-prema-garvam api nirdhunavāny athainā-
ntābhir mahādhikatamām anubhāvayāmi (84)

"'I will plunge the other *vraja-sundarīs* into an ocean of astonishment by revealing the boundless and incomparable agony that Rādhikā feels when She is separated from Me. They will then come to understand the depth of Her *prema* for Me, and that will dissolve the pride that appeared in their hearts when they thought that I loved them more than anyone else. After that, all the *gopīs* will firmly trust and believe that Śrī Rādhikā is supreme and beyond compare.

sambhoga eṣa sakalādhika eva vipra-
lambho 'pi sarva-śata-koṭi-guṇādhiko 'stu
tābhyāṁ śuciḥ parama-puṣṭim upaiti cāsyā-
ntā hrepayatv alam imāṁ tu gurū-karotu (85)

"'All the other beautiful young women will understand that just as the mellow of union (*sambhoga-rasa*) finds its absolute summit in Śrī Rādhikā, so Her feeling of separation from Me is incomparably greater than that of all the other *gopīs*. Only in Rādhikā is the transcendental mellow of amorous love (*śṛṅgāra-rasa*) nourished to the utmost point by union with Me and separation from Me. Thus the other *vraja-sundarīs* will become ashamed, and they will clearly see Rādhikā as their *guru*.'

kāmī harir bhavati no yad asau vihāya
premādhikā api raho ramate tu tasyām

ittham vadantya iha samprati yā ruṣāsyāḥ
ālīs tudanti bahu nāv api dūṣayanti (86)

tā eva koṭi-guṇitā virahe tv amuṣyāḥ
premāgni-bāḍava-śikhāḥ paricāyayāmi
yābhir balād upagatād avalihyamānāḥ
sva-prema-dīpa-dahanāyitam eva vidyuḥ (87)

"O friend, Śrī Kṛṣṇa also had another thought in His heart:
'The angry *gopīs* call Me lusty because I left them to play secretly
with Rādhikā. They think that they are more loving toward Me
than Śrī Rādhikā is, and this saddens Lalitā and the other *gopīs*
in Rādhikā's own group. The angry *gopīs* accuse both Rādhikā
and Me of having many faults. I will show them how the flames
of Rādhikā's *prema* increase a millionfold when She is separated
from Me. If those *gopīs* come close to Rādhikā while She is
feeling such separation, they will be burnt by these flames. Thus
they will be able to recognize that their own *prema* glows like an
insignificant lamp in comparison.

evañca setsyati mad-īpsitam aikyam āsāṁ
rāsākhya-nāṭyam anumaṇḍalatāṁ gatānām
madhye mayā saha rucā tu virājamānā-
menāṁ vilokya na bhaved api kācid īrṣā (88)

"'When the other *vraja-ramaṇīs* see Rādhā crying in separation
from Me, they will become sympathetic toward Her. Then, all of
them will come together to search for Me, and that is just what I
desire. Finally, at the time of the *rāsa* dance, they will all dance in
a circle, and they will not feel any jealousy when they see Rādhikā
shining brilliantly by My side, in the centre of the circle.

kaṣṭaṁ kadāpi sukha-sampad udarkam eva
mitrāya mitram api yacchati tad-dhitaiṣi

tīvrāñjanair yad api mūrcchayati sva-dṛṣṭi-
māyaty ati-dyuti-matiṁ kurute janas tām (89)

"'People make their eyes appear bright and beautiful by applying collyrium to them, even though that collyrium may cause them some discomfort. Similarly, well-wishers may create temporary difficulties for their friends that ultimately result in their friends' wealth or happiness. Even though I will cause pain to Rādhā by abandoning Her for some time, She will experience the highest bliss when We meet again.'

ity ātta-yuktir urasā sarasaṁ vahan māṁ
gatvā padāni katicin mṛdula-pradeśe
atrāsyatāṁ kṣaṇam apīti nidhāya tatrai-
vāste sma me nayana-gocaratāṁ jahat saḥ (90)

"O *devī*, as My beloved was deliberating in this way, He tenderly lifted Me up and carried Me for a few steps. Then He put Me down in a soft place, saying, 'My dear one, please sit here for a moment.' At that point He disappeared.

dṛṣṭvā mamātivikalatvam apāsta-dhairyyo
dātuṁ sva-darśanam iyeṣa yadā tadaiva
gopyaḥ sakhī-vitatayaś ca sametya tā mat-
sandhukṣaṇe samayatanta nitānta-taptāḥ (91)

"*Sakhī*, My beloved Śrī Kṛṣṇa became perturbed when He saw My grief in separation from Him, and He wanted to come before Me again. But, just at that moment My *sakhīs* and the other *gopīs* arrived. They were extremely distressed to see My suffering, and they tried to console Me.

yac cāvadhīt punar ariṣṭa-bakāgha-vatsān
viśva-druhaḥ kapaṭinīm api pūtanāṁ tām

doṣo na cāyam api tūccataraiva viṣṇu-
śaktir harāv ajani sādhu-janāvanīyam (92)

"Śrī Kṛṣṇa was not at fault in killing the bull-demon
Ariṣṭāsura, the crane-demon Bakāsura, the snake-demon
Aghāsura, the calf-demon Vatsāsura, or the deceptive *rākṣasī*
Pūtanā. It is the divine potency of Lord Viṣṇu, the protector of all
virtuous men, that kills demons, and that potency is within Śrī
Kṛṣṇa.

૰ૐ ૰ૐ ૰ૐ

Śrī Caitanya-caritāmṛta (*Ādi-līlā* 4.8, 13) states:

> *svayaṁ bhagavānera karma nahe bhāra-haraṇa*
> *sthiti-kartā viṣṇu karena jagat-pālana*
>
> *ataeva viṣṇu takhana kṛṣṇera śarīre*
> *viṣṇu-dvāre kṛṣṇa kare asura-saṁhāre*

It is not the work of Svayam Bhagavān Śrī Kṛṣṇa to remove the
burden of the universe; rather, it is the work of the maintainer, Śrī
Viṣṇu. ... During Śrī Kṛṣṇa's pastimes on Earth, it was Śrī Viṣṇu,
present within Kṛṣṇa's body, who actually killed the demons.

nārāyaṇena sadṛśas tanayas tavāya-
mity āha yad vraja-purandaram eva gargaḥ
tat-sākṣi-bhūtam iha daitya-vadhādi-karma
lokottaraṁ samudagād giridhāraṇādi (93)

"On the occasion of Śrī Kṛṣṇa's name-giving ceremony, the
sage Gargācārya told Vraja-rāja Śrī Nanda, 'O King of Vraja, your
son is just like Nārāyaṇa.'

૰ૐ ૰ૐ ૰ૐ

Kṛṣṇa's killing of demons, His lifting of Govardhana Hill and the
many other divine feats that He performed are proof of the great sage's
words.

kiñca sphuraty ayi yathā mama cetasīdaṁ
tenāpi nāpi kathitaṁ muni-puṅgavena
nārāyaṇo 'py agha-bhido na hi sāmyam asya
rūpair guṇair madhurimādibhir etum īṣṭe (94)

"O *devī*, at Śrī Kṛṣṇa's name-giving ceremony, Gargamuni, the best of sages, did not say that Śrī Nārāyaṇa's form, qualities, sweetness and other attributes will never be able to equal those of Śrī Kṛṣṇa, the enemy of Agha. But naturally it seems like that in My mind."

ॐ ॐ ॐ

Bhakti-rasāmṛta-sindhu (1.2.59) mentions:

siddhāntatas tv abhede 'pi śrīśa-kṛṣṇa-svarūpayoḥ
rasenotkṛṣyate kṛṣṇa-rūpam eṣā rasa-sthitiḥ

From the perspective of *siddhānta*, Śrī Nārāyaṇa, the Lord of Śrī Lakṣmī, is non-different from Śrī Kṛṣṇa. However, from the perspective of *rasa*, the form of Śrī Kṛṣṇa is *sākṣāt manmatha-manmatha*, He who even bewilders the mind of Cupid, who himself bewilders ordinary people's minds. This is achieved by Kṛṣṇa's four unique qualities: *līlā-mādhurī*, *prema-mādhurī*, *veṇu-mādhurī* and *rūpa-mādhurī*.[3]

ākarṇya karṇa-ramaṇīyatamāḥ priyāyā
vāco hariḥ sa-rabhasaṁ punar abhyadhatta
premokta eva khalu lakṣita-lakṣaṇo yaḥ
so 'yaṁ tvad-āśrayaka eva mayādhyavodhi (95)

The words of Śrī Kṛṣṇa's beloved Śrī Rādhikā were blissful nectar to His ears, and caused Him great joy. Still disguised as a

---

[3] (1) *līlā-mādhurī* – Śrī Kṛṣṇa is the performer of astonishing varieties of pastimes, of which *rāsa-līlā* is the most captivating; (2) *prema-mādhurī* – He is surrounded by devotees who possess incomparable *mādhurya-prema*, which develops to the stage of *mahābhāva*; (3) *veṇu-mādhurī* – the sweet and mellow sound of His flute attracts the minds of everyone within the three worlds; and (4) *rūpa-mādhurī* – His extraordinary beauty astonishes all moving and non-moving entities.

heavenly damsel, He said with great curiosity, "Rādhā, now I can fully understand that You alone are the shelter of the symptoms of the *prema* that You have been explaining.

> *doṣā api priyatamasya guṇā yataḥ syu-*
> *stad-datta-kaṣṭa-śatam apy amṛtāyate yat*
> *tad-duḥkha-leśa-kaṇikāpi yato na sahyā*
> *tyaktvātma-deham api yaṁ na vihātum iṣṭe* (96)

> *yo 'santam apy anupamaṁ mahimānam uccaiḥ*
> *pratyāyayaty anupadaṁ sahasā priyasya*
> *premā sa eva tam imaṁ dadhatī tvam eva*
> *rādhe śrutā khalu mayaiva tathaiva dṛṣṭā* (97)

"My dear *sakhī*, You have explained to Me the following characteristics of *prema*: even the faults of the beloved may be perceived as good qualities; the many troubles given by the beloved may appear to be nectar; one with *prema* is unable to bear even the slightest difficulty felt by the beloved; one with *prema* is unable to give up the body even if he wishes to; and at every step one perceives unprecedented glories in the beloved, even where there are none. Rādhā, this *prema* is in You alone. I have heard this earlier in the assembly at Haimavatī, and today I am witnessing it directly.

> *premī harir na hi bhaved iti satyam eva*
> *tac-ceṣṭitair anumime tam ime vadanti*
> *prāṇā mama tvad-anutāpa-davāgni-dagdhāḥ*
> *sakhyas tavātra nikhilā api yat pramāṇam* (98)

"But *sakhī*, I am telling You without any doubt that Śrī Kṛṣṇa has no *prema*. Please understand this to be true. I have concluded this after seeing His behaviour. The proof of this is found in Your *sakhīs* and in the flames of Your intense lamentation, which have scorched My life-air.

yac ca tvayoktam idam eva manogatam mat-
    preṣṭhasya tat tu vayam atra katham pratīmaḥ
no tan-mukhāt tvam aśṛṇor na ca tasya sakhyu-
    stau vā januṣya bhavatām kva nu satya-vācau (99)

"You have told Me the reasons why He left You at the time of
rāsa, but how can I believe what You say? You have not heard this
from His mouth, nor from any of His friends. And even if You did
hear it from them, so what? Have any of them ever spoken a true
word in their life?"

yarhy eva yad yad ayi mat-priya-cetasi syāt
    tarhy eva tat tad akhilam sahasaiva vedmi
rādhe viduṣyasi kim acyuta-yoga-śāstram
    śaknoṣi yena para-kāya-manaḥ praveṣṭum (100)

Śrī Rādhikā then said, "*Sakhī*, I am aware of all the moods in
the heart of My beloved Śrī Kṛṣṇa as soon as they arise."

To this the heavenly damsel replied, "Rādhā, have You studied
the scriptures that delineate the means by which one can meet
with Acyuta – the scriptures on *acyuta-yoga* which describe how
You are able to enter Śrī Kṛṣṇa's body and mind?"

devījano 'sya viratācyuta-yoga-siddhi-
    vyagras tathā katham aho vata mānuṣī syām
yat pṛcchasīdam ayi vaktum aśeṣam īśe
    ced viśvasiṣy aparathā tu kathā vṛthaiva (101)

Śrī Rādhā replied, "You are a celestial damsel, so You are
always eager to cultivate the perfection of *acyuta-yoga*. I am just
a human being; how can I be like You? Are You asking Me how
I can possibly know the mind of My beloved? I shall tell You
everything if You have faith that what I say is true; if not, why
should I waste My words?"

pratyāyane 'sti yadi yuktir atiprabhāvaḥ
kiṁ v āli te katham idaṁ na vayaṁ pratīmaḥ
no cet priyas tava guṇārṇava eva kintu
premī bhaved ayam idaṁ tu mataṁ tavaiva (102)

Hearing this, that heavenly damsel answered, "O Rādhā, if
You can convince Me with logic, and if You can awaken My faith,
then why would I not believe You? It is true that Your beloved
Śrī Kṛṣṇa is an ocean of good qualities, but it is only Your own
personal opinion that He has *prema*."

preṣṭhaḥ paro bhavati tasya mano na budhya
ity eva bhāty anubhavādhvani hanta yasyāḥ
saivocyatāṁ nu para-kāya-manaḥ praveśa-
vidyāvatīti parihāsa-vidā tvayādya (103)

Śrī Rādhikā said, "My dear *sakhī*, You joke most cleverly. You
say that You have acquired expertise in the art of entering the
body and mind of the lover or anyone else, but now You are
realizing that actually You are unable to understand the mind of
Your lover."

rādhe! tadā vilapitaṁ kim iti tvayoccai-
rjñātvā hṛdasya sukhinī katham eva nābhūḥ
satyaṁ bravīṣy api tu devy avadhehi kāpi
śaktir viveka-bhid abhūt tad-adarśanasya (104)

The celestial damsel said, "O Rādhā, if You know the mind
and heart of Your beloved Śrī Kṛṣṇa, why were You lamenting so
loudly when He left You? If You knew His heart, why did You not
become happy?"

Śrī Rādhikā replied, "*Devī*, Your point is valid, but please
listen carefully. I truly know Śrī Kṛṣṇa's heart, but still, when I
was in separation from Him, an indescribable potency arose and

overwhelmed Me. It stole all My discrimination and caused Me to lose consciousness and all awareness of My mind and body."

> *tvaṁ vetsi tan-mana ihāstu na me vivādo*
> *gāndharvike! tava manaḥ sa hi veda no vā*
> *vedeti kiṁ bhaṇasi bhoḥ śṛṇu yad-rahasyaṁ*
> *tattvaṁ tvayā yad abhavaṁ taralī-kṛtaiva* (105)

Śrī Kṛṣṇa disguised as a heavenly damsel said, "Gāndharvikā, I am not questioning whether or not You know Śrī Kṛṣṇa's mind; rather, I want to know whether He knows Your mind."

Śrī Rādhikā replied, "*Sakhī,* have You as yet inquired whether or not Śrī Kṛṣṇa knows My mind? Listen and I will tell You the secret of this. It is generally impossible to speak of this, but today I will reveal everything to You because Your *prema* has made Me restless."

> *rādhe! jano 'yam ayi yat taralī-kṛto 'bhūt*
> *premnā tvayaiva tad apṛccham idaṁ sva-dhārṣṭyam*
> *śuśrūṣate śravaṇam asya yathā rahasyaṁ*
> *vaktuṁ tathārhasi na gopaya kiñcanāpi* (106)

"Rādhā," the heavenly damsel said, "I have expressed My desire to hear the secret behind this matter, and in so doing, I have revealed My arrogance. I am only asking You this because Your love has made Me eager to hear it. I know that this is most confidential, but still, it is most appropriate to carefully tell everything to Your eager *sakhī*; it is not appropriate to withhold this information."

> *anyonya-citta-viduṣau nu parasparātma-*
> *nitya-sthiter iti nṛṣu prathitau yad āvām*
> *tac-caupacārikam aho dvitayatvam eva*
> *naikasya sambhavati karhicid ātmano nau* (107)

Śrī Rādhikā then spoke: "Common people say, 'Rādhā and Kṛṣṇa are eternally present in each others' hearts, and that is why They know each others' minds.' Factually, the real truth is this: We are one soul. It is not possible for one soul to become two.

ekātmanīha rasa-pūrṇatame 'tyagādhe
ekā susaṅgrathitam eva tanu-dvayaṁ nau
kasyiṁścid eka-sarasīva cakāsad eka-
nālottham abja-yugalaṁ khalu nīla-pītam (108)

"In a lake, two lotuses – one blue and one yellow – may bloom from a single stem. In the same way, Our two bodies, one blue and one yellow, are connected as one life. They are one supremely profound soul composed of topmost *rasa*. As bodies We are separate, but by nature We are one. Kṛṣṇa is by nature blissful (*ānanda*) and I by nature am joyful (*hlādinī*). Just as fire and its burning potency are one, there is no difference between the potency (*śakti*) and the possessor of the potency (*śaktimān*).

"We cannot be distinguished from each other when seen as a person and the person's potency, but for the sake of *rasa*, We manifest in separate forms as Rādhā and Kṛṣṇa. Without pastimes, We cannot relish each other; and without form, We cannot perform pastimes.

ॐ ॐ ॐ

With this truth in mind, *Śrī Gopāla-campūḥ* (*Pūrva-campū* 15.9) states:

imau gaurī-śyāmau manasi viparīrtau bahir api
sphurat tad tad vastrāv iti budha-janair niścitam idam
sa ko 'py accha-premā vilasad ubhayoḥ sphūrtikatayā
dadhan mūrttī-bhāva-pṛthag-apṛthag apy āvirudabhūt

The meaning of this verse (from *Śrī Gopāla-campūḥ*) is that Śrī Kṛṣṇa is fully present in Śrī Rādhā's heart, and Śrī Rādhā is fully present in Śrī Kṛṣṇa's heart. Śrī Rādhikā wears *śyāma*-coloured cloth, the colour of

Śrī Kṛṣṇa's complexion, and Kṛṣṇa wears yellow garments (*pītāmbara*), the colour of Rādhikā's. Seeing this, scholars learned in philosophical conclusions have ascertained that pure *prema*, which is impossible to describe in words, has manifested in two different forms. Furthermore, to perform enchanting pastimes, these forms are both different and non-different.

In *Śrī Caitanya-caritāmṛta* (*Ādi-līlā* 4.55–56) it is said:

> *rādhā kṛṣṇa-praṇaya-vikṛtir-hlādinī-śaktir-asmād*
> *ekātmānāv api bhuvi purā deha-bhedaṁ gatau tau*
>
> *rādhā-kṛṣṇa eka ātmā, dui deha dhari'*
> *anyonye vilāse rasa āsvādana kari'*

Śrīmatī Rādhikā is the very form of the transformation of *kṛṣṇa-prema*, and She is *kṛṣṇa-prema* in its most condensed state. She is the bliss-giving potency (*hlādinī-śakti*) of Kṛṣṇa's loving, sportive pastimes. Even though Śrī Rādhā and Śrī Kṛṣṇa are one soul, They have assumed two separate bodies to perform Their eternal loving pastimes in Goloka Vṛndāvana.

> *yat sneha-pūra-bhṛta-bhājana-rājitaika-*
> *vartty agravartty amala-dīpa-yugaṁ cakāsti*
> *tac cet are taratamo 'panudat parokṣa-*
> *mānandayed akhila-pārśva-gatāḥ sadālīḥ* (109)

"When a container filled with oil has a wick that is lit at both ends, the two flames dispel the darkness in both directions. Similarly, Our two bodies are joined together as one soul, destroying the darkness of each others' distress, and also giving pleasure to the *sakhīs* present with Us.

> *yady āpated viraha-māruta etad ātta-*
> *kampaṁ bhaved yugapad eva bhajec ca mūrcchām*
> *vyagrā sadāly atha tad-āvaraṇe yateta*
> *tat susthayec ca sukha-sadma-gataṁ vidhāya* (110)

"*Sakhī*, due to the blowing wind of separation from each other, the flames of Our two bodies tremble and We both faint at the same time. The *sakhīs*, all of whom are expert, anxiously try to stop this wind from blowing. They remove all Our distress and restore Our peaceful condition by arranging for Us to enter the house of happiness in each others' company.

sandarśitaṁ tad idam adya rahasya-ratnaṁ
svasvānta-sampuṭa-varaṁ sphuṭam udghaṭaya
sandeha-santam asahāri tavāstu bhavye
hṛdy eva dhāryam aniśaṁ na bahiḥ prakāśyam (111)

"O Kalyāṇi (auspicious one), today I have completely opened up the most precious treasure chest of My heart and shown You the supremely secret jewel of *prema*. May this remove the darkness of Your doubts completely. Always keep it in Your heart and never reveal it to anyone."

kṛṣṇo jagāda sakhi! yad yad idaṁ tvayoktaṁ
tat tat sa-yuktikam adhārayam eva sarvam
cetas tu me śaṭham aho haṭhavartty avaśyaṁ
tat te parīkṣitum ihecchati kiṁ karomi (112)

The celestial damsel (Śrī Kṛṣṇa) said, "My friend, I have clearly understood all that You have told Me, and I will keep it within My heart. But this crooked mind of Mine yearns to test the truth of Your words. How can I help this?

tvaṁ varttase 'tra sa tu sāmpratam ātma-tāta
gehe kadācid avanāya gavāṁ vane 'pi
ātmaikyam āli yuvayor yad iha pratīma-
stat kiṁ parīkṣaṇam ṛte samupaiti siddhim (113)

"*Sakhī*, as You sit here, Your beloved Śrī Kṛṣṇa may be in His father's house or in the forest tending the cows. I do believe that

You are one soul in two bodies, but only by testing it can it be actually proven.

> *yaiva smṛtiḥ sumukhi! yasya yathā yadā te*
> *saivāsya ced bhavati tarhi tathā tadaiva*
> *pratyakṣam eva yadi tāṁ kalayāmi sampra-*
> *tyatraiva vā sakhi tadaiva dadhe pratītim* (114)

"O Sumukhī (beautiful-faced one), if right now, at this very place, I directly perceive that Śrī Kṛṣṇa instantaneously and precisely knows what You are thinking, then O friend, My belief will become resolute.

> *dūre 'thavā nikaṭa eva sa te priyaḥ syā-*
> *dehīha satvaram iti smṛta-mātra eva*
> *āyāti cet tava samakṣam ayaṁ tadā vā-*
> *mātmaikyam ity avagamo dhinuyāt sadā mām* (115)

"Whether Your beloved is near here or far away, just think of Him and meditate on this: 'Please, come here quickly.' When I see Him present here before You, I will happily accept once and for all that You two are united as one soul.

> *vighnaḥ kvacit tu guru-nighnatayāpi daivād*
> *daityāgamād api kutaścana vāpi hetoḥ*
> *anyonyam apy atanu vāṁ smarato yadi syā-*
> *nno saṅgatis tad iha nāstitamāṁ vivādaḥ* (116)

"However, I will not say anything if the two of You are fully absorbed in thinking of each other but cannot meet because obstacles have arisen, such as the sudden arrival of a demon or Your having to obey the orders of elders.

> *yady apy amuṁ guru-pure sakhi saṅkucantī*
> *naivāhvayasy abhisarasyata eva dūram*

kiñcaikadāpi na tad āgamam īhase tvaṁ
svārthaṁ tv idaṁ tu nitarāṁ madirākṣi vidmaḥ (117)

kṛṣṇa-priye sakhi! tad apy adhunā mamānu-
rodhād amuṁ smara sa etu sukhaṁ tanotu
nātrāsti te guru-janāgamanāvakāśo
mat-saṁśayottham api khedam apākarotu (118)

"O *sakhī*, O You with intoxicated eyes (Madirākṣi), I know very well that when You are confined to the home of Your elders out of fear of them, You cannot call Śrī Kṛṣṇa to come to You. Your meeting with Him takes place far from Your home; You never desire that He come to You for Your own pleasure.

"But, now, My dear friend, O beloved of Śrī Kṛṣṇa, in accordance with My request, please remember Him just once. I would be overjoyed to see Him if He appeared here, especially since there is no reason to suspect the arrival of Your superiors. Please remove this painful doubt of Mine without hesitation."

ity arthitā sa-rabhasaṁ vṛṣabhānu-kanyā-
sanyāyam āha naya mā hasanīyatāṁ mām
brūṣe yathaiva karavāṇi tathaiva no cet
premaiva dhāsyati rujaṁ ciram ātta-lajjaḥ (119)

Śrī Rādhikā, the dear darling daughter of Śrī Vṛṣabhānu Mahārāja, duly deliberated upon the heavenly damsel's request and said, "O *sakhī*, do not make Me the object of ridicule. If I cannot satisfy Your request, I shall feel ashamed of My *prema* and thus I will be miserable forever.

vṛndārakeḍya! bhagavan! mad-abhīṣṭa-deva!
śrī-bhāskara! tri-jagad-īkṣaṇa-saukhya-dāyin
mat-sarva-kāma-da! kṛpāmaya! padminīśa!
satyānṛtādy-akhila-sākṣitayā pratīta (120)

gāndharvikā-giridharau bhavataḥ sadaikā-
tmānāv itīyam anṛtā na yadi prathāsti
sampraty asau giridharo 'tra tad ādadāno
man-netrayoḥ paricayaṁ svam ude 'bhyudetu (121)

"O Lord, who are worshipped by the demigods, O You who give pleasure to the living entities in all three worlds, O You who fulfil all My desires, O merciful one, O Padminīśa, O witness to all that is true and false, O My worshipful Lord, O Bhagavān Sūryadeva, if people speak the truth when they say 'Rādhā and Kṛṣṇa are eternally one soul', may Śrī Kṛṣṇa appear directly before My eyes so as to give pleasure to My intimate associates."

uktvedam eva vṛṣabhānu-sutātma-kāntaṁ
dhyātuṁ samārabhata mīlita-netra-yugmā
sā yoginīva viniruddha-hṛṣīka-vṛtti-
rāste sma yāvad avikhaṇḍita-mauna-mudrā (122)

tāvad vihāya sahasaiva hariḥ sa yoṣi-
dveṣaṁ sakhīḥ svam akhilāḥ paricinvatīs tāḥ
bhru-saṁjñayaiva vidadhan nija-pakṣa-pāte
cumban priyāṁ muhur avāritam āliliṅga (123)

Saying this, Vṛṣabhānu-nandinī Śrī Rādhikā closed Her eyes and meditated upon Her lover, Śrī Kṛṣṇa. She sat down like a *yoginī*, subduing the functions of Her senses and observing full silence.

In a moment Śrī Kṛṣṇa removed His disguise, thus revealing His identity to the other *sakhīs*. With the movement of His eyebrows He conveyed His desire that they play along with Him, and then He embraced His beloved Śrī Rādhikā and began to kiss Her freely again and again.

romāñcitākhila-tanur galad-aśru-siktā
dhyānāgataṁ tam avabudhya bahir vilokya

ānanda-līna-hṛdayā khalu satyam eva
yoginy arājata nirañjana-dṛṣṭir eṣā (124)

Śrī Rādhikā's whole body began to horripilate, and tears of joy flowed from Her eyes. As soon as She understood in Her meditation that Her beloved Śrī Kṛṣṇa had come, She opened Her eyes. Seeing Śrī Kṛṣṇa before Her, She became immersed in an ocean of rapturous bliss. Śrī Rādhikā appeared like a *yoginī* directly meeting *brahma*. The tears from Her eyes washed away Her collyrium.

saṁjñāṁ kṣaṇād alabhatātha paṭāñcalena
vaktraṁ pidhāya sudṛg ātanute sma lajjām
taṁ prāha saiva lalitā kim aho vilāsi-
nnāgā alakṣitam iha tvam atīva citram (125)

After a few moments, beautiful-eyed Śrī Rādhikā returned to Her senses and shamefully covered Her face with the end of Her garment. Śrī Lalitā addressed Śrī Kṛṣṇa, that crest jewel of all gallant lovers, "O sportive one, it is most astonishing that You have come here undetected.

antaḥ-pure kula-vadhū-kula-mātra-gamye
śakto na yatra pavano 'pi haṭhāt praveṣṭum
tatreti yas tu gatabhīḥ puruṣaḥ sa eṣa
gaṇyo 'tisāhasika-śekhara eka eva (126)

"Only the women of the family are allowed entrance into this private, inner chamber of the house. Even the wind cannot enter here. That male who comes here without fear must be the crest jewel of courageous men.

tatrāpi mad-vidha-sakhī-jana-pālitāyāḥ
sādhvī-kulāplavana-kīrtti-surāpagāyāḥ

snātvaiva mitra-yajanāya kṛtāsanāyā-
staṁ dhyātum eva vinimīlita-locanāyāḥ (127)

aṅgaṁ balāt spṛśasi yad-vṛṣabhānu-putryā
devāt tato dina-pater api no vibheṣi
na tvaṁ kim atra gaṇayiṣyasi loka-dharmau
lajjā tu keyam iti na hi paryyacaiṣīḥ (128)

"You are forcibly touching the body of Śrī Rādhikā, the daughter of King Vṛṣabhānu, even though She is constantly guarded by fierce *sakhīs* like me. Her fame is like the sacred river Mandākinī, in which chaste women ritually bathe by engaging in the purification of hearing and chanting. In other words, She is the best of chaste women. Even Arundhatī desires to attain Her chastity.

"After Śrī Rādhikā took Her bath, She sat with closed eyes to worship Mitradeva, the Sungod. [That is, on the pretext of worshipping the Sungod She meditated upon satisfying Her most beloved Śrī Kṛṣṇa.] You do not know the meaning of shame. Have You no fear of the Sungod? Have You no regard for social etiquette and moral virtues?

tan mādhavādya tava diṣṭam ahaṁ stuve ya-
dāryā gṛhe na hi nāpi patiḥ sa kopi
sakhyo 'balā vayam aho karavāma kiṁ te
bhadreṇa lampaṭa-vara tvam ito 'vito 'bhūḥ (129)

"O Mādhava, I praise Your good fortune that Śrī Rādhikā's mother-in-law Jaṭilā and Her angry husband are not at home. We *sakhīs* are but frail and weak women. How can we oppose You? O topmost amongst all debauchees, today by Your good fortune You have skilfully protected Yourself from this danger."

৯   ৯   ৯

Śrī Lalitā's words were full of irony. She actually meant: "O Kṛṣṇa, Śrī Rādhā's mother-in-law Jaṭilā and Her angry husband are not at home. I am Her friend, and since I always desire Her happiness, please sport with my friend Rādhikā without any fear."

kṛṣṇo 'bravīt kam api naiva dadhāmi mantuṁ
gośāla-catvaram anuśrita-khelano 'ham
daivāt samasmaram imam atha sadya eva
daivena kenacid ivāgamito 'py abhūvam (130)

Śrī Kṛṣṇa replied, "Lalitā, I am not to blame for what has happened. I was playing in the courtyard of the cowshed, when I suddenly remembered Śrī Rādhikā, and then some demigod instantly brought Me here."

rādhābhyadhatta lalite! kva nu varttate 'sau
devī pratītim upayāti vilokya no vā
devī tu dīvyati dṛśaiva gatādhir eta-
ddhāmāntar atra mudam ātanute tato naḥ (131)

Śrī Rādhikā said, "My dear friend Lalitā, Śrī Kṛṣṇa came here simply as a result of My remembering Him. But where has that celestial damsel gone? Does She believe Me now that She has witnessed this?"

Lalitā replied, "When that heavenly damsel saw the two of You meet, all doubt left Her and the pain in Her heart was dispelled. She is inside, arranging for our happiness."

devīti kāṁ bhaṇasi tāṁ paricāyayātre-
tyuktvā sakhīṁ harir athābruvad abruvāṇām
āṁ jñātam adya lalite khalu dhūrttatā vo
vyakteyataiva samayena babhūva diṣṭyā (132)

Śrī Kṛṣṇa said, "Please introduce Me to this heavenly damsel." When Śrī Lalitā did not reply, He said, "Aah, now I understand. Now, by good fortune, I have come to understand your cunningness.

kāpy atra siddha-vanitā kim u khecarī vā
devī sameti tata eva gṛhīta-vidyā
mām atyavaśyam iyam ātmavaśe vidhāya
dāsīyati pratidinaṁ prasabhaṁ prakṛṣya (133)

"Some adept young lady endowed with supernatural power, or some aerial demigoddess, must have come to your home, and your friend Rādhikā must have learned some supernatural *mantra* from her. Now Rādhikā has rendered Me weak and helpless, even though I am not controlled by anyone. Every day She forcefully allures Me and wants to make Me Her servant.

saivādya mahyam api kañcana mantram ekaṁ
rādhe dadātu bhava bhāvini me sahāyā
śiṣyaṁ tvam eva kuru mām athavā prapanna-
mutkaṇṭhitaṁ rahasi kutracanāpi nītvā (134)

"O Bhāvinī, O Śrī Rādhā, please arrange for this heavenly damsel to give Me a *mantra* too. I eagerly surrender unto You. Please take Me to a solitary place and make Me Your disciple."

vaṁśy eva rājatitamām atisiddha-vidyā
sāṅkaṁ tavānayati sādhu-satīḥ pura-strīḥ
tāñ cāpi corayasi yarhi tadā gatir me
kā syād ato nahi tayāpi sadārtha-siddhiḥ (135)

Śrī Rādhikā said, "In Your hand You hold Your shining flute, which is endowed with supernatural power and which can attract supremely chaste young married women to fulfil Your desires. Why do You need any other *mantra*?"

"The flute cannot always fulfil My task," Śrī Kṛṣṇa answered. "How can it help Me when you people steal it?"

devī hriyā tava gṛhāntar ihāsti līnā
tvām eva mantram upadekṣyati sā kathaṁ vā

> *utkaṇṭhase tad api cet praviśa svayaṁ bhoḥ*
> *sā cet dayeta bhavitā eva kārya-siddhiḥ* (136)

Lalitā replied, "O Kṛṣṇa, the celestial damsel became shy when She saw You so She hid in the house. Why would She teach You a *mantra*? If You are so eager, go into the house. If the heavenly damsel is merciful, She will certainly fulfil Your desires."

> *ity acyute viśati veśma jagāda rādhā*
> *kiṁ tattvam atra sakhi! māṁ vada saṁśayānām*
> *rādhe! na saṅkuca cala praviśāmi tasyāḥ*
> *sakhyās tavātra hariṇā kalayāmi saṅgam* (137)

Hearing this, Śrī Kṛṣṇa entered the house. Śrī Rādhikā asked, "Lalitā, what are you doing? Tell Me clearly. I do not understand what is going on, but I have a suspicion."

Lalitā replied, "My friend Rādhā, do not hesitate. Let us go into the house and observe Your friend meeting Śrī Kṛṣṇa."

> *ālīṣu manda-hasitāmṛta-varṣiṇīṣu*
> *kṛṣṇokti-pāṭavam athodabhinat tad uptam*
> *hṛd-vapram anvadhita tarka-tarus tato 'syā*
> *ṛddhaḥ phalaṁ bahu-rasaṁ nikhilāvabodham* (138)

Thereafter, the seed of Śrī Kṛṣṇa's skilful words was sown in the field of Śrī Rādhikā's heart. It sprouted and, showered with sweet laughter from the clouds of Śrī Lalitā and the other *sakhīs*, it grew into a tree of knowledge that gave fruits that were filled with *rasa*.

འ   ই   ই

Śrī Kṛṣṇa's clever talk, as potent as a *mantra* given by a demigoddess, put doubts in Śrī Rādhikā's heart. These doubts thickened with the laughter of the *sakhīs*. However, after carefully contemplating what had happened, She came to understand everything, and became overjoyed to learn that She had met with Śrī Kṛṣṇa, who is more dear to Her than millions of Her own lives.

antardadhe bahir agād athavātra devī
tan-mārgaṇāya tad itas tvarayā prayāmaḥ
vidyāṁ tvam eva sakhi! tāṁ upadiśya kṛṣṇa-
mānandayeti sahasā niragus tadālyaḥ (139)

Śrī Lalitā said, "It seems that the heavenly damsel has disappeared from this place or gone outside. Let us immediately go and search for Her. O friend Rādhā, please impart knowledge of the *mantra* to Śrī Kṛṣṇa and make Him happy." Thereupon, the *sakhīs* hastily left.

tat prema-samputa-gatair bahu-keli-ratnai-
stau maṇḍitāvajayatāṁ rati-kānta-koṭīḥ
santo 'pi yat śravaṇa-kīrtana-cintanādyai-
stau prāptum unnata-mudaḥ satataṁ jayanti (140)

Śrī Rādhā and Śrī Kṛṣṇa decorated Themselves with the jewels of amorous pastimes from the treasure chest of *prema*, and by so doing defeated millions of Cupids. This is not astonishing. Saintly devotees hear and chant about these gems of transcendental, amorous pastimes and meditate on them to attain service to Śrī Śrī Rādhā-Kṛṣṇa's lotus feet. Thus, they attain supreme bliss and eternally overcome lust.

ॐ   ॐ   ॐ

After one has tasted the *rasa* of transcendental pastimes, the desire for mundane enjoyment cannot remain in the heart. The heart and mind will then remain eternally immersed in relishing such *rasa*, leaving no place for thoughts related to the body or the senses.

ṣaṭ-śūnya-ṛtv-avanibhir ganite tapasye
śrī-rūpa-vāṅ-madhurimāmṛta-pāna-puṣṭaḥ
rādhā-girīndra-dharayoḥ sarasas taṭānte
tat-prema-samputam avindata ko 'pi kāvyam (141)

iti śrī-prema-samputaḥ sampūrṇaḥ

This poem about Śrī Śrī Rādha-Kṛṣṇa, entitled *Śrī Prema-samputa*, was manifested in the month of Phālguna in year 1606 of the Śakābda Era (AD 1684) on the bank of Śrī Rādhā-kuṇḍa and Śrī Śyāma-kuṇḍa by one who is fully nourished by drinking the sweet, nectarean words of Śrīla Rūpa Gosvāmī.

༔ ༔ ༔

Here, out of humility, Śrīla Viśvanātha Cakravartī Ṭhākura does not reveal his name.

iti śrīla-bhaktivedānta nārāyaṇa gosvāmī sampāditaṁ śrī-prema-samputa-bhāvānuvādaṁ sampūrṇaḥ

Thus ends the *bhāvānuvāda* of *Śrī Prema-samputa* of Śrīla Viśvanātha Cakravartī Ṭhākura by Śrīla Bhaktivedānta Nārāyaṇa Gosvāmī Mahārāja.

The Last Intellectuals

Other Works by Russell Jacoby

THE END OF UTOPIA: CULTURE AND IDEOLOGY IN
THE AGE OF RESIGNATION

THE LAST
INTELLECTUALS

American Culture in the
Age of Academe

With a New Introduction by the Author

RUSSELL JACOBY

A Member of the Perseus Books Group

Published by Basic Books,
A Member of the Perseus Books Group

Poem from C. Wright Mills, *The New Men of Power,* reprinted by permission of the publisher, Harcourt Brace Jovanovich, Inc.

Excerpts from *All That is Solid Melts into Air* copyright © 1982 by Marshall Berman. Reprinted by permission of Simon & Schuster, Inc.

Library of Congress Cataloging-in-Publication Data
Jacoby, Russell.
    The last intellectuals.

    Includes index.
    ISBN 0-465-03812-3 (cloth)
    ISBN 0-465-03625-2 (paper)
    1. Intellectuals—United States 2. United States—Intellectual life—20th Century 3. Universities and colleges—United States— Faculty. I. Title.
E169.12.J28   1987   973.9   87-47513

00   01   02   03

For Sarah and Sam

CONTENTS

PREFACE

"WHERE ARE our intellectuals?" In his 1921 book, *America and the Young Intellectual*, Harold Stearns (1891–1943), a chronicler of his generation, asked this question.[1] He found them fleeing to Europe, an act he supported and soon followed, joining what became the most celebrated of American intellectual groupings, the lost generation.

Stearns's question may speak to the present, but his answer does not. He believed that the hostility of a commercial civilization to youth in general, and to intellectuals in particular, drove young writers to Europe. This does not capture the current situation. Youth is lionized; intellectuals, if noticed, are usually blessed or subsidized. The young head for Europe not to flee, but for vacations, sometimes for conferences. Few American intellectuals live in exile. The question still stands. Where are the younger intellectuals? It is my starting point.

I have not located many—and I am using a criterion of "young," under forty-five or so, that will scandalize the authentically young. Nor are my standards absolute. The "last" generation of American intellectuals is my benchmark, those born in the first decades of this century. They possessed a voice and presence that younger intellectuals have failed to appropriate.

Yet this misleads; the issue is not a moral lapse but a generational shift. The experience of intellectuals has changed; this is not exactly news, but the causes are unexplored, and one consequence—at least—is unnoticed and profoundly damaging: the impoverishment of public culture.

Intellectuals who write with vigor and clarity may be as scarce as low rents in New York or San Francisco. Raised in city streets and cafes before the age of massive universities, "last" generation intellectuals wrote for the educated reader. They have been supplanted by high-tech intellectuals, consultants and professors—anonymous souls, who may be competent, and more than competent, but who do not enrich public life. Younger intellectuals, whose lives have unfolded almost entirely on campuses, direct themselves to professional colleagues but are inaccessible and unknown to others. This is the danger and the threat; the public culture relies on a dwindling band of older intellectuals who command the vernacular that is slipping out of reach of their successors.

In the following chapters I survey this breach in cultural generations; I offer some possibilities and appraise the costs. Nothing more. A small book confronting a large subject requires a thousand qualifications. I will skip most of them, but several are in order.

Apart from some references to novelists marking the landscape, I confine my account to nonfiction, especially literary, social, philosophical, and economic thought, where I believe the generational break is most emphatic, most injurious. I am excluding music, dance, painting, poetry, and other arts. No single proposition applies to all cultural forms. To be sure, none exist in isolation from the larger society; and I suspect a critical and generational inquiry into other areas might be revealing.

For instance, the migration of fiction into the universities—the establishment of "creative writing" centers and writers "in residence"; the rise of the academic or English department novel; the absence of an avant-garde for years, even decades—all this suggests that newer fiction registers the same pressures as nonfiction. The increasing prominence of novels by Latin Americans, Eastern Europeans, and black women also suggests that the creative juices flow on the outsides, the margins, as malls and campuses cement over the center.

Nevertheless the trajectory of fiction is more complex than nonfiction. Perhaps because the poets and novelists were always outsiders, only occasionally noticed, they can subsist as they always have, picking up crumbs off the table.[2] The plethora of small literary periodicals, sometimes called "little, little" magazines, that print fiction and poetry, indicates that imaginative literature flourishes.

Yet even the moving spirits of the "little, little" magazines allow that their moment seems over; that there are too many journals, the by-product of cheap offset printing and subsidies; and that they seem to have lost their zeal and direction. Insofar as they print exclusively fiction and poetry, unlike their distinguished predecessors, they also testify to cultural fragmentation. Few of these magazines, notes a coordinator of small literary journals, "take a critical stand; essays, even book reviews and correspondence, are less and less common." Nowadays they seem to be devoted to "knitting up the tattered edges of the present."[3]

My generalizations are based on American (and Canadian) intellectuals. I exclude the foreign-born and foreign-educated (the Bruno Bettelheims, Hannah Arendts, Wilhelm Reichs) not because of their minimal impact—the opposite is true—but simply to distill out the American generational life. Once they are excluded, their colossal impact can be glimpsed. The individuals I do include hardly add up to the whole. Every selection of intellectuals can be answered by another. There is no royal road to the zeitgeist. Intellectual life resists neat charts; to demand precision when culture itself is imprecise damns an inquiry to trivia. The discussion of a missing generation requires sweeping statements; it means scrutinizing some writers while ignoring others. It necessitates dealing in the glittery coin of generations, long a mainstay of cultural counterfeiters. It also means the risk of being wrong.

Preface

I will employ, but not exhaustively define, various categories—bohemia, intellectuals, generations, cultural life. Too
many definitions, too much caution, kill thought. Modern analytic philosophy, laboring for decades to establish sound conceptual methods, has only established its inability to think. Its bleak
record, of course, does not warrant reckless judgments. With
care the coin of decades and generations can be traded.

Since I probe, sometimes ungently, the oeuvre of younger
intellectuals, and I question the impact of universities on cultural
life, I should state: I do not write as an outsider. When I say
"they" or "younger intellectuals," I mean "we." When I take
up a "missing" generation, I am discussing my own generation.
When I question academic contributions, I am inspecting the
writings of my friends and myself. I have published articles in
academic journals and a book with a university press. I read academic monographs and periodicals. I love university libraries,
endless bookstacks, giant periodical rooms. I have taught at a
number of colleges. I do not for an instant pretend that I am
made of different and better stuff. My critique of the missing
intellectuals is also a self-critique.

I should add, however, that I am not a complete academic
insider. In a dozen years I have wandered through seven universities and several disciplines. I have more than once made a stab
at living as a free-lance writer. Perhaps I should also note that this
book was aided by no foundation largesse or university grants; I
cannot thank teams of research assistants and graduate students.
Nor can I thank the center for the advanced study of this-or-that
for a year of support.

At the risk of false advertising—pretending something is more
controversial than it is—I might state: no one will completely
agree with this book. It violates conventional loyalties. My
friends, generation, and self are not the heroes—or victims. I

prize a younger left intelligentsia that I believe has surrendered too much. I take as a measuring rod an older generation of intellectuals, whose work I often criticize; I value conservative intellectuals whose estimable vigor covers yawning hypocrisies and contradictions. Thought shrivels when it honors friends and labels before thinking.

Some final remarks: the title, "the last intellectuals," is deliberately ambiguous—it refers to a final generation of intellectuals, as well as to the generation most recently past (as in last year), implying there soon will be another. I write with no optimism, but not as a seer. As I was completing this work a number of books in diverse areas began to appear, each challenging a single discipline—books such as *The Tragedy of Political Science, The Rhetoric of Economics, International Studies and Academic Enterprise,* and *Radical Political Economy Since the Sixties*.[4] They do not uphold a single position, but they evidence discontent with excessive professionalization; they hint at a reversal, a delayed effort to recapture a public culture.

There are other signs. A specter haunts American universities or, at least, its faculties: boredom. A generation of professors entered the universities in the middle and wake of the sixties, when campuses crackled with energy; today these teachers are visibly bored, if not demoralized. One report found college and university faculties "deeply troubled" with almost 40 percent ready and willing to leave the academy.[5] This subterranean discontent might surface, reconnecting with public life. Conservatives suspect and fear this; hence they continuously rail against what they imagine as the threat from the universities. I think they are wrong. I hope they are right.

INTRODUCTION
TO THE 2000 EDITION

———

AT THE TIME *The Last Intellectuals* was published in 1987 I could not anticipate that my argument on the eclipse of public intellectuals would soon be disproved. I could not foresee the explosion of university-based public intellectuals who would enrich political and cultural life; nor did I imagine the battalions of new specialist intellectuals who would subvert the establishment from within. I failed to predict these things because I was wed to an obsolete model of intellectual life, privileging old white guys and gals from the past. My sharp-eyed critics upbraided me for these deficiencies.

If this admission is diplomatic, it is also disingenuous—and rubs against my own inclinations. *The Last Intellectuals* is hardly perfect, but happenings since its publication do not cause me to revise its main points. The book's working title, "The Last Generation: The Eclipse of Public Intellectuals," captured its tenor. I perceived a generational move from public intellectuals earlier in the century to university thinkers at its end. Intellectuals have not disappeared, but something has altered in their composition. They have become more professional and insular; at the same time they have lost command of the vernacular, which thinkers from Galileo to Freud had mastered. Where the Lewis Mumfords or Walter Lippmanns wrote for a public, their successors "theorize" about it at academic conferences.

Introduction to the 2000 Edition

Judging from its reviews, the book touched a nerve, a widespread feeling that intellectual life had shifted, perhaps contracted. At the very least it put into circulation a term, *the public intellectual*, which has traveled far beyond its pages. The phrase pops up in millions of places nowadays. One recent example is that of Alan Brinkley closing an appreciation of Henry Steele Commager by stating that he played the role of "what we now call a public intellectual."[1] As far as I know, I was the first to use this term.

I mainly attended to leftist thinkers and writers in the book, but in the last chapter highlighted the singular role of conservative intellectuals. Loyal to an old-fashioned intellectual style, some conservatives mounted an effective criticism of professionalization and academization. Distrusting the cost of bureaucratic success, they prized the lucid prose that career professionals often surrendered. It was partly for this reason that they loomed large in the "cultural wars" that have ebbed and flowed over the last fifteen years. It was easy to list the conservative tracts decrying educational misdeeds (*Illiberal Education, Tenured Radicals, The Closing of the American Mind*), but where were the rejoinders? The liberal professors growled and scowled, but had trouble answering in limpid English; instead they collected conference papers.[2] When their books finally appeared, they lacked bite. In the liberal view, education proceeded swimmingly; it had become more diverse, multicultural, and exciting, a fact only crabby conservatives failed to fathom. [3] A strange inversion had taken place; liberals and leftists, once critics of the establishment, had become its defenders.

Introduction to the 2000 Edition

The Last Intellectuals was widely discussed, often with great venom. Milk-toast professors turned purple. Thomas Bender, a New York University historian, damned the book as "careless, ill-conceived, and perhaps even irresponsible;" [4] Leo P. Ribuffo, a George Washington University professor, denounced it as "glib, superficial, and oracular."[5] What flustered the placid dons? Often my failure to acknowledge the brilliant work of their colleagues, friends, and selves. I had argued that a recent generation was "missing," that it lacked the profile and presence of earlier American intellectuals. I had specified that my argument "was not a statement about personal integrity or genius; nor does it depend on any particular writers or artists." I was trying to generalize about large-scale cultural and intellectual shifts. No matter.

"There's plenty of intellectual activity going on in America now," grumbled Walter Kendrick in one of the first reviews, which appeared in the *Voice Literary Supplement*. For instance, "The very existence of the *Voice Literary Supplement* (a *public intellectual* journal) proves that the situation isn't quite so bleak as Jacoby maintains."[6] This turned out to be a stock response. Reviewers championed themselves, their journals, and their friends as refuting my argument. "The reason Jacoby can't find young radical intellectuals is that he looks for them in the wrong places," claimed Lynn Garafola, a historian of dance. What are the right places? Periodicals like *Cineaste*, *Performing Arts Journal*, and *The Drama Review*; she finds many public intellectuals, some very close to home, actually one in her home (her husband, Eric Foner, author of "widely read volumes"), as well as people down the block such as "*October* editor Rosalind Krauss, an art critic so well known that a *New Yorker* profile (on someone else) opened with a descrip-

xvii

tion of her living room."[7] The last is particularly touching. A description of one's living room in a *New Yorker* profile (of someone else) ratifies status as a public intellectual. How could I miss that?

Beyond slighting their friends and acquaintances, my critics charged me with the primal crime for all progressives: nostalgia. For many of my reviewers history only advances, as if twentieth-century death camps improved upon nineteenth-century prisons. To suggest otherwise brands one a hopeless romantic. These reviewers operate with ossified categories: Either toot your horn for the contemporary intellectuals or cry in your soup for the past. I was emphatic in my book that 1950s figures were hardly giants of intellect and prose, and I offered, for instance, harsh assessments of Lionel Trilling and Sidney Hook. Moreover, I outlined the irreversible social conditions— demise of urban bohemia and explosion of university employment—that made independent intellectuals an endangered species. Nonetheless, a dozen reviewers complained that I longed for Lionel Trilling. This has become almost the standard line about *The Last Intellectuals*; it is a dirge for the scintillating cultural life of the 1950s. Not true.

Yet it would be churlish to say that my critics made no telling points at all or that nothing has happened since 1987 that would cause me to reformulate my arguments. Several reviewers, for instance, raised good questions about how to define an intellectual generation and how to identify public intellectuals. Others challenged the category of the public (and the public intellectual); some suggested teaching itself was a form of political activity. Inasmuch as intellectuals are now professors, and millions go to college, teaching constitutes a public engagement. In the limited space I have here, I mention three areas to rethink.

At the end of my original preface, I indicated possible change in the offing. Driven by academic discontent and boredom, professors might want to reinvent themselves as public writers. To a limited extent I think this has happened in the last ten years. In the domain of philosophy, for example, Richard Rorty represents an effort to invigorate a public philosophy, and he has been followed by a number of others. Historians and literary critics increasingly try to break out of closed discussions into a larger public. Yet these professionals are not heeding but bucking institutional imperatives that reward esoteric rather than public contributions. Will they be successful? It is not clear.

In the last decade, the emergence of what has been called the new black public intellectuals has generated much attention. For the first time in many years a group of African American intellectuals have burst upon the scene—figures such as Henry Louis Gates, Gerald Early, Adolph Reed, Jr., Randal Kennedy, and Cornel West. These are smart, hard-hitting and often graceful writers who weigh into public problems of race, sports, politics, law, and culture. They have been both acclaimed as successors to the New York intellectuals and criticized as publicity hounds who ignore earlier black intellectuals such as W. E. B. Dubois and C. R. L. James.[8] In no way did my book anticipate their appearance. Yet to conclude that their very existence refutes my argument seems facile. In fact, I see their success as weakening one frequent charge against *The Last Intellectuals*, a version of the nostalgia accusation. Many of my critics believed that an irrevocable demise of a literate public undermined public intellectuals, who necessarily yielded to professional thinkers more appropriate for an age of specialization. Yet it seems to me that the new black intellectuals demonstrate that a literate, indeed hungry, public still exists. What is lacking is the will and ability to address it.

Not by everyone. Another promising recent development is the increasing importance of what is sometimes called the new science writers, many of whom have been writing for decades. I had said nothing about them in *The Last Intellectuals*, but their growing impact seems to confirm that a public has not disappeared. While scientists are often belittled as technicians and positivists—usually by conformist postmodern theorists—a group of science writers has more or less filled the space vacated by humanists. I am thinking of people such as Stephen Jay Gould, Oliver Sacks, the late Carl Sagan, Jared Diamond, Jonathan Weiner, and Jeremy Bernstein, among others.[9] Here are professionals who do not disdain to write with clarity on matters of wide intellectual interest. Their success with a literate public raises numerous questions. What does it mean if humanists lose the ability to think and write lucidly, while scientists become penetrating, engaged, and accessible? "I deeply deplore the equation of popular writing with pap and distortion," says Stephen Jay Gould.[10] Few contemporary humanists or social scientists would agree. Why is that?

The Last Intellectuals was less a lament than a call for intellectuals to reclaim the vernacular and reassert themselves in public life. Some reviewers saw this as an injunction to sell out—or just plain sell—an anti-intellectual demand to exchange dense and unpopular work for media coverage. I don't think so. No one can do everything, but intellectual work need not be pitched in a single register. It should be possible for thinkers and writers to be both serious and accessible—not always at the same time, but over time. After all, those thinkers touted as the most original and complex have often sought a broad public. Even the famously difficult Adorno sweated over his radio lectures to ensure they would be clear and understandable. Ultimately, it is not only the larger public that loses when intellectuals turn inward to fetishize their profundity, but intellectuals themselves. Their work turns arid, their arguments thin, their souls parched. In the life of the mind, as in life itself, vitality requires resisting the lure of the familiar and the safe.

Russell Jacoby
February, 2000
Los Angeles

1. Alan Brinkley, "The Public Professor" (A review of *Henry Steele Commager* by Neil Jumonville), *New Republic,* September 27, 1999, p. 42.

2. One example is *The Politics of Liberal Education,* ed. by Darryl J. Gless and Barbara Herrnstein Smith (Durham, N.C.: Duke University Press, 1992).

3. For instance, see Lawrence Levine's *Opening of the American Mind* (and my review in *Dissent,* Winter, 1997, pp. 115–119).

4. Thomas Bender, *Intellect and Public Life* (Baltimore, Md.: Johns Hopkins University Press, 1993), p. 172.

5. Leo P. Ribuffo, Review: *The Last Intellectuals, Academe,* May-June, 1988, p. 83.

Introduction to the 2000 Edition

6. Walter P. Kendrick, Review: *The Last Intellectuals*, *Voice Literary Supplement*, September, 1987, p. 13.

7. Lynn Garafola, Review: *The Last Intellectuals*, *New Left Review 169* (May 1988), pp. 125–126.

8. A small part of the growing literature includes: Robert S. Boynton, "The New Intellectuals," *Atlantic Monthly*, March, 1995, p. 53 seq.; Michael Berubé, "Public Academy," *New Yorker*, January 9, 1995, p. 73 seq.; Sean Wilentz, "Race, Celebrity and the Intellectuals," *Dissent*, Summer, 1995, p. 253 seq; Michael Hanchard, "Intellectual pursuit," *Nation*, February 19, 1996, p. 22 seq.; "It's Not What You Know, It's How You Show It: Black Public Intellectuals," pp. 47–76 in Michael Eric Dyson, *Race Rules: Navigating the Color Line* (Reading, Mass: Addison-Wesley, 1996); and Ross Posnock, *Color and Culture: Black Writers and the Making of the Modern Intellectual* (Cambridge, Mass.: Harvard University Press, 1998).

9. See *The Literature of Science: Perspectives on Popular Scientific Writing*, ed. M. W. McRae (Athens, Ga.: University of Georgia Press, 1993).

10. Stephen Jay Gould, *Bully for Brontosaurus: Reflections in Natural History* (New York: Norton, 1991), p. 11.

The Last Intellectuals

CHAPTER 1

―――――――

Missing Intellectuals?

I

TO WALK INTO a familiar room and spontaneously identify a new object—a lamp, a picture, a clock—is a common experience. To walk into a familiar room and instantly name an object recently removed is rare. While our eyes and ears effortlessly register additions, "subtractions," objects or sounds that have been eliminated, often go unnoticed. Weeks, months, or years can pass without our recognizing their absence. One day, perhaps, on entering the room we feel a vague uneasiness surging up: something is missing. What?

This book is about a vacancy in culture, the absence of younger voices, perhaps the absence of a generation. The few—extremely few—significant American intellectuals under the age of thirty-five, even forty-five, have seldom elicited comment. They are easy to miss, especially because their absence is longstanding. An intellectual generation has not suddenly vanished; it simply never appeared. And it is already too late—the generation is too old—to show up.

The issue, if hardly discussed, is also charged; it provokes heated responses. Writers and editors draw back, as if insulted.

The Last Intellectuals

Aren't the young authors today—themselves and their friends—as talented and compelling as those from the past? Offended professors list Young Turks shaking up their fields. Leftists recoil, detecting the primal heresy, nostalgia, in talk of a passing generation. Aren't younger radicals, products of the 1960s, as brilliant as past radicals, and even more numerous? A recent elegy for the New York intellectuals in *The New York Times Magazine* sparked several angry replies: intellectual life is thriving outside New York; no need to bemoan the decline of Manhattan's intellectuals. The 1960s drove them into early retirement and senility. So much the better.[1]

This is whistling in the dark. I should say at the outset: the proposition of a missing generation does not malign individuals. It is not a statement about personal integrity or genius; nor does it depend on any particular writers or artists. Complex factors stamp or undercut the formation of an intellectual generation; it would not be the first time that one failed to galvanize. However, more is at stake than an interesting observation; the issue is the vitality of a public culture.

Nor is it a simple political issue, at least not in conventional terms. There has been much talk of the rise of neoconservatism and the demise of radicalism, even of liberalism. Of course, the dominance of neoconservatives and the eclipse of radical intellectuals correspond to shifts in political realities. Neoconservatives dine at the White House; they are blessed with public attention, grants, government support.

It might be satisfying to conclude that this fully explains the vagaries of intellectual life: younger intellectuals, generally more radical than the neoconservatives, are ignored for political reasons; they are out of step with the times. Perhaps. But this leaves too much obscure. Compared to the 1950s, the left has prospered. Marxist professors teach everywhere; radicals publish endlessly; and the wider left hardly fears a McCarthyite repression. Yet younger left intellectuals seem publicly invisible. Why? The political realities cannot be ignored, but deeper currents—social and economic—inform intellectual life.

To declare an intellectual generation "invisible" is fraught with difficulties. The statement seems to accept the judgment of the "public sphere"—newspapers, book reviews, talk shows— as truth itself; it risks confounding glitter with substance, TV exposure with intellectual weight. The public sphere is hardly neutral; it responds to money or power or drama, not to quiet talent or creative work. For decades, even for centuries, writers and critics have decried the press for distorting cultural life. Inasmuch as the public sphere is less a free market of ideas than a market, what is publicly visible registers nothing but market forces.[2]

If true, this observation easily degenerates into a cliché that the ruling ideas are the ideas of the ruling class; cultural studies vanish into economics. Intellectual life, which includes books, articles, magazines, lectures, public discussions, perhaps university teaching, is obviously subject to market and political forces but cannot be reduced to them. The impact of network television or national newsweeklies on cultural life can scarcely be underestimated; but it is not the whole story. The restructuring of cities, the passing of bohemia, the expansion of the university: these also inform culture. They are my subjects.

My concern is with public intellectuals, writers and thinkers who address a general and educated audience. Obviously, this excludes intellectuals whose works are too technical or difficult to engage a public. Nevertheless I believe it is a myth that private intellectuals thrive while public culture decays. The relationship between "private" and "public" intellectual work is complex. At least this can be said: there is a symbiotic relationship. The greatest minds from Galileo to Freud have not been content with private discoveries; they sought, and found, a public. If they seem too distant, too high a standard, the last generation of American intellectuals is my benchmark. They also embraced a public; the successor generation has not.

Perhaps there is no one to embrace. The public has changed during the last decades, even centuries. A public that once snapped up pamphlets by Thomas Paine or stood for hours listening to Abraham Lincoln debate Stephen Douglas hardly exists; its span of attention shrinks as its fondness for television increases.[3] A reading public may be no more. If younger intellectuals are absent, a missing audience may explain why.

This is true, but it is not the whole truth. A public that reads serious books, magazines, and newspapers has dwindled; it has not vanished. The writings of older intellectuals from John Kenneth Galbraith to Daniel Bell continue to elicit interest and discussion, which suggests that a public has not evaporated. The audience may be contracting, but younger intellectuals are missing. That is the emphasis here, less on the eclipse of a public than on the eclipse of public intellectuals.

To put it sharply: the habitat, manners, and idiom of intellectuals have been transformed within the past fifty years. Younger intellectuals no longer need or want a larger public; they are almost exclusively professors. Campuses are their homes; colleagues their audience; monographs and specialized journals their media. Unlike past intellectuals they situate themselves within fields and disciplines—for good reason. Their jobs, advancement, and salaries depend on the evaluation of specialists, and this dependence affects the issues broached and the language employed.

Independent intellectuals, who wrote for the educated reader, are dying out; to be sure, often they wrote for small periodicals.

Yet these journals participated, if only through hope, in the larger community. "We looked upon art as a sharing of life," stated the 1917 farewell editorial of *The Seven Arts*, a vital cultural monthly, "a communism of experience and vision, a spiritual root of nationalism and internationalism."[4] The contributors viewed themselves as men and women of letters, who sought and prized a spare prose. They wrote for intellectuals and sympathizers anywhere; small in size, the journals opened out to the world. For this reason their writers could be read by the educated public, and later they were. Schooled in the little magazines, the Max Eastmans or Dwight Macdonalds or Irving Howes easily shifted to larger periodicals and publics.

Today nonacademic intellectuals are an endangered species; industrial development and urban blight have devastated their environment. They continue to loom large in the cultural world because they mastered a public idiom. The new academics far outnumber the independent intellectuals, but since they do not employ the vernacular, outsiders rarely know of them.

Academics write for professional journals that, unlike the little magazines, create insular societies. The point is not the respective circulation—professional periodicals automatically sent to members may list circulation far higher than small literary reviews—but the different relationship to the lay public. The professors share an idiom and a discipline. Gathering in annual conferences to compare notes, they constitute their own universe. A "famous" sociologist or art historian means famous to other sociologists or art historians, not to anyone else. As intellectuals became academics, they had no need to write in a public prose; they did not, and finally they could not.

The transmission belt of culture—the ineffable manner by which an older generation passes along not simply its knowledge but its dreams and hopes—is threatened. The larger culture rests

7

on a decreasing number of aging intellectuals with no successors. Younger intellectuals are occupied and preoccupied by the demands of university careers. As professional life thrives, public culture grows poorer and older. An irony colors this inquiry into a missing generation. The intellectuals absent from public life are largely those who came of age in the 1960s—a short term for the upheavals that lasted almost fifteen years. How is it possible that these veterans of movements, who often targeted the university, derided their teachers, and ridiculed past thinkers could mature into such earnest professionals, quieter than older intellectuals? I offer no single or simple answer, yet the irony hints of the magnitude of cultural restructuring. By the 1960s the universities virtually monopolized intellectual work; an intellectual life outside the campuses seemed quixotic. After the smoke lifted, many young intellectuals had never left school; others discovered there was nowhere else to go. They became radical sociologists, Marxist historians, feminist theorists, but not quite public intellectuals.

How can the absence of a generation be inferred? There is no guide. A moment's reflection, I believe, hints of the vacancy. Name a group of important younger American critics, philosophers, or historians. Perhaps this is unfair; few names pop up. Yet it was not always difficult to name the "young" intellectuals. Once writers and critics regularly, often obsessively, monitored the new generation; they differed not so much over the names but over their merits. Today even the briefest list would include many blanks: leading younger critics? sociologists? historians? philosophers? psychologists? Who are they? Where are they?

A quick view of the fifties yields a score of active critics, young and old: Mary McCarthy, Philip Rahv, C. Wright Mills, Dwight Macdonald, Lionel Trilling, David Reisman, Irving Howe,

Arthur Schlesinger, Jr., Edmund Wilson, Lewis Mumford, Malcolm Cowley, Sidney Hook, and numerous others. Or consider the many vital works from the late 1950s and early 1960s: John Kenneth Galbraith's *The Affluent Society*, Betty Friedan's *The Feminine Mystique*, Paul Goodman's *Growing Up Absurd*, Jane Jacobs's *The Death and Life of Great American Cities*, C. Wright Mills's *The Power Elite*, William H. Whyte's *The Organization Man*, and Michael Harrington's *The Other America*.

Simply listing these books and authors suggests two striking truths about the current scene: the same books or individuals command the cultural heights today, and very few books or people have been added. Today, a quarter of a century later, we continue to listen to the same intellectuals, Norman Mailer or Daniel Bell or John Kenneth Galbraith or Gore Vidal, who first gained attention in the 1950s.

While isolated younger intellectuals have shown up—and usually receded—no generation has coalesced to challenge, or even to supplement, the older contributors. For a group of intellectuals to command the posts for thirty-odd years—from the 1950s to the 1980s—is amazing; in a society that prides itself on youth and dynamism, it is astonishing. While the aging industrial plant of America elicits much talk, the aging intellectual plant passes unnoticed. Where is the younger intellectual generation?

Over ten years ago a sociologist studying influential intellectuals commented on the absence of younger thinkers and critics. Charles Kadushin presented the findings of an extensive empirical study of American thinkers; he wanted to characterize— name and describe—America's "intellectual elite." To do this he interviewed 110 influential intellectuals, who were identified by regularly appearing in "influential" periodicals, such as *The New York Review of Books*, *Commentary*, *Harper's*, *Atlantic*, *The New Yorker*, and *The New York Times Book Review*.[5]

From his study Kadushin obtained cartons of interesting and not-so-interesting information, including a list of the most prestigious intellectuals. In 1970 the ten leading intellectuals were: Daniel Bell, Noam Chomsky, John Kenneth Galbraith, Irving Howe, Dwight Macdonald, Mary McCarthy, Norman Mailer, Robert Silvers, Susan Sontag, and "tying" at tenth place, Lionel Trilling and Edmund Wilson.[6] None could be considered young, with the possible exception of Susan Sontag (thirty-seven in 1970). The absence of the young even on the extended list of the "top" seventy intellectuals troubled Kadushin. He did not fault his research methods.

"The fact there are few young intellectuals [on the list] is not an 'error'; it reflects the structure of intellectual life in the United States at this time," concluded Kadushin. Young intellectuals are simply not present in cultural life, nor have they been for some time. Moreover, the aging "elite" did not recently fall into place; it had assumed prominence twenty years earlier. "The elite American intellectuals as we saw them in 1970," Kadushin noted, "were basically the same ones who came to power in the late 1940s and early 1950s."[7]

Kadushin asked this "elite" to identify younger intellectuals on the horizon; they were unable to do so. Doubting that this indicated a permanent vacancy, Kadushin surmised that "the heirs have not yet made themselves known." He confidently suggested that this situation would soon change. Fifteen years later this confidence looks ill-founded; the heirs have still not made themselves known. A list of significant intellectuals today would look very much like Kadushin's (minus the deaths)—and the list was yellowing fifteen years ago.

Other, more informal, surveys of the intellectual scene have also appeared since the Kadushin study. Although they do not deplore, or even note, a missing generation, their findings evidence the absence. Daniel Bell, for instance, mapped several generations of New York intellectuals. The most recent, a "second generation," included no surprises, no new names (Norman Podhoretz, Steven Marcus, Robert Brustein, Midge Decter, Jason Epstein, Robert Silvers, Susan Sontag, Norman Mailer, Philip Roth, Theodore Solotaroff).[8] Current anthologies of leading opinion display the same aging literati; the fiftieth anniversary issue of *Partisan Review* (1984)—almost 400 pages—reveals few younger faces. Even more popular efforts to parade young talent come up short. *Esquire* magazine regularly runs a fat annual issue on "the best of the new generation: men and women under forty who are changing America." They cast a wide net, filling the issue with sketches of bright young people. Leaving aside computer whizzes, architects, and art administrators, their 1984 and 1985 issues offer almost no writers or critics who are major figures outside their specialities.

Of course, none of these sources are beyond criticism. For example, Kadushin's study, awash in funds from five foundations, and painstakenly empirical and "scientific," is fundamentally circular. Influential intellectuals were asked to name influential intellectuals. How was the first group selected? By plowing through 20,000 articles in "influential" magazines the most frequent contributors were identified. Here is the flaw: the group to be interviewed was already preselected by the influential magazines. Moreover, whom did the influential intellectuals name as influential intellectuals? More or less themselves.

My own skimming of periodicals and random questioning of acquaintances have also confirmed the generational vacancy. *The New York Review of Books* might be offered as Exhibit A, evidencing the dearth of younger intellectuals. The important periodicals of America's past—*The Dial, The Masses, Partisan Review*—were closely associated with the coming-of-age of intellectuals, from John Reed to Max Eastman and Philip Rahv. Yet after almost twenty-five years, it is difficult to name a single younger intellectual associated with *The New York Review*. Of course, distinguished writers have, and do, appear in its pages, from Mary McCarthy to Christopher Lasch to Gore Vidal, but they are neither young nor unestablished.[9]

Exhibit B would be the results of my informal survey. For some years I have asked journalists, academics, and writers to name new American intellectuals of wide significance, not specialists. Professor X, celebrated for unreadable excursions into postmodernism, does not count; nor does Professor Y, touted for computerizing Marx's economic theories. My criterion is roughly the same that Harold Stearns employed in his 1921 inquiry of intellectuals: "publicists, editors of nontrade magazines, pamphleteers, writers on general topics."[10]

I have received few compelling responses, and usually no responses at all. Friends who pride themselves on their intellectual savvy and wit often rapidly reply: Foucault, Habermas, Derrida. The conversation goes this way: No, I re-emphasize, I'm looking for home-grown corn-fed real live Americans (or Canadians). I then hear: Kenneth Burke, Marshall McLuhan, Norman O. Brown, Sidney Hook. No, no, I restate, new, younger, fresh intellectuals of general importance. "Oh, younger American intellectuals? . . . in the last ten to fifteen years? . . . Yes, of course. . . . There is . . . Hmmmmmmm . . . Did you say, ten to fifteen years, not twenty-five? . . . Hmmm . . . Yes . . . Well . . . There is . . . no . . . ahhh . . . well. . . ." The conversation trails off, and my friends wander off, puzzling over the absence both startling and unnoticed.

It is startling and unnoticed; and it is more than an intriguing fact. Society increasingly relies on older intellectuals who bear the imprint of cultural and political battles from thirty years ago. Not the "greening" but the graying of American culture is the future.

II

IN TRACKING an elusive cultural life I cannot offer certified conclusions that refute all possible alternatives. My argument of a missing generation might be challenged by proposing that the new intellectuals thrive in journalism. I agree that "new" and not-so-new journalism (personal reportage, muckraking, rock criticism) testifies—or once testified—to a vigorous younger generation. Moreover, by virtue of abdication elsewhere journalists have assumed a critical, and increasing, importance. Yet the constraints of living solely from the press—deadlines, space, money—finally dilute, not accentuate, intellectual work. I discuss this briefly in the final chapter.

My argument might also be countered by responding that younger intellectuals have surfaced in film and television; or that new writers exist, even thrive, outside a public arena that has been closed to them by older editors and publishers. A new intellectual generation, however, is hardly visible in mainstream film or television; and it is doubtful whether editors, no matter how despotic or shortsighted, can regulate the generational flow.

Far more important are the economic winds that propel cultural life, and at times chill it. Of the thousands of statistics describing the transformation of the United States in the twentieth century, two may partly explain a missing generation: the increasing substitution of corporate employment for independent businessmen, workers, and craftsmen; and the post–World War II "explosion" of higher education. These currents carried intellectuals from independence to dependence, from free-lance writing to salaried teaching in colleges. Between 1920 and 1970 the United States population doubled, but the number of college teachers multiplied ten-fold, rising from 50,000 in 1920 to 500,000 in 1970.

The newly opened and enlarged colleges allowed, if not compelled, intellectuals to desert a precarious existence for stable careers. They exchanged the pressures of deadlines and free-lance writing for the security of salaried teaching and pensions—with summers off to write and loaf. When Daniel Bell left *Fortune* magazine in 1958 for a university life, he told Luce he had four good reasons: "June, July, August, and September."[11] "The trouble with everything but teaching," complained Delmore Schwartz to a fellow poet, "is that one spends so much time thinking of making money . . . that one is more distracted than ever."[12]

With few reservations, by the end of the 1950s, American intellectuals decamped from the cities to the campuses, from the cafes to the cafeterias. The losses seemed trifling; they gave up the pleasures of sleeping late, schmoozing with friends, and dreaming up their own projects; they also gave up the deep anxiety of selling their dreams to indifferent editors so as to eat and pay the rent. Insiders seldom romanticized the life of free-lance writing. "He never could understand," wrote Edmund Wilson of his friend the music critic Paul Rosenfeld, "that writing was a commodity like any other, which, from the moment one lacked a patron had to be sold in a hard-boiled way."[13]

The gains of academic life—salaries, security, summers—seemed hardly offset by the drawbacks: the occasional lectures at eight in the morning, the committee drudgery, and, sometimes, a new location distant from old friends. Yet the balance sheet does not include the real losses, less visible, but finally decisive. In recasting the lives of intellectuals, intellectual life was recast.

Intellectuals as academics no longer relied on either the small magazines of opinion and literature or the larger periodicals, such as *The New Yorker* or *Fortune*, as their outlets. Professional journals and monographs became their sustenance. Scholarly editors and "referees," professional colleagues of the same specialty, now judged their manuscripts, supplanting the general editors of *The New Republic* or *Partisan Review*. The ante was much smaller, at least initially. A manuscript rejected by the *Journal of Economic History* did not spell financial disaster. A salary was still paid, the contract still honored. Nevertheless, to obtain promotions and, finally, to retain a position, academics needed to gain the approval or recognition of colleagues.

The constraints and corruptions of academic life are hardly news. Savage criticism of American universities dates back to Upton Sinclair's *The Goose-Step* (1923) and Thorstein Veblen's *The Higher Learning in America* (1918), which Veblen intended to subtitle "A Study in Total Depravity."[14] The critical issue, however, is not the novelty of the situation but its extent. When universities occupied a quadrant of cultural life, their ills (and virtues) meant one thing. When they staked out the whole turf, their rules became *the* rules.

These rules did not encourage a leathery independence. Yet the "conspicuous conformity to popular taste" and the kowtowing to business—the "total depravity" that Veblen denounced[15]—lag behind the reality, the vast university system of the postwar years and its requirements. Political timidity was in the long run less essential than academic know-how and productivity. A successful career depended on impressing deans and colleagues, who were interested more in how one fit in than in how one stood out. It was also essential to feed the system. New academics wrote books and articles with an eye to their bulk—the findings, the arguments, the facts, the conclusions.

In their haste, they did not linger over the text. Academic intellectuals did not cherish direct or elegant writing; they did not disdain it, but it hardly mattered. Most scholarly literature included summaries of the argument or findings; the fact of publication far outweighed any quibbling over style. These imperatives increasingly determined how professors both read and wrote; they cared for substance, not form. Academic writing developed into unreadable communiques sweetened by thanks to colleagues and superiors. Of course, crabbed academic writing is not new; again, the extent, not the novelty, is the issue.

The absorption of intellectuals into the fattened university was, and is, a trend, not an "on and off" switch. Intellectuals did not suddenly enter the university and instantly spit out dreary prose. However, when this accelerating migration is viewed against the generational rhythms, the mystery of a "missing" generation is partially unraveled.

The generation born around and after 1940 emerged in a society where the identity of universities and intellectual life was almost complete. To be an intellectual entailed being a professor. This generation flowed into the universities, and if they wanted to be intellectuals, they stayed. The issue is not their talent, courage, or politics. Rather, the occasion to master a public prose did not arise; consequently, their writings lacked a public impact. Regardless of their numbers, to the larger public they are invisible. The missing intellectuals are lost in the universities.

For intellectuals born before 1940 universities did not play the same role. Colleges were small and often closed to radicals, Jews, and women. To be an intellectual did not entail college teaching. Harold Stearns's 1921 reflections on young intellectuals specifically excluded professors.[16] The college route was seldom emphatically rejected as not considered: it was not a real possibility. To be an intellectual, rather, necessitated moving to New York or Chicago and writing books and articles.

To these crude categories additional refinements can be made by identifying generations of 1900, 1920, and 1940. Intellectuals born at the turn of the century—Lewis Mumford (1895–), Dwight Macdonald (1906–82), Edmund Wilson (1895–1972)—represent classical American intellectuals; they lived their lives by way of books, reviews, and journalism; they never or rarely taught in universities. They were superb essayists and graceful writers, easily writing for a larger public. They were also something more: iconolasts, critics, polemicists, who deferred to no one.

The generation born around 1920—Alfred Kazin (1915–), Daniel Bell (1919–), Irving Howe (1920–)—might be called transitional. They grew up writing for small magazines when universities remained marginal; this experience informed their style—elegant and accessible essays directed toward the wider intellectual community. Later, in the 1950s, they often accepted university positions, which looked better and better as the nonacademic habitat diminished. In their mastery of a public prose they are loyal to their past; in a precise sense they are obsolete.

The full weight of academization hit the generation born after 1940; they grew up in a world where nonuniversity intellectuals hardly existed. As earlier generations of intellectuals seldom considered university careers, so the obverse became true: this new generation barely considered an intellectual life outside the university. In each case "consider" means to appraise the real choices; it reflects the transformed social realities, not simply the transformed desires.

These social realities did not only dictate a change in prose;

they encouraged a complete renovation of intellectual identity and self-identity. Almost from adolescence the post-1940 intellectuals grew up in a university environment; its trappings and forms became theirs. For instance, the planning and execution of a doctoral dissertation—often ridiculed by the outsider—loomed large. It was the ticket for a serious academic post, for life as an intellectual; it consumed years of nervous energy, if not research and writing. For many young intellectuals it was the cultural event and contest of their lives.

When completed it could not be ignored; the dissertation became part of them. The research style, the idiom, the sense of the "discipline," and one's place in it: these branded their intellectual souls. And more: the prolonged, often humiliating, effort to write a thesis to be judged by one's doctoral advisor and a "committee" of experts gave rise to a network of dense relations—and deference—that clung to their lives and future careers.[17] Even if they wished, and frequently they did not, the younger intellectuals could not free themselves from this past.

Yet earlier American intellectuals were almost completely spared these rites. Very few of the 1900 generation wrote dissertations; and when they did, the insignificance of the university in intellectual life prompted them to look beyond it to a larger public. Trilling alludes to this in recalling his dissertation. "Something of the intellectual temper of the time . . . is suggested by my determination that the work should find its audience not among scholars but among the general public."[18]

Trilling was much the exception in following the straight and narrow academic path. Few even of the "transitional" generation earned doctoral degrees. They entered the universities in the 1950s under circumstances that scarcely would be allowed later, as tenured professors at "major" universities without Ph.D.s; or they were awarded advanced degrees under clauses

rarely invoked again. Daniel Bell recalls that when he was about
to be granted tenure at Columbia University, an awkward question came up. They asked " 'Do you have a Ph.D.?' I said 'No.'
They asked, 'Why?' I said, 'I never submitted a thesis.' " This
was happily resolved by awarding him a Ph.D. for past work, his
book *The End of Ideology*.[19]

Such informality reflects a past era; it is next to impossible to
obtain university posts without a Ph.D., as did Irving Howe or
Alfred Kazin, or to be awarded degrees on the basis of past work,
as were Daniel Bell or Nathan Glazer. A younger intellectual
could no more show up for a dissertation "defense" with a collection of essays written for several magazines, which constituted
The End of Ideology, than he or she could show up without taking the requisite number of credits and seminars—and without
paying the proper fees. These academic obstacles or initiations
were much more than annoyances; stretched out over years they
defined young lives and finally the shape and color of an intellectual generation.

Nor was the possibility of intellectual life outside the university
enticing for post-1940 intellectuals. Writing as a free-lancer
made as much sense as homesteading: the open space did not
exist. The shrinking cultural space—acknowledged or unac-
knowledged—herded younger intellectuals into the university.
If academic salaries and security were the carrot, the decline of
traditional intellectual life was the stick.

To live from selling book reviews and articles ceased to be
difficult; it became impossible. The number of serious magazines
and newspapers steadily declined (and the pay scale of those remaining hardly increased), leaving few avenues; the signs all
pointed toward the colleges. If the western frontier closed in the
1890s, the cultural frontier closed in the 1950s. After this decade
intellectuals joined established institutions or retrained.

The dwindling space is not only a metaphor; it denotes the loss of living areas, the renovation of urban bohemias into exclusive quarters of boutiques and townhouses. Since 1900 the most prominent urban bohemia, Greenwich Village, beckoned America's intellectuals with the promise of emancipation, art, sexuality, and free thinking—all sustained by cheap rents. In the first decades of the century, John Reed, Floyd Dell, Max Eastman lived in, celebrated, and sometimes bemoaned the Greenwich Village bohemian life.

Although often written off as dead, Greenwich Village remained alive through the 1940s and 1950s. "I arrived one fall afternoon in 1949," wrote Michael Harrington, "put down my bags, and went out to find Greenwich Village." He found it, full of kindred spirits, "voluntary exiles from a middle class." For Harrington it ended when the "beats" of the fifties passed the torch to the counterculture of the sixties, when one night in the early sixties a "gawky kid named Bob Dylan showed up at the Horse [their tavern hang-out] in a floppy hat" and imitated Woody Guthrie.[20]

The demise of Greenwich Village, which of course cannot be neatly dated, ensured the eclipse of the new generation of independent intellectuals. Through the 1950s the Village functioned as an escape and refuge from conventional careers; even as a myth it offered the glimpse of an independent life. That imposters, frauds, and poseurs flocked to Greenwich Village is not the point; this was always true, and perhaps added to its charm: they flocked nowhere else. Without Greenwich Village young intellectuals could not challenge or imagine alternatives to university careers.

Even H. L. Mencken, not especially sympathetic to the bohemian village ("the Village produces nothing that justifies all the noise it makes"), confesses that "the spectacle gives me some joy," since it evidences "the natural revolt of youth against the pedagogical Prussianism of the professors." Is it a wonder, he asks, that after "one or two sniffs of that prep-school fog" we find the young would-be poet from the provinces "in corduroy trousers and a velvet jacket, hammering furiously upon a pine table in a Macdougal street cellar . . . his discourse full of inane hairsplittings about *vers libre*, futurism, spectrism, vorticism, *Expressionismus* . . . ?"[21]

No longer. Gentrification eliminated the cheap rents of Greenwich Village, squeezing out marginal intellectuals and artists. Areas that might have served as bohemian centers succumbed to real estate developers almost as soon as they emerged. Economic exigencies reshaped New York into a city of extremes, a city that could no longer sustain bohemians who were neither rich nor poor.

Urban bohemians elsewhere succumbed to the same economic pressures. Greenwich Village was the most prominent, but hardly the only bohemian center. North Beach in San Francisco and Venice in Los Angeles also attracted disaffected intellectuals and artists. Other cities boasted small, sometimes tiny and ephemeral, bohemian sections that served as way stations for young intellectuals. These can be easily denigrated. Nevertheless, the aerial view of society should not forget that in the lives of intellectuals—the lives of all individuals—it just takes several friends to make the difference; and these friends can meet in a coffeehouse in St. Louis or a bookstore in Seattle. Bohemia can be this small, this vital.

Even the isolated bookstore or coffeehouse has in recent decades closed, to reopen as a fitness center or a fern and wine bar. Cheap and pleasant urban space that might nourish a bohemian intelligentsia belongs to the past. The eclipse of these urban living areas completes the eclipse of cultural space. "The free spaces—both real and metaphorical—once occupied by bohemia have become narrower and harder to find," writes Jerrold Seigel in his study of bohemia.[22] New generations grow up in a world sharply subdivided into suburban malls, prosperous urban centers, and bleak ghettos for the poor. The geography—cultural and physical—offers few refuges for intellectuals seeking alternatives to city or suburban campuses.

III

CULTURAL LIFE is composed of the activities of intellectuals who do not simply write or think or paint but live and work in specific environments. This is hardly a novel truth, but it is easily forgotten; the ideas of Edmund Wilson or Geoffrey Hartman, a Yale English professor and a leading exponent of Derrida and deconstructionism, evidence different lives, different periods. I mention this because my account will be salted with mini-biographies; at least I will provide dates of birth, sometimes current activity. I do this not to litter the text but to provide an inkling of the generational process. It matters whether someone was born in 1910 or 1940, when they write for *The New Yorker* or *Bulletin of the Midwest MLA*.*

However, the lives and ideas of intellectuals are not identical.

---

* Nevertheless, to avoid unnecessary clutter I am placing in the index the years of birth and death of pertinent figures. In the text I give the ages (or years of birth) of American intellectuals and professors only when it seems immediately relevant. Some additional clarifications: In general I provide these facts in my primary discussion of individuals, which is not always when they are first mentioned. I am not including dates for authors whom I use as secondary sources, unless it seems apposite. I also omit dates for novelists and artists, since they are not my main concern. Unfortunately, I have not always been able to verify years of birth, especially of some younger intellectuals.

Biography cannot replace thought. For this study it is important to know when people were born, what they did or are doing; it is also insufficient. People cannot simply be reduced to their lives and occupations. Mind is more than matter.

Insurance executives can write fine poetry; Harvard professors can toss off ringing calls for revolution. In general neither do. It is well to remember but not be obsessed by this. Insurance executives usually write memos and reports, and Harvard professors monographs and grant applications. Mind is also matter, a lesson of both Marx and Freud. People are what they do, but not entirely.

Several cautions: propositions about intellectual generations do not target individuals, but neither can they bypass them. Critical statements must be anchored in judgments about particular people. However, if public culture is warped by money or politics, the intellectuals tossed up to view may signify little. Perhaps an aging generation commands the public's attention, while outside the limelight a youthful culture thrives. How can one be certain?

One cannot. However, a secret culture with no contact with the public world is improbable. Of course, judgments, if they are to be more than whims, must rest on something, beginning with the material at hand, the works of intellectuals. This remains the rub—which ones? An honest inquiry must ransack all sources and recognize that they are all prejudiced; that even the most prudent cultural conclusions assess not simply individual artists and writers but a preselected grouping. In a narrow sense, regardless of their fate, this grouping is successful—compared to those who have failed to make any public impression. In sticking to known intellectuals even the most heretical generalizations are conformist; they ratify the cultural sieve.

Yet there is no escape. A critic might challenge the prevailing opinion of Susan Sontag or Lionel Trilling, but it is impossible to challenge an entire slate of writers and offer at the same time another unknown slate. This may be obvious. Yet only those who imagine that a benign historical process advances the talented, and buries the untalented, believe that the visible culture includes everything worth seeing. I do not believe it. Nor do I want to romanticize the genius of the invisible and silent, a regular inclination of some historians. Yet I want even less to aggrandize celebrated intellectuals whose status is often due more to luck and friends than to intrinsic talents.

Another caution: at least since *The Dial* moved from Chicago to New York in 1918, Manhattan and its intellectuals have cast a spell that is difficult to resist. Not only the major publishers but the major intellectual journals remain clustered around New York: *The New York Times Book Review, Commentary, The New Yorker, The Nation, The New York Review of Books, Harper's.*

To bemoan this is a veritable occupation. West Coast writers and poets have long complained of inattention by New York publishers and critics. It would be satisfying to conclude that New York reigns by virtue of power and corruption. Perhaps. That the West Coast still has not generated an intellectual journal to challenge New York, however, is sobering. In population, mean income, and book sales, the Los Angeles metropolitan area equals or exceeds New York, but these numbers do not translate into cultural magazines. *The Los Angeles Times*, though no rival to *The New York Times*, is respectable; its Sunday *Book Review* magazine hardly is.[23]

In the 1980s, however, New York literary domination may rest on an optical illusion. As cultural activity drains off into scores of cities and universities, the aging capital still appears imposing. Each year it is smaller, but without a competing center, it casts long shadows. From Gainesville, Florida, or Portland, Oregon, New York appears like a cultural mountain.

The same illusion may plague my own treatment. Even as I deal in individuals and journals from the 1950s and earlier, I do not want to foster the illusion of their unassailable superiority; even as I argue that a generation is missing, I do not want to lionize the previous generations—and this is especially true of past New York intellectuals, who have produced fewer enduring works than is supposed. To put it sharply: if the intellectuals from the 1950s tower over the cultural landscape right into the 1980s, this is not because the towers are so high but because the landscape is so flat.

Of course, some work from the fifties—the writings of Dwight Macdonald, C. Wright Mills, Lewis Mumford—is first rate; and the list could be extended—but not very far. The literary, social, or cultural criticism of American intellectuals rarely dazzles. To obtain a perspective consider Lionel Trilling, often presented as the crème of American (and New York) intellectuals: cosmopolitan, thoughtful, elegant.

He was, but the strengths and sharp limits of Trilling coincide. The cadence of his prose and his measured liberalism distinguished Trilling, but not the brilliance, originality, or force of his thought. His reach, in fact, was limited, no further than Anglo-American literature; his social theory, thin; his philosophy, weak. His essays which often originated as lectures to admiring audiences, suffer on the cold page. What Trilling wrote of V. L. Parrington, in the opening essay of *The Liberal Imagination*, could almost be said of himself. He was not "a great mind . . . or an impressive one . . . what is left is simple intelligence, notable for its generosity and enthusiasm."[24] Even a sympathetic study of Trilling suggests his essays suffered from vagueness or "weightlessness."[25]

However, on a single but absolutely critical quality, the fifties intellectuals far surpassed their successors: they mastered a public prose. Not only Lionel Trilling, Paul Goodman, and John Kenneth Galbraith, but Irving Kristol and William F. Buckley, Jr., loom large because of their public idiom. Fifties intellectuals were *publicists*: they wrote to and for the educated public. The following generation surrendered the vernacular, sacrificing a public identity.

To be sure, sixties activists gained public attention. Yet intellectuals associated with the sixties failed to maintain a public presence; many departed for other careers; other disappeared into the universities. Today it would be difficult to name even a few important intellectuals who came of age in the sixties; and even the works of the period—*The Making of the Counter Culture, The Greening of America, The Pursuit of Loneliness*—lack the force of earlier social criticism. Of course, this restates the problem: who were the intellectuals of the sixties, and what became of them? Individual faces have shown up in the seventies and eighties and then receded. A generation is missing.

CHAPTER 2

The Decline of Bohemia

I

TO CHART the evolution of bohemia and its relation to cultural life raises thorny problems: how is bohemia defined? what makes it prosper or decline? and how, and when, does it affect intellectual and artistic activity? Robert Michels, best known for his "iron law" of bureaucratization, once proposed a "sociology of bohemia." For the young, Michels believed, bohemia was often a stage characterized by poverty, freedom, and hatred of the bourgeoisie. As a passageway, it might lead—and here Michels followed the classic portrayal by Henry Murger[1]—to the Academy of Arts, as well as to the hospital or the morgue.

In addition to transient youth or students, some more-or-less permanent residents, "surplus" intellectuals, constituted bohemia. For Michels, writing in the midst of the Great Depression, these intellectuals are "strictly" surplus in that society produces more than required, the consequence of "unregulated intellectual production." Not all intellectuals become superfluous. Michels divides them into two categories, the first manages to find lucrative employment in established enterprises. "Out of a sense of duty or of concern over losing their position" they loyally uphold Church, Family, and King. However, the surplus intellectuals, the second group, turn into floaters, outsiders, malcontents, who collect in bohemias to dream of the future or the past.[2]

Michels's case was suggestive, not conclusive; he underlined the realities neglected in most discussions of bohemia.[3] Very crudely, these realities define bohemia in two ways: they regulate the flow of people, and they shape the environment. If the human material is not available, bohemias might dry up; and if the habitat is too hostile, a colony may not take root. Any account of bohemia must not lose sight of these two elements: the residents (their origins, employment, unemployment) and the urban environment.

Bohemias live off of cities. Even the rural bohemian colonies typically thrive a short hop from a major urban center or as summer enclaves only.[4] However, it is not the size or wealth of a city that sustains a bohemia but the atmosphere or texture. Fragile urban habitats of busy streets, cheap eateries, reasonable rents, and decent environs nourish bohemias. These can be easily damaged by economic depression, prosperity, urban renewal, expressways, slums, or suburbs. When this delicate environment is injured or transformed, the "surplus" intellectuals do not disappear, but disperse; they spread out across the country. The difference is critical: a hundred artists, poets, and writers with families and friends in ten city blocks mean one thing; scattered across ten states or ten university towns, they mean something else.

To the skeptic the reliance of bohemian intellectuals on city life and institutions smacks of hypocrisy: the self-proclaimed outsiders flourish exclusively on the inside. They require the streets, cafes, and bars of urban civilization to escape the burden of urban civilization: work and routine. Alfred Polgar, an Austrian writer, once offered a "theory" of Cafe Central, a favorite haunt of pre–World War I Viennese intellectuals and bohemians; he called it an "asylum" for those unfit for life, those who renounce or have been renounced by "family, profession, party." It is a form of "organization for the disorganized."[5] Albert Salomon, a refugee scholar from Germany, concurred, dubbing the bohemian coffee house "the salon of homeless thinkers, poets, and scientists, the drawing room of underpaid writers."[6]

The hypocrisy of bohemia, however, is not simple dishonesty; it hints of a flagrant contradiction. The world of labor and wealth is armed against the idleness and utopia that it sometimes promises. Thinking and dreaming require unregulated time; intellectuals perpetually lingering over coffee and drink threaten solid citizens by the effort—or the appearance—of escaping the bondage of money and drudgery. Guardians of order have denigrated, almost for centuries, critics and rebels as mere "coffee house intellectuals."[7] In the catalog of bourgeois sins bohemian intellectuals earn a double entry, thinking too much and doing too little. Crown aristocrats have been no less disdainful. When the count who lurched Austria into World War I was warned that war might ignite a Russian revolution, he retorted, "Who is supposed to make that revolution? Herr Trotsky in the Cafe Central?"[8] (For several years Trotsky lived in Vienna, frequenting its cafes.)

Habitués of cafes, of course, returned the contempt of the good citizens. Bohemians have always set themselves apart from conventional society; the vocabulary, from "philistine" and "bourgeois" to "square" and "straight," of the 1950s reflects this distancing. The idiom includes such oddities as "pharmacists" from the bohemian Stray Dog cafe of pre–World War I St.

Petersburg. "A basic pre-requisite" of our world, recalled a Stray Dog regular, was "the division of mankind into two unequal categories: the representatives of art and the 'pharmacists,' the latter meaning everybody else no matter what profession they followed."[9] Once this vocabulary loses its sting, as it would by the 1960s, bohemia surrenders its raison d'être.

That urban cafes and streets sheltered marginal intellectuals seems clear enough, but how, or if, this environment colored their oeuvre and their lives is difficult to show. Walter Benjamin mused on the relationship of nineteenth-century Paris—its streets and arcades—to the new intellectual types, such as the man of letters who wandered about, retiring in the afternoon to a cafe to write cultural fillers for the press: "On the boulevard he kept himself in readiness for the next incident, witticism, or rumour. There he unfolded the full fabric of his connections with colleagues and men-about-town." To this life Benjamin attributed the popularity of the "feuilleton," the newspaper feature of many European dailies where intellectuals aired opinions about culture and life.[10]

In his own memoirs Benjamin recalled the cafes of his youth. "I see myself," he reminisces of the West End Cafe in Berlin, headquarters of bohemians, "waiting one night amid tobacco smoke on the sofa that encircled one of the central columns," though he admits he "did not yet possess that passion for waiting without which one cannot thoroughly appreciate the charm of a cafe."[11]

These reflections, drenched in the cafe life of central Europe—and they can easily be multiplied—mark the almost unbridgeable distance to the present.[12] They evoke a world before cafes and strolling succumbed to boutiques and highways. Parking lots, high rises, freeways, and now malls have remade cities, altering as well the cultural tempo. When Henry Pachter, a refugee from Nazism and once a devotee of Berlin cafes, taught college in the United States, he bemoaned that "there were no coffeehouses—and college cafeterias are notoriously unconducive to talk."[13]

The cold-at-heart might retort: there also was no Nazism. The task is to avoid heavy regrets for Old World institutions that did not flourish in North America and resist, as well, burdening daily life with the sins, or glory, of the zeitgeist. Yet a thick-skinned approach that dismisses the quotidian as irrelevant is hardly superior. The rhythm of the lives of intellectuals permeates their writings. This is not surprising. If telephoning supplants letters and cafes yield to conferences, thinking itself—its density and parameters—may echo the shifts. The decline of bohemia may entail not simply the decline of urban intellectuals and their audience, but of urban intelligence as well. To vary an old proposition, cafe society gives rise to the aphorism and essay; the college campus yields the monograph and lecture—and the grant application.

II

THE YEAR IS 1948. Some GIs, including a young New Yorker, Milton Klonsky, twenty-seven, gravitate toward Greenwich Village. They are searching for bohemia, which Klonsky does not find. The times have changed. "The good old days when nobody had a job and nobody cared were over," concludes Klonsky. Now it even takes "pull" to rent an apartment. Money reigns supreme. "Somehow the crass slogan of American business—'How much does he make?'—had been taken over by the Village: 'Where does he show?'—'What has he published?'" The GIs had come to the Village, "expecting to find the Golden

Age of the 20s or the Silver Age of the 30s, but hardly prepared for this, the Age of Lead."[14]

Yet Klonsky observes that the hopefuls were still arriving, "some to be free of their parents . . . some to trade in free love; some for art's sake." Others "come down from the provinces to be close to the Big Time and leave as soon as they can."[15] Graduates of "toney" women's colleges check in and—after a summer—out. Bohemian "fellow-travellers" keep up with the scene but settle elsewhere. Even the old residents, prosperous from the war and uptown money, have contracted expensive habits: analysts, families, nice apartments.

For Klonsky, success is killing bohemia. Not only does the dollar invade the old haunts, but the war levels the "moral dikes" of puritan America, allowing in bohemian waters. "There was as much freedom in the Village as before; but since this was equalled and even surpassed by Main Street, where was the defiance and the revolt against convention" which once infused Greenwich Village? Only the "jazz-narcotics coteries" and "the hipsters" continue to recall a life outside, perhaps against, society.[16]

That same year, 1948, Albert Parry, who wrote the classic account of American bohemianism fifteen years earlier (*Garrets and Pretenders* [1933]), returns to Greenwich Village to gauge the changes; he visits his old hang-outs, asks about the new talent, and also concludes that the bohemian golden era is over. For bohemians, he acknowledges, yesterday was always better. Nevertheless "the Village *is* changed." A few dancers and artists still show up; but the high rents filter out the unknown and undiscovered while "the genteel and dull and chamber-of-commerce elements" take over. The "shiny look" of prosperity glazes the Village; even the bohemian die-hards are leaving.[17]

Twelve months later, a twenty-one-year-old Michael Harrington pulls into New York from the Midwest and sets out to find a bohemian Greenwich Village. Unaware that it has been declared dead, Harrington discovers the bohemian "party" still on. Albert Parry, Henry Miller, Malcolm Cowley, and others who announced its demise are all wrong. "The Village did not die until I got there." He is not "simply indulging the nostalgia of an aging ex-Bohemian trying to immortalize his own youth. . . . I really did find a Bohemia of talent, and sometimes genius, in the New York of the late forties and fifties."[18]

He is not alone. The same year, 1949, a twenty-two-year-old John Gruen, later an art critic and journalist, arrives from Iowa City with his wife, Jane Wilson, a painter. As he recounts in his memoirs of the 1950s, *The Party's Over Now*, they settle in a single room, twelve by fifteen feet, on West 12th Street, convinced that only the Village harbors life and creativity. Like Harrington, they find a community of poets, writers, and artists— Jackson Pollock, Helen Frankenthaler, Robert Motherwell, Larry Rivers, and others—who in the 1950s still work and socialize outside the limelight.[19]

And others are arriving in the Village in 1949, including a thirteen-year-old Joyce Johnson, later an editor and writer, who seeks and finds bohemia. Johnson, who comes all the way from 116th Street, heads downtown with her best friend in search of unknown and forbidden territory. She has heard from some high school girls—Trotskyists who wear "dark clothes and long earrings"—that the Village harbors "romance and adventure." She expects to see a new world but finds only six stragglers in Washington Square Park singing against the falling rain. They suffice, however, to change her life, triggering her encounter with the beats.[20]

The reports of death and of life-after-death can be easily multiplied. Harrington swears the Village was jumping until the late

1950s. Others believe it peaked and died in the 1920s or earlier. "Greenwich Village had become commercialized during the war," declared Floyd Dell—only Dell was referring to World War I. "The little basement and garret restaurants," he recalled in his autobiography, "proved a lure to up-towners, who came into the Village with their pockets full of money and their hearts full of pathetic eagerness to participate in the celebrated joys of Bohemian life." For Dell it was over. "I loathed what the Village had now become. It was a show place." The real Villagers were leaving; and to fill the gap "there now appeared a kind of professional 'Villager.' "[21] Nor was Dell the first to bemoan the decline. "I have listened," he reported, to Sinclair Lewis and others "telling of those early days—the days of the 'real' Village, as they proudly say. . . ."[22]

The conflicting testimonies suggest the impossibility of dating the demise of bohemian Greenwich Village or any cultural community. The judgments are too disparate; the object—cultural vitality—too elusive. Individuals busy growing up and living their lives discover that they were in New York or Paris or Chicago after the decline. How do they know? They are informed by historians or memoirists that they arrived too late. What does it matter, especially if they found what they were looking for? Dell himself remarked that the newcomers experienced the Village blithely unaware of his judgment. "Here were the young people, as young as we had been, as gay and eager. They were the new Greenwich Villagers. They did not mind the changes, because they had never seen our Village."[23]

San Francisco bohemia exemplifies the problem: notices bemoaning its commercialization or demise reach back almost to its origin, at least to the inception of the Bohemian Club. Within a brief period, the Bohemian Club evolved from a loose collection of journalists and rebels to a retreat for the prosperous. In recent decades the San Francisco Bohemian Club and its summer estate in the redwood forests, the Bohemian Grove, have come to symbolize wealth and power. When New York Governor Nelson Rockefeller put in a 1963 appearance at the Bohemian Grove, testing his presidential prospects, *The New York Times* headlined the event as "Governor to Spend Weekend at Bohemian Grove Among State's Establishment."[24]

It was not always so. Founded in 1872, the Bohemian Club was associated with numerous West Coast writers and poets, including Ambrose Bierce, Jack London, and Mark Twain. Within a few years, however, it ran up against the common fate of bohemians: lack of money. Many could not afford to chip in for the rent; others took action. "It was soon apparent," recalled one well-heeled member, "that the possession of talent, without money, would not support the club." The logic was simple: "It was decided that we should invite an element to join the club which the majority of the members held in contempt, namely men who had money as well as brains, but who were not, strictly speaking, Bohemians." With this decision "the problem of our permanent success was solved."[25]

Not everyone was happy. In late 1880 some dissenting painters and writers, who called themselves Pandemonium, protested the "commercialism" and departed to recapture the original bohemian ethos—only to shipwreck on their lack of funds.[26] Later an anonymous member denounced the reign of Mammon among the members—to no avail: "In the beginning rich men were absolutely barred, unless they had something of the elements of true Bohemianism. . . . Now they get in *because* they are rich."[27] Oscar Wilde seemed to agree; he remarked on visiting the club that he had "never seen so many well-dressed, well-fed, business-like looking Bohemians."[28]

"When George Sterling's corpse was discovered in his room

at the Bohemian Club in November of 1926," states a historian of California, "the golden age of San Francisco's bohemia had definitely come to a miserable end."[29] Sterling, a minor poet and one-time follower of Ambrose Bierce, had stood at the center of Bay Area culture since the late 1890s.[30] If his suicide, on the evening of a dinner for H. L. Mencken, ended the golden era, it closed a chapter, not the whole book; San Francisco's bohemia percolated along and sometimes exploded right into the counter-culture of the sixties. The Bohemian Club may have turned fat and conservative, but other centers, such as the Black Cat Cafe, a link between the bohemia of the thirties and the gay culture of the sixties,[31] or the City Lights Bookshop, a home for bohemians and poets in the fifties, took up the slack.[32]

Is the conclusion that bohemia never dies or hardly changes? Is it possible that between 1910 and 1980 little has altered in the New York or San Francisco bohemian communities? There is surely evidence to suggest this, but before taking refuge in the comforting wisdom that bohemia—all culture—is relentlessly the same, that nothing changes in history, a critical distinction must be drawn: the experience of a few individuals and that of a whole generation are not identical. Some individuals may de-clare, believe, or discover that they are living in bohemia; this may be a constant, as true today as it was in the past. It is a different matter, however, for bohemia to shape an intellectual generation. For this, bohemia needs more depth or presence.

This distinction between individual and generational experi-ences is not contrived, for it regularly appears in cultural life. Unique communities—ethnic, religious, national—rarely van-ish in a flash. Even in their decline, they may engender individu-als whose experiences and references are not far removed from earlier inhabitants. It would be difficult, for instance, to dispute the importance of the Lower East Side or Brownsville for a generation of American Jews; it would also be difficult to maintain that these communities have retained their importance for later generations.[33] Their decline, however, does not mean that the old centers have completely disappeared or that all residents have departed. The evolution of bohemia raises the same issues, and necessitates drawing the same distinction—between some individuals and a generation. The task is to appraise how, or if, an intellectual generation experienced bohemia; not to determine the date when bohemia disappeared from the earth. The problem is when and why bohemia ceased to attract a younger intellectual generation.

Of American writers Malcolm Cowley (1898–) has undoubtedly offered the most influential account of bohemia and generations; his benchmark has been his own generation, intellectuals born around the turn of the century. According to Cowley, "writers do not come forward singly, at random intervals of time; instead they appear in clusters or constellations that are surrounded by comparatively empty years." He quotes F. Scott Fitzgerald, who wrote that a "real generation" has "its own leaders and spokesmen" and "draws into its orbit those born just before and just after."[34]

In Cowley's view World War I "physically uprooted" his generation and "infected" it with the "poison" of irresponsibility, danger, and excitement "that made our old life seem intolerable." After the war "most of us drifted to Manhattan, to the crooked streets south of Fourteenth, where you could rent a furnished hall-bedroom for two or three dollars weekly. . . . We came to the Village . . . because living was cheap, because friends of ours had come already . . . because it seemed that New York was the only city where a young writer could be published." For Cowley's generation the Village was not only "a place, a mood, a way of life: like all bohemias, it was also a doctrine."[35]

Yet as his generation arrived, success was threatening the Village. Cowley revises Max Weber's classic argument that the Puritan ethic—restraint, asceticism, guilt—lubricated the engines of capitalism. As Cowley puts it—and many scholars concur—the "production ethic" that preached "industry, foresight, thrift" belonged to an earlier machine age. Newer capitalism did not need work and saving but leisure and spending, not a producing but a consuming ethic.

In this conflict of an older "production ethic" and newer "consumption ethic," Greenwich Village played an unexpected role; its own devotion to pleasure and self-expression tallied with the consuming ethos. Bohemia proved to be the vanguard of the market. "Living for the moment," once a radical idea, promoted buying for pleasure; price and utility ceased to restrain. Even "female equality," dogma if not reality in bohemia, helped double cigarette consumption.

The ease with which Sigmund Freud's austere teachings served in America to intensify consuming illustrates the vigor of the recast ethic. The American Tobacco Company hired Edward Bernays, Freud's nephew, to draw up a campaign to encourage women to smoke. Bernays turned to A. A. Brill, an early American psychoanalyst, and learned that smoking represented sublimated oral eroticism, symbolizing for women emancipation, even "torches of freedom."[36] Bernays, employing this discovery, enlisted women to smoke in the 1929 Easter parade on Fifth Avenue. "Our parade of ten young women," he trumpeted, "lighting 'torches of freedom' on Fifth Avenue on Easter Sunday as a protest against women's inequality caused a national stir."[37]

Advertisers hawked a bohemian protest once reserved for the few; Americans lined up. "The Greenwich Village standards,"

Cowley observed, "with the help of business, had spread through the country." People smoked, had affairs, partied in every state. If the Village was dying, as the press regularly announced, "it was dying of success."[38] "In effect," concludes a recent study of the Village, "the rebels had served as the research and development wing of American society, and in the 1920s a middle-class culture co-opted, at least in part, its counter-culture."[39] Throughout the country the middle classes exchanged a simple code of "self-restraint" or a "Protestant ethos of salvation through self-denial" for consuming as a way of life.[40]

Harrington and other commentators have shifted Cowley's argument forward some thirty years; for them the sexuality, subversion, and madness of a "sixties generation" commercialized, popularized, and finally killed a bohemian ethic. Greenwich Village abandoned its raison d'être. "Somewhere around the early sixties," Harrington believes, "America lost that faith in its own philistine righteousness and Bohemia began to die."[41] Ronald Sukenick, novelist and critic, agrees; an underground Village culture died in the sixties, when it went public. "By the time Allen Ginsberg in an Uncle Sam top hat appeared in a subway ad for *Evergreen Review* with a caption saying 'Join the Underground,' a whole generation of Americans in the 60s were doing so."[42]

There is no need to choose between Cowley and Harrington; they may both be right. Cowley witnessed an earlier and Harrington, a later, perhaps final, stage of the democratization of bohemia. Eventually bohemia, commercialized and popularized, surrendered everything but a few monuments in New York and San Francisco. By the 1960s intellectuals no longer responded to its pull; they no longer had to, since bohemia, renamed the counter-culture, had entered the mainstream. Moreover, the very fabric, the urban texture that sustained bohemia, had by the late 1950s unraveled. Bohemia had lost its urban home and identity. For the generations born in the 1940s and after, bohemia ceased to be either an idea or a place.

III

THE DEMISE of urban bohemia is inextricably linked to suburban expansion. Bohemia and suburbia are not related by cause and effect; rather they express different aspects of the same constellation, the city under the dominion of the automobile. In the 1950s cities became undesirable or unlivable, and the new highways enabled a population on wheels to flee, devitalizing central blocks and neighborhoods. *From Downtown to No Town* reads the subtitle of a book on urban America.[43]

The cover of *Time* in the summer of 1950 pictured William J. Levitt, who pioneered the mass production of suburban homes, before a neat row of identical houses with a caption reading *"House Builder Levitt. For Sale: a new way of life."* And it was a life; not only did Levitt houses come with washing machines and built-in televisions, the deeds specified weekly mowing of lawns (in season) and prohibited fences and outdoor laundry lines. Americans jammed Levitt's sales offices.[44]

The 1950s did not invent suburbs, which as villas, gardens, and walks outside the town reach back almost to the origin of the city.[45] Nor did the 1950s invent the rationale for suburbs. A 1925 study called decentralized suburbs the answer to the evils of crowded cities. "A crowded world must be either suburban or savage."[46] Already in 1900, Adna Weber wrote, "The 'rise of the suburbs' furnishes the solid basis of a hope that the evils of city life . . . may be in large part removed."[47] Even the focus on healthy city street life has a long history. "The problems of the street are the first, the last, and the greatest of the material problems of the city," wrote Delos F. Wilcox in 1904. "It is the street that makes the city possible to begin with."[48]

At least this is clear: the pace and extent of suburbanization in the fifteen years following World War II far surpassed anything before—or since. The automobiles, new highways, and federal policies encouraged, perhaps dictated, the suburban migration and, in the process, gutted the cities.[49] The construction of single-family houses jumped from about 100,000 in 1944 to almost 1.7 million in 1950, a historic high. Suburbia was growing almost ten times faster than central cities. "Because the federally supported home-building boom was of such enormous proportions," writes Kenneth T. Jackson, a historian of suburbia, "the new houses of the suburbs were a major cause of the decline of central cities."[50]

The vast federal investment in highways, signified by the Interstate Highway Act of 1956, intensified the dispersal. Highways absorbed 75 percent of postwar government transportation monies; 1 percent went toward urban mass transit. "The interstate system helped continue the downward spiral of public transportation and virtually guaranteed that future urban growth would perpetuate a centerless sprawl," writes Jackson.[51] Public transportation, already weakened by far-flung urban developments that were difficult to service,[52] was being dismantled. "The current objection to mass transportation," Lewis Mumford noted in 1958, "comes chiefly from the fact that it has been allowed to decay."[53] As it deteriorated, more people visited the car dealer. In 1950 New York subways carried two million riders each day. As fares increased and service declined, half the people deserted the mass transit system, and the number of cars entering Manhattan doubled.[54] One comparison: in 1946 two million cars were built; in 1953, six million.

The suburban explosion yielded a vast literature, fiction and nonfiction, from Herman Wouk's 1955 best-selling novel, *Marjorie Morningstar*, to William H. Whyte's 1956 study, *The Organization Man*. After a 500-page fling, Wouk's bohemian characters snap up commuter tickets. " 'I'm ready to quit, Marjorie,' " Noel the artist declaims. " 'That should be good news to you. All I want to be is a dull bourgeois. . . . Staying up till all hours, sleeping around, guzzling champagne, being oh so crazy, oh so gay, is a damned damned damned damned BORE. . . . I want to get some dull reliable job in some dull reliable advertising agency.' " Too late. Marjorie chooses the suburbs and Milton, the lawyer. He was "reliable, sound and sure," offering the conventional wedding and life she always wanted.[55]

The suburban explosion also produced a highway czar, Robert Moses. Lewis Mumford, Moses's most persistent critic, concludes that "in the twentieth century, the influence of Robert Moses on the cities of America was greater than that of any other person."[56] For over forty years, the redoubtable Moses rammed expressways, tunnels, and bridges throughout New York, city and state. In the mid-fifties he planned to sink a major highway through the heart of Washington Square Park—only seven acres—in order to hook up with another expressway, crossing lower Manhattan. Jane Jacobs's *The Death and Life of Great American Cities* was partially provoked by the successful battle she and her neighbors mounted to preserve Greenwich Village and its Washington Square Park from the New York roadbuilders commandeered by Moses.

The story of Moses illuminates—he did not cause—the deurbanization of America. The new highways that Moses promoted and engineered enabled suburban colonies to flourish. City bohemias eroded as suburbs prospered. Robert Caro, in his extraordinary biography of the extraordinary Moses, *The Power Broker: Robert Moses and the Fall of New York*, identifies 1955 as the irrevocable "turning point" for New York and its suburbs; this was the year that Moses, vetoing proposed transit tracks, began the Long Island Expressway, damning the island to the same sprawl that his parkways had already encouraged.

Just a listing of some Moses projects suggests his impact: Major Deegan Expressway, Van Wyck Expressway, Sheridan Expressway, Bruckner Expressway, Cross Bronx Expressway, Long Island Expressway, Harlem River Drive, West Side Highway, Southern and Northern State Parkways, Brooklyn-Queens Expressway, Saw Mill River Parkway, Cross Island Parkway. Bridges: Triborough, Verrazano, Throgs Neck, Henry Hudson, Bronx-Whitestone. Parks: Jones Beach (perhaps his greatest creation), Sunken Meadow, Montauk, Orient Point, Fire Island, Captree. Plus dams and housing projects. And this is a very partial catalog.

With passion and iron endurance Moses devoted his life to revamping the metropolitan region so that car owners could drive out to his parks or commute into Manhattan. Moses worshipped the private automobile. On his orders bridge overpasses for parkways were built with insufficient clearance for buses, effectively barring city residents without cars. As his chief engineer later explained,

Mr. Moses had an instinctive feeling that someday politicians would try to put buses on the parkways . . . and he used to say to us fellows, "Let's design the bridges so the clearance is all right for passenger cars but not for anything else." . . . He knew . . . you can't change a bridge after it's up. And the result of this is that a bus from New York couldn't use the parkways if we wanted it to.[57]

That Moses himself, like many New Yorkers, never learned to drive—he was chauffered about—hints of madness in his vision.

Of course, it is not possible to accuse or honor a single individual for shaping modern New York. Moses remade the map of New York, but he worked in tandem with potent economic forces; even the formulation "Moses built" misleads, as if by his own hands he dug out roadbeds rather than hammering together power blocs of politicians, developers, and labor unions. Nonetheless, even cities do not expand or contract without human intervention. If Moses marched in step with history, he also barked some decisive commands; and his palpable successes were widely imitated by many urban developers. He is a symbol—and more than a symbol—for the car and the suburb.

The 1950s registered the demise of urban bohemia and the ballooning of suburbia. This was not only a demographic shift; it was cultural as well. Bohemia had lost its raison d'être; bourgeois society, always nipping at its heels, finally caught up. At the same time the fragile environs that sustained urban bohemias suffered a series of blows. By the end of the fifties younger intellectuals, usually raised in the suburbs, rarely moved to New York or Chicago or San Francisco to fashion lives as independent writers. Rather they streamed toward spacious college towns, safely distant from blighted cities.

IV

FEW OBSERVERS or historians admit that in cultural clashes boredom often has the final word: no one shows up for another round. The issue of suburbia, which provoked innumerable reports, novels, and magazine articles in the 1950s, finally sank out of sight. When in recent years, even decades, has a major magazine or television report covered suburban life? To the new generations, those who did not move to the suburbs but were raised there, the endless debate on the ills and pleasures of suburban life failed to elicit much interest. Suburbia was suburbia, familiar and universal. It was hardly a controversial topic. If only by lack of interest, the subject seemed closed.

Not quite. The new generations did contribute something. While they did not argue the merits of the suburbs, many by the 1980s have voted "with their feet." In recent years significant numbers—not a flood—of children of parents who enthusiastically escaped from the cities have moved back. If cities have regained public attention and some revitalization, this is due to two imports from the suburbs: people and shopping malls.

Neither promises to restore the conditions of urban community. The shopping mall was suburbia's answer to de-urbanized sprawl; as downtowns died or were killed, they were reborn as distant concourses accessible only by highways. Shoppers preferred the big chain stores surrounded by endless parking. "Suburbanization and the Baby Boom created and defined the needs and desires of this culture," reports William Kowinski in his personal account of malls, *The Malling of America.* "The highways finally defined how and where that culture would flourish."[58]

Yet nostalgia often clouds discussions of malls; a vibrant city seems to lurk in the past. Malls displaced downtowns crowded with people and stores, throbbing with life, day and night. Was it so? Kowinski concedes that the downtown of his childhood was hardly idyllic; and the new malls offer, especially to youth, a place to gather, which otherwise they do not have.

It offers little more, and usually less. It is difficult to get misty-eyed about malls, big or small, covered or uncovered, with or without fountains, glass elevators, and local craft exhibitions. Malls are selling machines. Unlike city streets, they are designed and run by private corporations so that every square foot, including benches and fountains, promotes a shopping mood. One corporation calls the shots, including which stores may open or stay; rents are usually based on square footage of rental space, plus a percentage of gross receipts. Obviously stores that do not yield enough do not have their leases renewed, ensuring that the mall remains homogeneous; a bookstore with too much browsing has no future. The store hours are also determined by the corporation, and since few people live close by and none live in malls; they are deserted after 6:00 or 9:00 P.M.

Malls are an American success story. With parking and highway access they multiplied with postwar suburbia; in 1946 there were only eight shopping centers; by the end of the 1950s, four thousand dotted the United States.[59] That these suburban artifacts, which once spelled the death of downtowns, are now prescribed for urban ills and are increasingly built in city centers adds irony to irony. Victor Gruen, a major mall developer, originally envisioned the malls as bringing cities to the suburbanites suffering from isolation.

After the war, Gruen, a refugee architect from Austria, emerged as a one of the first mall designers and builders. He began as a reformer with a dream. The shopping mall would replace the commercial strips—ugly, unfocused, unsocial—springing up in suburbia. More than stores with parking lots, the mall would offer space for walking, talking, and sitting. It would, almost, recreate the city.

Visions of European markets and his own Vienna infused Gruen's hopes for malls. "We must sensitively observe the colorful, stimulating and commercially busy urban scene in the market squares in Central European cities." He instructed mall developers that "our new shopping towns" can "fill an existing void," providing a "community," or a new version of the old town squares and market places.[60]

Gruen prospered and his firm, Victor Gruen Associates, became, and remains, a major mall developer. Yet the reality of the malls never came close to his vision; he saw the malls as surmounting, not extending, suburban sprawl. Gruen was a mall developer who thought more like Lewis Mumford and Jane Jacobs than Robert Moses. He decried the effect of the automobile. "Why danger labels only on cigarettes?" he asked. "Why not on cars?"[61]

He drew back from the new developments that were neither city nor country. "Shopping centers are referred to as villages, and everywhere one finds Town and Country shops, and Country Clubs. . . . The names of subdivisions refer to nonexistent lakes, woods, glens, dales. . . ." Gruen concluded it was time to reclaim the cities; the belief of the 1950s in decentralized suburbia "has now been shattered." He urged readoption of "the values of centralization and urbanism."[62] Eventually a disillusioned Gruen returned to his beloved Vienna, where he wrote on the dilemmas of progress, the evils of automobiles.[63]

The other suburban import promising to restore city vitality is people. A major surprise of the last decade is the return or reappearance of city dwellers—"gentrification" or renovation of older urban neighborhoods by new, young, and affluent residents, a process visible from Vancouver to Baltimore.[64] While everything about this phenomenon—its extent, impact, and meaning—is controversial, these new residents seem to be "children of the suburbs," who for reasons of living or life-style prefer a downtown existence.[65]

The first generation wholly raised in suburbia appears unenthusiastic about the greenery, backyards, and shopping centers that dazzled their parents from the crowded cities. "A suburban address was the status symbol for many newly forming households of the 1950s and 1960s," notes one survey of gentrification. "Today, a rising proportion of the affluent offspring of these suburbanities find a center city address fashionable."[66] Moreover, single men and women, including single parents—an increasing proportion of the population—seem to require, at least prefer, urban to suburban living, since it offers more possibilities for socializing, child care, shopping, eating.[67]

A new preference for downtown living is not simply a cause but an effect of the transformation of cities: the departure of old industries and the growth of downtown "smokeless" businesses—financial, advertising, technical. The people who arrive are the new work force, replacing the old blue-collar laborers. "The new 'means of production'—in modern offices—are now surrounded by their own 'working-class districts' of high-rise apartments, brownstones, and converted loft buildings." The conversion of lofts from light manufacturing to upscale homes is a particularly elegant sign of a recast urban economy, where new consumers have replaced old producers. Moreover, the lofts themselves, insofar as they are not occupied by artists but by financial analysts and corporate lawyers, testify to "the same spatial values as a typical suburban home . . . a preference for lots of air, light and open space."[68]

In numbers and extent gentrification and loft-living is confined; it has not spread through vast urban tracts. Rather it is restricted to select areas, usually blocks of decent older housing stock, close to downtowns and near to parks, rivers, or harbors. This revitalization hardly reverses urban decline. New affluence coexists with old decay; one street succumbs to poverty while the adjoining street prospers. Gentrification has also brought in its wake accelerating rents and a new homogenization; both of these threaten city diversity and bohemian culture.

None of this is especially new. Jane Jacobs in 1961 commented upon the dangers of urban success, at the time a rarity. Desirable neighborhoods attract the affluent, who squeeze out the less affluent.

So many people want to live in the locality that it becomes profitable to build, in excessive and devasting quantity, for those who can pay the most. These are usually childless people . . . and . . . people who can or will pay the most for the smallest space. Accommodations for this narrow, profitable segment of population multiply, at the expense of all other tissue and all other population. Families are crowded out, variety of scene is crowded out, enterprises . . . are crowded out.[69]

The pressures of gentrification eliminate not only low-rent housing but also modest restaurants, cafes, and bookstores. From Santa Monica to Brooklyn Heights new boutiques, card shops, ice cream bars, and pricey cookie outlets drive out less profitable stores. "Bookseller Fights Back," reports *The New York Times* on a classic battle in Brooklyn Heights between an old community bookstore devoted to literature and an ice cream boutique. With the chain ice cream outlet offering twice the rent, the landlord tried to evict the bookstore. "At issue," stated *The New York Times*, "is a landlord's right to raise commercial rents, a move that can force 'mom and pop' stores out of newly affluent neighborhoods." The article also noted that "down the block" a national chain bookstore (Waldenbooks) "does a lively trade in best sellers."[70] With some changes, this article can apply to scores of cities.

Both in choice of neighborhoods and in the accelerating rents, gentrification undercuts urban bohemias; the dependence of writers and artists' communities on cheap housing cannot be overemphasized. If low rents vanish, a community cannot coalesce. Lionel Abel, who moved to New York in 1929 at the age of nineteen, stayed with relatives; he explains that it took him more than a year to afford his own room in the Village. Finally "a publisher . . . had given me a contract to make a translation of Rimbaud's poems, and on the advance for this I was able to live in the Village."[71] Today an advance for a similar project would hardly pay a New York rent, no matter how modest.

Intellectuals of the 1950s, when they reflected on the "death of bohemia," regularly indicted the refurbished housing and onerous rents. "The past always lingers on," wrote William Phillips in 1952, but the cold-water flat is gone, taking with it the wandering, jobless writers and artists.[72] Higher rents obviously do not spell the end of artistic life; but they do require more income, more commissions, more connections. For the young or unestablished the rents simply are not possible.

Of course, poverty and low rents also make up the mythology of bohemian life; they are easy to ridicule as harmless dreams of ex-bohemians who were never impoverished. It is true that standards of living are always relative. Intellectuals enmeshed in destitute families cannot afford to escape to bohemia, no matter how low the admission price; bohemian poverty requires an emancipation from desperate poverty. As Irving Howe recounts, Yiddish intellectuals in America were "too poor to venture on the programmatic poverty of bohemia. . . . These intellectuals were thrown in with the masses of their people, sharing their poverty, their work, their tenements."[73]

The skeptic, unconvinced that suburbia, malls, or gentrification undercuts bohemias, might argue that insofar as only small urban sections are refurbished, other tracts are ripe for settlement by marginal writers and artists. Moreover, bohemias have never been static and in New York have shifted from Greenwich Village to the south (SoHo) and perhaps now are migrating to the East Village or to other cities, such as Hoboken or Newark, New Jersey.[74]

This is true, but it does not address the rate of transformation. Absolute novelty is not the issue. Neither commercialization nor bohemian migrations are new. The difficulty is calculating the tempo of transformation, not simply its fact; this may be decisive. If commercialization is not unique to the 1970s or 1980s, its velocity may be; bohemian development is now orchestrated and financed. "Far from being an indigenous or a spontaneous artists' community, SoHo was really a creation of the investment climate," concludes Sharon Zukin.[75]

The Greenwich Village of cheap rents and restaurants lasted at least seventy-five years; SoHo, perhaps ten years, and the East Village, even fewer. Craig Owens, an editor of *Art in America*, views the East Village renaissance as the "Manhattanization" of New York, the uprooting of diverse groups by the young, affluent professionals. According to Owens, the East Village art scene is no bohemia, but a commercial imitation. "What has been constructed in the East Village is not an alternative to, but a miniature replica of the contemporary art market—a kind of Junior Achievement for young culture-industrialists."[76]

This may be unfair, yet it speaks to the accelerating merchandising of culture. Bohemian communities may germinate but cannot take root before the boutiques and condominiums crowd them out. The hysteria of development poisons the conviviality of artists and perhaps the creativity as well. "It used to be possible—not easy, but possible," notes a grim account of costly real estate driving artists out of Manhattan, "for ordinary talented New Yorkers to work at art for other reasons than the promise of big money and instant fame. In the present circumstances, those artists in the East Village, or SoHo or Theater Row, who do it *only* for fame and money are understandable." Due to rent hikes the numbers of theaters, dance schools, and bookstores have dropped dramatically in New York; cheap housing, loft space, and neighborhood bars and restaurants have become a dim memory.[77]

To be sure, insofar as gentrification is spatially confined, other urban sections are available to writers and intellectuals. Yet sheer availability has never been the issue. An ineffable mix of modest rents and restaurants in pleasant surroundings nurtures bohemias. Gentrification lives with its opposite, urban collapse; it is news to no one that cities are increasingly stratified; slums adjoin luxury condominiums. Neither encourages communities of writers and artists.

The stout at heart, of course, may live in the slums of the South Bronx and write or paint. A few scattered individuals, however, do not constitute a community. Newcomers who have neither funds nor well-paying jobs will quickly discover that rents in decent areas of New York or San Francisco are prohibitive; they may find city tracts where rents are possible but life seems difficult. And they decide: why try? Why not live and write in the countryside of Vermont or Montana or Arkansas? Why not indeed?

The move to the countryside is an old story. The 1960s counterculture inspired many to desert cities for the countryside; and the sixties ethos tapped a venerable American spirit of self-sufficiency, as well as a Yankee distrust of urban sin and dirt.[78] Even the beats of the 1950s played a role; they came from the city with a rural message. These complementary impulses ensured that new bohemian recruits no longer collected in the major cities, where the obstacles to living steadily augmented; rather, they dispersed across the continent, often settling in rural areas in search of a different life. Once a commitment to urban life was surrendered, however, bohemia could never be the same.

The extent of such migrations, which continued into the 1970s, is difficult to measure. From Vermont to New Mexico to the Pacific Northwest—and scores of other locales—colonies of bohemians, ex-bohemians, and veterans of the sixties survive and sometimes flourish as part-time farmers, shopkeepers, and craftsmen. On slow days newspaper editors dispatch reporters to write up a local group. "Rural Homesteaders Seek Self-Sufficiency and Cherish Solitude," reads a typical piece on eighty families who grow their own vegetables, collect honey, raise sheep, and make yogurt in upstate New York. The article notes that "a revolt against society" motivated most of these new homesteaders to abandon the cities; they "hail from a 'back to the land' movement of the late 1960s and early 1970s," which the sober *New York Times* defines as "a somewhat misty-eyed retreat to the countryside in search of what was thought to be a rural utopia."[79]

The very difficulty of gauging the breadth of these colonies illustrates the critical transformation: when bohemia became rural, it also became invisible. This is not a minor shift from city to countryside; invisibility deprives bohemia of the seductive force that radiated from its urban quarters. This force was crucial for the vitality of bohemia. By attracting new individuals it allowed for replenishment; and it enabled bohemia sometimes to affect the larger culture. But at the same time that the cities turned inhospitable—and partly for this reason—bohemians abandoned them for the highways, campuses, and countryside. Nowadays suburban and city youth neither see nor feel a tug from bohemia; and even if some did, no one could find it.

CHAPTER 3

———

On the Road to Suburbia: Urbanists and Beats

I

WHILE THE REBELLIONS of the 1960s can be and have been documented in exhaustive detail, the 1950s appear increasingly puzzling, as well as crucial. The 1950s encompass rapid suburbanization, the rise and fall of McCarthyism, and the beats. These years also witnessed a new national crisis: juvenile delinquency, the subject of endless investigations. Yet newspaper editorials also bemoaned another, almost opposite, phenomenon, apathetic and conformist youth. How did the upsurges of the sixties emerge from this constellation? "No one surveying the campus scene in 1959," concludes one study, "could have predicted the 1960s."[1]

Perhaps one clue can be found in the restructured urban environment. By the end of the 1950s not only the urban habitat but its intellectuals and bohemians were transformed. For this reason the last bohemians—the beats—and the last urbanists are of exceptional interest: they denote the passing of one cultural type and the emergence of another. The beats are bohemians in the era of interstate highways. After the beats urban bohemia and bohemians are historical facts, not living reality. The 1950s urbanists—Jane Jacobs, Paul and Percival Goodman, William H. Whyte, Lewis Mumford—grappled with the city in its crisis hour; they represent the last of a breed, intellectuals committed to an educated public.

As individuals, the 1950s urbanists and bohemians did not associate. Jane Jacobs and Jack Kerouac, for instance, inhabited completely different personal worlds. Nor were the urbanists and beats symmetrical social formations. The urbanists were classic American intellectuals, independent writers and critics. They wrote cogently about the city, but few followed in their steps. The beats, on the other hand, almost constituted a cultural movement. Arriving with an ethos, if not a program, they partly engendered, and merged with, a 1960s counterculture.

However, both signify not only a geographic but a cultural fracture and shift in their responses to the atrophying metropolitan environment. The fifties urbanists address the city strangled by cars and highways. Their own lives testify to its demise; they are the last urbanists who live fully as city people, free-floating intellectuals. Their successors abandon the cities for the universities. The beats play a parallel role. They are the last bohemians as the cities turn increasingly difficult and stratified, quarters for the very rich and the poor. After the beats, bohemia strikes out from its urban enclaves and enters the mainstream. In the urbanists and beats it is possible to glimpse midcentury American culture as it migrates from cities to campuses and suburbs.

Of course, the writings of the fifties urbanists do not mark the end of intelligent analyses of cities. Younger observers and scholars continue to confront the metropolitan environment. Yet the rapid expansion of urban studies in the universities (under various rubrics: urban history, city planning, regional studies, urban geography) has hardly supplemented public writings on the city. Rather, the dwindling universe of independent journalists and scholars takes its toll. For this reason urbanism shares with other fields a peculiar cultural trajectory: a rising curve of compelling writings that crests at the end of the 1950s, and afterward a steep decline with few additions by younger thinkers fired by the same caliber of imagination, boldness—or writing.

Even the most talented and productive of the younger urbanists, such as David Harvey (1935–), a professor of geography and author of *Social Justice and the City* (1973), are little known outside restricted academic circles.[2] Harvey's most recent books, *The Urbanization of Capital* (1985) and *Consciousness and the Urban Experience* (1985), reveal why: they are designed for professional sympathizers and friends of the author.

In the current academic fashion his new books arrive bristling with self-importance. However, these volumes, subtitled *Studies in the History and Theory of Capitalist Urbanization*, reek of too many lectures, seminars, and conferences. Nor does it help that Harvey ventilates the text with his favorite source—himself. He begins by telling us that "it has been my ambition, ever since the writing of *Social Justice and the City*, to progress toward a more definitive Marxian interpretation of the history and theory of urbanization under capitalism than I there achieved." And he concludes his more definitive interpretation by quoting himself.[3] In between these two points—whatever the theoretical innovations—is a prose desert, certain death for anyone unprepared for an extreme academic environment. A sample passage from his conclusion reads:

On the Road to Suburbia: Urbanists and Beats

An inspection of the different moments and transitions within the circulation of capital indicates a geographical grounding of that process through the patterning of labor and commodity markets, of the spatial division of production and consumption (under sociotechnical conditions that are in part an adaption to geographical variations), and of hierarchically organized systems of financial coordination. Capital flow presupposes tight temporal and spatial coordinations in the midst of increasing separation and fragmentation. It is impossible to imagine such a material process without the production of some kind of urbanization as a 'rational landscape' within which the accumulation of capital can proceed.[4]

If this is not sufficiently clear, he adds, "The connection between city formation and the production, appropriation, and concentration of an economic surplus has long been noted." Noted by whom? Harvey cites himself. Unfortunately, the few books by younger urbanists which are less self- and professionally involved suffer almost from an opposite ill of vagueness and imprecision.[5]

Compared to this literature, the books grouped around the years 1959–60 breathe of public discussions, open, engaged, and lucid: Jane Jacobs's *The Death and Life of Great American Cities* (1961); *The Exploding Metropolis* (1958), edited by William H. Whyte; Lewis Mumford's *The City in History* (1961); Percival Goodman and Paul Goodman's *Communitas* (1960);[6] Murray Bookchin's *The Limits of the City*.[7] These works, all by independent scholars and writers, are unsurpassed by younger intellectuals.[8]

As suburbanization peaked, Jane Jacobs published her passionate and influential text, *The Death and Life of Great American Cities*. A resident of Greenwich Village, she was committed not to bohemia but to its prerequisites: communities and neighborhoods, street life and night life. She argued persuasively that

the professionals—the planners, consultants, and engineers—
devitalized the city in the name of reform; that their geometrical
blocks, superhighways, and zoning-by-use effectively, sometimes
deliberately, gutted neighborhoods; that the city regressed into
homogeneous units that undermined continuous human activity
(e.g., financial areas deserted after 5:00 P.M., residential high
rises far from grocery stores and busy streets).[9]

By virtue of its author and contents, *Death and Life* illuminates the cultural universe. Jane Jacobs (1916–) is a classic intellectual of the last generation; a journalist from Pennsylvania, she
moved to New York to write, eventually joining the staff of *Architectural Forum*. Perhaps her distance from institutions and
the profession allowed her to challenge urban planners; she as-
cribes her irreverence simply to walking and observing unen-
cumbered by conventional planning wisdom.

"Reformers have long observed city people loitering on busy
corners, hanging around in candy stores and bars and drinking
soda pop on stoops," Jacobs wrote, "and have passed a judgment,
the gist of which is 'This is deplorable! If these people had decent
homes . . . they wouldn't be on the street!' " For Jacobs this judgment "represents a profound misunderstanding of cities."[10]

Her book savages city planners for their estrangement from
the city itself, their devotion to anti-urban straight lines, massive
projects, and blueprints. She prefers knowledge rooted not in
statistical surveys but in urban life. She states, for instance, that
all the professional studies of downtown Brooklyn "cannot tell
us as much . . . as is told in five short lines of type in a single
newspaper advertisement." The advertisement lists the hours of
a chain bookstore; its Brooklyn branch closes early, while the
Greenwich Village and Times Square branches remain open till
midnight.[11] For Jacobs these facts evidence the stagnation of
downtown Brooklyn. Her book includes a page of "Illustrations"

with no illustrations; the page reads, "The scenes that illustrate this book are all about us. For illustrations, please look closely at real cities."

While neither cars nor suburbs were her main concern, Jacobs's book closes with the specter of "vapid suburbanization" and "dull, inert cities."[12] This was the issue and the threat that all the fifties urbanists addressed. Ruptured by highways, bled by suburbs, the classic city was expiring. "Perhaps our age," reflected Mumford in 1958, "will be known to the future historian as the age of the bulldozer. . . . Nowhere is this bulldozing habit of mind so disastrous as in the approach to the city." The "fatal mistake" has been sacrificing all transportation to the private motor car. He anticipated a future where the city is a "mechanized nonentity," a "tangled mass of highways, interchanges and parking lots."[13]

"Downtown Is for People," an early version of Jacobs's *Death and Life*, appeared in the collection *The Exploding Metropolis*, edited by William H. Whyte. Two years earlier Whyte had published *The Organization Man*, a critical inquiry into suburban life and mores. He did not wish to join the chorus lamenting superficiality. "There will be no strictures in this book against 'Mass Man,' . . . not will there be any strictures against ranch wagons, or television sets, or gray flannel suits. They are irrelevant to the main problem, and . . . there's no harm in them."[14]

Like Jane Jacobs, William H. Whyte (1917–) is a classic public intellectual of the 1950s; and like Jacobs, he was born in Pennsylvania, became a journalist, and then an editor of a New York magazine (*Fortune*). His collection, *The Exploding Metropolis*, attacked the new religion of automobiles and suburbs. Whyte's opening essay, "Are Cities Un-American?" declared an urban love affair: "This is a book by people who like cities." The book also raised an alarm; suburbia threatened to dissolve the urban centers. If it was to remain a cultural force, "the city must have a core of people to support its theatres and museums, its shops and its restaurants." Whyte added, "Even a Bohemia of sorts can be of help."[15]

For thirty-odd years Whyte has monitored urban culture and activity. He lectures and writes against the latest urban fashions, barren concrete fortresses enclosing miles of underground concourses.[16] He has been called a "free-lance *agent provocateur*," abetting those who want to make cities livable.[17] *The Social Life of Small Urban Spaces*, his inquiry into street life, questions the megastructures and shopping malls assaulting city life. Alluding to the Detroit Renaissance Center, Atlanta Omni International, and Los Angeles Bonaventure Complex, he notes that "the ultimate development in the flight from the street is the urban fortress." These centers seek to salvage the downtown but are designed as "wholly internalized environments. . . . Their enclosing walls are blank, windowless, and to the street they turn an almost solid face of concrete or brick." For the pedestrian they are uninviting, even impenetrable; with underground entries and parking, they tempt only the automobile.[18]

While Whyte dislikes sharp judgments, he is hardly dispassionate, and occasionally he sounds like Jacobs or C. Wright Mills, when attacking the new professionals. In *The Organization Man*, he warned of the younger urbanists who neglect issues for techniques.

Not so very long ago, the younger social scientist was apt to see his discipline as a vehicle for protest against society. . . . The seniors that set the fashion for him were frequently angry men . . . and did not conceal strong opinions. . . . But this is now old hat: it is the "bleeding-heart" school to the younger men . . . they do not wish to protest; they wish to collaborate.[19]

Whyte sensed the future: the fifties urbanists would have few successors. He also alluded to the passivity of the younger generation, a regular refrain in the 1950s. Commentators often lamented the conformist and apathetic youth. Yet few realized that as the cities turned inhospitable, not only were the intellectuals departing for campuses, but the last bohemians were taking to the road.

II

MALCOLM COWLEY, who continued to monitor the literary scene, weighed in during the decade, offering "that I can compare what is happening in the 1950s with my memories of what happened after another world war." Of course, the new reality did not measure up to the old; now few youth displayed "the personal recklessness of their predecessors." Writing and criticism had become careers, not callings. Novelists had "stopped acting like bohemians or proletarians, and it was getting hard to tell a writer from anybody else. Many of the younger ones lived on residential streets, owned their homes—or were trying to buy them—and were active members of the Parent-Teacher Association." Others had "gone straight from studying creative writing into teaching it, without any interlude for writing creatively, or even commercially."[20]

Editorial writers concurred; they regularly reported that the campuses were quiet—too quiet; youth seemed "silent," "conformist," "apathetic." Ludwig Marcuse, a German refugee professor (no relation to Herbert Marcuse), writing in *Partisan Review*, dubbed American youth "the oldest younger generation."

He believed that his own generation had developed "individuality, enthusiasm, war on parents and teachers." This legacy evaporated; youth was now silent, unemotional, pliant. It was not disillusioned for it had no illusions. "There is no Younger Generation," concluded Marcuse. There were only eighteen- to twenty-eight-year-olds.[21]

In *Harper's Bazaar* Caroline Bird labeled youth the "unlost generation." She asked why the new generation seemed "so unambitious, so over-adjusted and apathetic," and proposed that since childhood the young had been schooled to cooperate, in effect, to conform. Moreover the new generation was rebelling—against the rebellion of its parents, the lost generation that had been "awash in words" in its quest for utopia. Youth now was "revolting against the cult of personal experience, against sexual experiment, against infatuation with talk, against skepticism."[22]

Some contested these dirges for rebellious and bohemian generations. In 1958 Otto Butz, a professor at Princeton University, troubled by the laments of complacent and smug youth, published a symposium in which "eleven college seniors look at themselves and their world." The soul-searching essays encouraged Butz to see the contributors as constituting an "unsilent generation."[23] The essayists, however, neither identified themselves—the contributions were anonymous—nor aired any heretical ideas. If these youths were "unsilent," a reviewer remarked, it is because they expressed uncertainty about careers, military service, and religion. "But in terms of this definition, almost everyone is 'unsilent.' ..."[24] Nevertheless, this mild probing cost Butz his Princeton appointment.[25]

The persistent mourning for the passing of rebellious youth has to be set against its opposite, the national mobilization against juvenile delinquency. For the public of the 1950s, "juvenile delinquency" supplanted a memory of a rebellious, even unconventional youth. A thousand conferences, agencies, committees, and newspapers alerted the country to the danger. Juvenile delinquency was the only rebellion around, and it had to be stopped.

Articles on teenage delinquency gushed forth. Experts labeled it a "national epidemic," projecting some two and a half million cases. "Unless this cancer is checked early enough," warned one popular book, *1,000,000 Delinquents* (1955), "it can go on spreading and contaminate many good cells in our society. . . . Juvenile delinquency is already creeping from the wrong side of the tracks to the right side."[26] Hollywood joined in, with young, angry stars James Dean and Marlon Brando in films such as *The Wild One* (1954), *Rebel Without a Cause* (1955), and *The Blackboard Jungle* (1955).[27]

In films, newspapers, and congressional committees juvenile delinquency seemed everywhere; yet if it hinted at the future, a sixties youth culture,[28] contemporary observers missed it. Few identified familiar signs of bohemian or protesting youth. Robert Lindner in *Must You Conform?* and Paul Goodman in *Growing Up Absurd* did view juvenile delinquency as a mangled or self-destructive protest, but they were largely ignored. A suffocating conformism provoked the "mutiny of the young," stated Lindner. " 'Better' schools will not help, nor will more stringent laws, harsher punishments, the Boy Scouts, Police Athletic Leagues, Visiting Teaching programs, social work in distressed areas"; these all served to tighten the noose.[29]

The nation, however, seemed convinced that juvenile delinquency signified a threat to life, liberty, and happiness. Yet the obsession with youth crime cannot be accepted at face value. A recent assessment challenges its basic premise: "What every participant in the broad public discussion assumed to be true— that delinquency had increased in quantity and severity since

World War II—now seems questionable. . . . Despite inflammatory headlines and the repetition of charges about brutality, the incidence of juvenile crime does not appear to have increased enormously during this period."[30]

Then why the ruckus? James Gilbert believes that police "prodded by government and private pressures groups" asserted a new authority over young people, whose behavior seemed to be slowly shifting. For instance, violations of curfews, which many communities introduced for their youth, showed up as statistical jumps in juvenile "crime." The numbers meant that the local police had caught some after-hours teenagers; and the figures were then displayed by journalists and experts as evidence of mounting crime. In this way the California Youth Authority announced that one out of four seventeen-year-olds was delinquent in 1957.[31]

The increase in juvenile delinquency, even if it were only curfew violations and other minor infractions, testified less to crime than to an emerging juvenile mass culture that threatened traditional codes. The greater access to money and especially to automobiles, which allowed the young to escape watchful parents, fostered their identities as individuals with specific sexual, musical, and consuming needs. For conservatives juvenile delinquency, like communism, subverted the American Way. "Not even the Communist conspiracy," stated a United States senator in 1954, "could devise a more effective way to demoralize, disrupt, confuse, and destroy our future citizens than apathy on the part of adult Americans to the scourge known as Juvenile Delinquency."[32]

Yet history was preparing a small joke. As the authorities denounced juvenile delinquency, outside the limelight more insidious threats, the last bohemians, were gathering. At the end of Cowley's mid-1950s survey, he identified one group that violated generalizations about gray and cautious youth; these young "refused to conform and waged a dogged sort of rebellion . . . against the whole body of laws, customs, fears, habits of thought, and literary standards that had been accepted." "Individual and nihilistic," they liked to be "cool" and underground. For the best account of this "beat generation" Cowley recommended an "unpublished long narrative" called *On the Road* by an unknown author, Jack Kerouac.[33]

III

THE BEATS seemed designed to humble cultural commentators. Sermons bemoaning conformity did not allude to the living refutation, the beats; and lectures about juvenile delinquency failed to mention this greater danger. Few knew about the beats until the second half of the fifties. When they finally captured the public imagination, spurred by Allen Ginsberg's *Howl* (1956) and Kerouac's *On the Road* (1957), their finest hours were fading. Though no one knew it at the time, the public fascination with the beats announced a zig in the zeitgeist.

The beats, however, are more than a lesson in the risks of cultural forecasting. They are the last bohemians, and the first of the 1960s counterculturalists. In the account of the demise of bohemia, the beats are the missing agents. They carried bohemia into the age of suburbia where it spread and disappeared. If bohemia died of success, the beats both administered the last rites and invented a new popular version. Accounts of the sixties give a nod toward the beats, but more than a nod is required. Not the revived Marxism or Maoism but the sexuality, drugs, mysticism, and madness of the sixties owe much to the beats.

In 1957 Kerouac was thirty-five, and his autobiographical *On the Road* documented lives from ten years earlier. The first self-identified beat novel, *Go*, by Kerouac's friend John Clellon Holmes, appeared in 1952 and—as he later remarked—disappeared in 1952. With the same cast as *On the Road*, *Go* portrays the beats as urban bohemians.

He came to know their world . . . of dingy backstairs "pads," Times Square cafeterias, bebop joints, night-long wanderings, meetings on street corners, hitchkiking, a myriad of "hip" bars all over the city, and the streets themselves. . . . They kept going all the time, living by night, rushing around to "make contact," suddenly disappearing into jail or on the road only to turn up again and search one another out. . . . Once Pasternak [Keroauc] said to him. . . . "You know, everyone I know is kind of furtive, kind of beat. They all go along the street like they were guilty of something, but didn't believe in guilt. I can spot them immediately! And it's happening all over the country, to everyone; a sort of revolution of the soul. . . ."[34]

Five years later, when *On the Road* appeared, times had changed; a voracious public descended upon the beats. *Life* magazine marveled in 1959 that the "biggest, sweetest and most succulent casaba ever produced by the melon patch of civilization"—the United States—has incubated some of "the hairiest, scrawniest and most discontented" fruit flies of all time, "the improbable rebels of the Beat Generation." They sneer at "virtually every aspect of current American society: Mom, Dad, Politics, Marriage, the Savings Bank, Organized Religion," as well as the automatic dishwasher and the split-level house. *Life* identified them as mainly "shabby and bearded men" and "pallid and sullen girls" who inhabit North Beach in San Francisco, "dreary pads" in Venice (Los Angeles), or cheap cafeterias in Greenwich Village.[35]

For some older sympathizers, the beats refuted pronouncements of the death of bohemia. Lawrence Lipton (1898–1975), a minor novelist and poet who wrote the first popular account of the beats, *The Holy Barbarians* (1959), celebrated the return of an old bohemian ethos.[36] He recalled that when meeting the poet Kenneth Rexroth "for the first time in Chicago back in the late twenties he was as beat as any of today's beat generation. So was I. So were most of my friends."[37]

Rexroth (1905–82) agreed, although he sighed that "at my advanced age" he was "a little tired of being the spokesman for the young." The "voluntary poverty, absolute artistic integrity, social disengagement, commitment to personal values" of the beats signaled the beginnings of a new literature, perhaps a new society.[38]

To Lipton the beats reach back to the 1920s, not to the flappers but to the "spirit of revolt" that wafted through the studios of Greenwich Village and Chicago's Near North Side, through declassé neighborhoods of major cities across the continent. In those years "we were expropriating" from the upper classes their leisure arts, sins, and "privilege of defying convention." This is what Lipton dubbed "the democratization of amorality," which began after World War I and, with some interruptions, continues to permeate society. For Lipton the beats were not the last but the latest bohemians.[39]

Like Rexroth, Lipton believed that the future belonged to the beats, quiet rebels distant from the corruption and violence of American society. Yet neither the beats' well-wishers nor their critics fathomed the cunning of history: just as bohemia was being throttled in the cities, the beats arrived to spread the message far and wide. They did this brilliantly. Two features set them apart from earlier bohemians and turned the beats into gifted propagandists: their devotion to the automobile, the road, and travel, which kept them and then a small army of imitators crisscrossing the continent; and their populism, their love of the American people.

In his classic anthology, *The Beat Scene*, Elias Wilentz, proprietor of the 8th Street Bookshop, a Village beat hangout, stated that all the contributors "are Bohemians but all have been labeled as 'beat.' "[40] Yet the populism of the beats distinguished them from "classical" bohemians who were almost defined by their disdain of the philistine masses; and it brought the beats in contact with poets, such as William Carlos Williams, who worked in an American vein.[41] The bohemian elitism of the beats, which is reflected in the idiom of "straights" and "squares" is drowned by their romanticization of common lives and peoples, sometimes a celebration of kitsch.

We were the first American generation, said Holmes much later, to grow up with popular culture and unashamedly love it.[42] In *On the Road*, Sal reports that "I have finally taught Dean that he can do anything he wants, become the mayor of Denver . . . or the greatest poet since Rimbaud. But he keeps rushing out to see the midget auto races. I go with him."[43]

Sal stumbles upon a evening softball game with neighbors relaxing, rooting, watching. "Just sandlot kids in uniform. Never in my life as an athlete had I ever permitted myself to perform like this in front of families and girl friends and kids of the neighborhood. . . . Always it had been college, big-time, sober-faced," writes Kerouac, who had entered Columbia University on a football scholarship, "no boyish, human joy like this."[44]

These are not cultural aristocrats decrying—or fleeing—the vulgar masses; rather, *On the Road* celebrates everyday life and its pleasures. Dean's "criminality" was not

something that sulked and sneered; it was a wild yea-saying overburst of American joy; it was Western, the west wind, an ode from the Plains, something new, long prophesied, long a-coming. . . . All my New York friends were in the negative . . . putting down society and giving their tired bookish or political or psychoanalytical reasons, but Dean just raced in society, eager for bread and love.[45]

This populist-bohemian attack on his New York "friends" was not lost on New York intellectuals; they had little liking for sixties rebels and not much for their predecessors, fifties beats. Norman Podhoretz, in his essay "The Know-Nothing Bohemians," defended civilization from the barbarians: "There is a suppressed cry in those books [of Kerouac]: Kill the intellectuals who can talk coherently, kill the people who can sit still for five minutes at a time." "The Bohemianism of the 1950s" is "hostile to civilization; it worships primitivism, instinct, energy, 'blood.' " For Podhoretz, "This is the revolt of the spiritually underprivileged."[46]

Podhoretz thought he glimpsed a link between the beats and the delinquents, a common hatred of civilization and intelligence. "I happen to believe that there is a direct connection between the flabbiness of American middle-class life and the spread of juvenile crime in the 1950s, but I also believe that juvenile crime can be explained partly in terms of the same resentment against normal feeling and the attempt to cope with the world through intelligence that lies behind Kerouac and Ginsberg."[47]

However, Podhoretz and other critics could hardly combat the appeal of the beats. The message of the beats was their lives, which were not enclosed by thickets of snobbishness or set off in urban bohemias, but publicly paraded with a missionary zeal. "And it's happening all over the country, to everyone; a sort of revolution of the soul." Suffused by populism, the message or the constantly moving messengers proved irresistible to youth. "In three hundred pages," complained Paul Goodman in his review of *On the Road*, "these fellows cross America eight times, usually camping on friends or relatives."[48]

Gary Snyder, the poet, characterized Neal Cassady, whom Kerouac fictionalized as "Dean" in *On the Road*, as a "Denver grandchild of the 1880s cowboys with no range left to work on."

Cassady's type is that frontier type, reduced to pool halls and driving back and forth across the country. . . . What was intended to be done [in America] was that you should step forth into wild space; what you end up doing a hundred years later is driving back and forth in cars as fast as you can. Initially you were moving very slowly in a totally wild area. What you end up doing is going very fast in a densely populated area. Space becomes translated into speed. What got Kerouac and Ginsberg about Cassady was the energy of the archetypal west, the energy of the frontier. . . .[49]

This relentless activity eventually found a receptive audience, new colonies that swallowed up the beats and bohemia into something called the sixties, hippies, and the counterculture. Culture and demography began to intersect. As the beats and would-be beats took to the road they stumbled on new youth centers, college campuses crammed with the baby boom generation. Almost by virtue of the numbers, youth on these campuses formed a critical mass, a unique social formation.

"Once they arrived at college," explains a chronicle of the baby boom generation, "the teeming numbers of students overwhelmed the teachers and educators waiting for them. . . . The result was that the baby boom began to undertake its own socialization in places like Berkeley, Boston, Austin, New Haven, and Ann Arbor. Communities of students and ersatz students circled the major universities like penumbras around a hundred suns." In small cities, such as Ann Arbor and Madison, students, staff, and hangers-on comprised almost 30 percent of the population.

"Youth was no longer a stage of life but a community."[50] In these youth "ghettos" the beats found a home.

Of course, it is not quite so simple. While the beats exported a bohemian cultural message, the politics of the sixties did not derive from them. Some of the beats adjusted to the new idiom and concerns, but others, notably Kerouac, could not fathom the anti-Americanism of the young. Sean Wilentz, a professor of history (and son of Elias Wilentz), recalls that when his father's bookshop moved in the midsixties, many beats helped and partied afterward.

> All went swimmingly until midday, when news arrived from Harlem that Malcolm X had just been murdered. Bewilderment, then tension, hit the room. My clearest memory is of LeRoi Jones immediately leaving the proceedings. I sensed that the Village would never be the same. The next time I saw Jones in the shop, his name was Baraka.[51]

Yet the beats became bohemian messengers in the age of the highway and the declining city. They were not suburbanites, but they responded to the same realities, inhospitable cities and new highways. Once the cultural explosions of the sixties dissipated, the role of the fifties bohemians became evident. The beats not only widened and concluded the democratization of "amorality," they not only abetted—to use Malcolm Cowley's terms— the replacement of a consuming for a work ethic, but they also anticipated the de-urbanization of America, the abandonment of the cities for smaller centers, surburbs, campus towns, and outlying areas. In the period of urban sprawl, the beats were the last bohemians.

CHAPTER 4

New York, Jewish, and
Other Intellectuals

I

"IS THE INTELLECTUAL OBSOLETE?" asked H. Stuart Hughes in 1956, scanning the cultural horizon. Troubled by McCarthyism and a popular anti-intellectualism, he believed that America allowed little room for the "freely-speculating mind." The range of debatable issues had narrowed. Moreover, expanding universities and government bureaus hired experts and technicians, not critical writers and thinkers. "We are living in a society and in an era where there is scope for comparatively few intellectuals." Overwhelmed by the "almost irresistible pressures" of conformity, America's intellectuals faced a "dubious future."[1]

Hughes's was not an isolated voice. Numerous commentators, in articles with titles such as "The Intellectual: Will He Wither Away?" or "The Twilight of the Intellectuals," joined in.[2] "The intellectual in 1953," concluded Arthur Schlesinger, Jr., "faces an incalculable but depressing combination of factors."[3] For some observers, it was not persecution or indifference but affluence that threatened intellectuals. In John W. Aldridge's view, American intellectuals, disenchanted with communism and European elite culture, succumbed to "money, status, security and power."[4] "Economically," remarked Merle King in *The New Republic*, "the intellectual is better fed, better housed and more elegantly pampered than ever before."[5]

Ten years earlier, at the war's end, *Partisan Review* had already raised an alarm: professionals and academics were replacing unaffiliated intellectuals. A new "American academic type," a by-product of the "Managerial Revolution," was "everywhere ascendant," announced Newton Arvin in 1945. This new breed discarded "wide-ranging, curious, adventurous, and humane study" for "results" and office management. With fields and sub-fields, committees and organizations, the new academics were preparing to put "our literary heritage on a firm fiduciary basis."[6] Another critic concurred; college teachers who lived conventional lives and thought conventional thoughts were phasing out free-lance, bohemian, and avant-garde intellectuals. "The academic hierarchy . . . enforces caution on the imaginative or adventurous thinkers"; even in their personal lives, professors could not afford to be "conspicuously out of line."[7]

These laments might be dimissed as an old refrain. Intellectuals have always been obsessed with themselves, regularly bemoaning their impotence, corruption, or imminent demise. For the skeptic the wailings of 1950s intellectuals simply mark another chapter in an old story. Yet this skepticism may be too trusting, too willing to believe that nothing changes. To avoid turning into its opposite, skepticism must also be skeptical of itself.

The larger vision suggests that the years following World War II marked a swing period between two intellectual types: independents and bohemians receded before academics and professionals. Of course, intellectuals did not suddenly abandon their apartments and garrets for suburban homes and office complexes, but the accelerating trend in the 1950s left few untouched. By the end of that decade intellectuals and university professors had become virtually synonymous; academics even filled the pages of small magazines, once outposts beyond the campus. *Partisan Review* itself, the symbol of irreverent New York intellectuals, finally passed into university hands, its editors largely English professors.[8]

The writers of the 1950s palpably sensed what the next generation could not, the restructuring of their lives. "I was my own staff researcher," recalled Alfred Kazin of his years in the Reading Room of the New York Public Library, "a totally unaffiliated free lance and occasional evening college instructor who was educating himself . . . in the middle of the Great Depression."[9] For intellectuals coming of age in the sixties and after, life outside universities was not even a memory. However, intellectuals like Philip Rahv, Alfred Kazin, and Irving Howe became professors only after years as free-lance writers and editors.

Others, such as Lewis Mumford, Edmund Wilson, Gore Vidal, or Dwight Macdonald, never made the transition. All, however, were aware of the migration and its consequences. In the early part of the century, recalled Malcolm Cowley, teaching and writing had been "separate worlds"; but today, no longer "independent craftsmen," writers assume roles as professors or as well-paid employees in government or magazine bureaus.[10]

The evidence of change seemed everywhere; universities and national magazines eagerly hired intellectuals; either Luce publications or *The New Yorker* sent checks to Dwight Macdonald, Alfred Kazin, Edmund Wilson, John Kenneth Galbraith, Norman Podhoretz, Daniel Bell, and many others. Major publishing houses launched "little" magazines for young and avant-garde writers. Pocket Books founded *discovery*; Avon offered *New*

Voices, Doubleday put out *New Writers*, and New American Library, the paperback publisher of Mickey Spillane, established the most successful series, *New World Writing*. One issue ran "Jazz of the Beat Generation" by a "Jean-Louis," an excerpt from Kerouac's unpublished *On the Road*.[11]

To Isaac Rosenfeld (1918–56), a Chicago essayist, these developments signified that an intellectual life of poverty and protest belonged to the past. "The writer very seldom stands over against the world as he used to, and when he does, the danger is that he may be attitudinizing." Even the bohemia that sheltered poor writers and artists showed signs of renovation. "The garret still exists, but the rent has gone up."[12]

Yet nostalgia should not skew the record. If some intellectuals believed the new situation implied decline, most thought it spelled progress. Critics such as Trilling, Riesman, Bell—the list could be easily expanded—applauded or accepted the new reality. "In many civilizations there comes a point at which wealth shows a tendency to submit itself, in some degree, to the rule of mind and imagination . . . [to] taste and sensitivity," stated Lionel Trilling in a 1953 discussion of intellectuals.[13]

He announced the good news: "In America the signs of this submission have for some time been visible." Prosperity has undermined the proverbial alienation of American intellectuals, who are now "close to the top of the social hierarchy." Even professors, traditionally ridiculed and underpaid, obtain new status and good salaries, making academic careers attractive to those who once spurned them. "One cannot but be struck by the number of well-to-do students," crowed Professor Trilling, who "now elect the academic life."[14]

In slightly different form, Trilling's comments appeared in a much-cited *Partisan Review* symposium, "Our Country and Our Culture" (1952), in which numerous intellectuals celebrated their new status. The editors of the symposium remarked that only ten years earlier intellectuals regularly savaged America for its philistinism and emptiness. "Since then, however, the tide has begun to turn, and many writers and intellectuals now feel closer to their country and its culture." They put it sharply, "for better or worse, most writers no longer accept alienation as the artist's fate in America; on the contrary, they want very much to be a part of American life. More and more writers have ceased to think of themselves as rebels and exiles."[15]

Several respondents, including Philip Rahv and Norman Mailer, disagreed. Rahv reflected on the passing of "the intellectual bohemian or proletarian," a by-product of postwar prosperity, which "at long last effected the absorption of the intellectuals into the institutional life of the country." For Rahv intellectuals now viewed America from the inside. "We are witnessing a process that might well be described as that of the *embourgeoisement* of the American intelligentsia."[16]

The dissenters, however, were a distinct minority. Intellectuals "have arrived, they count," commented David Riesman; and like Trilling, he noted with pleasure that the wealthy now prize culture. "Many of the former enemies of the intellectuals from the upper social strata"—lawyers, doctors, executives—are now "taking up" culture. Too many intellectuals, however, remained fixated on European models, believing that their status depended more on a "widening circle of dislikes than on a widening circle of sympathies."[17] Max Lerner offered his own autobiography as an "exhibit." He was then working on a study of American civilization that ten years earlier he himself would have judged "sentimental, conformist, even chauvinist." But times had changed, and his "long suppressed" love for America was finally being "released."[18]

The fifties intellectuals receive, and deserve, attention for several reasons. As the last public intellectuals they loom large in the cultural firmament. They have viewed from outside, as their successors could not, the professionalization of cultural life; and perhaps because of their origins as free-lance authors, their writings often shine. They write to be read. Many continue to play active roles in letters and politics. They have presided over the intellectual scene for decades.

Moreover, they largely defined a cultural politics that not only has survived relatively intact but in the recent period has dominated American letters. It is often forgotten that the "neoconservatism" of the 1980s is a restatement, frequently by the same figures, of the conservatism of the 1950s. "By now the 'new conservatism' is an old story."[19] This statement—made three decades ago—indicates the conservative continuity through the entire postwar period. To be sure this conservatism was, and to some degree is, "liberal"; its architects were generally former radicals with lingering commitments to reform. Moreover, pure conservatism never acquired deep roots in the United States—a point Trilling made in his *The Liberal Imagination*. Nevertheless, this liberal conservatism has structured American culture since the war.

The success and presence of fifties intellectuals through the eighties is not simply due to their genius. After ebbing in the 1960s, some realities of the 1950s, especially a cold war ethos and anticommunism, revived and sparked interest in the original cultural script and cast. It is also due to something else. Few younger intellectuals have arisen to challenge the old guard. The visibility of last generation intellectuals reflects the absence of new public thinkers. With little to measure it against, the work of fifties intellectuals may appear more impressive than it actually was or is. A study that is unsparing toward young intellectuals must be equally unsentimental about the elders.

Even a cursory survey of these elders reveals that they were not a random collection of intellectuals. Rather, in the 1950s New Yorkers and Jews commanded the cultural heights, and often defined the terms and scope of debate. Any study of recent American intellectuals must assess the New York and Jewish contributions. Typically these studies emphasize the immigrant roots, Marxism, brilliance, and versatility of the New York intellectuals. Yet a fresh scrutiny partially revises conventional wisdom. The talent and vigor of the New York and Jewish intellectuals cannot be challenged. In retrospect, however, their radicalism seems shaky, and their accomplishments not small, but smaller than supposed.

II

COLUMBIA UNIVERSITY offers a clear view of 1950s intellectual life. Three colleagues at Columbia, Lionel Trilling, the literary critic, Richard Hofstadter, the historian, and C. Wright Mills, the sociologist, cover the spectrum, from Jewish to non-Jewish, from right to left. It was Mills, who objected most strongly to Trilling's formulations on intellectuals; and it was Hofstadter, who marked out a middle path. Their differences, however, should not obscure what they shared: they saw themselves not so much as professors but as intellectuals addressing a public on public issues; and they all sought and found a larger audience.[20] This should not be forgotten.

Where Trilling celebrated cultural progress, Mills bemoaned decline, the degeneration of political discourse into slogans and toothpaste commercials. The President of the United States

(Dwight D. Eisenhower) read cowboy stories, while know-nothing technicians made fateful government decisions. At this very moment, argued Mills in 1955, when a stringent opposition has disappeared, intellectuals embrace a "new conservative gentility." Instead of criticizing the mediocrity and mindlessness, they savor their new status; instead of acting as the "moral conscience of society," they confound prosperity with advancing culture. Mills named Trilling as one of many intellectuals succumbing to this confusion.[21]

Mills's remarks displeased Trilling, who fired off a rejoinder, initiating a series of notes that ended in a personal break. Trilling explained that he was reporting, not celebrating, the new status of intellectuals. "I was trying to refer to circumstances which require that masses of people have an intellectual training. . . . All these people . . . are touched with the pride of ideas. . . . A kind of cultural revolution has taken place . . . [which] brings with it many possibilities of revision and improvement."[22]

An unyielding Mills replied that Trilling blurred the vital distinction between humanist intellectuals and policy experts who were obviously prospering. Talk about American civilization subordinating itself to "mind . . . taste and sensitivity" was wildly off the mark. Trilling should have been emphasizing the dominance of technicians and consultants, and this was "not the burden of your essay."[23]

In idiom and temper Mills belonged to a world apart from Trilling's—and Hofstadter's. From the end of the war until his death, he railed against intellectuals who traded ethics and vision for salaries and status. "American intellectuals," he wrote in 1944, "are suffering the tremors of men who face overwhelming defeat," a situation they camouflage by "busy work and self-deception."[24]

Mills's *White Collar* (1951) continued the attack on profes-

sors and intellectuals. "Men of brilliance, energy and imagination" are not drawn to universities. Nor do colleges "facilitate,
much less create, independence of mind." The professor is a
"member of a petty hierarchy, almost completely closed in by its
middle-class environment and its segregation of intellectual from
social life ... mediocrity makes its own rules and sets its own
image of success." The larger group of intellectuals are not in
better shape; they have deserted politics for administration and
personal success. "The loss of will and even of ideas among intellectuals" is not simply due to "political defeat and internal decay
of radical parties." They have accepted, sometimes with a personal lament, their places in state or media bureaucracies.[25]

These blasts irritated Hofstadter, a fact Mills discovered when
he solicited opinions of *White Collar*. "You detest white-collar
people too much," Hofstadter wrote Mills, "altogether too
much, perhaps because in some intense way you identify with
them. . . . If the situation is characteristically as bad as you say—
which I doubt—then in a book which candidly seeks to express
emotion as well as to analyze, why no pity, no warmth?"[26] Hofstadter, whose evaluation soured relations with Mills, wanted a
more judicious evaluation of white-collar workers, professors,
and intellectuals.

Richard Hofstadter (1916–70), whose own measured contribution came at the end of the fifties debates, was a hard-working,
thoughtful historian; he twice won the Pulitzer Prize, for his *The
Age of Reform* (1955) and *Anti-Intellectualism in American Life*
(1963). Much of his work challenged a naive liberalism. "Those
of us who grew up during the Great Depression and the Second
World War," he explained in one of his last books, "could no
longer share the simple faith of the Progressive writers in the
sufficiency of American liberalism. We found ourselves living in
a more complex and terrifying world."[27]

The same age as Mills, Hofstadter was born in Buffalo, New York, and majored in history and philosophy at the University of Buffalo before moving to New York City in 1937 and hooking up with the New York intellectuals. Alfred Kazin, who became his good friend, recalls visiting him in his "first" New York apartment. "He looked marvelous, fresh, the all-American collegian just in from Buffalo with that unmistakable flat accent."[28] With his wife, Felice Swados, Hofstadter joined the Communist Party, which explains, according to a recent account, his "cautious response to McCarthyism."[29] As the disenchantment with the working class and the Soviet Union deepened, Hofstadter and other New York leftists reexamined the place of intellectuals in American society.

His *Anti-Intellectualism in American Life*, which summarized past discussions about intellectuals, carefully picked out a path between acceptance and stridency. His was a "personal book," a response to the "political and intellectual conditions of the 1950s." McCarthyism and Eisenhower's resounding defeat of Adlai Stevenson in 1952 renewed the endemic anti-intellectualism of American society. The time was ripe for a reexamination, Hofstadter wrote, because John F. Kennedy's presidency was burying anti-intellectualism. "If there was then a tendency to see in McCarthyism, and even in the Eisenhower administration, some apocalypse for intellectuals in public life, it is no longer possible, now that Washington has again become so hospitable to Harvard professors and ex-Rhodes scholars."[30]

The book closed with a generational perspective on current disputes. "Two decades of disillusioning experience" rightly disabused the "older generation of intellectuals" of its cult of alienation, once a moral and political imperative. Nevertheless, Hofstadter, writing in the early sixties, observed a revival of the "old commitment to alienation" by dissenting writers of a "rising generation." The dissenters responded to the fact that America was absorbing intellectuals "just at the moment . . . when their services as an independent source of national self-criticism [were] most desperately needed." They argued "with good reason" that more than ever America required vigorous critics.[31]

Hofstadter laced into a ten-year-old essay by Irving Howe, "This Age of Conformity" (1954), perhaps the classic 1950s statement of independent intellectuals. Hofstadter called it "a kind of manifesto of the intellectuals of the left." Like Mills, Howe took issue with Trilling's celebration of the intellectuals' new respectability. Identifying the "break-up of bohemia" as accelerating intellectual conformity, Howe remarked, "Where young writers once faced the world together, they now sink into suburbs, country homes and college towns." The "absorption" of intellectuals by universities meant "they not only lose their traditional rebelliousness but to one extent or another *they cease to function as intellectuals.*"[32]

Howe forcefully stated the case:

The university is still committed to the ideology of freedom and many professors try hard and honestly to live by it. If the intellectual cannot subsist independently, off his work or his relatives, the academy is usually his best bet. But no one who has a live sense of what the literary life has been and might still be . . . can accept the notion that the academy is the natural home of intellect.[33]

When writing this essay, Howe himself was positioned between two lives, independent intellectual and professor. He explains in his autobiography that "by the early fifties word began to reach New York that it might be possible to find a job—no one I knew thought of it as a career—teaching in a university." Though they lacked advanced degrees and academic scholarship, Howe and other literary figures were wooed by expanding universities. The post that Brandeis University offered him could not be refused—here Howe typifies the careers of many fifties intellectuals—since it meant "a steady job" and freedom from "the irksome reviewing I did for *Time*."[34]

In his book, Hofstadter delightedly referred to Howe as Professor Howe, since by 1963 the independent critic had become the entrenched professor he had warned against.[35] Hofstadter recoiled from "the prophets of alienation" like Howe, dissenters who calculate intellectual merit by "the greatest possible degree of negativism." They believe that an intellectual's responsibility is not "to be enlightening about society but rather to make an assertion against it."[36]

The dissenters threatened to become "strident"—or worse; alluding to Norman Mailer and the beats, Hofstadter used terms like "moral nihilism," "romantic anarchism," "adolescent rebellion." He scorned the belief that creativity needs bohemias or that "accredited institutions" contaminate intellect. To charge betrayal when intellectuals join established institutions crudely misconstrues the complex relationship of the intellectual and power.

Between the lure of success and a cult of isolation stood a "personal choice." Hofstadter counseled that intellectuals should become neither "technicians concerned only with power" nor "willfully alienated" critics "more concerned with maintaining their sense of their own purity than with making their ideas effective." His book concluded with a ritual praising of the "variety of styles of intellectual life" that "liberal society" makes possible. He feared only that "single-minded men" might dominate the future.[37]

Hofstadter's closing had a responsible and judicious ring: servants of power and prophets of alienation equally threatened the well-being of the pluralistic Republic. Yet the neat symmetry is somewhat misleading. Hofstadter was not a simple figure with simple faith. If he was a "secret conservative," as Kazin called him in *New York Jew,* he was also a hidden radical. Even after his relationship with Mills had deteriorated, he expressed guarded approval of Mills's stance and efforts.

Hofstadter offered some sharp criticism of *The Power Elite* (1956), Mills's moral and political indictment of the concentration of American power, but added that Mills was the first forthright sociologist since Veblen. "The sight of an American academic," Hofstadter wrote in this unpublished review, "trying courageously in these times of danger and complacency, to confront the large issues of the world from a notably rebellious point of view is in itself a thing to command attention and respect."[38]

Nevertheless, publicly Hofstadter stood almost midway between the enthusiasm of Trilling and the harshness of Mills. Trilling occupied a liberal right, settling into an easy, sometimes ironic, acceptance of society. Mills assumed the role of the American rebel, an outsider with no manners; and Hofstadter delicately plied the center, critical but harboring few grievances. Christopher Lasch remarked upon Hofstadter's "faith in Columbia University" and his "supreme confidence in the historical profession."[39] In their choices and fates the three Columbia University colleagues almost present a microcosm of 1950s intellectuals.

Is there a lesson here about radicalism and Jewish and non-Jewish intellectuals? Trilling, the first Jew in the English Department at Columbia, always amazed at and appreciative of his good fortune, never ceased to be the responsible professor. Mills, a muckraker and moralist, an outsider to New York intellectual life, even at Columbia University, kept his distance; he once called himself "the outlander, not only regionally, but down bone deep and for good," adding that "my Texas grandfather has something to do with that."[40] And halfway between Trilling and Mills was the "half" Jew, Hofstadter, upholding a critical liberalism that looked both ways. Kazin remembered his clean collegiate looks. but "he was soon telling Jewish jokes, jokes about Jews, doing impersonations of Jews." Hofstadter "was secret in many things, in some strange no man's land between his Yiddish-speaking Polish father and his dead Lutheran mother."[41]

III

IN PLOTTING cultural life often the less original thinkers register most faithfully the zeitgeist. In his evolution and politics, Norman Podhoretz exemplifies the trajectory of New York Jewish intellectuals. Like the others, he was first of all a publicist—a journalist, a book reviewer, and an essayist who wrote well and easily. He established a voice and a presence. From the back cover of his first book, *Doings and Undoings*, the young Podhoretz stares out, tie loosened, eyes squinting, cigarette dangling—someone to be reckoned with. He is described as "the most brilliant young critic of our day."

From the first, as well, he spelled out a conservatism that he only once lost sight of. In 1957 a twenty-seven-year-old Podhoretz touted the mature life against revolution and bohemia. "On the whole," he proclaimed, postwar America offered "a reasonably decent environment for the intellectual." This situation required a new intellectual garb since "the old style of 'alienation,' represented by commitment to the ideal of Revolution and an apartment in Greenwich Village" smacked of the 1930s. The 1950s called for a "new style of 'maturity,'" that assumed "the real adventure of existence was to be found not in radical politics or in Bohemia but in the 'moral life' of the individual . . . in a world of adults."[42]

For Podhoretz "the trick" was to "stop carping at life like a petulant adolescent" and get "down to the business of adult living as quickly as possible." This was not "conformity" but the realization that "the finest and deepest possibilities" of life could be found *within* 'bourgeois' society."[43]

Twenty-five years later, after a short detour opposing bourgeois society, or at least the war in Vietnam (a fact he no longer remembers),[44] Podhoretz repeats his old wisdom. In almost the same words from decades earlier—although somewhat more hysterically—he advises his son in an afterword to his memoir *Breaking Ranks* that radicalism constitutes "a refusal . . . to assume responsibility . . . in a world of adults." It is a "contemptuous repudiation of everything American and middle-class." Of course, Podhoretz has learned some things in the intervening years. He warns his son of a "spiritual plague," coursing through the nation's bloodstream, which attacks "the vital organs of the entire species, preventing men from fathering children and women from mothering them." To be adult, he tells his son, is to be a father. "There can be no abdication of responsibility more fundamental than the refusal of a man to become, and to be, a father, or the refusal of a woman to become, and be, a mother."[45]

Podhoretz personifies the continuity of a conservatism—or a new conservatism or a liberal conservatism—through the postwar decades. Of course, he does not represent all New York Jewish intellectuals, but he is hardly an isolated or rare case. Yet according to standard interpretations, Jews as political radicals are "over-represented" in cultural and social life; an impoverished immigrant people with a vast pride and love of culture, they naturally rebelled against discrimination and injustice.

"The Jewish contribution to the Left in the United States during the twentieth century," begins a book on Jewish radicalism, "ranks the highest of any immigrant or ethnic group. . . . American Jewry has provided socialist organizations and movements with a disproportionate number—sometimes approaching or surpassing a majority—of their leaders, activists, and supporters."[46] Another study demonstrates that Jewish predominance continued into the New Left, especially in its early stages: Jews, 3 percent of the United States population, constituted a majority of the New Left's membership and its leaders.[47]

This seems true enough. Yet the familiarity with this proposition undermines a dispassionate evaluation of its validity for New York intellectuals. An overview of many New York and non–New York careers suggests not a flat refutation but a critical revision. "In 1972 alone," states a study of American conservatism, "[Nathan] Glazer, Sidney Hook, Lewis Feuer and Seymour Martin Lipset appeared in [the conservative] *National Review*. What did these men have in common? None had been previously known as a conservative. All were Jewish. Three (Glazer, Feuer, and Lipset) had been at Berkeley (birthplace of the student revolution) early in the 1960s. . . . Perhaps most interesting was the fact that all had at one time been 'radical.' "[48]

If Jewish intellectuals gravitated toward radicalism in large numbers, they also hastily beat a retreat. By the 1950s not simply Glazer, Hook, Feuer, and Lipset but Irving Kristol, Lionel Trilling, Daniel Bell, Leslie Fiedler, and scores of others traded in their red pasts for blue chip careers. In contrast non-Jewish (and usually non–New York) intellectuals seemed more willing or able to retain radicalism throughout their careers.

Generalizations of this type are vulnerable to a series of convincing objections. It would be easy to list non-Jews who rapidly abandoned their radicalism. Moreover, all intellectuals responded to the dominant political and social realities: not ethnic

peculiarities but historical events drove intellectuals from the earlier ramparts. Irving Howe underlines the disillusionment with
communism, the impact of McCarthyism, and the prosperity of
the postwar period—plus simple aging—to explain the growing
conservatism of Jewish intellectuals.[49] This cannot be denied.[50]

Nevertheless, the chart of the larger currents should not neglect the smaller eddies, which are critical precisely because they
sustain a sometimes rare species, the American radical; and these
eddies seem tinted by ethnic or religious hues. Again, this is a
delicate and elusive matter, which, of course, is no reason to
avoid it.

The long view suggests not how many, but, compared to the
non-Jews, how few Jewish intellectuals remained radicals and
dissenters. This could almost be seen in pairs of kindred Jewish
and non-Jewish intellectuals: Lionel Trilling (1905–75) and
Dwight Macdonald (1906–82); Daniel Bell (1919–) and C.
Wright Mills (1916–62); Norman Podhoretz (1930–) and Michael Harrington (1928–). Other non-Jews could be added: Edmund Wilson, Gore Vidal, Paul Sweezy, John Kenneth Galbraith, Christopher Lasch. But the list of Jewish public
intellectuals who remained devoted to a radical vision seems
shorter.

Scenes from the 1960s: Lewis Feuer, a professor at Berkeley
and once a New York socialist, glimpses the end of civilization
in the Berkeley campus protest.[51] He describes the student
movement as a magnet for "the morally corrupt," those advocat-
ing "a melange of narcotics, sexual perversion, collegiate Castro-
ism."[52] Feuer never recovers from the fright. On the other coast
three students, one carrying a can of beer, are applauded after
berating a faculty meeting at New York University. A scandal-
ized Sidney Hook, once a Marxist, calls the event "the most
shocking experience in my life."[53] Meanwhile, uptown Dwight

Macdonald wanders around Columbia University and concludes that the student disturbances are a justifiable response to an intolerable situation.[54] He and his wife befriend many student radicals.

IV

IS THIS TYPICAL, the New York Jewish intellectual denouncing youthful radicalism while the non-Jewish counterpart offers sympathy? Is it possible that Jewish intellectuals visited radicalism, while more non-Jewish intellectuals stayed the winter? Is it possible that a solid American background provided more sustenance for the long haul than the immigrant past common to many of the Jews?

Estrangement from a Christian civilization, runs the usual argument, edged Jews into reformism or revolution. Yet this argument can be reversed, or at least recast: personal alienation does not engender a hardy radicalism. The angst that expresses the pain of separation also craves union—or its substitute, recognition and acceptance. The social critique founded solely on alienation also founders on it.

The economic realities of Jewish and immigrant life go far in explaining a vulnerability to conventional success, money and recognition. Those who worked too hard with their hands wanted their children to do better with their heads. "I entered C.C.N.Y. [College of the City of New York] in 1936," recalls Irving Howe. "It was understood that a Jewish boy like me would go to college. How could it be otherwise when the central credo of the immigrant world was 'my son should not work in a shop' ? That was the beginning and the end of all desire and wisdom."[55]

Moreover, for Jewish intellectuals to complete college or secure academic posts was especially sweet; compared to the Christians, it often marked firsts for their families.[56]

No dense Freudian theory is necessary to explain that economic deprivation and cultural estrangement often led to an identification, and overidentification, with the dominant culture.[57] Jewish intellectuals from Yiddish-speaking families— Trilling, Fiedler, Howe, Kazin—often fell in love with American and English literature. The phenomenon is familiar, but its relevance for American intellectuals has not been noticed. The "foreigner"—the Jewish intellectual—embraced his new cultural home, sometimes dispatching critical acumen for recognition and approval. The native son, lacking a similar estrangement, kept a distance, often turning to foreign sources. While Trilling drenched himself in American and English literature, Wilson studied Russian. Sidney Hook stuck to John Dewey, while C. Wright Mills wandered into the thicket of German neo-Marxism.

Is it possible that solid American backgrounds allowed—obviously did not compel—a distancing that sustained radicalism for the long haul? That the anxiety of illegitimacy, or persecution, did not haunt the all-American intellectuals? That their sometimes more monied or aristocratic background gave them better footing? Did more principles and less angst infuse the radicalism of non-Jewish intellectuals? Did the radicalism steeped in anxiety slide into conservatism, while the Texan, Puritan, or Scottish identities of Mills or Wilson or Vidal or Galbraith gave rise to a bony radicalism more resistant to economic and social blandishments?

Trilling and Mills exemplify the contrasts between Jewish and non-Jewish intellectuals. Trilling typifies the successful and moderate Jewish professor with a radical past; Mills, the American rebel suspicious of compromise and adjustment. Trilling's Yiddish-speaking parents (his father was a tailor and an unsuccessful furrier) encouraged his studies; it was assumed that he would attend college, and like other Jewish intellectuals, he commenced a lifelong commitment to English literature. His talent and devotion paid off: Trilling, who entered Columbia University as an undergraduate, was the first Jew tenured in its English department.

Everything about Trilling, from his name to his demeanor, implied a successful adjustment to Anglo-American culture. As his wife later wrote, "in appearance and name" Trilling made a "good gamble" for an English department looking for its first Jew. "Had his name been that of his maternal grandfather, Israel Cohen, it is highly questionable whether the offer would have been made."[58] As a polished and judicious commentator on humanism and literature, Trilling earned an endowed chair, showers of awards, honorary titles, national recognition. For intellectuals caught between a leftist, often ethnic, past and cold-war prosperity, Trilling struck the right tone; he contributed to "reconciling a depoliticized intelligentsia to itself and the social status quo."[59]

For some of his old acquaintances, on the other hand, Trilling had gone too far; Alfred Kazin recoiled from his "exquisite sense of accommodation," his nerveless abstract prose, his penchant for words like "scarcely," "modulation," "our educated classes." "For Trilling I would always be 'too Jewish,' too full of my lower-class experiences. He would always defend himself from the things he had left behind."[60]

The differences with Mills are instructive. Mills also came from a modest economic background: his father was an insurance salesman in Waco, Texas; his mother, a housewife. Nothing else tallies with Trilling. Mills did not seek an academic career, nor was he encouraged as a scholar; he enrolled in Texas Agricultural and Mechanical College to become an engineer. When he transferred to the University of Texas, he stumbled upon philosophy and sociology. Until his last years he retained doubts about an academic life, distrusting professional conventions, which he frequently flouted. While he obviously prized his Columbia University position, unlike Trilling, he did not settle happily into it; his colleagues found him abrasive and strident.

For an immigrant family, a university career—status, salary, and security—signified unalloyed advance. Herein lies a critical difference between an American and an immigrant experience. Mills recalled a family past—his grandparents—of independent ranchers. Whether this was fact or fiction hardly matters, for it shaped a vision of self and world: life as an employee in an office—university, government, or publishing—did not measure up no matter the title, money, or respect. The same could be said of other venerable intellectual radicals, such as Wilson or Vidal or Galbraith; they looked back to families of independent farmers, statesmen, or rebels that seemed to provide a secure base for a radical life. This is captured in the title of Galbraith's memoir of his Scottish-Canadian past, *Made to Last*.[61]

In his autobiography, Kenneth Rexroth, poet and lifelong bohemian, pondered the role of genealogy in casting a peculiar American rebel. He believed his own past provided "a kind of family epic in which I thought, and still think of myself, as called to play a role." An ancestory of "Schwenkfelders, Mennonites, German revolutionaries of '48, Abolitionists, suffragists, squaws and Indian traders, octoroons and itinerant horse dealers, farmers in broad hats, full beards and frogged coats, hard-drinking small-town speculators" engendered a personality resistant to conformity.[62]

Rexroth did not think that his past was atypical. "Most American families that go back to the early nineteenth century, and certainly those whose traditions go back to the settlement of the country, have a sense of social and cultural rather than nationalist responsibility. The sense that the country is really theirs, really belongs to them, produces radical critics, rebels, reformers, eccentrics."[63]

Wilson and Vidal have aired kindred thoughts. Gore Vidal once noted that he shared with Wilson a "sense" of America and roots in a Puritan tradition.[64] Wilson recollected in *Upstate* that even after a thirty-five-year absence, he felt he belonged in the town of his youth, his parents, his grandparents. Everyone knew him or the family; everyone was related; several houses belonged to family connections. "Our position was so unquestioned in this little corner of Lewis County [New York] that I have never ceased to derive from it a certain conviction of superiority."[65] As a "member of a half-obsolete minority" of Americans, it was for Wilson just a short step to solidarity with even "more old-fashioned Americans," the New York State Indians, the Iroquois, in the battle with developers.[66]

Mills's family (or his sense of it) does not compare with Rexroth's or Wilson's, yet the faint image of his grandfather, a Texas cattle rancher killed in a gunfight, wafts through his work. It is almost possible to detect in Mills the fleeting figure of another Waco resident—also gunned down—the rebellious journalist William Cowper Brann, who published *The Iconoclast*. "We are solemnly assured," Brann wrote, "that the world is steadily growing better; and I suppose that's so, for in days of old they crucified men head downwards for telling the truth, while now they only hammer them over the head with six-shooters and drag 'em around a Baptist college campus with a rope. All that a reformer now needs is a hard head and a rubber neck."[67] (This proved optimistic: Brann's feud with a Baptist school, Baylor

University, ended with his assassination—and the killing of the assassin, since Brann managed to return a shot.)[68]

Next to the larger-than-life figures of ranchers and gun-toting journalists, his own father, the insurance salesman, appeared colorless. Mills's *White Collar*, his broadside against the new bureaucratic classes, including academics, whom he roasts in a chapter entitled "Brains, Inc.," is at least half autobiographical. He traces the decline of the old independent groups, the farmers and small entrepreneurs, tough, democratic individuals, and the rise of insecure and craven employees of corporations and the state. The evolution of his own family from ranchers to salesmen, Mills once revealed, entailed a painful loss. "I have been writing *White Collar* since I was ten years old and watched my white-collared father getting ready for another sales trip."[69]

In the New York world Mills viewed himself, a friend recalled, as an outsider, a Texan and often a Wobbly, those ornery American anarchists who "opposed nearly everything and everyone, and valued most of all their independence. Whenever he liked someone, he'd say, "That guy's a real Wobbly.'"[70] Mills's first book, *The New Men of Power*, bears as an epigram an anonymous Wobbly poem:

> When that boatload of wobblies come
> Up to Everett, the sheriff says
> Don't you come no further
> Who the hell's yer leader anyhow?
> *Who's yer leader anyhow?*
> And them wobblies yelled right back—
> *We ain't got no leader*
> *We're all leaders*
> *And they kept right on coming.*[71]

Of course, it is easy to overdo this, and Mills himself may have overplayed the Texas rebel. "He commuted to Columbia in a rather bulky getup suggestive of a guerrilla warrior going to meet the enemy," recalled a friend. "He usually wore camping boots . . . a helmet or cap used for motorcycle riding, and was strapped around with army surplus duffle bags or knapsacks filled with books and notes."[72]

It is hardly surprising that Mills felt a deep affinity for another abrasive critic with roots in independent farming, Thorstein Veblen, whom he considered a "sort of intellectual Wobbly" and "the best critic of America that America has ever produced." (Nor is it surprising that another stony critic of America, Lewis Mumford, looked to Veblen, and alluded to Veblen's own fondness for the Wobblies.[73]) Mills's introduction to Veblen's *The Theory of the Leisure Class* reads much like Mills on Mills. "In character and career, in mind and in everyday life, he was the outsider." He "hated sham, realistically and romantically protesting against it by his manner of living as well as by his life work." Veblen, Mills tell us, "was a masterless, recalcitrant man, and if we must group him somewhere in the American scene, it is with those most recalcitrant Americans, the Wobblies. On the edges of the higher learning, Veblen tried to live like a Wobbly. It was a strange place for such an attempt."[74]

For Mills, also, it was a strange place for such an attempt. Of course, Mills cannot represent all non-Jewish intellectual dissenters, but there was something peculiarly American about his stiff-neckedness. When Dwight Macdonald met Mills, he remarked on their temperamental affinity. "We were both congenital rebels, passionately contemptuous of every received idea and established institution."[75]

To believe that Mills or Wilson or Rexroth or Vidal, and others, found resources for a rebellion in their all-American family pasts is perhaps to succumb to myths they themselves invented. Yet these myths enabled them to resist the lure of success, so tempting to more desperate immigrants. Trilling's pleasure that the rich respect professors and Podhoretz's glee that he has "made it" have to be set against Mills's ode to failure as certifying integrity. "Veblen's virtue is not alienation; it is failure. . . . There is no failure in American academic history quite so great as Veblen's."[76] For Mills, these are words of praise.

Several qualifications to this discussion must be introduced. The shift of Jewish intellectuals to the right has frequently been noted. Yet it is easy to overstate this migration; it is also easy to confuse the visible public intellectuals with the larger, more submerged, and perhaps more stable, radical Jewish community of social workers, lawyers, editors, teachers, unionists, and political activists. The new conservatism may be confined to the more public intellectuals. And even within this select grouping, of course, some Jewish intellectuals continue to place themselves on the left. In this category belong people associated with *Dissent*, like Irving Howe, or *The Nation*, like Norman Birnbaum; and there are others. Nevertheless, this does not dispense with the issue. While "some" is imprecise, it appears that more Jewish intellectuals now, especially in comparison to the past, identify with conservatism.

The short or shrinking list of Jewish radical intellectuals includes a disproportionate number from one sector of the political spectrum: anarchism. Perhaps this is also true of the non-Jewish radicals. The pink thread of the Wobblies and Veblen runs through the cloth of American dissenters.

Of the Jewish radicals, Paul Goodman, Noam Chomsky, Murray Bookchin, and to some degree Isaac Rosenfeld represent versions of anarchism. The peculiar resiliancy of anarchists, of course, is not mysterious. To the extent that they are anarchists, they distrust large institutions, the state, the university, and its functionaries. They are less vulnerable to the corruptions of title and salary because their resistance is moral, almost instinctual.

This, of course, is what Marxists charge: anarchists think ethically, not strategically. Yet exactly this reveals their long-run (and short-run?) strength. Marxist intellectuals can and do convince themselves to subordinate mind and ethics to a larger goal or distant cause that frequently slips out of sight. Anarchist intellectuals are less susceptible to this logic. To use the language of historical materialism, it is no accident that currently an anarchist, Noam Chomsky, is the most energetic critic of intellectuals apologizing for American foreign policy.

While Paul Goodman and Noam Chomsky are familiar figures, Murray Bookchin remains neglected.[77] Bookchin might almost symbolize the distortion of public attention; his work is deeper and longer than most lionized intellectuals, but he has received scant notice.

Bookchin (1921–), raised in New York by his Russian-speaking social revolutionary grandmother and mother (Yiddish and English were his second and third languages), passed through the familiar shifts of his generation. As he explains, "My own life in the thirties closely follows that of people like Irving Howe" (whom he did not know). He joined the various Communist youth groups—first, the Young Pioneers. "We were everywhere with our drum corps. . . . Those who could afford it attired themselves in blue uniforms and, instead of raising the clenched fist, raised an open palm over their right temple, to denote the 'five-sixths' of the world that were not conquered by socialism." Later he became a member of the Young Communist League. However, the Popular Front, Moscow Trials, and definitively the Soviet-Nazi pact drove him into opposition, to

Trotskyism, and to dissident Trotskyist groups. After a stint in the army, he wound up as a foundryman and auto worker in the United Auto Workers. Ten years of factory work convinced him that the proletariat was finished as a revolutionary, even radical force, and he enrolled in a technical school on the GI Bill.

Bookchin did not drift from Trotskyism to liberalism or conservatism but to anarchism; moreover, two subjects that most radicals habitually ignored early marked Bookchin's anarchism: ecology and cities. Bookchin's first important work, *Our Synthetic Environment*, appeared in 1962 (under the pseudonym Lewis Haber). As he explains in its republication, arriving some six months before Rachel Carson's *Silent Spring*, it was all but drowned by her book.

When noticed, Bookchin was erroneously considered her follower or written off as too utopian. Unlike Carson he tackled not only pesticides but food additives, chemicalized agriculture, X-rays, fallout, and bloated cities. For reviewers this was too much. "No one is going to stop the world so that some who would like to get off will be able to," decided *The New York Times* reviewer, "or, as with Mr. Herber, spin us backward in time." Bookchin closed *Our Synthetic Environment* with a vision of "a new synthesis of man and nature, nation and region, town and country."[78]

However inauspicious its reception, this book began a writing career that is still picking up steam; his books *The Limits of the City, Post-Scarcity Anarchism, Spanish Anarchists, Ecology of Freedom* champion an ecological and anarchist perspective. He writes as a polemicist, historian, and philosopher.

Unlike many of his communist generation, Bookchin's unhappiness with the 1960s was not from the right but the left: the Marxists were too conservative, too wedded to tinkering with capitalism. His most celebrated pamphlet of the sixties, "Listen,

Marxist!" blasted the revival of dead and deadly Leninist slogans in the New Left. Bookchin came out swinging: "All the old crap of the thirties is coming back again."[79]

He remains a scathing critic of academic radicals and milk-toast reformers.

Radical politics in our time has come to mean the numbing quietude of the polling booth, the deadening platitudes of petition campaigns, carbumper sloganeering, the contradictory rhetoric of manipulative politicians, the spectator sports of public rallies and finally, the knee-bent, humble pleas for small reforms—in short, the mere shadows of the direct action, embattled commitment, insurgent conflicts, and social idealism that marked every revolutionary project in history.... What is most terrifying about present-day "radicalism" is that the piercing cry for "audacity"—"L'audace! L'audace! Encore l'audace!"—that Danton voiced in 1793 on the high tide of the French revolution would simply be *puzzling* to self-styled radicals who demurely carry attaché cases of memoranda and grant requests into their conference rooms ... and bull horns to their rallies.[80]

Bookchin's radicalism derives from at least two sources. Like the best of revolutionaries, his vision of the future, especially the future city, is drenched in the past. "We lived in cultural ghettos, but intensely creative ones and, economically, *very* communal ones," he remembers of his childhood. "It is easy to forget how richly articulated the immigrant socialist movement was in that time and the extent to which that cultural wealth has been lost today. There were choral groups, lecture groups, educational groups, mandolin groups."[81]

For Bookchin, the present and future demand nothing less. His anarchism enables him to stay the course. "I hold this commitment [to anarchism] with pride, for if nothing else it has been an invisible moral boundary that has kept me from oozing over to neo-Marxism, academicism, and ultimately reformism."[82]

The history of anarchism has its share of sinners and opportunists, but few anarchists joined former Trotskyist and Marxist intellectuals in registering for rooms in the motel of state. Insofar as the cultural benchmark for anarchists is a pre-industrial order, they can sometimes offer a more penetrating critique of industrial civilization than mainline Marxists, who oil rather than rebuild society. While Marxists dream of Five Year Plans, anarchists, whose critique is ethical as well as political, nurture the utopian flame.[83]

V

SOME YEARS AGO Daniel Bell observed that memoirs of the New Left and the beats flood the world, but aside from several older novels (by Tess Slesinger and Mary McCarthy) and a single memoir (Podhoretz's *Making It*), little has appeared by New York intellectuals. "There are almost no memoirs, no biographical accounts, no reflections." For Bell the autobiographical dearth explains the emphatic contribution of New York intellectuals, which includes himself, to American culture. Ashamed of their immigrant and drab origins, the New Yorkers turned to culture with a vengence. They did not want to discuss their family pasts; they wanted to discuss ideas. "The very nature of their limited backgrounds indicates what really animated and drove them was a hunger for culture."[84]

Bell's remarks were off the mark—and not only because of unfortunate timing.[85] Bell announced the absence of New York memoirs in 1976, on the dawn of an outpouring: Irving Howe, William Phillips, Lionel Abel, William Barrett, and Sidney Hook offered their reminiscences.[86] Bell also managed to forget that two volumes of the best memoir of the lot, Alfred Kazin's *Walker in the City* and *Coming Out in the Thirties*, had appeared some time earlier (his third volume, *New York Jew*, was published in 1978); and that Podhoretz's *Making It* was partially patterned on Mailer's 1959 *Advertisements for Myself*.

It is true that New York intellectuals established a high profile in American culture, often overshadowing non–New Yorkers; and this is due in part to the reasons that Bell—and many before him, including Veblen—outlined.[87] Jews became intellectuals for the same reasons they became shopkeepers: they were not automatically excluded, and they commanded the prerequisities, wits and gumption.

Yet familiarity imbues this argument with more truth than it may contain; the superiority of New York Jewish intellectuals is assumed, not established. In discussions of the 1950s, for instance, there is much talk of Trilling or Rahv or Podhoretz and little of William H. Whyte, Kenneth Burke, or John Kenneth Galbraith. This is reasonable, even just, if it is believed that the New Yorkers made themselves into premier intellectuals while the others were something else: popularizers or commentators. But this is questionable.

By quality alone, it is simply not possible to sharply distinguish the oeuvre of New York intellectuals from that of non–New Yorkers. Essay by essay, book by book, the collective work of New York intellectuals is neither so brilliant nor so scintillating that all else pales. It is almost more feasible to reverse the common opinion: the significant books of the fifties were authored by non–New Yorkers. The books by C. Wright Mills or Jane Jacobs or Rachel Carson possessed an energy and originality that the New Yorkers' books rarely matched.[88]

If this is true, then New York intellectuals receive the lion's share of attention less by reason of genius than by sociological luck: their New York location and their personal and physical proximity to the publishing industry. In addition, their tireless monitoring of themselves lays the groundwork for further studies (and myths). For those padding cultural histories with reports on what writer X said to editor Y at Z's party, the New York scene is a motherlode. It would be more difficult to fluff up a study of Norman O. Brown or Kenneth Burke, around whom there were no circles and little gossip.

Cultural attention and intrinsic merit rarely tally, but even within the rarified universe of Freud studies, New Yorkers tend to edge out non–New Yorkers; for instance, the writings of Lionel Trilling and Norman O. Brown on Freud belong to approximately the same period. For concentrated intellectual probing Brown's *Life Against Death* may have no match in American studies of psychoanalysis; compared to this book Trilling's Freud writings are casual and familiar.[89]

Trilling, however, wrote a partially autobiographical novel, offered several essays about himself and his milieu, and, as a New York intellectual, figures in a number of memoirs. His collected works are published replete with a reminiscence by his wife, Diana Trilling. Some books on Trilling have appeared, and more are in the offing. Brown, on the other hand, was never part of the New York scene; *Life Against Death* is appreciated, indeed treasured, but its author is rarely written about. For American cultural history he hardly exists *not* because of a minimal contribution but because of a minimal impact on New York circles.

To characterize the complex world of New York intellectuals is, of course, exceedingly difficult. Yet automatic deference to its unparalleled brilliance and heady intellectualism should be resisted. A cool appraisal of New York intellectuals reverses Bell's judgment: they are best—most convincing, articulate, observant—when they are discussing their own lives, but the compelling theoretical works by New York intellectuals are in very short supply. Bell got it exactly wrong: precisely because of their immigrant past and fragile situation, New York intellectuals specialize in the self; theirs is the home of psychoanalysis, the personal essay, the memoir, the letter to the editor. In style and subject matter their writings are generally highly subjective. Of course, this is not a failing. An intensely personal voice permeates their most brilliant writings, for instance Kazin's work— including, obviously, his autobiography.

Even the most philosophical of the New York intellectuals failed to produce an imposing theoretical oeuvre. If Trilling was the New Yorker's consummate literary critic, their "professor of English who could really think, whose writing . . . moved to the movement of ideas,"[90] Sidney Hook was their philosopher. Bell dedicated *The End of Ideology* to Hook: "I owe most . . . to Sidney Hook . . . one of the great teachers of the generation."[91] Irving Kristol also designated Hook as the "great teacher" of their group.[92] Others concurred; Dwight Macdonald, William Phillips, William Barrett, Nathan Glazer, even Howe and Kazin, all praised Hook as the philosophic genius of the group. "Sidney Hook is America's Number One Marxist!" proclaimed Macdonald. By virtue of his productivity, theoretical acumen, and feistiness, Hook would seem to deserve all accolades.[93]

Hook's early work justified these appreciations. His *Towards the Understanding of Karl Marx* (1933) and *From Hegel to Marx* (1936) brought originality, breadth, and European thought to an American Marxism dulled by dogma and provincialism. These books, which sought to give a John Dewey twist to Marxism, have rightly been called "absolutely the best" American books on Marxism of the thirties.[94]

Yet Hook's later works sadly lack the force and excitement of these books. Herein lies an old tale: as a Marxist sympathizer he wrote thoughtful and philosophical books; as a sworn enemy of Marxism, he fell into a philosophical rut, endlessly recasting the same positions. Of course, it is daunting to summarize the oeuvre of an individual who lists more than twenty books to his credit. Yet the numbers are more intimidating than the contents. Hook's books are almost exclusively anthologies he edited or compilations of his own essays that had appeared in diverse periodicals. Essays and lectures compose books like *Reason, Social Myths and Democracy* (1940); *Academic Freedom and Academic Anarchy* (1970); *Revolution, Reform and Social Justice* (1975); *Philosophy and Public Policy* (1980), *Marxism and Beyond* (1983). Books with titles indicating coherent philosophical efforts, such as *The Quest for Being* (1961) or *Pragmatism and the Tragic Sense of Life* (1974) are filled with lectures, forum contributions, and magazine pieces. For instance, *The Quest for Being*, which is typical, contains two lectures, several essays from *Festschrifts* and philosophy journals, two contributions from *Commentary*, five from *Partisan Review*, and an exchange of letters.

There is nothing wrong with assembling lectures and essays; but in repeating the same arguments and points they do not elaborate a philosophical position. And repeat they do: reading Hook in 1985 is very much like reading him in 1975, 1965, 1955, 1945, and almost 1935. No book by Hook is complete without a reiteration of the threat to democracy from communism and its supporters. Even books that might seem distant from his usual concerns, for instance, *Philosophy and Public Policy* and *Pragmatism and the Tragic Sense of Life*, are filled with familiar Hook essays ("Law and Anarchy," "Are There Limits to Freedom of Expression?"). His *Education and the Taming of Power* (1974), a classic Hook grab bag of essays, including one from the mid-1930s, is dedicated "To those who have suffered without yielding in the cause of scholarship and academic freedom at home and abroad at the hands of political tyrants, cowardly administrators, colleagues and student mobs."[95] In his most recent book, Hook is still quoting from an American communist newspaper of 1937 as proof that communist professors "violated the norms of academic freedom and integrity."[96]

Like other New York intellectuals, Hook is primarily a political essayist. Since the 1930s he has written almost no sustained book; he is a philosopher who has contributed almost nothing to philosophy.[97] His complete bibliography suggests he delighted in letters to the editor, rejoinders, and replies to rejoinders; their subject is usually the communist threat and someone's misunderstanding of it.[98] Even the editor of the Hook *Festschrift*, which gushes with praise, calls him a master of *"applied* intelligence,"[99] meaning he wrote little philosophy.

The problem is not the essay form, which hardly precludes philosophy, but what Hook did with it, which was very little. Unlike the essays of other New York intellectuals, Hook's lack elegance. They seem hurried, written by an angry author, and they do not improve when collected together. Chapter one of *Education and the Taming of Power* begins this way: "The time for plain speaking about American education in our day is long past due. A hoax is being perpetrated on the American public in the name of educational 'reform,' 'innovation,' and 'freedom.' " Chapter two opens with "There is great deal of nonsense talked about philosophy of education."[100] Hook is more a stump orator than a philosopher.

Hook recently pondered why in the renaissance of Marxist scholarship, his own work is not cited. More than a score of books "in which I have discussed some aspects of Marxism," he complained, go unmentioned in a new "dictionary" of Marxism.[101] The reason may be that for decades Hook has contributed nothing to Marxist scholarship. Long ago he ceased to grapple with Marxism or philosophy. Hook is an essayist, polemicist, raconteur. He specializes in politico-cultural stances, but since his Deweyian expositions of Marx in the mid-1930s, he has not produced an original and coherent philosophical work.

If Hook is ignored by current Marxist scholars, an "extra" theoretical reason plays a role: leftists feel little affection for a philosopher who has worked nights to establish the grounds to exclude subversives, communists, and student radicals from universities. Hook's publications relentlessly raise the alarm that leftists, communists, radicals, and what he calls "ritualist liberals" endanger freedom. He is slower to register any other threats, although the blinkered vision is exactly what he holds against the left.

The only time that Hook raised the issue of Nazi anti-Semitism in the prewar period was to score points against communism. "Let us remember," he wrote in 1938, "that it was from Stalin that Hitler learned the art of uprooting and wiping out whole groups and classes of innocent citizens. We cannot with good conscience protest against Hitler's treatment of the Jews and remain silent about the six million . . . who fill the concentration camps in Russia." In his study of New York intellectuals, Alexander Bloom comments that "so entrenched was he [Hook] in the anti-Stalinist campaigns that he could not discuss" on its own terms the Nazi war against the Jews.[102]

VI

UNTIL RECENTLY arguments about "intellectuals" took their cue from the Dreyfus Affair of the 1890s. The artists, writers, and teachers, including Emile Zola, who challenged the state's prosecution of Dreyfus became known as the "intellectuals." For the anti-Dreyfusards they were a new and objectionable group. As one anti-Dreyfusard wrote,

The interference of this novelist [Zola] in a matter of military justice seems to me no less impertinent than, let us say, the intervention of a police captain in a problem of syntax or versification. . . . As for this petition that is being circulated among the *Intellectuals!* the mere fact that one has recently created this word *Intellectuals* to designate, as though they were an aristocracy, individuals who live in laboratories and libraries, proclaims one of the most ridiculous eccentricities of our time.[103]

Moreover, the Russian term "intelligentsia," which dates to the 1860s,[104] gradually passed into English or at least rubbed off on "intellectuals," darkening its oppositional hues. The intelligentsia, which prepared the way for the Russian Revolution, was almost exclusively defined by "its alienation from and hostility towards the state."[105]

This history colored subsequent discussions. Some thinkers wanted to overcome this past; others to reclaim it.[106] When H. Stuart Hughes looked into the future of intellectuals, he also looked to their past in the 1890s. (Perhaps his most important book surveyed intellectuals at the turn of the century.)[107] Nevertheless, the 1950s and 1960s bleached out much of the original pigments. Discussions about intellectuals do not cease, but the terms change. Where once there was talk of intellectuals as critics and bohemians, now there is talk of intellectuals as a sociological class. The shift in idiom illuminates the shift in lives.

The old questions seem less urgent, since they had been answered not by agreements or conclusive arguments but by events. As with the controversy about suburbia, "progress" is marked less by resolution than neglect; heated issues slip out of sight because they reflect a past no longer encroaching upon the present. In the 1980s few are asking about the future of independent or bohemian intellectuals. This is settled: there is no future. Instead, commentators and scholars ask if intellectuals constitute a "new class."

Of course, there is still no agreement, but the reformulation of the question registers the restructured lives. Intellectuals live less as independent writers or poets and more as professional groups, interest coalitions, perhaps classes. For some, like Alvin Gouldner, the "new class" of intellectuals and technicians constitutes "the most progressive force in modern society."[108] Irving Kristol disagrees; the new class is an "ambitious and frustrated class."[109] An editor of *The Wall Street Journal* has discovered—or hallucinated—that "many of the great fortunes built from business empires have now been captured by intellectuals, and are now being used . . . to attack business and advance the New Class."[110]

To Daniel Bell "new class" is a "muddled" category. Instead, he proposes to classify intellectuals by their institutional attachments, which he numbers at five: business, government, university, medical, and military.[111] Bell's list indicates the distance traveled. The sociological idiom of class and institutions supplants talk of independent intellectuals, who survive as curiosities.

Today intellectuals travel with curricula vitae and business cards; they subsist by virtue of institutional backing. The standard first or second question among academics is not "who?" but "where?" meaning with which institution someone is affiliated; it makes a difference. In 1964 Lewis Coser called Edmund Wilson a "monument" from a "half-forgotten past."[112] Twenty years later that past is fully forgotten. To put it sharply: in the 1950s, the future of unaffiliated intellectuals engendered discussion; in the 1980s, the future of an intellectual class. The substitution of class for intellectuals encapsulates the change.

The novelty, as fact or term, of "new class," is again not the issue. When Newton Arvin identified a new academic species, the managerial professor, he alluded to James Burnham's *The Managerial Revolution* (1941), which announced a new society, beyond socialists and capitalists, of "managers"; and Burnham, an ex-Trotskyist, borrowed his idiom from the old Trotskyist argument about who ruled the Soviet state—new capitalists or new bureaucrats? The term, however, arose much earlier; it has been employed in political controversies for at least a century.

This is not simply an antiquarian point; for if many intellectuals moved from left to right, they also retained and revamped their old vocabulary. The collection *The New Class?*, mainly by conservatives, is dedicated to Max Nomad (1881-1973), who prior to World War I collaborated with the Polish revolutionary Jan Machajski (1866-1926) in several revolutionary schemes. Machajski forcefully enunciated a theory of intellectuals as a new dominating class. In a series of books Nomad did the same, presenting Machajski's ideas to American culture.[113] As Nomad's work abundantly shows, neither the vocabulary nor the concept of intellectuals as a class is new. Today these fringe concerns— Nomad's writings never gained much attention—inch into the center while the debate on independent intellectuals lapses.

Not only the issue of intellectuals as a class signals the times; almost everywhere the iconography of the professor has been redesigned. Through the 1950s the professor appeared in American fiction as a harmless misfit wandering through society; he was Professor Pnin of Vladimir Nabokov's *Pnin* (1957), literally lost en route to a Friday lecture; or he was Professor Muleahy of Mary McCarthy's *The Groves of Academe* (1952), whose car— "the roof leaked; the front window was missing; the windshield wiper was broken"—reflected his life.[114]

Perhaps these characters still exist, but they have become too rare for fiction to employ, even to lampoon.[115] Contemporary fiction needs material that smacks of the times. To cast a professor as a scatter-brained pedant would damn a book as a quaint period piece; rather an absurd erotic or professional ambition imbues the current professor. In Don DeLillo's *White Noise*, Murray calls in his colleague, Jack, for advice. Murray bursts with praise and admiration. Jack invented Hitler Studies, which has become a small industry in the academic world. Everyone honors, defers, and toadies to Jack; he is invited to numerous conferences. "You've evolved an entire system around this figure [Hitler], a structure with countless substructures. . . . I marvel at the effort. It was masterful, shrewd and stunningly preemptive. It's what I want to do with Elvis [Presley]."[116]

A reviewer of a recent satiric academic novel summed up the situation:

Once upon a time, if you wanted to get people to laugh at professors, you would portray them as goggle-eyed intellectuals so disoriented from the practical world that they wore unmatched shoes and spoke in Sid Caesarian German about incomprehensible nonsense. Today . . . the figure of the absent-minded professor has been replaced by a pack of smoothies. . . . Instead of retiring from the world of events, the new comic professor has the world too much with him. He craves big money, drives sporty cars, covets endowed chairs, and hops from conference to conference in pursuit of love, luxury and fame.[117]

* * *

In 1965 Harold Rosenberg reviewed the past discussion of intellectuals on intellectuals. Rosenberg (1906–78), trained as a lawyer, led a checkered career as a poet and government and advertising consultant before becoming the art critic for *The New*

Yorker and, in the 1960s, a professor at the University of Chicago. In this he mirrored the life of last generation intellectuals.

His essay "The Vanishing Intellectual" reconsidered the literature, including Hofstadter's *Anti-Intellectualism* and Coser's *Men of Ideas*. Rosenberg did not share the worry that intellectuals might disappear; he believed that intellectuals assumed various guises and disguises and that they regularly showed up after being consigned to the historical dustbin. Intellectuals eluded all categorization, escaped all prognoses of their imminent demise. Rosenberg was confident that intellectuals would always be with us.

Rosenberg concluded his essay by noting that a journal Coser co-edits, *Dissent*, recently carried a report of student activity at the University of California, Berkeley. The report called Berkeley "a melting pot of campus intellectuals, aesthetes, and politicoes"; it described the crowds at the campus cafeteria and at Telegraph Avenue coffee houses: "Here . . . are a surprisingly large proportion of the most intellectually serious and morally alert students on campus." For Rosenberg the moral was clear: "So much for the 'death of Bohemia' in the twenties and the vanishing of the organizationally unattached intellectual."[118] For Rosenberg and for many, young and old, the sixties explosions ended all doubt about conformist or vanishing intellectuals. Yet when the dust—and dirt, rocks, and boulders—had settled, the doubt returned.

CHAPTER 5

===

The New Left on Campus I: The Freedom to Be Academic

I

IN A *Prophetic Minority* (1966), Jack Newfield (1938–) surveyed the origins and impact of the New Left. His book, perhaps the best of the early studies, argued that the New Left—"the prophetic minority"—was destined to assume increasing importance. He guessed that in fifteen years "Bob Dylan's poems will be taught in college classrooms" and the Beatles' movies shown in art houses. He also hazarded that the New Left theorists would emerge as society's next eminent intellectuals. By the 1980s "Tom Hayden, Norman Fruchter, Robb Burlage, Mario Savio, Dick Flacks, Bob Parris, and Carl Oglesby will be major social critics."[1]

As a cultural seer, Newfield made a respectable showing. Beatles' movies are sometimes booked by art houses, and Bob

Dylan, if his poems are not studied, still performs. As an intellectual forecaster, however, Newfield scored zero. To be sure, "major social critics" is an imprecise category. Nevertheless, some twenty years after he drew up the list, none of its figures could remotely be considered major social critics or prominent intellectuals. Of course, Tom Hayden (1939–), a California reform Democrat (and husband of Jane Fonda), is well known, but he is hardly a commanding intellectual. Several have disappeared from public life (Mario Savio [1942–], Bob Parris [1935–]); one is a professor of sociology (Richard Flacks [1938–]); and the others remain active in urban, regional, or peace politics (Norman Fruchter [1937–], Robb Burlage [1937–], Carl Oglesby [1935–]). The issue is not the value of their contributions but their relationship as intellectuals to a larger public.

Mistakes are possible, and Newfield, a senior editor and columnist at *The Village Voice*, may simply have guessed wrong. Hindsight is more reliable than foresight, and it should not be difficult to look back and answer two questions: who were the intellectuals of the 1960s, and what became of them?

The first question is, of course, hardly simple; many even contest its legitimacy. Conservatives and radicals, who agree on little, sometimes concur that the sixties and intellectuals did not mix. For conservatives the sixties represented an irrational sexual and political explosion that wrecked the culture. "The 60s were like a tidal wave that swept over America," writes Joseph Epstein. "The wave has begun to roll back, but in its wake the shore is revealed to be littered with broken glass, dead animals and all kinds of garbage."[2] According to *The New Criterion*,

We are still living in the aftermath of the insidious assault on mind that was one of the most repulsive features of the radical movement of the

Sixties. . . .The effect on the life of culture has been ongoing and catastrophic. . . . It would probably take the combined talents of a Gibbon and a Tocqueville to tell the whole shabby story . . . but one does not have to be a genius to recognize some of the more egregious results of this flight from intelligence. . . .[3]

Some radicals might almost agree but regret that the effect has not been ongoing or catastrophic. Both perspectives bestow different values on the same scenario: the "direct action," drugs, sexuality, and rock 'n' roll of the sixties displaced or challenged intellectuals.

This is true—to a point. To view the sixties exclusively through the lens of intellectuals would be a serious mistake. Nevertheless, it is equally erroneous to disregard the impact of writers, philosophers, and political theorists. In every phase of the sixties, student protest organizations—Student Peace Union (SPU), Students for a Democratic Society (SDS), Student Non-Violent Coordinating Committee (SNCC), Northern Student Movement (NSM)—played decisive roles. College "teach-ins" galvanized the opposition to the Vietnam War; and the last chapters of the sixties were written at Kent State University and Jackson State College, where in May 1970 National Guardsmen and police shot and killed protesting students. Of course, students and intellectuals are not identical; yet campus politics of the sixties cannot be disassociated from books, ideas, or intellectuals, all of which suffuse a student universe.

Who were the sixties intellectuals? Probably most were not American: Jean-Paul Sartre, Albert Camus, Frantz Fanon, Herbert Marcuse, Isaac Deutscher, Wilhelm Reich. Students did not necessarily grasp, even read, Sartre's *Being and Nothingness* or Marcuse's *One Dimensional Man*, but these individuals and their writings glowed with protest, revolution, and morality that sharply broke with American liberalism. When he spoke at a Berkeley teach-in in 1965, Isaac Deutscher, the independent Marxist, received a standing ovation from an audience of twelve thousand.[4] This hardly indicated that the audience had plowed through his three fat volumes on Trotsky; rather, Deutscher exemplified an engaged intellectual willing to challenge American (and Soviet) official wisdom.[5]

It would be difficult to imagine an American intellectual who would elicit this response, except for C. Wright Mills, and he died in 1962. Some American intellectuals played small roles in the sixties, but then fell away; others played roles despite themselves: Paul Goodman, Norman Mailer, Michael Harrington, William H. Whyte, Rachel Carson, John Kenneth Galbraith, Betty Friedan. Mills, however, almost bridged the gap between the intellectuals of the fifties and the new figures of the sixties. The contribution of Mills illuminates not only the cultural scene of the early New Left but the fate of its intellectuals.

II

"TODAY in the United States," Mills stated flatly in 1959, "there is no Left." He presented a catalog of resignation and retreat: weary ex-communists, who substitute nationalist celebration for politics; professional ex-communists who "sour" the atmosphere; "Young Complacents," who desert politics for prospering careers; academics who "are fully rational, but . . . refuse to reason." The very bleakness of the political landscape gave Mills some hope. "In the present situation of the impoverished mind and lack of political will, United States intellectuals, it seems to me, have a unique opportunity to make a new beginning."[6]

A year and a half later, Mills published a "Letter to the New Left" with a strikingly different tone; he announced the new beginning. In the interim Fidel Castro had driven Batista from power, and Mills had published an exuberant defense of the Cuban Revolution, *Listen Yankee!* He noted that the "end of ideology" ideology that assumed—or desired—the disappearance of real issues had seen its day. Around the globe a new political wind gave a chance to the theory, morality, and utopianism of a New Left. "Let the old men," he closed, "ask sourly 'Out of Apathy—into what?' The Age of Complacency is ending. Let the old women complain wisely about 'the end of ideology.' We are beginning to move again."[7]

For Mills the "we" were intellectuals. All his work dwelled on the task and impact of intellectuals. He traced the decline of public intellectuals; he sought to awaken intellectuals; and he tried to be a public intellectual himself. To Mills, intellectuals constituted the New Left.[8] "We cannot create a left by abdicating our roles as intellectuals to become working class agitators or machine politicians. . . . We can begin to create a left by confronting issues as intellectuals in our work." We must, he declared, act as intellectuals, as "public men."[9]

A revitalization of intellectuals required more than moral courage. In the Jeffersonian democracy of early America, Mills believed, intellectuals lived in and among the educated citizens, their audience. Now institutions and corporations prevented intellectuals from addressing a public. Mills often referred to Thomas Paine, whose world allowed "a direct channel to readers"—the pamphlet. For intellectuals to pen pamphlets today roughly corresponded to writing poems for the drawer; the mass magazines, too dependent on advertising and circulation, could not risk heretical opinions. "Between the intellectual and his potential public stand technical, economic and social structures which are owned and operated by others," noted Mills.[10]

No matter. If moral courage did not suffice, it was nonetheless a prerequisite. Mills always wrote as a moralist, partisan, critic. He lamented the intellectual surrender of the 1950s: the conformism, the caution, the loss of the utopian vision. "In class, status, and self-image" the intellectual "has become more solidly middle class, a man at a desk, married, with children, living in a respectable suburb. . . . The writing of memoranda, telling others what to do, replaces the writing of books, telling others how it is."[11] He called upon intellectuals to uphold "the politics of truth." "The intellectual ought to be the moral conscience of his society."[12] In *The Causes of World War Three*, he decried the "cultural default," the loss of intellectual nerve. What should we do? "We ought to act as political intellectuals . . . as public intellectuals."[13]

For a historical moment, Mills seemed to be everywhere. His books, *The Causes of World War Three* and *Listen, Yankee!* (which was excerpted in *Harper's*), sold hundreds of thousands of copies. His views were regularly solicited—perhaps too much so; he suffered a heart attack on the eve of a television debate on Cuba.[14] Yet Mills's spirit, language, and example stamped the early New Left. The founding statement of SDS, an argument for a new campus politics (Port Huron Statement [1962]), borrowed his ideas and idiom. Tom Hayden, its main author, had already written a thesis on Mills. For New Left intellectuals or would-be intellectuals Mills was essential, even a hero.[15]

The moment passed. Of course, Mills's oeuvre survived the

demise of the New Left, but his successors became sociologists, not public intellectuals. In the 1950s, apart from Mills, there was scarcely another publicly radical sociologist. Today leftist, Marxist, or feminist sociologists can, and do, fill convention halls. They seem everywhere. The change is startling—and partly deceptive. The increased numbers do not translate into public intellectuals; out of the hundreds, perhaps thousands, of left-wing sociologists, it is difficult to name one with the presence of Mills.

This is due not to the quirks but to the contours of history. Radical sociologists may dream of revolution, but they bank on their profession. Professionalization also spells privatization, a withdrawal from a larger public universe. Mills was a scrappy public thinker, who was also a professor; today radical sociologists are first professors and rarely, if ever, public intellectuals. The volume that appeared in Mills's honor in 1964, *The New Sociology*, is dedicated "To the American graduate students of Social Science." But more than twenty years after its publication, its younger American contributors have not crossed from sociology to public writing. In this they exemplify the larger movement of New Left intellectuals.[16]

As they obtained university slots, New Left intellectuals acquired the benefits: regular salaries, long vacations, and the freedom to write, and sometimes teach, what they wanted. Of course, it was not this simple. Vast insecurities beset the academic enterprise. One's future depended on a complex set of judgments made by colleagues and administrators. Academic freedom itself was fragile, its principles often ignored. Nor were these violations confined to meddling trustees and outside investigators. The threat emerged, perhaps increasingly, from within; academic careers undermined academic freedom. This may be a paradox, but it recalls an inner contradiction of academic freedom—the institution neutralizes the freedom it guarantees. For many professors in many universities academic freedom meant nothing more than the freedom to be academic.

III

MILLS HAD BEEN a graduate student at the University of Wisconsin, Madison, a school with a long tradition of independent radicalism. One Madison journal, *Studies on the Left*, which carried the imprint of Mills and his mentor, Hans Gerth, exemplifies the hope and fate of younger intellectuals. If, by the end of the fifties, disillusionment and McCarthyism had gutted the old communist left, it also opened a breathing space for leftists without old loyalties.[17] In 1959 those who launched *Studies*, an essential journal for intellectuals of the early New Left, envisioned themselves as future professors. "As graduate students anticipating academic careers," stated its inaugural editorial, "we feel a very personal stake in academic life." They called for the revitalization of radical scholarship. "It is our conviction that academic acceptance of the radical scholar's work . . . would . . . revitalize all of American intellectual life."[18]

Yet *Studies* fled from academic complacency and specialization, moving in 1963 from the campus town of Madison to New York to breathe the air, if not partake of urban political ferment. This move did not resolve its persistent arguments about intellectuals and their commitments. Several years later three editors—Norman Fruchter, Tom Hayden, and Staughton Lynd—dissatisfied with the journal's self-contained theorizing resigned to assume more active political roles. If most editors and associates of

Studies did become professors, these three and some others, such as Saul Landau (1936–), member of the Institute for Policy Studies, Washington D.C., and film maker; Lee Baxandall (1935–), publisher, nude beach activist; and James Weinstein (1926–), publisher of the socialist newspaper, *In These Times*, made lives outside the university. The problem is that neither the academics—Martin Sklar (1935–), Ronald Radosh (1937–), Warren Susman (1927–1985), Michael Lebowitz (1937–), James Gilbert (1935–), Joan Wallach Scott (1941–), and others—nor the nonacademics have quite made the transition to public intellectuals. The trajectory of two *Studies* editors, Staughton Lynd and Stanley Aronowitz, highlights the limited choices.

Their careers are almost mirror images. Lynd was a professor who became a labor activist; Aronowitz, a labor activist who became a professor. Staughton Lynd (1929–) is the child of an academic family; his parents (Robert S. and Helen M. Lynd) authored a classic sociological work, *Middletown*. The moralism and pragmatism of Robert S. Lynd, a Christian and a reform minister who became a dissenting sociologist, made a lasting impression on Staughton, whose own writings are imbued by an ethical spirit.[19] Staughton Lynd followed a high academic road, from schooling at Harvard and Columbia to teaching American history at Yale. However, intense political work in the sixties—civil rights, antiwar, and draft resistance—drew him in another direction, disrupting his relationship to the university.

At a Berkeley teach-in in 1965, Lynd replied to a political science professor, Robert A. Scalapino, who damned the event as a "travesty" of scholarship. Lynd challenged the purity of reputable scholarship that Scalapino had invoked.

I am employed by Yale University, the institution which produced the architect of the Bay of Pigs, Richard Bissell; the author of Plan Six for Vietnam, W. W. Rostow . . . and McGeorge Bundy [presidential assistant and vigorous defender of the Vietnam War]. Hence if Professor Scalapino is an expert on Vietnamese insurgents, I consider myself something of an expert on American counterinsurgents. I think I know something about the Ivy League training which these unelected experts receive: a training in snobbishness, in provincial ethnocentrism, in cynical and manipulative attitude toward human beings.[20]

Yale did not appreciate these sentiments, and when it booted him out, Lynd's discontent with the university prompted him to try another career. He saw no way to inject humane values and action into his field, history, and "I sure wasn't going to . . . score brownie points with senior conservative historians for the rest of my life to prove that, even though I was a radical, I could be a good historian, too."[21] After a career as a history professor, Lynd became a law student. In 1976 he moved to Youngstown, Ohio, to practice law, representing steelworkers who opposed mill closings.

His writings reflect his trajectory; his first book was an academic monograph, *Anti-Federalism in Dutchess County, New York* (1962). Later, he tackled the history of radicalism in America (*The Intellectual Origins of American Radicalism* [1968]), draft resistance to the Vietnam War (*The Resistance* with Michael Ferber [1971]), and the experience of working-class organizers (*Rank and File: Personal Histories by Working-Class Organizers* with Alice Lynd [1973]). More recently, he has written on labor law and steelworkers' resistance to plant closings. His *Labor Law for the Rank and Filer* (1978) is a pamphlet, designed for unionists and organizers, summarizing federal labor legislation.

The Fight Against Shutdowns (1982) is an account of plant closings in Ohio, where Lynd served as legal counsel for several unions and community organizations. "I was a historian before I became a lawyer," he explains. "After our struggle ended, it was natural to think of telling the story as best I could." He adds that "I have deliberately placed rank-and-file steelworkers in the center of the narrative. I think they belong there."[22] This anti-elite, populist, and moral stance has consistently marked Lynd's writings and activities.

The value of Lynd's efforts as a labor lawyer or chronicler is not in question; and on occasion in newspapers and magazines, he addresses more general political issues. His own career, however, inadvertently testifies to a specialization that no one seems able to buck. He renounced the narrowness, perhaps elitism and sterility, of the university; but he has not become (perhaps he has not wished to become) a more general intellectual. Today he writes as a socially committed labor lawyer.

Aronowitz (1933–), on the other hand, began as a union organizer, and unhappiness with its limits drove him to the university. Several years ago two small academic journals, *New German Critique* and *Social Text*, whose editors include Aronowitz, held a conference in Madison. Paul Breines (1941–), a history professor, once associated with *Studies*, mused on the irony that Aronowitz had now come to Madison as a professor and editor. He recalled the earlier years, when *Studies* had left Wisconsin.

Part of the reason for its move from Madison to New York City was to be located more suitably for building ties to leftist activity beyond the campus confines. The recruitment of Stanley Aronowitz, at the time an organizer for the Oil, Chemical and Atomic Workers' Union, was to further this aim. Through him *Studies* . . . was not only reaching into the working class, but bringing the working class into the journal.

Now, with some water under the bridge, Stanley Aronowitz, one of three editors of *Social Text*, is a tenured professor. He is seeking among other things exactly what *Studies on the Left* had found in him in the first place.[23]

Aronowitz is himself almost a transitional figure, illustrating the passing of the older independent intelligentsia and the rise of the professors. His career runs parallel to that of Michael Harrington, whom, in fact, Aronowitz met at the famous Greenwich Village hangout, the White Horse, at its last hurrah in the late 1950s. Aronowitz recalls listening to "the refugees of the political intelligentsia" who had remained in the cities despite the suburban exodus of the fifties.

The McCarthy era, the obvious deterioration of the labor movement's militancy, the advent of consumer society—nothing could daunt the small band of radicals who downed gallons of beer every Friday at the White Horse. How appropriate it was that they should jostle in that packed room with the Beats and the veterans of an already eclipsed literary radicalisms [of the thirties].[24]

He is also transitional in that his first book, *False Promises* (1973), an original mix of autobiography and thoughts about working-class life, bespeaks the domain of the free-wheeling intelligentsia. Aronowitz, suspended from college in 1950, assumed a series of factory jobs that led to union activity. He was offered a position in the Oil, Chemical and Atomic Workers' Union, where he stayed for many years, resigning in 1967.[25] Afterward he participated in antipoverty programs and alternative schools, eventually finding a post at a Staten Island community college.

Today he is a professor of sociology at the Graduate Center of the City University of New York. His more recent work—its idiom and its problems—reflects his new environs. For instance, an essay littered with references to Foucault, Derrida, and Lacan (in his *Crisis in Historical Materialism*) begins this way: "The problem of the commensurability of discourses is a way of describing an antinomy regarding the structure of human knowledge: can we speak of a unitary science, or is the object of our knowledge constituted by structures/discourses that are fundamentally discontinuous?"[26] This is a thousand leagues from *False Promises*.

Of course, this is unfair. By virtue of his union past Aronowitz remains devoted not simply to a new academic audience, or even a single discipline, but to addressing, sometimes in *The Village Voice*, a wide series of issues before a lay public. His recent *Working Class Hero*[27] marks a return to (and a revision of) themes of his *False Promises*.[28] There may be several clues here to the contours of intellectual life. If the oeuvre of Aronowitz shines, this may be due not only to his sheer talents but to his unique trajectory; he stands at the end of the tradition of urban nonacademic intellectuals. And at that end the progression from labor and antipoverty organizer to full professor takes a toll even on the wiliest. The talented intellectuals of *Studies on the Left* display the gamut of choices; they also reveal its limits, the nature of cultural activity in an age of institutions.

IV

NEVER BEFORE in American history did so many left intellectuals seek and find university positions. Radicals of the early part of the century almost never became college teachers. Max

Eastman completed all his requirements for a Ph.D. in philosophy but neglected to pick up his degree. Why should he? Scott Nearing, one of the very few socialist professors, had been fired.[29] It also cost thirty dollars to print a thesis, and Eastman could not see himself as an academic. Rather, he became a freelance lecturer and writer, finding his calling when summoned by the editors of "a bankrupt magazine of unpopular opinions." "You are elected editor of the *The Masses*," stated the complete text of the offer. "No pay."[30]

As the postsecondary school systems gradually expanded, however, even radical intellectuals could find employment. Of course, the size of the university was not the only factor; the political climate was also decisive. In the 1930s at least several hundred professors, perhaps more, had links to the Communist Party; nevertheless, few ventured forth as public radicals. In any event, they had no future. Not only had the Depression limited new positions, McCarthyism effectively rendered universities off-limits to leftists. McCarthyism, of course, refers to the anti-communism orchestrated by Senator Joseph McCarthy in the early 1950s. However, as a loose term for systematic harassment and persecution, it dates back at least to 1940, when a committee of the New York State Legislature (led by Assemblymen Herbert Rapp and Frederic R. Coudert) began to investigate subversives on college faculties.

Figures on the numbers of communists and radicals in the universities are notoriously difficult to establish. This is clear, nevertheless: McCarthyism in its various guises successfully purged or silenced academic radicals. Fifty-eight teachers were dismissed in New York City alone, perhaps a hundred in the country. At the end of the McCarthy period, concludes one study, "Marxism disappeared from the campus. Most of its main practitioners were exiled from the academy and the tradition of left-wing scholarship . . . was broken."[31]

The numbers of those dismissed or hounded out only tell part of the story. Most major universities either investigated themselves or were investigated by the state. Those fired rarely found new teaching posts.[32] "None of the three dismissed faculty," notes an account of the witch-hunt at the University of Washington, "ever got jobs in higher education again." After futile attempts, one discharged professor ended his days on public relief.[33] The sorry tale is recounted in Ellen W. Schrecker's *No Ivory Tower*. "The academy did not fight McCarthyism," she concludes. "It contributed to it."[34]

The specter of dismissal and unemployment raised by the fate of some professors could and did silence entire faculties, which had no more, and probably less, courage than any random grouping of individuals. "Now consider the case of the professors of economics," stated H. L. Mencken of the earlier Nearing firing, "who have *not* been thrown out. Who will say that the lesson of the Nearing *debacle* has been lost upon them?"[35] Of course, from the point of view of the individual, the distinction between dismissal and silencing is not trifling. For the wider culture, however, the distinction is less critical; from this perspective, a radical (or conservative) who has been silenced does not exist.

"Silencing," however, can be rendered more precise. What is often obscure in the history of academic freedom is its almost inverse relationship to professionalization. Not classroom teaching but public statements or political affiliations have provoked hostility to professors. When threatened they have withdrawn, naturally, into their speciality. Professionalization has served as a refuge; it has also entailed a privatization that eviscerates academic freedom.

This seems the lesson of one famous case of academic freedom. In 1894 Richard T. Ely of the University of Wisconsin was charged with "justifying and encouraging" strikes and boycotts, specifically of a local plant. His trial before the University of Wisconsin Regents concluded with a ringing defense of academic freedom. In a statement, part of which continues to adorn the Wisconsin campus, the Regents declared that "whatever may be the limitations which trammel inquiry elsewhere we believe the great State University of Wisconsin should ever encourage that continual and fearless sifting and winnowing by which alone the truth can be found."[36]

Yet these eloquent words concealed a defeat perhaps more illuminating for the future; for Ely, a mild socialist, drew the conclusion after the trial that it would be better, as his biographer writes, "to concentrate on 'scientific' investigations in the future rather than 'popular' writing."[37] When he became editor of a book series several years later, he was unhappy with its title, *The Citizens Library*, because it seemed too popular and unscientific. The moral he drew from his own case—stay away from public controversy—was reinforced by the fate of his former student, Edward W. Bemis, embroiled in trouble at the University of Chicago.

Bemis had long advocated public ownership of railroads. In the year of the great Pullman railroad strike that was shaking Chicago, Bemis, teaching at the University of Chicago, sided with the strikers. The president of the University of Chicago, which had been founded with John D. Rockefeller's money, did not appreciate Bemis's stand: "It is hardly safe for me to venture into any of the Chicago clubs." He directed Bemis to "exercise very great care in public utterance about questions that are agitating the minds of the people."[38] At the end of the school year Bemis was sacked; all efforts at redress failed.

Why the differences in their fates? Part of the reason, it seems, is that Bemis remained incorrigibly devoted to public discourse. In fact, Bemis had written to Ely congratulating him on his exoneration. However, he added a regret. "I was sorry only that you seemed to show a vigor of denial as to entertaining a walking delegate or counseling strikers as if either were wrong."[39] Bemis continued to bemoan that Ely had withdrawn from public life. He wrote to Ely some years later, "I wish you might occasionally return to your practice of years ago of writing advanced articles of social reform in the most popular magazines."[40]

Their academic futures duly reflected their contrasting relations to the public. As Walter P. Metzger writes, Ely "remained in a full state of academic grace for the rest of his life." However, Bemis became "an academic Ishmael, with a reputation as a partisan and a malcontent that he never was able to live down. Except for a brief and ill-starred tenure at Kansas State, he received no further academic appointments."[41]

Of course, the Ely and Bemis chapters do not exhaust the history of academic freedom and its lessons. Another event, the formation of the New School for Social Research, also is instructive of the relationship between academic freedom and professionalization. The founders of the New School not only ardently defended academic freedom, they protested the insularity of university life and thought. While the New School is often associated with the influx of European refugee scholars in the 1930s, it was actually founded by American refugee scholars after World War I—professors fleeing the established universities.

During the First World War, the president of Columbia University, Nicholas Murray Butler, established a board to ferret out subversive and disloyal professors.[42] It unearthed several: J. McKeen Cattell, who for years had argued for faculty control of universities ("a democracy of scholars serving the larger democracy"[43]), and Henry Wadsworth Longfellow Dana, who opposed United States participation in the war. Both were discharged.[44] Their dismissal engendered a strong protest and some resignations. Charles A. Beard and James Harvey Robinson, Columbia's most illustrious historians, resigned. Together with others, including Thorstein Veblen and John Dewey, they founded the New School for Social Research, an institution exclusively defined by faculty and students without meddlesome administrators.[45]

A common dissatisfaction with the sterility of academic life motivated the New School's founders. They accepted Veblen's indictment that "American universities continued to encourage publications largely for the sake of institutional prestige, reward mediocrity as often as merit, and exert enormous pressure on dissident faculty to conform"; and they rejected "the assumptions of the new professionalism," which obscured moral and political issues.[46] Alvin Johnson, who came to preside over the new outfit, regarded the London School of Economics as a model and wanted to create a new institution devoted to "advanced adult education."[47] Robinson, weary of academic routine and conformity, also envisioned adult education as the heart of the New School.[48] These proposals did not go far enough for Beard. He desired a complete break with the established university—even its odor: he suggested that the New School locate "over a livery stable, garage or brewery where even the olfactory stigmata of conventional education would be effectively obscured."[49]

In the 1930s Johnson set up a University in Exile at the New School for European refugee scholars; this became the Graduate Faculty. Although "accredited," the Graduate Faculty, according to Lewis Coser, was "nevertheless not fully part of American cultural and intellectual life."[50] This was a blessing: it allowed the New School to support scholars who found little place elsewhere. In recent years the original ambiance is hardly in evidence; yet the founding of the New School by protesting faculty and its illustrious history as a refuge for dissident thinkers may hold a lesson. When academic freedom succumbs to professionalization, it becomes purely academic.

V

BY THE EARLY SIXTIES, McCarthyism was largely spent, and universities no longer feared a hostile government and climate. Rather, higher education was turning fat and self-confident. Demographics is part of the story: children of new postwar families constituted a grouping larger than any previous generation. The baby boom generation was entering college in unprecedented numbers. Almost all the statistics show sharp absolute and relative increases: not only did millions more young people enter college in 1960 than in 1900, but the percentage of youth who completed high school and continued on to college climbed steadily as well. In 1900 college was strictly an elite affair, with about 4 percent of eighteen- to twenty-two-year-olds attending; by the late sixties, some 50 percent of the eighteen- to nineteen-year-old group were entering postsecondary educational systems.[51]

After the launching of Sputnik in 1957, federal and state monies poured into the universities; over a single decade (1960–70) some states (for example, New York and Massachusetts) increased their spending six- and sevenfold. Massive new campuses, such as Cleveland State University, Chicago Circle (University of Illinois), and the State University of New York at Albany opened in the sixties. Old ones expanded and refurbished. "In the course of the 1960s," noted one commentator, "old private colleges, shabby city universities, and forlorn rural colleges projected and accomplished the completion of hundreds of student unions, libraries, and performing-arts centers. . . . Little Wells College . . . got a new library of extraordinary proportions. . . . Sooty Wayne State University decorated itself with a convention center of marble and crystal."[52]

These trends translate into sizable jumps in numbers of students and faculty. "In 1900 there were about 250,000 American university students. Today, the City University of New York alone has more than that."[53] Graduate students—those enrolled in programs after receiving B.A.'s—increased from about one hundred thousand in 1939–40 to over one million in 1970. Faculty, which numbered thirty-six thousand in 1910, swelled to over a half million in 1970.[54] For a historical moment these faculties beckoned radical intellectuals not simply with jobs but with more: the cultural and political fires were burning brightly on campuses.

The relationship of New Leftists to the university fluctuated wildly, depending on the year and the political faction; for some, the prosperous universities were simply new homes where they had moved after high school and intended to stay. Others denounced the colleges as tools of imperialism or as an escape from real political activity. Many young intellectuals, such as those around *Studies on the Left*, believed that universities could harbor a new radical culture.

131

Some theorized that professors with or without students formed a "new" working class; universities replaced or supplemented factories as the locus of capitalism.[55] By designating teachers and students as "new" workers, university Marxists could legitimate their own activities. "Neo-capitalism," it was argued, entailed a "proletarianization of students and academics at the same time that the knowledge industry became an essential cog in the machine producing surplus-value."[56] Leftists slept better dreaming that they were part of the working class.

Even those who departed to work as community or labor organizers were seduced back by universities that seemed alive with energy, or they returned as the larger ferment abated. After several years outside school New Leftists with an intellectual bent often realized that the best chance for a life of thinking and writing lay with the university. A sign of the trajectory that many took: a former SDS president stated in 1968, "I . . . have no further academic plans."[57] Today Todd Gitlin (1943–) is professor of sociology at the University of California, Berkeley.

The wider "movement" and its intellectuals probably never saw eye to eye about the university. While activists often disdained academics, New Left intellectuals largely envisioned themselves as future professors. Herein lies an irony that hints of institutional strength. Unlike the old left, the New Left frontally attacked the university. Yet young intellectuals entered it with less regrets. Maurice Isserman, in his careful account of the formation of the New Left, comments on this.

When Howe had attended City College he had done so with the "certainty" of never getting an academic job. . . . In the early 1960s, [for New Left intellectuals] "the only question was where were you going to get tenure." New Leftists paradoxically would adopt a much more hostile political stance toward the universities than Howe ever had and yet, at the same time, feel much more at home and less ambivalent about making a career within the confines of those same universities. The transformation of the intellectual class from a marginal, adversarial role to a securely institutionalized one went on apace in the 1960s regardless of the momentary radical ascendancy on the campuses.[58]

In their 1966 book, *The New Radicals* (dedicated to C. Wright Mills), Saul Landau and Paul Jacobs reprinted the opening editorial of the 1959 issue of *Studies on the Left*. They noted that the *Studies* editors, who were then radical graduate students, had "thought that similar groups of graduates existed at other universities and that *Studies* would become the organ for a New Left theory. Similar constellations, however, did not develop. . . ." They added that "the notion that the radicals should leave the world of the university had not yet received the wide approval it was to get later."[59]

These statements by Landau and Jacobs were skewed by the times; the 1959 *Studies* editorial, anticipating numerous radical graduate students and young faculty, was hardly off the mark. By 1966 the notion that radicals could and should stay in the university was enjoying unprecedented success, and similar groupings of graduate students and young professors did emerge in many schools. In the mid-sixties several professors, including *Studies* associates, launched the Socialist Scholars Conference as a forum for radical scholarship. They optimistically assumed that fifty scholars in the country might contribute papers, and perhaps several hundred might show for the first meeting. The inaugural conference in 1965 drew a thousand people; by 1967 almost three thousand New Left scholars and hangers-on attended an electric and free-wheeling forum in midtown Manhattan.[60]

Although the door slammed shut before many could gain entry, the New Left established a visible, often self-confident, presence on the university faculties. How large a presence? *The Wall Street Journal*, an unreliable source on these matters, figures twelve thousand Marxists now teach in American colleges.[61] Yet it is impossible to determine. An inkling of the size, and change from the past, might be obtained by comparing the mid-fifties and the mid-eighties. A discussion of public radicals in the universities in 1955 might take a dozen pages, perhaps less; after surveying C. Wright Mills and Paul Baran, it would begin running out of steam.[62]

Today a discussion of radicals in the University could fill several volumes—and in fact has. Bertell Ollman (1935–), a professor of political science, and Edward Vernoff, a teacher and editor, have compiled a three-volume survey, *The Left Academy: Marxist Scholarship on American Campuses*, which goes over the writings of left-wing professors discipline by discipline. "A Marxist cultural revolution," begins their tour, "is taking place in American universities. . . . It is a peaceful and democratic revolution, fought chiefly with books and lectures. . . ."[63]

Each essay runs over the major names and books and lists additional bibliography; nearly all the disciplines have dissenting journals, such as *Dialectical Anthropology, Insurgent Sociology, New Political Science, Radical History Review*, and *Antipode*. Nor is Ollman and Vernoff's survey exhaustive. Indubitably, radicals have established themselves in colleges and universities; left-wing professors, books, magazines are common; conferences of "socialists scholars" and feminist historians draw thousands.

None of this is news to conservatives, who regularly charge that the universities have succumbed to leftists. Conservative periodicals, such as *Commentary* or *American Scholar* or *Modern Age*, print articles almost monthly lamenting that left academics have seized the universities. "Those of us who received graduate degrees in the humanities from American universities in the 1960s," begins a typical piece, "know that a major change took place in the academy about that time." This change is what the author calls "an invasion and conquest" by left professors espousing "dialectical methodologies."[64]

This conservative nightmare lifts with any daytime inspection of universities. What happened to the swarms of academic leftists? The answer is surprising: Nothing surprising. The ordinary realities of bureaucratization and employment took over. The New Left that stayed on the campus proved industrious and well behaved. Often without missing a beat, they moved from being undergraduates and graduate students to junior faculty positions and tenured appointments.

The ordinary realities comprise the usual pressures and threats; the final danger in a liberal society is unemployment: denial of tenure or unrenewed contract. In a tight market this might spell the end of an academic career. The years of academic plenty were long enough to attract droves of would-be professors; they were brief enough to ensure that all saw the "No Vacancy" sign. Professionalization proceeded under the threat of unemployment. The lessons of the near and far past, from McCarthyism to the first stone thrown at the first outsider, were clear to anyone: blend in; use the time alotted to establish scholarly credentials; hide in the mainstream.

Nor does it take much to intimidate professors; news travels fast and well. All know cases of teachers forced out, not because they were imperfect professionals but because they were something more: public intellectuals and radicals. Inevitably the cases reported in the news are those that take place in the elite and Ivy League schools; and simply by virtue of the publicity they are often "happily" resolved.

For instance, Paul Starr (1949–), a young sociologist at Harvard University, several years ago published *The Social Transformation of American Medicine*, to what *The New York Times* called "extraordinary praise." In 1984 Starr received the first Pulitzer Prize ever awarded to a sociologist. His future at Harvard seemed secure—until 1985, when he was dismissed, or, more exactly, denied tenure, effectively releasing him. Why?

It seems that Starr wrote for a larger public; hence his contribution to professional sociology was suspect. The (former) departmental chair hinted that Starr wrote too much journalism, straying outside professional sociology. "If I want to be a free-lance journalist," offered this professor, "then I should quit Harvard and go be a free-lance journalist." *The New York Times* noted that Starr "worked alone, took an interest in public issues. . . . He rarely wrote for an audience of professional sociologists. . . . The 'mainstream' behaves quite differently. . . . Its dialogues are academic, conducted in professional journals."[65]

Starr was hardly thrown to the wolves. By reason of the publicity and his achievement he instantly received a position at Princeton. Coincidently, Princeton recently let go a young historian, David Abraham (1946–), according to his detractors, for sloppy scholarship; according to his supporters, for his politics. Yet his case also was not typical, if only because it generated endless articles in newspapers and journals.[66] Yet what happened to Starr or Abraham in Ivy League schools, duly reported by the press, happens continuously, and goes unreported, elsewhere. It is necessary only to cross the Charles River from Harvard University to Boston University to find several cases that barely elicit any notice.

Henry Giroux (1943–), a young professor of education, identified with a critical and dissenting tradition. He published widely, with many articles and several books, one introduced by Paulo Freire, the Brazilian educator. Several deans and appropriate committees unanimously recommended him for tenure. The final decision, however, rested with the university president, John Silber, a conservative little known for his devotion to civil rights. He is quoted as saying, "It would be a pleasure to rid Boston University of Henry Giroux." He appointed Nathan Glazer, the neoconservative, to an ad hoc committee to review all the other committees and recommendations. Glazer penned a savage political attack on Giroux, suggesting that he belonged to a political "sect" and had no place in higher education. Although he was outvoted (two to one) in the ad hoc committee, Silber accepted Glazer's recommendations and discharged Giroux.[67]

No one noticed or reported this—and Boston University is a major university in a major city. Dismissals with political overtones at Harvard or Princeton may make the news; something similar at Boston University might elicit some passing comments. But what happens when a young professor is sent packing for political reasons from Southwestern Oklahoma State University in Weatherford, Oklahoma, or even well-known universities outside the usual news belts, such as Washington University in St. Louis? Few outside the local community will know or care.

Paul Piccone (1940–)—to summarize one case of academic life outside the limelight—translated, edited, and wrote on European social thought and Marxism; he published extensively not only in the journal he edited, *Telos*, but elsewhere; his essays, often anthologized, appeared in six languages. He was a veritable dynamo of a scholar and editor; he wrote a prize-winning book on Italian Marxism, which was published by the University of California Press. He came up for tenure at Washington University in St. Louis with enthusiastic support from a wide spectrum of scholars, including Daniel Bell ("I would unhesitatingly recommend Mr. Piccone for promotion and tenure. . . . [He] has been in the forefront of a necessary effort to introduce a larger philosophical dimension in the thinking of American sociology"), Herbert Marcuse (". . . Professor Piccone's work has been of the greatest significance"), Jürgen Habermas (". . . one of the most influential among those philosophers who attempt to develop a social theory. . . . I highly respect the work and the inspiring influence of Paul Piccone").[68]

His department evaluated the record and voted unamiously to recommend Piccone for tenure, noting "he is one of the most eminent figures in his field of specialization and has both a nationwide and a worldwide reputation . . . an especially effective scholar and researcher . . . his publications . . . in many cases [are] brilliant. . . . Washington University is indeed fortunate to have a person of such high intellectual calibre and whose reputation is outstanding."[69]

Washington University decided that it was not fortunate to have such a person. Piccone was turned down for tenure; he was turned down on the appeal and on the appeal of the appeal. In the face of his record and recommendations, the administration decided that Piccone had wandered too far from the mainstream; his contribution, stated a dean who reviewed the matter, "bears a problematic relation to the main currents of development in the social sciences," as if the main currents were the only currents. In other words, swim with us or get out. Piccone never found another regular post. None of this, of course, ever caused a moment's concern elsewhere.[70]

The situation is worse at community colleges, where the tradition of academic freedom hardly exists.[71] Moreover, in all of higher learning the cases that provoke some attention are necessarily those involving tenure, where committees and administrators meet and write up recommendations. Yet increasing numbers of academics, perhaps as many as a third of the nation's faculty, are not employed in 'tenure-track' positions; they teach part-time or on single (renewable or unrenewable) year contracts. To let these people go requires no committee reports or recommendations; they are dismissed unless rehired. Hence they are particularly vulnerable to pressures of professionalization; a half-step off the beaten path and they are applying for unemployment benefits (for which they are frequently not eligible).[72]

Sociologists and more sober conservatives concede that left-wing professors are less left-wing than they are professors. The rapid expansion of the universities, notes a sociologist, meant that many younger professors came out of the sixties student movements, a situation that might have led to crisis and generational conflict. No need to fret, however; it is already clear that "the normal politics of the academic profession, which is by and large supportive of established institutions, has reasserted itself."[73]

This was a conclusion some conservatives had already reached. *Radicals in the University*, a study published by the Hoover Institution, the conservative think tank, allows that since radicals captured the Modern Language Association (MLA) in 1968, nothing has changed. "In retrospect, the spectacular 1968 successes of the radicals have proven to be ephemeral. MLA is little different from what it was before 1968."[74] A conservative who wandered into the American Philosophical Association convention was pleasantly surprised: radicals had made hardly any impression.[75]

CHAPTER 6

───

*The New Left on
Campus II: The Long
March Through
the Institutions*

I

WHEN THEY ENTERED the universities, last generation intellectuals sometimes reflected with nostalgia on the demise of
bohemian and independent thinkers—their own past. Even as
professors, this generation retained its commitment to a larger
public. The New Left sprang into life around and against universities; its revulsion seemed visceral. Yet New Left intellectuals
became professors who neither looked backward nor sideways;
they kept their eyes on professional journals, monographs, and
conferences. Perhaps because their lives had unfolded almost entirely on campuses they were unable or unwilling to challenge
academic imperatives.

Younger professors, however, did not accept passively the academic disciplines they found. By establishing a credible body of radical, feminist, Marxist, or neo-Marxist scholarship, they assailed the venerable, sometimes almost official, interpretations dominant in their fields. The extent of this literature, the outpouring of left academics, is extraordinary, without precedent in American letters. In several areas the accomplishments of New Left intellectuals are irrevocable.

Yet it is also extraordinary for another reason; it is largely technical, unreadable and—except by specialists—unread. While New Left intellectuals obtain secure positions in central institutions, the deepest irony marks their achievement. Their scholarship looks more and more like the work it sought to subvert. A great surprise of the last twenty-five years is both the appearance of New Left professors and their virtual disappearance. In the end it was not the New Left intellectuals who invaded the universities but the reverse: the academic idiom, concepts, and concerns occupied, and finally preoccupied, young left intellectuals.

"Professors Woods, Perry, and Hocking are moderately talented and enterprising young men with whom philosophy is merely a means for getting on in the world," declared Professor E. B. Holt of several younger teachers in his department. "I do not respect them; I will not cooperate with them; and I am happy to be in a position now to wipe out the stigma of being even nominally one of their 'colleagues.' " With this statement Holt in 1918 resigned from Harvard University and moved to an island off the Maine coast.[1]

The sworn enemies and bitter critics long produced by academic life, however, cannot simply be dismissed as failed or rejected scholars. Max Weber, very much a successful professor, once suggested that all prospective academics should answer the following question: "Do you in all conscience believe that you can stand seeing mediocrity after mediocrity, year after year, climb beyond you, without becoming embittered and without coming to grief?" He added, "I have found that only a few men could endure this situation."[2]

The two most savage attacks on American university life are steeped in the muckraking of the early part of the century. Both Thorstein Veblen's *The Higher Learning in America* (1918) and Upton Sinclair's *The Goose-Step* (1923) denounced the heavy hand of business stifling universities. Chapters with titles such as "The University of Standard Oil" (University of Chicago) and "The University of the Steel Trust" (University of Pittsburgh) composed Sinclair's book. Yet a cataloging of corporate control and miscontrol did not exhaust their efforts; both Sinclair and Veblen addressed the effects on teachers and research.

Sinclair recalled his experience as a student at Columbia. "It was a peculiar thing, which I observed as time went on—every single man who had anything worth-while of any sort to teach me was forced out of Columbia University in some manner or other. The ones that stayed were the dull ones, or the worldly and cunning ones."[3]

Distempered critics, commented Veblen, the distempered critic, charge that social scientists are restrained in their research by conservative controls. Not so. Professors are given complete freedom of research and allowed "the fullest expression to any conclusions or convictions to which their inquiries may carry them." No external barriers restrict the professor. However, "their intellectual horizon is bounded by the same limits of commonplace insight and preconceptions" as their conservative overseers. For academic success "a large and aggressive mediocrity is the prime qualification."[4]

H. L. Mencken's scathing attacks on academics stem from the

same period. He presented his biases: "All my instincts are on the side of the professors. I esteem a man who devotes himself to a subject with hard diligence. . . . I am naturally monkish." However, investigation did not yield a flattering picture. The professor, menaced from above and below, is "almost invariably inclined to seek his own security in a mellifluous inanity—that is, far from being a courageous spokesman of ideas and an apostle of their free dissemination . . . he comes close to being the most prudent and skittish of all men." The behavior of professors during World War I is his proof.

> They constituted themselves, not a restraining influence upon the mob run wild, but the loudest spokesmen of its worst imbecilities. They fed it with bogus history, bogus philosophy, bogus idealism, bogus heroics. . . . I accumulated, in those great days, for the instruction and horror of posterity, a very large collection of academic arguments, expositions and pronunciamentos. . . . Its contents range from solemn hymns of hate . . . official donkeyisms . . . down to childish harangues.[5]

After Veblen and Mencken, corrosive critiques of the academy abate—until C. Wright Mills. If Mills prized intellectuals, he doubted whether universities could protect or nurture dissenters. On the eve of their expansion, Mills characterized universities as "still the freest of places in which to work." Nevertheless, "the professor, after all, is legally an employee, subject to all that this fact involves." The institutions "naturally select" pliable individuals, who are influenced "how, when and upon what they will work and write." Not blacklists, secret police, and arrest but insecurity threatens academic intellectuals.

> The deepest problem of freedom for teachers is not the occasional ousting of a professor, but a vague general fear—sometimes politely known as "discretion," "good taste," or "balanced judgment." It is a fear which

leads to self-intimidation. . . . The real restraints are not so much external prohibitions as control of the insurgent by the agreements of academic gentlemen.[6]

Recent analyses of academic life—more sociological and statistical—lack the verve of Veblen or Mills. Yet the picture they present is also sobering. They do not consider the "occasional ousting" of a professor or the role of big business; rather, they assess the imperatives of employment and advancement in the academic world. To succeed neither brilliance nor public contribution count, since both are viewed with suspicion—signs of a nonprofessional bent—but conformity and "contacts," connections with reputable institutions or people.

One survey of American professors dryly states that initially "it is much more the prestige of one's terminal degree and one's graduate sponsor than one's scholarly productivity which will lead to a good academic appointment." Later professional achievement, however, does not correct but reinforces this imbalance; early success ensures future success. "Once having secured the right initial appointment, which is more a function of prestige than demonstrated competence . . . subsequent appointments are determined by the prestige of that first appointment." University success, Martin Finkelstein concludes, summarizing studies of academic careers, depends more on "the prestige and visibility afforded by institutional affiliation" or "the prominence and power of contacts" or "the prestige of one's doctoral institution" than on "either the quality or the number of one's scholarly publications."[7]

Lionel S. Lewis's research confirms that the original doctoral institution—where one went to graduate school—constitutes the decisive ingredient for academic success. "Entree into any but the most marginal departments is indeed restricted for those who would hope to find a position solely on the basis of their teaching ability or research accomplishments."[8]

Lewis managed to obtain secret documents of academic success—letters of recommendation solicited by applicants for faculty slots. From these letters, he learned that interpersonal skill and charm outweighed scholarship, even intelligence. "After reading well over three thousand letters of recommendation . . . from a number of disciplines . . . it would not be overstating the case to say that, on the whole, academics are obsessed by the desire to be surrounded by individuals marked by charm, a conforming personality and skills in interaction." For the professors, integrity, genius, or productivity took a back seat, and often no seat, to collegiality, the ability to fit in. Universities that might seem to be "the last sanctuary for individual initiative in a society dominated by corporate psychology," Lewis closes, have become "havens" for "patronage, committee decisions, conviviality, callousness and provincialism."[9]

In plain English, these studies suggest that where one went to school and whom one knows, not what one does, are critical. Not quality of work but social relations permeate academic success. Of course, this can be exaggerated: a deadbeat graduate of Harvard University may fare no better than one of Middle Tennessee State University. There are no guarantees or automatic awards; yet an examination of academic careers indicates a decisive tilt toward the well connected. The professor at Black Hills State College in Spearfish, South Dakota, who received his doctorate from the University of South Dakota and who has published a fine book with the University of Nebraska Press, will be professionally invisible. The professor at Princeton University, who received a doctorate from Yale and published a dissertation with MIT Press, will be an esteemed expert, regularly cited, invited, and funded.

Even the latest research invention, footnote citation "indexes," encourages deferential and toothless scholarship. *The Social Science Citation Index,* a massive volume appearing three times a year, draws from thousands of journals the footnote references to particular articles and books. By looking up a specific author, say C. Wright Mills or Daniel Bell, one finds a list of the journal articles where Mills or Bell has been cited. In principle this allows a researcher to find material where Mills or Bell, or related matters, are discussed—or at least footnoted.

However, this index is increasingly touted as a scientific method for identifying scholars who have impact in their field; it is also being used as a guide for promotion and awards. Presumably the more references to a professor, the greater the stature. Many citations to an individual's work indicates he or she is important; conversely few or no references implies someone is unknown and irrelevant. "If citation indexing becomes a basis for promotion and tenure, for grants and fellowships," comments Jon Wiener, "the implications for one's own footnotes are clear. In the marketplace of ideas, the footnote is the unit of currency. . . . One should definitely footnote friends . . . and do what is possible to see that they footnote you in return. . . ."[10]

Like any quantitative study of reputation, the index is circular. It measures not the quality of work but clout and connections. If used to evaluate careers, however, the lessons for the striving professor are clear: cast a wide net, establish as many mutual relations as possible, do not isolate yourself from the mainstream. It pays not simply to footnote but to design research to mesh smoothly with the contributions of others; they refer to you as you refer to them. Everyone prospers from the saccharine scholarship.

II

THE STUDY of professions is itself an occupation; but inquiries into academic professionalization—salaries, class backgrounds, ethnic and sexual composition, status—fail to gauge the essential cultural dimension. It is frequently missed or understated: professionalization leads to privatization or depoliticization, a withdrawal of intellectual energy from a larger domain to a narrower discipline. Leftists who entered the university hardly invented this process, but they accepted, even accelerated it. Marxism itself has not been immune; in recent years it has become a professional "field" plowed by specialists.

It is possible only to suggest with the broadest strokes how several disciplines have succumbed to professionalization. Mills, again, is instructive, since his first work charted the retreat of American philosophy to campus enclaves. His doctoral dissertation examined the "professionalization of philosophy" since the Civil War, the migration of philosophy into universities. In the twentieth century full-time philosophy professors with their own organizations and journals replaced the lawyers, librarians, and scientists, the "relatively free intelligentsia," who once constituted American philosophy. Mills even offered some figures on the "decline" of philosophy, its shrinking presence in the public arena. He surveyed the number of articles on philosophy in general magazines and found that as the professional journals proliferated, the "volume of attention" in the general media diminished.[11] Philosophers increasingly preferred to address each other.

Although Mills cast some doubts about Dewey's accomplishments, he prized the pragmatist as the last public philosopher, a thinker whose devotion to a democratic audience and "liberal and free" knowledge set him against the professional drift.[12] This may still characterize Dewey's place in philosophy. Of course, Dewey is not forgotten. Yet his status in philosophy departments may be like Freud's in psychology, dispatched in an introductory lecture as an unscientific, although honorable, precursor.

Throughout his long and productive life, Dewey always criticized academic philosophy. He presented his ideas in and for the public; he was a publicist, who lamented philosophical scholasticism. "The monastic cell has become a professional lecture hall; an endless mass of 'authorities' have taken the place of Aristotle," he wrote in one of his earliest essays. "*Jahresberichte*, monographs, journals without end occupy the void. . . . If the older Scholastic spent his laborious time in erasing the writing from old manuscripts . . . the new Scholastic . . . criticizes the criticisms with which some other Scholastic has criticized other criticisms. . . ."[13]

His *Reconstruction in Philosophy* decried the philosophic "withdrawal from the present scene." For Dewey "the distinctive office, problems and subject matter of philosophy grow out of stresses and strains in the community life." To this community life philosophy must return "to regain the vitality it is losing."[14] These words come from Dewey's 1948 new introduction to his 1920 text. They imply a consistent vision; they also imply that twentieth-century philosophy heeded Dewey little.

From the beginning of his career Dewey sought a public. As a young instructor, he tried to launch *Thought News*, a cross between leaflet and journal that planned to inject philosophy into the daily world. This "newspaper" promised not to discuss "philosophic ideas per se but . . . [to] treat questions of science, letters, state, school and church as parts of the one moving life of man and hence common interest, and not relegate them to separate documents of merely technical interest."[15] As an established professor he wrote regularly for *The New Republic* and participated in a thousand causes and committees alerting the public to one evil or another. One example: at the age of seventy-eight(!), Dewey chaired the Commission of Inquiry in Mexico City investigating the Soviet charges against Trotsky.[16]

Yet Dewey was not an exception; he almost represented a philosophical generation. Bruce Kuklick, in his book on Harvard University philosophy, *The Rise of American Philosophy* (which does not treat Dewey, who taught in Chicago and New York), concludes that since William James and George Santayana, Harvard professors have surrendered their public. Kuklick closes his account reflecting on the "triumph of Professionalism." The philosophy professors who emerged after World War II "were unaware that American philosophy was once important outside the university; and if they were aware, they were contemptuous of the fuzziness, lack of clarity and woolly-mindness of their predecessors. . . . From its pre-eminent nineteenth-century role as the guide of life, mid-twentieth-century Harvard philosophy reflected the irrelevance of speculation to life." The new philosophers "spend their time in administration, in committee work, placing graduate students, in organizing conferences, and in running journals. When narrow professionals turned to their scholarship, they thought of their work as a game . . . a way, not of confronting the problem of existence, but of avoiding it."[17]

This is the conclusion of Kuklick, a historian and outsider to philosophy; but in recent years specialists themselves have begun to raise cautious alarms about their own disciplines. They ask whether professionalization or privatization has proceeded too far; whether it might be necessary to reclaim a public culture. In philosophy, literature, economics, political science, and international studies, books and articles have questioned the cost of professionalization. Works, such as William M. Sullivan's *Reconstructing Public Philosophy*, Gerald Graff's *Literature Against Itself*, David M. Ricci's *The Tragedy of Political Science*, challenge entire fields, often indicting an underlying professionalization.

For the philosophical effort, John Dewey has loomed large, at least for William M. Sullivan, who has sought to reinvigorate a public philosophy. "Since the death of John Dewey ... no professional American philosopher has played a major role in American cultural and political life outside specialized circles," writes Sullivan.[18] He calls for a public philosophy that is "closely tied to the mores, the practical understandings of everyday life. If it is to maintain its authenticity and power to infuse the public acts of individuals with significance, it can neither be an intellectually detached theory about politics nor a mere set of slogans."[19]

A similar note is struck by John E. Smith in *The Spirit of American Philosophy*. Smith, who also draws upon Dewey, regrets that American philosophy has become "completely an academic affair." The wholesale victory of British analytic philosophy has reduced philosophy to "an internal dialogue among professionals." Most philosophers have abandoned links to wider issues, neglecting history, literature, religion, and art. "The decline of philosophy as an influential voice" in cultural life might be reversed, he hopes, if it reappropriates a broader conception of experience and reason.[20]

Richard J. Bernstein, author of a book on John Dewey, records the "growing uneasiness in philosophy," adding that this salutary unrest is partially sustained by a renewed appreciation of Dewey. "It is not accidental that a philosopher like Richard Rorty, who has brilliantly criticized much of the sterility and irrelevance of recent philosophy, cites Dewey," calling for "a return to the spirit of Dewey's pragmatism."[21]

It is likely that these appeals will have little impact, since philosophy has proved almost immune to reform. Of course, the self-examination of every discipline proceeds at its own speed. The philosophic self-scrutiny, however, may well be the weakest, because American philosophy has promoted a technical expertise that repels critical thinking; its fetish of logic and language has barred all but a few who might rethink philosophy, an endeavor sometimes pursued by colleagues in political science, sociology, or history.

As in any discipline, notes of reform and self-criticism can be glimpsed—sometimes in the least promising places.[22] Nevertheless, philosophy seems the most routinized of the humanities, the least accessible to change. For this reason, unlike sociology or literature or history, dissenting journals in philosophy have had short lives and a feeble impact. The fate of one philosophic magazine, *Telos*, may be illustrative. Graduate students in the philosophy department at the State University of New York at Buffalo founded *Telos* in 1967. Dissatisfied with the dismissal of European philosophy by their professors, they organized their own seminar on Jean-Paul Sartre, after which they decided to launch a new journal.

In the words of the editor, Paul Piccone, they proposed to rescue philosophy from "triviality and meaninglessness."[23] The first issues set the tone for what became regular *Telos* features: long, dense articles introducing and analyzing little-known Continental philosophers, usually with a phenomenological bent, such as Enzo Paci and Karel Kosik. By the third and fourth issues, *Telos* moved on to evaluating French structuralism, Antonio Gramsci, Herbert Marcuse, and Georg Lukács (whose main work was still unavailable in English). "It is now recognized," states one survey of its history, "that *Telos* has been one of the most important vehicles for making continental Marxism available to English-speaking readers."[24]

After almost twenty years *Telos* still publishes and evaluates European philosophical and social thought. What has its impact been on American philosophy? In a word: nil. The stony ground of professional philosophy proved untillable. This is reflected in *Telos*'s own self-identification. Originally called "the official publication of the Graduate Philosophy Association of the State University of New York at Buffalo," it later redubbed itself "a philosophical journal *definitely outside* the mainstream of American philosophical thought." This was an understatment, and eventually the journal abandoned reference to philosophy; it has since called itself, among other things, "an international interdisciplinary quarterly" and, most recently, "a quarterly of critical thought."

The distancing from professional philosophy was not simply a theoretical matter. Almost none of the young philosophers who established *Telos* ever obtained academic posts in philosophy. The journal itself located no philosophy department willing to sponsor it. For a while a sociology department (at Washington University) tolerated *Telos*, but some seventy thick issues since its founding, *Telos* (and its long-time editor, Paul Piccone) has been associated with no department or university. Moreover, among its large group of editorial advisers—more than twenty-five—only two or three hold positions in philosophy; most teach in political science, sociology, history, or literature departments.

To be sure, *Telos* may represent a theoretical mode no more lucid or public than the philosophy it could not subvert. Nevertheless, its failure to establish even a minimal presence in philosophy suggests that the profession is armed against critical inquiry. When a discipline sustains dissenting thinkers or journals, it testifies to a willingness to reconsider its idiom and tasks and even to dream of reclaiming a public.

The self-scrutiny has been more promising in other disciplines, such as literature or international studies, where the self-destruction has not been so complete. International studies, almost unknown as an academic discipline before World War II, presents a classic example of professionalization and its costs. When the United States government and private foundations rediscovered the world, especially during and after the war, they threw money at universities to study it. Robert A. McCaughey, in a recent book on international studies, subtitled *A Chapter in the Enclosure of American Learning*, argues that the founding and funding of international studies programs led to the transfer of knowledge and interest "from the American intellectual community at large to the universities"—with dubious results.[25]

In the universities, he tells us, learning succumbed to the usual realities. For the young academic to write for a general audience or periodical was "to risk being thought insufficiently serious . . . aspiring international studies junior faculty gained greater stature—and more likely access to tenure—for publishing articles in either their area or their disciplinary journals." These pressures took a toll; the discipline turned inward. The prosperous new field of international studies, McCaughey concludes, failed to enrich public cultural life, rather it became "primarily and almost exclusively" an academic fiefdom.[26]

While eschewing sharp judgments, McCaughey indicates that the international studies scholars were more subservient to foundations and government than earlier independent advisers; the academic experts rarely chanced bucking official policy. During the height of the Vietnam War protests, when it might be supposed that they had something to contribute, international studies scholars were "conspicuous" by their absence.[27] Of course, this fact is open to various interpretations. Were these scholars absent because their fearless sifting of the truth led them to support the American strategy? Or did they suspect they endangered future grants and advancement by openly questioning United States policies?

Another assessment suggests that many "qualified experts" questioned the government in the "learned" literature but did not step forward as public opponents. Why? Because they could not afford to earn the disfavor of their colleagues, who were linked by inclination, money, and values to the administration. "The political scientist clearly risks his career when he takes a stand on a political matter."[28]

McCaughey does not pursue a generational angle, but others have noted a fateful progression, where younger and more docile academic experts supplant older independent advisors in foreign affairs and service. The so-called China Hands, by virtue of family, birth, or business, knew about China and possessed the wherewithal to challenge the official position on Chiang Kai-shek—and they paid for it by being dismissed or relegated to insignificant posts. More recent experts, the products of graduate schools and the elite institutes of international studies, know less and are less willing to question government decisions.

David Halberstam attributes some of the Vietnam debacle to the purge of the China Hands, and their replacement by Harvard intellectuals, "the best and the brightest," who knew Asia only through texts and monographs. John Paton Davies of the Foreign Service, who had lived in China, was finally drummed out of government in 1954, after undergoing nine security investigations. (He was cleared reluctantly fourteen years later.) Halberstam comments that Davies's exit marked for the United States "the end of one kind of reporting and expertise in Asia. The best had been destroyed and the new experts were different, lesser men. . . . The Americans who followed John Davies would be very different, they were determined to impose American versions and definitions of events upon Asian peoples. It became easier to be operational rather than reflective."[29]

Political science is a much broader and more diffuse domain than international studies, but recent appraisals by David M. Ricci in *The Tragedy of Political Science* and Raymond Seidelman and Edward J. Harpham in *Disenchanted Realists* detect advanced symptoms of the general ailment; political science has contracted into a dull self-contained professional pastime. Who are the important political scientists? Ricci asks. There seem to be none. He suggests that "the declining number of great thinkers and the growing prominence of universities" are related. Moreover, the eclipse of general intellectuals means that American citizens now rely on the professionals for information. Yet the work of these specialists reflects their own university situations, not the needs of the public.[30]

Seidelman and Harpham trace the rise and fragmentation of professional political science, concluding that its hopes, when the discipline was founded, to fuse knowlege with an informed citizenry, have receded.

Both the faith and the focus guiding the American science of politics has given way to hyperspecialization, resulting in the neglect of major political issues and questions. . . . Simultaneously, the outside audience of political science has narrowed and sometimes even disappeared. . . . The American science of politics formed and grew with the expectation and hope of winning the attention and deference of a mass public and enlightened, progressive elites . . . [but] political science is now an institution, not a crusade.[31]

With different material Ricci makes a similar argument. The American Political Science Association has expanded, but meetings and publications are "less interesting and intelligible to nonacademic generalists." The accumulation of jargon in the field registers not the needs of truth but academic empire-building, where professors can lord over microfields. The vocabulary, which political science shares with sociology and international studies, reduces human and social conflict to diagrams and computer printouts; these disciplines view society as an engineering problem.

A standard textbook, writes Ricci, lists traditional words and recommends that political scientists replace them with a professional idiom.

Among the old would be words like "absolutism," "justice," "nation," "patriotic," "rights," "society," and "tyranny." Among the new would be "attitude," "conflict," "cross-pressure," "game," "interaction," "pluralism," "socialization," and "valuation." . . . Notwithstanding formal justifications, the primary reason . . . for ceaselessly creating new terminology in political science has less to do with the substance of science than with the form of organized enterprise.[32]

The pressures of careers and publishing intensify the parceling of knowledge. Insofar as the quantity of publications, not the quality (which ranked fifth in one study), counts—and can be counted—the tendency is to "constantly refashion the scope of political science into smaller and smaller realms of expertise." As the intellectual yards subdivide, the number of competitors also dwindles, making it easier to set oneself up as an expert. Within a six-year period the profession officially acknowledged thirty-three new subfields. Articles which were once readable, at least interesting to others, have become utterly closed and enclosed.[33]

Even the subjects broached reflect caution and careers. Political scientists regularly seem to ignore the most pressing issues. For instance within a ten-year period (1959–69), the three leading political science journals published but one article on Vietnam (out of 924 pieces!). During this same period, the main journal, *American Political Science Review*, published a single study on poverty and three on urban crises. Insofar as young political scientists need research grants and recommendations for support—and the more recommendations the better—bland topics and technocratic approaches minimize opposition. To portray political scientists as searching for truth might get a few laughs; most of them are looking for grants.[34]

Sociology hardly seems better. More than fifteen years ago Alvin Gouldner published a free-wheeling critical appraisal of sociology, *The Coming Crisis of Western Sociology*. His hope that academic and Marxist sociology would transform each other has ironically come true, although not as he wished; it is more and more difficult to tell them apart. However, his assault on a sociological functionalism that embraced a technical vocabulary depreciating violence, power, and inequality as social issues still rings true. In Talcott Parson's 800-page sociological tome, *The Structure of Social Action*, four pages are devoted to violence.[35]

Gouldner argued that the lives of sociologists themselves affected their discipline. Some, wrote Gouldner, are "gentlemen professors" and "gentlemen farmers."

Most live suburban existences; not a few have summer homes; many do extensive travelling. . . . The daily texture of the sociologist's life integrates him into the world as it is. . . . It is a world in which the sociologist has moved onward and upward. . . . Their own personal experience of success suffuses with congenial sentiment their conception of society within which this happened.[36]

Gouldner even charged that Parson's functionalism dominated the profession, not because of its theoretical superiority; rather, Parson's association with Harvard bestowed on his system an automatic prestige. As expanding sociology departments hired Harvard graduates, Parson's theories were spread far and wide.[37]

Things have changed since Gouldner's book; but not much. Even Parsonian theory, for some years hardly visible, may be returning.[38] Recently a sociologist surveyed the official sociological journal, *American Sociological Review*, over a forty-five-year period (1936–82). Patricia Wilner expected to find the sociologists addressing critical political and social events—the cold war, McCarthyism, protest movements; she initially wondered how she would classify all these articles. But she found very few, for less than 5.1 percent of the 2,559 articles addressed such issues. During this period of massive social and political dislocation, the dynamics of mate selection proved irresistible to sociologists—it was their favorite topic. Moreover, contributions by one author have rapidly declined, supplanted by articles by teams and groups. "Issues filled by single authors nose-dived from 69.4 percent to 2.4 percent! This remarkable change indicates a move from 'entrepreneurial' to 'corporate' research, and the rise of funded research."[39]

What is to be done? For political science, Ricci offers a strategy, which unfortunately testifies to the power of the profession. He knows that any young academic who frontally challenges the discipline will be shown the door. "At the outset of one's teaching career," he counsels, "it is advisable to display unexceptional qualities of professional competence, expressing sound opinions and publishing unremarkable writings. This tactic will help young scholars to gain tenure." Once the academic is established, "boldness becomes more feasible"; it might even be possible to write up "some" thoughts in "plain English."[40] Unfortunately, Ricci does not realize, or has forgotten, that his strategy smacks of age-old advice—and suffers from the age-old failing: nothing changes. When finally the requisite rank and security have been attained, the talent, even the desire, for bold thinking has long since atrophied.

Seidelman and Harpham partly respond to Ricci's suggestion. In a contracting academic market, the old wisdom of "publish or perish" no longer suffices.

Today it is entirely possible to publish *and* perish if the publishing is not done in the right journals with the right publishers and to universally laudatory reviews. This is hardly a system designed to welcome pariahs. . . . By the time the lucky point-scorer receives the hard-won prize of tenure at a major institution, who could—or would—rock the boat?[41]

The field of economics displays similar features. In "The Poverty of Economics," Robert Kuttner, an independent economist, charges that the profession suffers from conformity and irrelevance. Economists increasingly employ complex mathematical models not simply because they might illuminate reality but because they facilitate publishing; the models allow economists to write articles without amassing any new information. He reminds us that Wassily Leontief (1906–), one of the profession's most celebrated mathematicians and a Nobel Prize winner, has often decried the profession's cult of mathematized formula building.[42]

Leontief complained in a 1970 address to economists that "the mathematical-model-building industry has grown into one of the most prestigious, possibly the most prestigious branch of economics." Unfortunately, "uncritical enthusiasm for mathematical formulation tends often to conceal the ephemeral content of the argument." Most of these models "are relegated to the stockpile" after publication because they have no application or validity; others fall out of favor only because a newer and more sophisticated version is served up. Moreover, this state of affairs seems to be self-perpetuating; younger economists have received the message. They "advance their careers by building more and more complicated mathematical models." Leontieff called for economists to return not only to empirical inquiry but also to the "wider public" they had abandoned.[43]

More recently, Leontief examined the profession's leading journal, *The American Economic Review*, over an eight-year period (1972-76; 1977-81) and found that most articles employed mathematical models without any data; only 1 percent employed direct information generated by the author. "Year after year economic theorists continue to produce scores of mathematical models . . . and econometricians fit algebraic functions of all possible shapes to essentially the same sets of data." Neither advances the understanding of the "structure and operation of a real economic system." The situation, Leontief concluded, seems permanent as long as senior economists "continue to exercise tight control over the training, promotion, and research activities of their younger faculty members."[44] According to Kuttner, Leontief has "so despaired of his profession that he [has] ceased publishing in economic journals."[45]

In his survey of the profession, Kuttner detects a generational rhythm; the only economists who still confront the economic reality lucidly are aging or retired. "A generation ago economics was far more committed to observation, disputation and its own intellectual history. The lions of the mid-century had lived through depression and war, had watched real economic institutions totter, had worked in economic agencies. . . . Most of them are now gone." What Kuttner calls "the great idiosyncratic economists of the last generation," including John Kenneth Galbraith (1908-) and Albert Hirschman (1915-), "disseminated their work to a broad audience but left few spores within the profession." (One might add Robert Heilbroner [1919-] and Robert

Lekachman [1920–] to this list.) These heretics agreed that "if they were young assistant professors attempting to practice their brand of economics today, they would not get tenure." The orthodoxy is reinforced "by the sociology of the profession, by the politics of who gets published or promoted and whose research gets funded."[46]

From deep within the profession, a gentle criticism, which is also a self-criticism, has recently emerged. Donald N. McCloskey, long associated with the University of Chicago "school" of economics, judges that Anglo-American economics "notwithstanding its gleams of steely brilliance" has yielded "by now many crippled economists," who are "bored by history," "ignorant of their civilization," "thoughtless in their ethics, and unreflective in method."[47]

McCloskey also examined the contributions to *The American Economic Review* and discovered that of 159 full-length papers during the period 1981–83 "only 6 used words alone." The obsessive use of statistics, diagrams, and "explicit simulation" has damaged the field. Contributions are "no longer even superficially accessible to lay people; and young economists overvalue a narrow, and occasionally silly, ingenuity of technique." For McCloskey, the crusading "scientism, behaviorism, operationalism, positive economics"—the fetish of science generally—has "outlived its usefulness."[48]

While he does not explain why economists joined this crusade, McCloskey alludes to a peculiar vulnerability of New York intellectuals to the cult of science. He sifts through *Railroads and American Economic Growth* (1964), a book which established the reputation of Robert W. Fogel, whom he calls "the Napoleon of the cliometric revolution in economic history."[49] Fogel inaugurated a scientific approach to economic history that has been widely imitated.

Born in the Bronx, Fogel (1926–) came to economics late, after a youth devoted to radical politics. An uncertain position in an uncertain discipline—"a distinctly right-wing and *goyisch* field," according to McCloskey—prompted his scientistic rhetoric and approach.

The necessities of academic politics required it. There were and are no departments of economic history in North America. . . . Economic history in 1964 was on the defensive in American departments of economics, dismissed as antique by the new technocrats strutting about the camp in their gleaming armor. . . . It was essential that young economic historians prove themselves technically able. . . . Fogel repeatedly displays the brightness of his economic armory.[50]

Fogel's work since his railroad book amply illustrates the costs of professionalization; he continues militantly to uphold what he calls "scientific" history (against "traditional") history. In Fogel's vision "scientists" are hard-working researchers with laboratory coats who use sophisticated statistics; traditional historians are dreamers, poets—the literati. The findings and reports of the scientific economists are not even intended to be read by the unwashed. "The majority of cliometricians," Fogel tells us, believe that the "proper audience" for their works are "not those who read history for pleasure"—the disdain here is palpable—"but those who are capable of assessing and validating the fruits of scientific labors—not a broad public, but a narrow group of highly trained specialists."[51]

Massive team efforts, according to Fogel, are the "hallmark" of cliometric history. "One recent paper," he announces proudly, "involved no fewer than ten authors." Since they treasure "facts and behavioral regularities," personal "voice" is considered a "failing." Fogel and his specialists gather in institutes dreaming of new colonies. He lists past victories. "The cliometric approach developed most rapidly in economic history and has been the predominant form of research in this field. . . . The majority of the articles published in the main economic history journals of the United States," Fogel crows, "are now quite mathematical, and cliometricians predominate in the leadership of the Economic History Association."[52]

Although Fogel enjoys professional success, the ability of his numbers to illuminate the historical reality remains questionable. In 1974 Fogel, with Stanley L. Engerman (1936–), published *Time on the Cross: The Economics of American Negro Slavery*, a two-volume work, which boasted that its scientific and quantitative approach put slave history on a new basis. Yet its deficiencies index the ills that haunt the fetish of methods: figures and methods mask the reality itself. "Scientific" history turns into science fiction.

At least in part, *Time on the Cross* sought to establish that slave labor was more productive than scholars previously thought and that this productivity depended less on external punishments than on an inbred work ethic. Herbert G. Gutman, in his blistering attack, *Slavery and the Numbers Game*, found their evidence and approach woefully inadequate.[53] For instance, Fogel and Engerman examine the records of one plantation owner who over several years kept track of when he whipped his slaves. They make the requisite computations and conclude, "The record shows that over the course of two years a total of 160 whippings were administered, an average of 0.7 whippings per hand per year."[54] For Fogel and Engerman, this was almost scientific proof that slaves were not driven to work by punishments, since the whippings were too infrequent to be effective.

Gutman demonstrates that Fogel and Engerman miscalculated the number of slaves on the plantation; but even within their terms, he questions the significance of the figures—"0.7

whippings per hand per year." What does it mean? In fact, re-translated it means that "a slave—'on average'—was whipped every 4.56 days. Three slaves were whipped every two weeks." This suggests a more harrowing level of violence. Fogel and Engerman's flawed method, Gutman argues, risks obscuring the reality. "It is known, for example, that 'on average' 127 blacks were lynched every year between 1889 and 1899. How does one assess that average? Assume that 6 million blacks lived in the United States in 1889. . . . Is it useful to learn that 'the record shows an average of 0.0003 lynchings per black per year so that about 99.9997 percent of the blacks were not lynched in 1889?" For Gutman this significance of social violence cannot be deduced from averages.[55]

Gutman's intervention was characteristic and signals that some historians swim against the tide of professionalism. History has always attracted radicals and Marxists seeking to rediscover the untold history of a nation or labor or women or minorities. Those from the left, like Gutman, who entered the profession have remained loyal to this commitment in a double sense; they have wished not simply to reclaim the past but to reclaim it for the participants—for a public. For this reason, American historians writing on labor, slavery, the family, women, and the origins of the cold war have informed, even influenced public discussions. William A. Williams (1921–), Eugene Genovese (1930–), Howard Zinn (1922–), Christopher Lasch (1932–), and others have offered readable books—from *The Tragedy of American Diplomacy* (1959) to *The Culture of Narcissism* (1979)—that speak to public issues.

Herbert Gutman's own work is typical in that he sought to bring history out of the academy into the open air. The son of Jewish immigrants, Gutman (1928–85), who was active in left politics, attended Queens College and Columbia University before shifting for his doctoral work to the University of Wisconsin, Madison, traditionally a home of an independent left and labor studies.[56] Later he taught at Fairleigh Dickinson University in New Jersey and the University of Rochester, before returning to New York at City University.

Gutman's writings were less technical monographs than public interventions. His book, *The Black Family in Slavery and Freedom, 1750–1925*, was directly provoked, as he states in its first sentence, "by the bitter public and academic controversy surrounding Daniel P. Moynihan's *The Negro Family in America: The Case for National Action.*"[57] Gutman targeted the belief that the black family had been destroyed and disorganized by American society; he wanted to show that it contained remarkable resiliency and vitality. He also wanted to undercut the policy implications of the Moynihan report that the cause of black poverty lay with the black family and not, as Gutman believed, with structural unemployment and racism.[58]

Gutman, a pioneer in the "new" social history researching the ignored underside of history—the invisible workers, blacks and minorities—feared that this history might forget its public obligations; he warned against "the balkanizing thrust in the new social history." Too much history is "too narrowly classificatory, too narrowly statistical and behavioral. . . . The new social history suffers from a very limiting overspecialization."[59] Unhappy with this academization, Gutman launched a still ongoing enterprise to make history public, the American Social History Project, which is bringing out a popular two-volume history of American labor, *Who Built America?*, as well as a series of slide shows and films designed for a wide audience.[60]

Gutman's work is undeniably powerful and influential. Yet is it possible that it belongs to a cultural world almost abandoned?

Might Williams or Gutman or Lasch be "transitional" intellectuals with an obsolete commitment to a public outside the profession? Lasch, once a colleague of both Gutman and Genovese, remarked on the differences between his generation of historians and that of his teacher, Richard Hofstadter. His own generation had difficulty sharing Hofstadter's confident professionalism: "We find ourselves uncomfortable in academic life and often at odds with the profession and the university."[61] Yet perhaps this discomfort impelled them to find an audience outside the university. Ironically the New Left historians seem more settled into university slots, more satisfied with a campus audience. Although some of these historians—again partly inspired by Gutman— have very recently sought to "remedy" the "neglect of popular history and the general public,"[62] it is difficult to identify the successors to Williams or Gutman or Lasch.

Precisely this issue has been raised by a young historian. "Where are the young left historians?" asks Casey Blake (1956–), a professor at Reed College. "Busy in the tasks of academic advancement," he writes, "radical historians roughly between the ages of 25 and 35 have paid little attention in recent years to the larger issues. . . . Young left historians too often produce work that merely fills out previous theses or applies them to new social groups or geographical areas with rather predictable results."[63] If this is accurate—Blake exempts some feminist historians—then the future of radical history will be little different from that of other disciplines.

III

NOWHERE HAS the impact of the New Left on the university been as great as in Marxist thought. Twenty-five years ago Marxism was almost absent from campuses; today, subdivided into political science, sociology, history, literary theory, and other fields, it is taught at most major universities.

As in many American industries, imports dominate the Marxist academic market—for roughly the same reasons as with cars. Although the final product is sometimes assembled inside the United States, foreign Marxism seems snappier, better designed; it accelerates more easily. It is more finished and polished. Why stick with clunky American models? A recent survey of philosophic Marxism by an American professor contains chapters on Georg Lukács, Karl Korsch, Antonio Gramsci, Max Horkheimer, Jean-Paul Sartre, and Jürgen Habermas, but only passing references to any American contributors.[64]

In the larger area of Marxist studies, however, one American is frequently put forward as a candidate on a par with the Europeans. Fredric Jameson has been labeled the most original and influential young Marxist thinker today. It is "generally recognized," states the introduction to a volume devoted to him, that Jameson is "a—and perhaps the—leading Marxist critic of our time."[65] His books, from *Marxism and Form* (1971) to *The Political Unconscious* (1981), are fundamental reference points; and their author has attained the academic heights, having been courted by major universities—Yale; University of California, Santa Cruz; and Duke University, where he currently teaches. Few will contest that Jameson is a thinker of rare energy and commitment. Few could doubt, also, that his world is that of the university: its jargon, its problems, its crises. While the Marxist and radical critics of the past—Lewis Mumford, Malcolm Cowley—never deserted the public, Jameson never sought it; his writings are designed for seminars.

That Jameson's work has already spawned a sizable secondary literature illustrates the shift. No one was needed to guide a reader through Mumford or Wilson or Trilling for the simple reason they were their own best introductions; they wrote to be read. Within three years of the publication of Jameson's *The Political Unconscious*, however, a university press published a book to help the uninitiated understand it.[66] This book, *Jameson, Althusser, Marx: An Introduction to "The Political Unconscious,"* offers an unobstructed view of academic gamesmanship.

Out-of-touch professors are informed that Jameson's work assumes "a good deal of serious thinking that has gone on in recent years about narrative." They are also told that his ultimate aim is "the opening up of the individual text into that *hors texte* or unspoken (non-*dit*) ground of intolerable contradiction that it cannot acknowledge."[67] But what "it," or more exactly, our author, cannot acknowledge is that the real text is the advance and self-advance of careers.

The world is slithering toward nuclear disaster, global pollution, and starvation, but one Marxist critic writing on another brightly trades in Marxist academic futures. What does the market look like? Excellent for coming years, though the quality is not quite up to the Parisian standard. "We are . . . in the midst of an explosion in theory, and a number of younger theorists especially show signs of rapid development, but so far Jameson is the only one working in English who writes as the peer of the French poststructuralists."[68]

Jameson cannot be burdened with the sins of cultists; however, it is worth examining a fragment of Jameson's writing in which he tackles a public issue. In a recent essay, Jameson identifies architecture as a salient example of "postmodernism," a favorite topic of literary critics. For Jameson, postmodernism signifies the "effacement" of the frontier between high culture and so-called mass or commercial culture; it implies the emergence of new kinds of "texts." The postmodernists have broken with the elitism of earlier critics who distained popular culture. "The postmodernists have in fact been fascinated precisely by this whole 'degraded' landscape of schlock and kitsch, of TV series and *Reader's Digest* culture, of advertising and motels. . . ."[69]

From this angle Jameson examines various postmodernist "texts" including a "full-blown postmodern building" that offers "some striking lessons about the originality of postmodernist space." This building is the Bonaventure Hotel in Los Angeles, designed and developed by John Portman, who is also the architect of the Peachtree Plaza Hotel in Atlanta and the Renaissance Center in Detroit. Portman's signature has been the many-storied atrium, a sweeping interior space lined with balconies and boutiques and enhanced by open lobbies, reflecting pools, and waterfalls.

Glass elevators glide up through this shimmering space and, in the case of the Bonaventure, out, almost into the open, where Los Angeles spreads out below. Atop the main tower, which is equidistant from four identical cylinders containing the hotel rooms, revolves a circular bar. Even Portman's harshest critics concede that his frank devotion to profitable and popular buildings is refreshing. He does not suffer, noted an Italian critic, "from those complexes that torture the European intellectual."[70] Perhaps for this reason people seem to like his work—at least, out-of-town visitors are often brought by friends to ride the elevators.

What does Jameson make of this? He cannot sufficiently praise or describe the Bonaventure. He suggests that it transcends conventional terms, even conventional experience.

We are in the presence of something like a mutation in built space itself. . . . We . . . the human subjects who happen into this new space, have not kept pace with that evolution. . . . We do not yet possess the perceptual equipment to match this new hyperspace. . . . The newer architecture . . . stands as something like an imperative to grow new organs, to expand our sensorium and our body to some new, as yet unimaginable . . . dimensions.[71]

This excited introduction spurs Jameson on; in keeping with a postmodern ethos, the Bonaventure decisively rejects elitism. Unlike the classic modern buildings, which were imposing and distant, the Bonaventure is "inserted" into the city fabric. Its entrances exemplify this very different relation to the city. Sumptuous old hotels staged the "passageway from city street to the older interior." The buildings of the International Style were acts of "disruption."[72]

With the Bonaventure, however, the entrances are small, "lateral" and "rather backdoor affairs." "What I first want to suggest about these curiously unmarked ways-in is that they seem to have been imposed by some new category of closure governing the inner space of the hotel itself." To this new space corresponds "a new collective practice, a new mode in which individuals move and congregate . . . a new and historically original kind of hyper-crowd."[73]

Nor is this all. Again and again Jameson confesses that he is at a loss for words, since the postmodern "hyperspace" of the Bonaventure transcends individual perception and cognition. However, his enthusiasm for its elevators and escalators, which are "dialectical opposites," calls forth some additional thoughts. They illustrate something of the narrative form, where visitors are led through various paths.

In the *Bonaventure*, however, we find a dialectical heightening of this process: . . . the escalators and elevators here henceforth replace movement but also and above all designate themselves as new reflexive signs and emblems of movement proper. . . . Here the narrative stroll has been underscored, symbolized, reified and replaced by a transportation machine which becomes the allegorical signifier of that older promenade . . . and this is a dialectical intensification of the autoreferentiality of all modern culture.[74]

There are several problems with this Marxist homage to the Bonaventure: the first is the Bonaventure itself. The Marxist cultural critic decked out with the latest advances in deconstructionism and semiotics cannot discover what the simplest inquiry shows. The building that Jameson believes is transcendently postmodern, requiring new organs to fathom it, is palpably premodern; it hints less of futuristic space than moats and feudal castles. The Bonaventure reduces contact with outsiders by the use of massive walls and minuscule entrances. It has been described as a perfect exemplar of fortress architecture.

Jameson considers the curiously invisible entrances as representing some new category of space. Not quite. They are small and unmarked to keep out the local population, predominantly poor and Hispanic. One reviewer called the main entrance "a small hole punched in a vast four-story-high wall of concrete."[75] For the Bonaventure, built on urban renewal land, is not for local inhabitants; the real entrances are by automobile for visitors and businessmen. The hotel is practically inaccessible to pedestrians, as anyone can verify who has sought to enter by foot; from the sidewalk it is a "bunker."[76]

The incoherence of the Bonaventure, which leaves almost all visitors confused, has less to do with new dialectical space than with the old incoherence of architects more interested in dazzle than design. A review of the building, which is positive but not uncritical, states that while the "entire complex works well as a landmark and visual focus, the vast concrete podium on which the towers sit does not respond well to the environment." The

171

limited street access threatens the entire project. The interior space is "large and certainly exciting," this review continues, but it is also "disorientating and lacks clarity and focus."[77]

This hotel's myriad columns and continuous gray concrete curving staircases serve only to confuse, rather than strengthen, the impact of the central space. . . . The Bonaventure Hotel is a labyrinth of such complexity that hotel guests have complained justifiably about going up into the wrong tube and wandering about literally in circles. Recent attempts to identify the four identical towers with narrow colored banners proved a feeble gesture when viewed against the vast canyons of the central space.[78]

That a leading Marxist critic can wax eloquent about the "insertion" of the Bonaventure into the city without stumbling on the fact that it expressly excludes, as well as devitalizes, the city suggests that the Marxist theoretical "explosion" has the force of a seminar coffee break. That a—the?—leading Marxist critic enthuses over hyperspace, new collective activity, hypercrowds; that it takes a reviewer unfamiliar with *Dictionary of Marxist Lingo* (revised) to raise questions about pedestrian access and spatial incoherence indicates a theory feeding upon itself. The problem is not only Jameson's surplus jargon but the jargon itself: everything is text and more text. The metropolis itself vaporizes. To be sure, this is just a passing exercise for Jameson; his major writings concern themselves with literature. Yet his piece exemplifies the failings of a new academic Marxism.

This new Marxism converges with, indeed partly promotes, a "poststructuralism" that concentrates on texts, signs, and signifiers as the stuff of intepretation. Insofar as this method, inspired by Jacques Derrida and Roland Barthes, posits, "there is nothing outside the text" and "interpretation of any signifying chain is necessarily only another chain of signs,"[79] it both surrenders attention to a social or material context—or fails to appreciate its import—and encourages endless spirals of commentary.

Gerald Graff, an English professor, has decried these approaches that imply literature is only about itself. He believes the fashion of meta-intepretations—more and more strained and belabored intepretations feeding on interpretations—is the form of professionalization in an age of advanced capitalism. With only a trace of irony, Graff states:

> Just as a postscarcity economy may require the liquidation of traditional moral restraints, academic professionalism may require radical critical innovation as a condition of its expansion. Where quantitative "production" of scholarship and criticism is a chief measure of professional achievement, narrow canons of proof, evidence, logical consistency and clarity of expression have to go. To insist on them imposes a drag upon progress. Indeed, to apply strict canons of objectivity and evidence in academic publishing today would be comparable to the American economy's returning to the gold standard: the effect would be the immediate collapse of the system. The new wave of paracritical and metacritical improvisations in criticism . . . may be a necessary spur to industrial growth at a time when the conventional modes of professional publication have worn thin.[80]

Charles Newman, reflecting on the professorial obsession with metatheory, agrees. "Theory becomes an infinitely expendable currency, the ultimate inflation hedge."[81] In different terms, literary theory expands as literature dwindles. The theory of fetishism, which Marx set forth, turns into its opposite, the fetishism of theory.

The devotion of Marxist (and non-Marxist) literary thinkers to self-devouring theory, it might be supposed, could not infect Marxist professors of economics, inevitably more attentive to social and economic realities. The species of Marxist economic professors is itself new to the American environment. "If there is a single professor in the United States who teaches political economy and admits himself a Socialist," wrote Upton Sinclair in his vast 1923 tour through American academia, "that professor is a needle which I have been unable to find in our academic hay-stack."[82] Today Sinclair would find dozens of needles.

Radical and Marxist economists have established a presence in several universities. For some years their organization, the Union for Radical Political Economists (URPE), and their journal, *Review of Radical Political Economics*, have been the most successful of New Left academic institutions. Unlike other left professionals, the radical economists retain a commitment to a larger public; they regularly hold conferences and summer "schools" specifically geared for interested outsiders. Almost alone among the left academic groupings, their organization publishes pamphlets and books for a lay audience. For instance, URPE edited a book on the crisis in state cutbacks of social services. This volume, *Crisis in the Public Sector: A Reader*, seeks not only to instruct but "to assist the process of organizing a response to the public sector crisis and the current mood of 'cut-backs.' "[83]

All of this is reason for celebration; it should also be put in perspective. The achievement of the radical economists has been limited, in spite of their numbers and indisputable talent. It is not possible to name a book by a younger radical economist in the same league—in writing or verve—as those by last generation radical economists from Paul Sweezy to John Kenneth Galbraith. Even the best work of this younger group, for instance, James O'Connor's *The Fiscal Crisis of the State*, tends to be diffuse and involuted; the writing seems increasingly to bear the homogenizing mark of university "dialogue."

Democracy and Capitalism, for example, the latest book by Samuel Bowles and Herbert Gintis, two outstanding URPE thinkers, challenges conventional political theory; yet it also exudes its idiom and concerns. The authors justify ignoring twentieth-century European Marxism and its "elegant critical pursuits" (such as psychology and philosophy!) because these "theories generally have not incorporated the logic of individual choice into their conceptual apparatus, have not understood the critical importance of the micro social aspects of macrosocial activity, and have not embraced the emancipatory status of individual liberty."[84] This (dubious) proposition opens the way—is already the way—to the language and ideas of academic political theory.

Despite their salutary efforts, and occasional successes, in the long run few radical economists seem able to resist professional imperatives. Radical political economy has steadily adopted, or succumbed to, the form and style of standard economics.[85] This, in fact, is the conclusion of Paul A. Attewell in his study, *Radical Political Economy Since the Sixties.* He suggests that initially the sixties generation engendered an "academic left scholarship" that challenged the prevailing economic knowledge. However the fervor, identity, and perhaps raison d'être of radical political economy ebb each year.

The story Attewell recounts is familiar; young Marxist professors face the hostility of the profession. Under the tenure system they are "dependents" with alloted time to prove their respectability. "This pressure," Attewell writes, "shows itself as an attempt to adopt academic style and to 'scientize' Marxist scholarship." Increasingly, reports Attewell, most radical economists "legitimate their work by adopting a scholarly style, by publishing in respected journals, and by emphasizing the rigorous empirical

175

foundations of their arguments, which often use quantitative techniques of analysis." While retaining their radical identities, usually by the choice of topics, "the professional pressures" have led them "to embrace the mainstream canons of academic method and discourse."[86]

The vulnerability to academic constraints sets the new Marxists apart from last generation Marxist economists situated outside or on the outskirts of universities. Perhaps for this reason, unlike Paul Baran and Paul Sweezy, who were able to update Marxism lucidly (in *Monopoly Capital*), the combined oeuvre of the more numerous younger Marxist economists seems weaker in content and impact. In the world of Marxist political economy, the generational divide yawns as wide as elsewhere.

Although often ignored, the writings by the associates of *Monthly Review* and, specifically, the books by Paul Baran, Paul Sweezy, Harry Braverman, and Harry Magdoff formed a school that in coherency, originality, and boldness no other American Marxism has come close to matching. When Marxists of other countries turn to American contributors, it is primarily to these authors. However, the *Monthly Review* school lacks pupils to carry on its work. If it is possible to point to absences elsewhere— the absence of successors to Trilling or Wilson or Mumford or Mills—the absence of successors to Sweezy and Baran is glaring.

To identify *Monthly Review* Marxism as a "school" beyond the academy is, of course, too simple. Paul Baran (1910–64)[87] led a life typical of the European left-wing intellectuals: many exiles, many countries, many careers. He was born in Russia and educated in Frankfurt and Moscow, but the rise of Hitler and the consolidation of Stalinism put him on the road. After a stint in the family business in Poland, Baran emigrated to the United States and enrolled at Harvard. He served in various agencies during the war, including the United States Strategic Bombing

Survey under John Kenneth Galbraith, who called him "one of the most brilliant and, by a wide margin, the most interesting economist I have ever known."[88]

In the war's aftermath, he again wandered about—Department of Commerce, Federal Reserve Bank—until Stanford University offered him a position in 1949, an act the administration soon came to regret. Paul Sweezy explains, "Since the Cold War and the witch hunt were still in their early stages and had not yet cast their baleful shadows across the country's campuses, no one was unduly troubled by his outspoken Marxism: many liberals, and even some conservatives, were still naive enough to welcome someone who could expound views radically different from their own."[89]

The naiveté dissipated, and Baran was much bothered, and sometimes demoralized, by quasi-official harrassments over his course load, salary, and leaves of absence, which left little doubt that the university wanted to be rid of him. This intensified after the Cuban Revolution, which Baran openly welcomed, traveling in 1960 to the island and meeting with Castro.

A friend reported to Baran that he saw both a stack of letters from Stanford alumni calling for his firing and the official response by the Stanford president. The president's reply, recounted Baran, "did not point out that the University was committed to the principle of academic freedom or anything of that sort, but stressed its having the very difficult problem of my having tenure. The business of freezing my salary, far from being treated as a secret, is being widely advertised (among donors) to show that nothing would be done to 'encourage me to stay here.'" Baran added that he should be "above all this," but "it burns me all up" and "plays havoc with the nervous system."[90] Three years later, in 1964, he died of a heart attack.

Paul Sweezy's (1910–) path was almost the reverse; he attended Phillips Exeter Academy and commenced an all-Harvard career: undergraduate, graduate student, and instructor in the economics department. Harvard University Press published his dissertation (on the English coal trade). During the war Sweezy took a leave, assuming a position in the Office of Strategic Services (OSS), a haven for many academics and left-wing intellectuals. After the war and following a period of study, he resigned his Harvard position, recognizing that "his political and intellectual views would prohibit his tenure at Harvard."[91]

Within several years Sweezy founded *Monthly Review*, an independent socialist periodical, which he still edits today. Its first issue featured Albert Einstein's "Why Socialism?" The journal also established a small publishing arm, Monthly Review Press; its first title was I. F. Stone's book on the Korean War, *The Hidden History of the Korean War*. The other Monthly Review principals will be mentioned briefly. Harry Braverman (1920–76), originally a metal worker and a Trotskyist activist, eventually became an editor at Grove Press. After some years he resigned when they refused to publish a book by Bertrand Russell on Vietnam, and joined Monthly Review Press. Harry Magdoff (1913–) worked as an economist for a series of New Deal and World War II agencies; like many leftists in the fifties he bounced around without secure employment—stockbroker, insurance salesman—until he entered publishing, joining *Monthly Review* as a co-editor with Sweezy in 1969.

At their best the Monthly Review books possess a clarity and originality rare among Marxist writings; they include Sweezy's *The Theory of Capitalist Development* (1942), which still may be unsurpassed for its exposition of classical Marxist theory and debate; Baran's *Political Economy of Growth* (1957), a decisive work in opening up the discussion of "underdevelopment"; Baran and Sweezy's *Monopoly Capital* (1964), which, bearing the imprint of the New Left, is the most accessible Marxist critique of American society; Magdoff's *The Age of Imperialism* (1969), a Marxist primer on American foreign policy; and Braverman's *Labor and Monopoly Capital* (1974), a thoughtful study that has spurred much discussion about the "de-skilling" of labor.[92]

The force of these works cannot be attributed simply to the lives of the authors; but neither can it be cleanly separated from them. The *Monthly Review* authors stood largely outside the universities and they wrote for the educated reader. Their books are not rehashings of Marxist dogma; nor are they monographs for colleagues. "The desire to tell the truth," wrote Baran, is "only *one* condition for being an intellectual. The other is courage, readiness to carry on rational inquiry to wherever it may lead . . . to withstand . . . comfortable and lucrative conformity."[93] They are last generation Marxist intellectuals, having more in common with Edmund Wilson and Lewis Mumford than with the university Marxists who follow them. Like *The Death and Life of Great American Cities*, *Monopoly Capital* and *Labor and Monopoly Capital* have academic successors, but none with the same vigor and language.

Insight into the Marxist generational shift can perhaps be glimpsed from the following: when Paul Baran died in 1964, *Monthly Review* published a memorial volume, "a collective portrait."[94] It included some thirty-eight statements about Baran by friends and associates. The vast majority of these were by older intellectuals—foreigners, or foreign-born and foreign-educated Americans. The list of contributors ran from Joan Robinson, Isaac Deutscher, and Ernest (Che) Guevara to Eric Hobsbawm, Otto Kirkheimer, and Herbert Marcuse. It also included reflections by four younger North Americans, students or friends of Baran: Peter Clecak (1938–), John O'Neill (1933–), Maurice Zeitlin (1935–), and Freddy Perlman (1934–85).

Who were these four and what became of them? The first three were instructors or assistant professors when Baran died; today they are established professors of American studies or sociology at major North American universities (University of California, Irvine; UCLA; York University, Toronto). They have made substantial contributions to scholarship, but little in the style or vein of Baran. The last, Freddy Perlman, founded an anarchist press in Detroit, Black and Red, which over the years has published pamphlets and books. His press and name might be recognized by a few cognoscenti of left literature.[95]

Twenty years later a *Festschrift* for Sweezy and Magdoff appeared with many contributions from North Americans.[96] Of the approximately seventeen younger American authors, none has yet written a book of the caliber of *Monopoly Capital* or *Labor and Monopoly Capital*; all but one of these authors teach at universities. Of course, like any list this hides a series of different situations and aspirations; it is more than possible that none of the contributors has wanted to write a work in *Monthly Review* style; and it is possible that some still do. Nevertheless, the overview of Marxism and radical political economy suggests that its development parallels other disciplines and subdisciplines: colleagues have replaced a public, and jargon has supplanted English. American Marxists today have campus offices and assigned parking spaces.

IV

THE RISE of radical geography illustrates the general problem that haunts Marxist and neo-Marxist scholarship—success. Richard Peet (1940–) recounts that he and his friends knew "nothing" of a radical geography tradition when they began their studies. "The very idea of a radicalized geography was beyond our comprehension." While enrolled in graduate school at the University of California, Berkeley, the student movement spurred them to rediscover and reinvent this tradition, although geography was the "last" department to be affected by radicalism.

As beginning professors they dispersed, accepting teaching posts across the nation. At Clark University in Worcester, Massachusetts, Peet and others decided to create a forum for friends and sympathizers. In 1969 these young scholars founded *Antipode*, a journal of radical geography. With early issues broaching subjects that traditional geography rarely addressed—the geography of poverty, underdevelopment, urbanism—the journal served as a catalyst for graduate students and younger faculty. David Harvey's work, which was just beginning to appear, inspired other geographers to delve into Marxism.

By the early eighties times had changed, and radical geographers sought to establish themselves within the profession. The Union of Socialist Geographers became an official subsection (Socialist Geography Specialty Group) of the Association of American Geographers. "Even radical academics with safe, tenured jobs" had to respond to the times if "they want to have students in their classes, or gain scholarly respect with their publications," comments Peet. The flow of articles to their journal, even the interest in it, flagged. "The very generation of Marxist geographers we had helped to radicalize" no longer submitted articles to *Antipode*. " 'Publish in a respected journal' had replaced 'support the movement.' "[97]

Yet *Antipode* survived and made the decision, at least in form, to professionalize: since 1986 it has been published by an established scholarly press, Blackwell's. "My own feelings about this," states Peet, "are essentially optimistic—that the academic respectability provided by a professional publisher will intersect with a renewed energy and commitment . . . allow[ing] *Antipode* to progress to a new level of quality and influence."[98]

The trajectory is typical, and it would be flip to challenge the inescapable realities or to deny the accomplishments. The flowering of left scholarship, the weakening of political protest, and the defense of the university beachheads seem an almost natural and inevitable progression that has affected radicals, Marxists, and neo-Marxists in all disciplines. Moreover, the gains seem, if not irrevocable, unprecedented. For the first time marginal or lost traditions of radical geography, sociology, history, and other disciplines have entered the bright light, where they can be examined and taught, while enlisting additional students. In the long run this may prove decisive.

Yet a sticky matter should be aired: if left intellectuals have succumbed to the imperatives that herded them into the universities, they are not innocent victims. Left intellectuals did not naively or unwillingly accept the academic regimen; they also embraced the university themselves. The critique of academization by a university left is curiously muted—softer than a conservative critique. Of course, a radical critique is not totally absent; it looks back to Veblen and Mills and forward to Noam Chomsky, perhaps its boldest current guardian.

An anarchist suspicion of intellectuals as power brokers pervades Chomsky's approach. For his criticism of American intellectuals, Chomsky invokes not simply classic anarchists, like Bakunin, but the most politically eccentric of New York in tellectuals, Dwight Macdonald. Chomsky begins his "The Re sponsibility of Intellectuals" (1969) with Macdonald. "Twenty years ago, Dwight Macdonald published a series of articles in *Politics* on the . . . responsibility of intellectuals. I read them as an undergraduate, in the years just after the war, and had occasion to

read them again a few months ago. They seem to me to have
lost none of their power or persuasiveness."[99] In Macdonald,
Chomsky sensed a kindred soul, an individual bucking institutions and leftist pieties.[100]

For Chomsky the new liberal and technical intelligentsia junks
truth and morality for specialization and power. He cites Zbig-
niew Brzezinski, who applauds the shift. "The largely humanist-
orientated, occasionally ideologically-minded intellectual-
dissenter . . . is rapidly being displaced . . . by experts
and specialists, who become involved in special governmental
undertakings. . . ."[101]

Yet Chomsky raises the sensitive issue that left-wing intellectuals are prone to enter governments and institutions. "One factor in the betrayal of the promise of socialist revolution has been
the willingness of the technical intelligentsia to assimilate itself
to a new ruling class." And this willingness is a factor at work in
Eastern Europe as well as western democracies.[102] Left intellectuals in Chomsky's view are not simply defeated; they sometimes
cooperate and collaborate. Chomsky, however, is an unusual and
somewhat isolated figure: an anarchist skeptical of intellectuals
in institutions is rare in the American left.

The much more significant progressivism, liberalism, and
Marxism projected a universe where intellectuals would reform,
if not rule society.[103] They would man its bureaus and agencies.
This prospect undermined a critique of intellectuals, for it was
always possible to misread the situation—perhaps intellectuals
were actually reforming society.[104] To put this another way: the
academization of a left-wing intelligentsia was not simply imposed, it was desired. For the leftists, appointment to state or
academic bureaucracies constituted small steps on the path
to power—or so they fantasized. Careerism and revolution
converged.[105]

Early in the century the progressive historian Frederick J. Turner succinctly expressed the hope of intellectuals as official reformers.

> By training in science, in law, politics, economics, and history the universities may supply from the ranks of democracy administrators, legislators, judges and experts for commissioners who shall disinterestedly and intelligently mediate between contending interests. . . . It is hardly too much to say that the best hope of intelligent and principled progress in economic and social legislation and administration lies in the increasing influence of American universities.[106]

This idea partially propelled the migration of left intellectuals into the university; it was hardly a question of "selling out." Rather, radical intellectuals were not inherent opponents of institutional power, and when the possibility emerged to enter, perhaps to utilize, these institutions, they did so. If quick to record violations to academic, and sometimes racial and sexual, freedoms, they typically proved oblivious to the costs of institutionalization.

For instance, the radicals in political science, according to Seidelman and Harpham, "did not abandon professionalism for politics; rather, they asserted their politics through the profession." The Caucus for a New Political Science, founded by radicals in 1967, successfuly democratized official political science organizations: it contested elections within the discipline; it set up new panels at conferences; and it established a new journal, *Politics and Society*. But it succeeded as a new professional group "not as a united intellectual movement or as a group of intellectuals seeking ties with a public outside the discipline itself. Indeed the Caucus's activities centered exclusively on the politics of political science itself." Eventually it "narrowed its goals to the concrete, material and limited demands of an interest group within the discipline. . . . Polemics, critiques and political activity became an effort to educate and mobilize other professionals."[107]

This is still generally true; the "politics" of academic life supplant larger politics. Of left professors, Marxist academics may be the most culpable, the most eager to embrace institutional imperatives (and benefits). From Marxism itself they inherit a sober scientific approach, discounting useless moral protests. To accept and utilize the university makes good political sense. Perhaps for this reason no-nonsense Marxist academics frequently seek to establish not simply the credibility of their ideas but institutes or power bases, dense networks of professors, graduate students, publications, and foundation monies. They want institutional clout and prestige.

A recent volume on "historical sociology," largely by and about left professors, is filled with reports on the status and success of the "field." Theda Skocpol announces that several of its main figures have done quite well.

[Charles] Tilly has attracted large amounts of research funding over the years, built a major research center at the University of Michigan, and serves as a professional gatekeeper in three or four disciplines. [Immanuel] Wallerstein enjoys broad international prestige . . . and has managed to embody his world-system perspective in a research center and journal, . . . in yearly conferences at revolving university locations . . . and in a section of the American Sociological Association that controls several sessions for every year's annual meeting.[108]

This perpetual monitoring of the field, charting the major contributors and their successes, which is a regular feature of Marxist and neo-Marxist writing about everything from feminist history to Marxist anthropology, suggests less about ideas and more about property and careers.[109]

When talk comes around to one's lifework, the motive most left scholars ascribe to themselves or others, of course, is not the establishment of institutional power; rather, they seek to establish a body of "counter" or Marxist culture that in the United States never existed. With frequent references to Gramsci and his ideas of ideological hegemony,[110] left scholars envision their teaching and writing as laying the cultural foundations for a political renaissance; they seek to develop a convincing "new" sociology, "new" political science, "new" history.

This surely has some plausibility: compared to almost any country, the American left suffers from ignorance of its past and of the larger history of radicalism. In most western democracies socialists and Marxists can claim an honorable cultural tradition, often with links to universities. In the United States, however, a dissenting or Marxist culture has never been firmly established; it is diffuse, fragile, and regularly lost. Left academics study the past, the state, the economy to escape finally from this failing.

Yet at what point does left scholarship lose its élan, even its raison d'être? At what point does it simply become more specialized knowledge, little different—neither better nor worse—than other contributions? Much Marxist scholarship, although not all, took its cue from a structural or "scientific" school with its own secret affinity to professionalism.[111] In its longing to be rigorously scientific, Marxism frequently began to look like the social science it wanted to subvert.

If Marxist sociologists broke with the values and culture of the mainstream, their love for "objective" and "structural" analyses brought them back to it, leading them to dismiss culture, ideology, and subjectivity as so much inconsequential poetry.[112] If Marxist political scientists depreciated conservative theorizing, they offered in its place technical models of the state that seemed hardly superior; the Marxist theories possessed the aura of penetrating the deep secrets of capitalism but rarely progressed beyond dense formulas. "Academic Marxists have typically chosen a path of retreat," concluded Carl Boggs, "from explicitly political phenomena in favor of abstract treatments of productive forces, state functions and class relations."[113]

Often this Marxist penchant for bloodless schematas is acknowledged and paraded. "The essays in this book," states Erik Olin Wright, a Marxist sociologist, in his introduction, "have been heavily shaped by the academic context in which they were written." He wishes to "engage in debate with mainstream social theory" and "simultaneously . . . develop a style of empirical research which advances Marxist theory."[114] Perhaps this is laudable, but it suffers from several flaws. There is no empirical research, as he admits. "While none of the essays constitute an empirical investigation . . . they are all intended to help establish the theoretical preconditions."[115]

Moreover, Wright's theoretical preconditions derive from the French brand—now recalled because of major design flaws but once exported by Nicos Poulantzas and Louis Althusser—in which vapid definitions and pronouncements decorate occasional examples and baroque diagrams. To lighten his task Wright offers six modes of "more differentiated schema of structural causality" ("structural limitation," "selection"—with "two complementary forms . . . 'positive' and 'negative' "—"reproduction/non-reproduction," "limits of functional compatibility," "transformation," "mediation") that allow him to map lucidly the relationships of the state, economic structure, state intervention, and class struggle. He notes, "This model could of course be made more complex. Other elements could be added, such as the role of ideology."[116]

The real problem is that this kind of Marxism has gained the worst of all worlds; it has not really joined the mainstream, but it has successfully abandoned the vigor of Marxism. A fair sample of the light that has been shed might be Wright's conclusion to one section:

The central message from the model of determination in Figure 2.3 is that it is essential to analyse the complex dialectical relationships between class structure, class formation and class struggle in any analysis of classes. . . . Any adequate political understanding of the possibilities and constraints present in a given social formation depends upon showing the ways in which class structure establishes limits on class struggle and class formation, the ways in which class struggle transforms both class structure and class formation, and the ways in which class struggle mediates the relations between class structure and class formation.[117]

This might be called Marxist voodoo.

Another book from the sixties illustrates the danger threatening Marxist scholars. Immanuel Wallerstein and Paul Starr put together two volumes about student and university protests, which presented a spectrum of opinions. In his conclusion to *The University Crisis Reader* (1971), Wallerstein offered some of his own thoughts about radicals in the university. "There is much hard intellectual work to be done by the left," he stated. "This intellectual work will never be done well if it is isolated from praxis, from involvement in a political movement and political action. But neither will it be done well if it is isolated from the pressures of competing intellectual ideas in the mainstream of intellectual debate, which in America is still located in the university."[118]

These words signaled the times, as did the fate of the sentiments: they did not survive the seventies intact. As the possibility of "political action" declined, only half, or less than half, the program remained: "hard work" in the middle of "the pressures of competing intellectual ideas in the mainstream of intellectual debate." This call for respectable scholarship is beyond reproach, yet it is dogged by the question, at what point does radical scholarship cease to be radical? Like so many books of the sixties, *The University Crisis Reader* was dedicated to "the memory of C. Wright Mills." Fifteen years after this anthology appeared, it seems that competing with the mainstream has been costly.

Wallerstein himself has cut a wide swath through sociology and history, as Theda Skocpol observed. Among other things, he has published two weighty tomes titled *The Modern World-System*; and he has founded not only a journal (*Review*) but an outfit, which he heads, called the Fernand Braudel Center for the Study of Economies, Historical Systems and Civilizations (State University of New York at Binghamton). His achievements have been considerable, and he has persistently sought to enlarge standard approaches to national economies and history.

He has recently stated that the student movement, which it is fashionable to minimize, led in fact to important ideological "explosions." Yet his very appreciation, laden with the new academic jargon, suggests the distance traveled.

In terms of epistemology, we are seeing a serious challenge to both universalization and sectorialization and an attempt to explore the methodology of holistic research, the implementation of that *via media* that had been excluded by the nomothetic-idiographic pseudo-debate.... What is really new, however, is the historiographical challenge.... We are living in the maelstrom of a gigantic intellectual sea-change, one that mirrors the world transition from capitalism to something else (most probably socialism).... This ideological shift is itself both one of the outcomes and one of the tools of this process of global transition.[119]

Whatever the value of Wallerstein's global approach and logic—and it may be valuable—it is far from the spirit of C. Wright Mills, muckraker, moralist, public intellectual. Moreover, as in much Marxist and neo-Marxist writing, the drumbeat of academic troops can be heard. Wallerstein has championed the "system" approach to world economics; he has also established a system—his own, a mini-empire of journals, centers, and publications.[120]

The final report on universities and the New Left is not in. The complexity and size of higher education forbid confident conclusions. The general tendencies, however, are clear. The academic enterprise simultaneously expands and contracts; it steadily intrudes upon the larger culture, setting up private clubs for accredited members. That it is difficult for an educated adult American to name a single political scientist or sociologist or philosopher is not wholly his or her fault; the professionals have abandoned the public arena. The influx of left scholars has not changed the picture; reluctantly or enthusiastically they gain respectability at the cost of identity. The slogan that was borrowed from the German left to justify a professional career—"the long march through the institutions"—has had an unexpected outcome: at least so far, the institutions are winning.

CHAPTER 7

After the
Last Intellectuals

I

AS EXEMPLARS of last generation intellectuals, Lewis Mumford (1895–) and Edmund Wilson (1895–1972) seem almost too perfect. In life and prose they summon up a world distant from the new academics. Mumford, who has been called America's last private scholar, inherited little money and has rarely been the beneficiary of foundation largess. Nor has he worked as a salaried editor, researcher, or teacher. In an age of institutions, Mumford is attached to no institution. He has managed what was once very difficult and is now almost impossible—to live from his writings. His twenty-eight books, from *The Story of Utopias* (1922) and *Technics and Civilization* (1934) to *The City in History* (1961) and *The Myth of the Machine* (1967–70), constitute a singular oeuvre, almost unequaled in American letters.

His life bears the stamp of his times: old New York and Greenwich Village. Mumford walked, savored, and wrote about New

York's museums, libraries, ferries. "Surely the ferryboat was one of the great inventions of the Nineteenth century. . . . Even the short trips to Jersey City from downtown New York provided a touch of uncertainty and adventure, allowing for the tide, dodging other boats and ships, all with a closeness to the sea and sky and the wide sweep of the city itself. . . ." Bohemian Greenwich Village provided the requisite ambience: ". . . I, too, belonged to the Younger Generation; rebellious; defiant of conventions, but not yet wholly disillusioned; and Greenwich Village was our rallying ground." Veblen served as a model. As an editor of *The Dial*, Mumford knew Veblen, describing him as a fellow "heretic in the academic world" who, like Mumford himself, refused to "recognize the no-trespass signs" of specialists.[1]

Mumford mainly wrote, as he would state later, around and past the academics to the intelligent readers.[2] "Until the Great Depression of the 1930s there was a sufficiently wide variety of weeklies and monthlies, some like 'The Dial' and 'The American Mercury,' paying a modest two cents a word, some like 'Harper's' and 'Scribner's,' paying more, so that I never was compelled to undertake a subject that did not, in some way, further my own purposes." This was the golden age for young writers, with publishers offering liberal advances for bold projects. "It would seem almost sadistic to give the present generation of writers an account of the liberated state of publishing then in almost every field."[3] Later, he occasionally taught college, but he did so as a visitor, eschewing a permanent post. He cherished an independence that he feared would wilt once burdened with university obligations and protocol.[4]

It seems proper that Mumford initiated the last generation's final sally against the encroaching academization of culture. In 1968 Mumford came across a new edition of his favorite writer, Emerson, whom he considers "a mountain spring" watering all

American letters.[5] Published by Harvard University Press, this complete and scholarly edition of Emerson's journals was an "approved" text of the Modern Language Association.

Mumford was appalled. Teams of academics had transmuted Emerson's fluid prose into sludge. In the name of accuracy, the good professors had flagged every inconsequential divergence between various manuscripts and published editions. They used twenty different diacritical marks, which became part of the printed text, that "spit, and sputter at the reader, not only to indicate cancellations, insertions or variants, but also unrecovered matter, unrecovered cancelled matter, accidentally mulitilated manuscript, even erasures."[6]

For Mumford, the academic enterprise had gone amuck. "Thus these 'Journals' have now performed current American scholarship's ultimate homage to a writer of genius: they have made him unreadable." A friend had begged him not to criticize this scholarly edition, since Mumford was an unaccredited outsider.

True, but I am a faithful Emerson reader; and, as it turns out, that academic disability is perhaps my chief qualification for writing this criticism. For who is to question such an authoritative enterprise . . . except those whose reputations and promotions could not possibly be jeopardized by passing an unfavorable verdict upon it?[7]

Mumford's frontal attack on the academic establishment stirred into action another old war-horse. Edmund Wilson, born the same year as Mumford, shared much with him: an all-American past; a long and productive life of independent writing; a refusal to specialize. If anything, Wilson was more jealous of his independence and more suspicious of the university. After World War II, when he had acquired a wide reputation, he sent a preprinted postcard to those requesting his services. On the card

> it was noted (with a check against the appropriate box) that Edmund Wilson does not ... write articles or books to order; does not write forewords or introductions; does not make statements for publicity purposes; does not do any kind of editorial work, judge literary contests, give interviews, broadcast or appear on television; does not answer questionnaires, contribute to or take part in symposiums. ...[8]

Wilson's almost willful obsolescence set him apart and against. Already in 1944, when a professor asked for a complete bibliography of his published writings, Wilson realized his time and generation were over; he had become an object of study, someone to gape at. He belonged to a group, almost "extinct and a legend" in which "the practice of letters was a common craft and the belief in its value a common motivation." Many are now troubled by "a writer who works up his own notions and signs his own name." Professors want to classify and analyze, not to play a role in literature. "For the literary man in a college, incorporated in that quite different organism, the academic profession, with its quite other hierarchies of value and competition for status, the literary man of the twenties presents himself as the distant inhabitant of another intellectual world; and he figures as the final installment of the body of material to be studied."[9]

Inspired by Mumford, Wilson looked at some other scholarly editions sponsored by the Modern Language Association. He found the same profligate pendantry, a vast scholarly libido channeled into textual annotations mangling America's authors. Thirty-five scholars were busy going through variant texts of Mark Twain; eighteen of them were "reading Tom Sawyer backward, in order to ascertain without being diverted from this drudgery by attention to the story or style, how many times

"Aunt Polly" is printed as "aunty Polly." While universities lavished funds and research on unreadable scholarly editions, often of unimportant books or authors, cheap usable editions of essential American writings hardly existed. For Wilson this all demonstrated that the academic enterprise had become a bloated boondoggle.[10]

This blast by America's aging but leading man of letters elicited a small storm of protest—and some agreement. The MLA published a booklet of replies, ominously titled *Professional Standards and American Editions: A Response to Edmund Wilson*. To leave no doubt that this was the establishment talking, the president of the Guggenheim Foundation wrote the preface. Gordon N. Ray set the record straight: Wilson and his supporters represented obsolete amateurism in the age of high-performance professionals. Wilson's attack

derives in part from the alarm of amateurs at seeing rigorous professional standards applied to a subject in which they have a vested interest. Here, at least, the issue is not in doubt. As the American world has come to full maturity since the second World War, a similar animus has shown itself and been discredited in field after field from botany to folklore. In the long run professional standards always prevail.[11]

II

AS A STATEMENT of fact few could contest this judgment. Professionals in high theory or mass culture or international terror have staked out the future. To describe someone as a "man of letters" in the 1980s is almost derogatory, hinting of village poets or family historians.[12] An unexpected source, however, has yielded some stiff-necked men of letters loudly decrying the reign of the technocratic academics: the new and not-so-new conservatives. Exposés and denunciations of academic sophistry and careerism can often be found in conservative journals, such as *The New Criterion, Commentary, American Scholar*, but rarely in left and liberal ones. Conservatives honor men of letters, regularly attacking professors and academic hustlers. Why?

In principle, conservatives have been less tempted by institutional or government solutions to social ills. At least since Edmund Burke, they have objected to experts, lawyers, or professors meddling in government or society; this is the crux of the conservative critique of the Enlightenment. They have prized the man of letters devoted to letters, not politics. An opponent of Thomas Jefferson raised this charge: he is "a man of letters, and should be retired as one. His closet, and not the cabinet, is his place." Another suggested that Jefferson's merits "might entitle him to the Professorship of a college, but they would be as compatible with the duties of the presidency as with the command of the Western army."[13]

This commitment to the aristocratic man of letters fires a critique of the university that has no left counterpart. The titles alone of books by conservatives index their concerns: *The Degradation of the Academic Dogma* by Robert Nisbet, *The Fall of the American University* by Adam Ulam, *Decadence and Renewal in the Higher Learning* by Russell Kirk, *The Decline of the Intellectual* by Thomas S. Molnar. These works all indict the endemic careerism and corruption of bloated universities. The authors' loyalty to the obsolete man of letters enables them to condemn academics swarming for grants and advancements. Russell Kirk, a central figure of post–World War II conservatism, resigned from his university post in the early fifties, already protesting automatic growth and academic bureaucratization.

The intensity of the conservative attack on the university almost transcends political labels. Nisbet, in *The Degradation of the Academic Dogma,* occasionally sounds like a wide-eyed radical unmasking colleagues as capitalist tools. He deplores the conquest of the university by capitalism: "The first million dollars given to a university" was a million too much. "The first man who, having enclosed a piece of the university, bethought himself of saying, 'This is my institute' and found members of the faculty simple enough to believe him, was the real founder of the university's higher capitalism."[14]

Entrepreneurs and hucksters have replaced disinterested scholars and researchers. An "academic bourgeoisie" complete with shoddy goods and conspicuous research has sprung up. "Scratch a faculty member today," Nisbet reports, "and you almost always find a businessman." "The entrepreneurial spirit" spreads throughout the university, corrupting everything and everyone.

A veritable faculty jet set came into being, to excite envy—and emulation. . . . I firmly believe that direct grants from government and foundation to individual members of university faculties, or to small company-like groups of faculty members, for the purposes of creating institutes, centers, bureaus, and other essentially capitalistic enterprises within the academic community to be the single most powerful agent of change that we can find in the university's long history. For the first time in Western history, professors and scholars were thrust into the unwanted position of entrepreneurs in incessant search for new sources of capital, of new revenue, and . . . of profits. . . . The new capitalism, *academic capitalism,* is a force that arose within the university and that has had as its most eager supporters the members of the professoriat.[15]

The same homage to the aristocratic man of letters explains some of the conservatives' success and public presence; they object to academic entrepreneurialism and its language. Unlike left academics, more easily seduced by professional journals, jargon, and life, the conservatives are committed to lucid prose; for this reason they are readable and are read. While several periodicals of the left devoted to the general reader have appeared in recent years, for instance *Salmagundi* or *Grand Street*, the proliferating radical journals are geared to sympathizers in various disciplines; the uninitiated could hardly plow through *Enclitic* or *Social Text*. The conservative journals, however, adopt a public idiom; an outsider can pick up and read *The New Criterion*.

Moreover, the conservative journals seem willing not only to challenge new academic wisdom but to highlight its function, shoring up insecure professors. A typical essay in *Commentary* questions the mania for theory by literature departments. "The terms that now cause pulses to race—deconstruction, disseminations, epistemes, the mirror stage, and the like—are so undescriptive of literary detail that they tend not so much to explain literature as to replace it." Geoffrey H. Hartman, a Yale literary critic whom Frederick Crews quotes, states that he and his colleagues resist the attitude that "condemns the writer of criticism or commentary to nonliterary status and a service function." The literary critics respond by the cult of high Theory, including the cult of the high Theorists—themselves.[16] Another *Commentary* piece judges, "this eagerness for a whole new set of terms that can be maneuvered around and behind and beyond literature has the look of a program of system-wide retooling in an industry that has discovered it is antiquated."[17]

The conservative critique comes alive, sniffing academic wheeling and dealing and its debased prose, where the left often slumbers. However, the vigorous right-wing attack soon flags. Conservatives' opposition to professionals founders on their suspicion of all intellectuals, at least of all those who do not know their place.[18] They inch toward anti-intellectualism, praising the experts they sometimes challenge. Their man of letters stays out of trouble by staying in a specialty.

From the Dreyfus affair to the Vietnam War, conservatives howled that intellectuals meddled in matters outside their training. In words almost identical to those deployed against Zola and the Dreyfusards, a conservative has attacked scholars who protested the Vietnam War.

Small cliques speaking for the professoriat . . . come forward . . . not as scholars in relevant fields but as professors, simply as professors. By virtue of being professors—professors of biology, assistant professors of English, instructors in Romance Languages—they claim the right to challenge the Government to public debate on whatever issues they please. No one would maintain that plumbers, just by virtue of being plumbers, had any such right, or physicians, lawyers, engineers, merchants, bankers, or labor leaders, except perhaps where the issue touched on their special field of interest and competence.[19]

Ironically, the conservative critique of professions turns into its opposite, a defense of special interests and fields. They object to the poets or plumbers speaking about foreign policy, instead of poems and sinks, as if the divisions of labor were cast in heaven. Herein lies a critical difference with the sometimes overlapping anarchist critique of professions.

The critique of intellectuals as servants of power by an anarchist like Chomsky does not aim to confine intellectuals to their labs and fields. If anything, he wants intellectuals to speak up as citizens or citizens to assert themselves as intellectuals. The hostility toward unaccredited outsiders keeps specialists in business; it also works, notes Chomsky, to silence critics, who are inevitably outsiders—for instance himself, a professional linguist criticizing foreign policy.

"In discussion or debate concerning social issues or American foreign policy," writes Chomsky, "the issue is constantly raised, often with considerable venom. I've repeatedly been challenged on ground of credentials, or asked, what special training do you have that entitles you to speak of these matters. The assumption is that people like me, who are outsiders from a professional viewpoint, are not entitled to speak on such things." The problem is that the appropriate disciplines successfully filter out dissenters "so that by and large a reliance on 'professional expertise' will ensure that views and analyses that depart from the orthodoxy will rarely be expressed."[20]

Conservatives, however, cherish a more benign view of professionals tending their own fields. Yet even this is not a consistent principle. Their man of letters is not to be found above or outside the fray, cleaving to arts and letters, but on its right flank; they do not allow that an independent intellectual can also be a critic of society. For most conservatives this is a contradiction, proof of corruption, loyalty to alien powers, and un-American activity. In the conservative lexicon, "politics" itself is a dirty word, which somehow the left introduced into the university; at least politics is the special province of politicians, who never mess with art and scholarship. Once upon a time culture and scholarship stood apart from politics. The left drove them together.

This skewed notion of politics drowns their own defense of standards and values. Hilton Kramer's *The New Criterion* and Joseph Epstein's *American Scholar* persistently accuse the left of injecting politics into culture. "The intrusion of politics into culture," states Epstein, is "one of the major motifs" of the last twenty-five years.[21] Not only do they imagine that at some point culture was uncontaminated by politics; but for them politics can only mean left-wing politics. Their own politics is not politics. Yet rarely have general periodicals devoted to the arts and scholarship been as emphatically political as *The New Criterion* and *American Scholar*. Alfred Kazin remarks that *American Scholar*, the journal of the Phi Beta Kappa Society, was never associated with any particular politics—until a neoconservative began saving it from politics.[22] The same might be said of *Commentary*. It may have once been liberal and tolerant of radicals, but it was never so relentlessly political until it became conservative.

This one-eyed definition of politics cripples the conservative critique of the university. When conservatives see leftists in the university, they cry "politics." However, they are silent about the much more numerous conservatives. Why? Are they outside politics? One radical law professor in a conservative department; two Marxists economists in a Keynesian or monetarist discipline; a group of left-wing literary critics in the vast literary enterprise— these isolated, and sometimes not-so-isolated, individuals cause conservatives to announce the decline of the university and civilization. Politics has taken over.

Yet it is not difficult to demonstrate that the active and committed conservatives far outnumber the miscellaneous radicals and leftists. The emergence of left-wing literary theorists regularly occasions attacks in the conservative journals. But why not attack the far more significant institutes of Russian studies or international affairs, even schools of business and management? With a few exceptions, conservatives not only man these outfits but play much more important political and cultural roles than the usually beleaguered left professors. Is the Harvard Business School or the UCLA School of Management nonpolitical? Departments of political science and economics house untold numbers of scholars who advise the United States Government. This, too, is "politicized" scholarship. Why the fiction that the universities have been politicized by some left scholars?

A conservative symposium on the "politicization of scholarship" tackles "the deformation of scholarship and teaching in American Universities by radical ideology." Professor Balch informs us that "the origin of virtually all of this is on the Left." The situation is serious, perhaps terminal. "The prime concern for alarm is the gradual conversion of many educational institutions from open forums . . . into organizations with established ideological lines. . . ." The future looks bleak. "With tenure in hand, and with control secured over many departments, schools, journals, and professional associations . . . the politicization of the academy by the Left" is almost unstoppable.[23]

Other contributors also raise the alarm: Marxism has dominated "many departments and even some fields." Scholarship has been replaced by "ideology," "traditional discipline" by "radical attacks on Western culture." According to Stanley Rothman, who is identified as the Mary Huggins Gamble Professor of Government at Smith College, radicals gain positions of power and then "press for hiring scholars who share their outlook." Traditional scholars are "demoralized." Certain topics are taboo; it is difficult to discuss the possibility that "some group differences in performance on IQ tests might have a genetic component" or that poverty is a "function of personal limitations rather than simply the fault of the system." According to Rothman, "American colleges and universities are very different places in the 1980s than they were in the 1950s."[24]

The conservative critique of the university lapses into conservative ideology. Politicized scholars and universities, we are to believe, were unknown in the blissful 1950s—the years the government instigated the purge of leftists from colleges and schools. Why is this news to the Mary Huggins Gamble Professor of Government? From vague allusions we are to conclude that Marxists "dominate" departments and fields, but nothing is said of the conservatives who control most departments of economics or philosophy or political science or psychology. Radicals, we are told, try to hire radicals—as if conservatives for years, decades, or centuries have not staffed universities with conservatives. We are to presume that conservative ideas have difficulty getting a hearing—as if the entire structure of government, from the American president to most college presidents, does not emphatically lean to the right.

For conservatives a critical vision is itself evidence of personal failings or foreign ideas. For instance, Lewis Mumford might seem a conservative hero, an authentic man of letters, who has stayed clear of big government, big universities, and big grants. The problem is that Mumford has mounted a withering critique of American society. How can Edward Shils, a conservative, explain that? Easy. While Shils acknowledges Mumford's independence and intelligence, he concludes that he has not "been strong enough to withstand the force of misleading traditions." What are these "misleading traditions"? "The dislike of contemporary American society and culture has been a postulate of many American intellectuals. . . . They acquired the attitude from Europe. . . . Lewis Mumford . . . has not been successful in freeing himself from the fundamental antimonian prejudices that this tradition infused into him."[25]

The distaste, even contempt, for critical thinking—it is not only wrong, it is foreign—becomes even less innocent when coupled with the conservative penchant to undermine freedom of speech. They object to academic freedom not because it is too feeble or narrow but because it is too strong and wide. William Buckley's book on Yale, which inaugurated his career, is subtitled *The Superstitions of "Academic Freedom."* Like many conservatives, Buckley believed the threat to academic freedom was academic freedom itself.

"It is therefore an appalling yet indisputable fact that because of the restraints of 'academic freedom' . . . scores of influential professors . . . are allowed—in fact encouraged—to teach just as they will, to traffic within loose limits, in whatever values they choose," wrote Buckley.[26] His roster of trafficking professors, who should have been cashiered, was quite long; it included not only socialists, Keynesians, and "collectivists" but one Yale professor who at an American Social Hygiene Association conference attacked as "unrealistic" and "outworn" the ethical and religious sanctions against premarital sexual intercourse. "As a professor, Mr. Murdock has wide influence," Buckley noted darkly, "and it cannot be expected that his remarks and attitudes will have no influence on his students."[27]

Russell Kirk affirmed his belief in academic freedom—then took it back: "But when certain persons in the Academy abuse their power and proceed to sneer at human dignity and the whole fabric of order and justice and freedom, then the license of those persons justly may be curtailed."[28] He cautioned not to impair "the principle itself" when expelling professors who have "lost their right to the benefits of academic freedom"; and he thoughtfully bestowed "some discretion" on university officials. "If they decide that a professor despite being a Communist is no discredit to the Academy, then they ought to be allowed to retain him." In any event, for Kirk "much of the whimpering" about academic freedom comes from boredom; this freedom is needed only by a select few.[29]

For decades conservatives like Sidney Hook have sought to rid educational institutions of communists and subversives. Hook's activities have not endeared him to liberals. William O'Neill suggests, however, that civil libertarians have "misread" Hook, who was freedom's best friend. Not exactly.[30] Hook's *Heresy, Yes. Conspiracy, No* (1953) argued it was reasonable, and desirable, to exclude communists from the school system. Moreover, his language and approach were calculated to maximize the inquisition. He estimated a thousand communists were teaching in New York City alone.

> Even if each teacher, on a conservative estimate, taught only a hundred students in the course of a year, this would mean that every year one hundred thousand students in New York City alone would be subject to educationally pernicious indoctrination. Of these ... hundreds would have been influenced by their teachers to join Communist youth organizations from which the Communist movement draws its most fanatical followers.[31]

He concludes that nothing justifies exposing "growing minds" to the "dark mark" of communism.[32] This is the conservatives' leading philosopher calling for a purge—a thousand communist teachers in New York City alone—far more terrible and extensive than that which actually occurred.

Hook's eagerness to define the limits of academic freedom did not fade with the fifties. The student movement inspired him persistently to distinguish between academic freedom and "anarchy."[33] The rights guarded in the First Amendment ("They are first not because they are in the First Amendment, an historical accident ...") are "strategic." "Sometimes in the interest of preserving the entire structure of our desirable freedoms, we may be compelled to abridge one or another of our strategic freedoms."[34]

The conservatives' critique of big universities and big bucks is also more than a bit compromised by their embrace of big universities and big bucks. Few have resigned like Russell Kirk. They attack the noxious impact of the dollar from cool corporate offices. If left-wing academics appear sweaty, clamoring for positions and appointments, perhaps it is because they have traditionally been blacklisted, locked out in the street. It looks rather unseemly—from the top floors where the conservatives lament the decline of scholarship. No academic left can tap funds of the magnitude available to conservative intellectuals. No slick and expensive left journal has ever appeared like *The New Criterion*, handsomely funded by a conservative foundation, an arm of the Olin Corporation, which originally provided Park Avenue office space for Kramer's periodical.[35] Nor does the left include individuals like Richard Mellon Scaife, a great-grandson of the founder of the Mellon bank fortune, with millions available to fund conservative projects and journals.[36]

American corporations increasingly spread their political views by supporting or paying conservative intellectuals. For instance, Smith Kline Corporation, a major drug company

allocates a generous share of its national media budget neither to promoting Contac pills nor Sine-Off. . . . Instead, it buys space to permit featured intellectuals to express themselves on issues of moment. The title of one [two-page] advertisement appearing in *Newsweek* and elsewhere is indicative: "To afford lasting gains in quality of life, we must renew America's aging industrial base, concludes distinguished sociologist Amitai Etzioni."[37]

When was the last time such corporations paid for a two-page spread by a radical professor?

Nor are there many—any?—left professors who have been appointed to funded chairs at major universities. A single issue of the conservative *Public Interest*[38] identifies some of its contributors as Henry Ford II Professor of Social Science, Harvard University (Daniel Bell); John M. Olin Professor of Social Thought, New York University (Irving Kristol); Albert Schweitzer Professor of the Humanities (Emeritus), Columbia University (Robert Nisbet); Shattuck Professor of Government, Harvard University

(James Q. Wilson). Are these people lamenting the impact of money on scholarship?

Sometimes they do not. They object, almost, to the opposite, the effort to belittle or resist the reign of the dollar. This was Buckley's position: the university should serve the money behind it. No freedom is abridged; freedom of the consumer, the rich who fund Yale, is strengthened.

Let us examine the situation of Mr. John Smith, a socialist professor of economics at Yale, and survey his fate under my proposed plan. First of all, let us bar him from teaching because he is inculcating values that the governing board at Yale considers to be against the public welfare. . . . No freedom has yet been abridged in the case of Professor Smith. Rather, the freedom of the consumer has been upheld.[39]

Buckley's "plan" anticipates all eventualities. Discharged from Yale, Mr. Smith is free to find employment at a college "interested in propagating socialism." No luck or no such college? Then Mr. Smith should respond to the needs of the market and try something else, such as carpentry.

The ethos here is simple, whoever pays the tab does the ordering. Culture and scholarship should celebrate capitalism because they are sustained by it. Many conservatives are driven to distraction by individuals who violate this precept. Little irritates them more than left intellectuals who are not starving; social critics in their view should be poor, hungry, or sick. To denounce society and live off it strikes them as an intolerable contradiction.

This theme recurs throughout Epstein's *Ambition*, as well as in Kenneth S. Lynn's *The Air-Line to Seattle*. The authors are incensed by left intellectuals who dare criticize the system that supports them—sometimes nicely—as if only recluse farmers can be social critics. Epstein growls about the "revolutionary lawyer quartered in the $250,000 Manhattan condominium, the critic of American materialism with a Southampton summer home, the publisher of radical books who takes his meals in three-star restaurants."[40]

There is no need to toast such individuals, but the proposition that well-heeled intellectuals must praise society substitutes accounting for thinking. Lynn reexamines Emerson's life and suggests he married for money, to gain an inheritance. If this is true, it may be worth knowing, but Lynn concludes that Emerson was a supreme hypocrite in his gentle attacks on a commercial civilization; instead of questioning vulgar prosperity, he should commend all to do as he did. As Emerson was advising students to spurn business and dedicate themselves to the life of the mind, he neglected to add that he himself was "an American scholar who was living on a subsidy and that the source of that subsidy was the business fortune of a Boston merchant."[41]

A supreme irony lurks in these arguments: conservatives profess no love for economic determinism, which is their objection to Marxism; they protest the subordination of mind to matter, of thought to economic power. Yet they are more determinist than most Marxists. For conservatives the business of culture is not only a fact, it is an ethical command; because American intellectuals live in and from a capitalist society, they should sing its praises. Many conservatives want to tighten the noose, not cut the rope.

The conservative critique of professionals—and professors— that begins boldly concludes lamely. Of course, there is no monolithic conservatism with a single position on academic freedom or culture. It is well to remember that H. L. Mencken, much loved by conservatives for his blasts at professors and purveyors of nonsense, held a more complicated and heretical position. He was no friend of the left, but he shot in both directions.

Ideas of the socialist Scott Nearing found no favor with Mencken. "They seemed to me to be hollow and of no validity.... They have been chiefly accepted and celebrated by men I regard as asses." Mencken forcefully stated his credo: "I am in favor of free competition in all human enterprises.... I admire successful scoundrels, and shrink from Socialists as I shrink from Methodists."[42]

However, when the University of Pennsylvania discharged Nearing, Mencken knew the story. Nearing was not packed off because he was "honestly wrong." "He was thrown out because his efforts to get at the truth disturbed the security and equanimity of the rich ignoranti who happened to control the university. ... In three words, he was thrown out because he was not safe and sane and orthodox. Had his aberration gone in the other direction, had he defended child labor as ardently as he denounced it ... he would have been quite ... secure in his post...."[43] Mencken closed his reflections on Nearing by reiterating his distaste of socialism.

But I should be a great deal more comfortable in those convictions and instincts if I were convinced that the learned professors were really in full and absolute possession of academic freedom—if I could imagine them taking the other tack now and then without damnation to their jobs, their lectures dates, their book sales and their hides.[44]

H. L. Mencken is to conservatives as C. Wright Mills is to radicals: honored and forgotten.

III

NOT ALL left and liberal academics have retreated to professional enclaves while the conservatives monopolize public discussions. Some on the left continue to address a wider audience.

THE LAST INTELLECTUALS

If a disproportionate number are located in New York City, the reasons are close at hand: the lingering tradition of the New York intellectuals, the concentration of the remaining nonacademic periodicals, the raw power of the city. Unlike large campuses in smaller cities, an insular existence is less possible in New York. A professor wraps up his lecture at the University of Michigan in Ann Arbor or at the University of Kansas in Lawrence and encounters only students, researchers, and faculty on his way to lunch. In New York he or she bumps into the city.

Richard Sennett (1943–) and Marshall Berman (1940–) are not only young New York professors (New York University and City University of New York); they might represent the last hurrah, perhaps toot, of New York intellectuals. They write as urban dwellers for urban dwellers. Like the last generation, their talents are broad, and their approach is more literary and impressionistic than coldly methodological. Unlike standard monographs, their books resist easy classification. *The Fall of Public Man, Authority*, and *All That Is Solid Melts into Air* range widely, drawing on case studies, novels, poetry, personal experience. The grit and craziness of New York infuse their work. Most importantly, their topics of urban life, public discourse, authority, and modernism are vital issues which they address in a vital way. All this sets them apart from most academics.

Nor are they completely alone; the list of New York intellectuals might include Stanley Aronowitz, Morris Dickstein, and a few others, who all write for general periodicals. Yet the strain shows. The zeitgeist, if not armed, is watchful. Contemporary New York professors may be dressed as yesterday's New York intellectuals but they remain today's professors. The differences tell. Compared to average academic fare, the writings of Sennett and Berman shine; compared to the last generation's, theirs are drab and pretentious, even sloppy.

"The idea for this book," Sennett tells us in the first sentence of his *Uses of Disorder: Personal Identity and City Life,* "came to me during a walk with Erik Erikson one morning in a New England graveyard."[45] Not the walk, but the sentence suggests the distance traveled from the last generation. Humorless pretense replaces wit and irony. Berman modestly suggests that his own work follows the lead of Walter Benjamin's, but is "more coherent." Benjamin "lurches," while "I try to recapture the most constant currents of metabolic and dialectic flow."[46]

The best work of last generation writers was acid, polemical, deft. Books like *Fall* and *All That Is Solid* seem to be based on the opposite principle: they are diffuse, vague, uncritical. Few pages attain clarity; few seem crafted. Sheldon Wolin, himself a maverick academic, called *Fall* "shoddy in execution" and almost incomprehensible in its method, repetitiousness, and fractured English.[47] While several brief sections are lucid, the whole seems almost deliberately vague.

If *Fall* seems murky, Sennett's *Authority* is opaque—or pedestrian. Sources are not identified; the argument is uncertain; the book hardly written. "I think it is possible from an enquiry into how people now feel authority, fraternity, solitude, and ritual to derive ideas of a more political and visionary sort."[48] The style might be called degraded academism or degraded journalism. There are many allusions to scholarly literature, with no footnotes (which is fine), but there is also no punch or elegance; dead language clots the text.

What I shall explore in this chapter is how the occasions for this reading might occur. . . . My aim is to show how disrupting the chain of command in these special ways does not create chaos, or destroy the sense that someone with strength is in charge, but rather offers the subjects a chance to negotiate with their rulers and to see more clearly what their rulers can and cannot—should and should not—do.[49]

211

In his *Fall* and *Authority*, Sennett refers to scores of authors or commentators, but none is criticized or corrected. Sennett writes about authority, but no authorities are challenged. In Sennett's intellectual world everyone adds a little piece to the story; everyone points out, reminds, or discovers something that Sennett finds interesting. The pluralism and graciousness are estimable but also costly, resulting in a shapeless pastiche. Sennett is a New York intellectual without the caustic intelligence that marked the species; rather he nods to and compliments everyone he encounters. The warm collegiality that flows through his books douses the spark of ideas.

Marshall Berman is feistier. Yet his arguments about modernism make Hegel's night in which all cows are black look like high noon; his terms and arguments are so wide and diffuse anything and everyone can be included. Modernism is energetic, wonderful, tragic, painful, exhilarating, dialectical. So is Marx's thought. So is Nietzsche's. So is everyone's. Who could disagree, but who also can follow Berman's obviously vigorous arguments? These continuously dilate into lax generalizations and upbeat speeches. He concludes his discussion of Marx with these words:

I have been trying in this essay to define a space in which Marx's thought and the modernist tradition converge. First of all, both are attempts to evoke and to grasp a distinctively modern experience. Both confront this realm with mixed emotions, awe and elation fused with a sense of horror. Both see modern life as shot through with contradictory impulsions and potentialities, and both embrace a vision of ultimate or ultramodernity ... as the way through and beyond these contradictions.[50]

This may be true, but it is applicable to many nineteenth- and twentieth-century thinkers. Repeated twenty times in twenty forms, as Berman does, these vague thoughts lose all precision. In Berman everything that is solid melts into air.

Even at his best, when discussing city life and streets, Berman sprays all surfaces with his day-glo paint of contradictions, renewals, anguish. He waxes eloquent about Jane Jacobs, who, of course, fought development and urban renewal; for Berman, her *Death and Life of Great American Cities* is a fundamental modernist text, which played "a crucial role in the development of modernism." Yet he discovers "that beneath her modernist text there is an anti-modernist subtext, a sort of undertow of nostalgia. . . . Jacobs, like so many modernists, . . . moves in a twilight zone where the line between the richest and most complex modernism and the rankest bad faith of modernist anti-modernism is very thin and elusive, if indeed there is a line at all."[51]

From here it is only a short step to deciding that Jacobs and her historic opponent, Robert Moses, are both modernists. Of course, this is difficult to swallow, since Berman poignantly describes how Moses destroyed the Bronx. He introduces a distinction to explain this: "The evolution of Moses and his works in the 1950s underscores another important fact about the postwar evolution of culture and society: the radical splitting-off of modernism and modernization."[52] What might this mean? Berman employs his trusty idiom of contradictions, renewal, dialectics to show the way.

All this suggests that modernism contains its own inner contradictions and dialectics; that forms of modernist thought and vision may congeal into dogmatic orthodoxies and become archaic; that other forms of modernism may be submerged. . . . If we learned through one modernism to construct haloes among our spaces and ourselves, we can learn from another modernism—one of the oldest but also, we can see now, one of the newest—to lose our haloes and find ourselves anew.[53]

Sennett and Berman have abandoned a New York intellectual style not only in their incorrigible diffuseness but also in their perpetual good cheer. Lest they be accused of negativism, constructive ideas dot their books. Sennett's work teeters on the edge of pop psychology with little tips on life and its problems. His suggestions at the end of *Authority* could be lifted, mangled English and all, from a primer about discontent on the job.

These, then, are five ways to disrupt the chain of command, all based on the right and the power to revise through discussion decisions which come from higher up: the use of the active voice; discussion of categorization; permitting a variety of obedience responses to a directive; role exchange; face-to-face negotiation about nurturance. These disruptions are opportunities to connect abstract economic and bureaucratic forces into human terms. . . . And it is by these disruptions that the fear of omnipotent authority might be realistically lessened.[54]

Berman is more ambitious. He is an evangelist of the human spirit and an urban populist; wherever he turns he finds signs of renewal, strength, community. His aim is to appropriate "modernism" so that "we will see that there is more depth in our lives than we thought. We will feel our community with people all over the world. . . . And we will get back in touch with a remarkably rich and vibrant modernist culture . . . a culture that contains vast resources of strength and health, if only we come to know it as our own."[55] Berman hits all the buzzwords: roots, community, strength, health. This is psychobabble for aging leftists.

He concludes his book on an upbeat note with a suggestion or more exactly with a "modernist dream" that might help salvage the Bronx. "I want to use modernism to generate a dialogue with my own past . . . my Bronx." A "modernist vision and imagination can give our maimed inner cities something to live for, can help or force our non-urban majority to see their stake in the city's fate, can bring forth its abundance of life and beauty."[56]

Berman dreams of the Bronx Mural. This would be painted on the retaining wall that runs along the Cross-Bronx Expressway, which mortally wounded the borough. "The mural would have to be executed in a number of radically different styles. . . . Children of the Bronx would be encouraged to return and put themselves in the picture: the Expressway wall is big enough to hold them all. . . . To drive past and through all this would be a rich and strange experience. Drivers might feel captivated by the figures, environments and fantasies. . . ."[57]

As if shooting past the mural on the way to work or inching past it in New York traffic, would not be a sufficiently rich and strange experience, Berman caps it with an equally rich and strange idea: a "gigantic ceremonial arch" would mark the end of the highway.

This arch would be circular and inflatable, suggesting both an automobile tire and a bagel. When fully pumped up, it would look indigestibly hard as a bagel, but ideal as a tire for fast getaway; when soft, it would appear leaky and dangerous as a tire but, as a bagel, inviting to settle down and eat.[58]

So Berman's modernist-antimodernist dream. Of course, not all the details are worked out. When will the arch be pumped up or deflated? What color will it be, tire color or bagel color? (There is also an awkward question about Professor Berman's familiarity with bagels: he seems to think they change shape when stale.) Obviously, this is fantasy, but as a vision it is as inspired as the giant doughnuts and hot dogs of some fast food joints. As an idea, it is half-baked.

As usual, Berman covers his ideas with a wordy icing:

I could go on talking about more exciting modernist works of the past decade. Instead, I thought to end up with the Bronx. . . . As I come to the end of this book, I see how this project, which consumed so much of my time, blends into the modernism of my times. I have been digging up some of the buried modern spirits of the past, trying to open up a dialectic between their experience and our own, hoping to help the people of my time create a modernity of the future.[59]

The sentences seem lifted from an endless lecture. The original New York intellectuals were known as big talkers—and spartan writers; they wrote graceful and finely tuned essays. The successors lost this talent. Sennett and Berman are garrulous writers; the elegant essay has become the sloppy book. Sennett writes, "Experience of diversity and experience in a region of society at a distance from the intimate circle; the 'media' contravene both these principles of publicness. Having said this, I am uncomfortable with it as a self-contained formula."[60]

These are not stray examples. These books lack balance and grace. While their styles are not the same—Berman's adopts the personal, Sennett, the bureaucratic—their books seem only partially written. They meander and poke around, and the digressions do not hone the argument. It is here where form passes into content; both *Fall* and *All That Is Solid* are remarkably opaque books. They provide less light than a sense of generalized urgency, perhaps a feeling.

For this reason many readers and critics are fond of these books; the arguments or contents recede before the topic and atmosphere. Even with a dash of originality few books examine broad social issues for a reading public; readers are gratified when a book does. It hardly seems to matter how the books proceed, or if they do; whether after a chapter or two they are readable, even coherent; whether anyone can figure out what Sennett has argued; or whether by page 350 Berman is dreaming of inflatable bagels. None of this matters. These books live by virtue of their titles, their subject matter, and the authors' general effort to write for the public. Yet the achievements mark not a vital New York culture, in which ideas and language still count, but its afterlife.

One additional index of New York cultural life should be mentioned: *The New York Review of Books.* The evolution of *The New York Review* is a short course on the fate of independent writing, younger thinkers, and Jewish New York intellectuals. From its beginnings during a 1963 newspaper strike, when *The New York Times Book Review* addicts began suffering withdrawal symptoms, *The New York Review* has exuded the bravado of New York cultural life.

Predictably it was Norman Podhoretz who boasted in "Book Reviewing and Everyone I Know" (1963) that "just about everyone I know has contributed" to the first issue. He named Elizabeth Hardwick, Dwight Macdonald, Irving Howe, Alfred Kazin, Philip Rahv, Norman Mailer, William Phillips, Mary McCarthy, and some others, including one contributor "I never heard of before."[61]

A young critic, writing in *The New Yorker* blasted Podhoretz (and several other reviewers) for crude self- and group promotion. "There are several remarkable things about this essay," Renata Adler wrote in 1964, with divine foresight of Podhoretz's later career. "First, 'everyone I know' occurs fourteen times (aside from its appearance in the title) . . . Mr. Podhoretz clearly does not consider himself a speaker in isolation. . . . Moreover, such unembarrassed statements as 'Among our most talented literary intellectuals (including just about everyone I know) reviewing is regarded as a job for young men on the make' . . . imply that the New Reviewers regard criticism less as a sympathetic response to literature than as an opportunity for an assertion of personality."[62]

Adler glimpsed the future: she described this brand of reviewing as ". . . an elaborate system of cross-references that amounts to mutual coattail-hanging; a stale liberalism gone reactionary . . . false intellectualism that is astonishingly shabby in its arguments . . . a pastiche of attitudes and techniques vying to divert the attention of the reader from the book ostensibly under review to the personality of the reviewer. . . ."[63]

While these barbs were directed at Podhoretz (who edited *Commentary* and much later "broke" with *The New York Review*), they were also aimed at the insular world of New York intellectuals, whose favorite periodical—for a while—was the *Review*. Some ten years later a book-length study argued that *The New York Review* was almost a closed shop. "If you are young, gifted, and white, don't call the *New York Review*. And they probably won't call you, either. . . . In general, the *Review* has a wretched reputation when it comes to dealing with young and/or 'unimportant' writers. . . ."[64]

Yet these criticisms missed something. *The New York Review* buzzed with energy and excitement during its first decade— perhaps fueled by its intense crisscrossing relationships. Today, however, it looks very different. Approaching its twenty-fifth anniversary, not only has it shifted from left to right but, more revealingly, it has refashioned its identity. For contributors the *Review* increasingly relies not on mere professors but on Ivy League professors, professors with titles and chairs, and especially professors from Oxford or Cambridge. Its few independent writers are old contributors like Gore Vidal and Theodore Draper. While it continues to publish serious and sometimes provocative pieces, reading *The New York Review* summons up Oxford teas rather than New York delis.

An unscientific check of ten random issues from early 1985 confirms the transformation. Excluding poems and minor pieces, out of 116 major reviews, over half were by British writers and professors; of these, 20 were from Oxford and Cambridge. The embrace of the English academics and Ivy League professors by *The New York Review* confesses the demise of the free-wheeling New York intellectual life it once championed.[65]

Of course, it may confess something more. The absence of new and young writers at *The New York Review* has long been noted. Does this simply reflect an absence in the culture or also the blindness of its editors? Richard Kostelanetz (1940–), a young writer who has carefully, perhaps obsessively, monitored the state of his generation,[66] concludes that not talent but an interlocking directorate of New York intellectuals headquartered at *The New York Review* keeps young writers out of the limelight. In a book-long tract Kostelanetz marshalled his evidence that the New York brokers allowed no one younger than Susan Sontag and Philip Roth, both born in 1933, to enter the big time. For Kostelanetz, the missing younger writers are the suppressed writers.[67]

To be sure, this argument can easily be denigrated as the consolation of talentless and rejected authors. To explain their lack of success they hallucinate conspiracies directed against themselves and their friends. Kostelanetz may be his own worst enemy. Nevertheless, the rancor of its critics should not be a pretext to avoid probing *The New York Review*.

The most serious of the charges against the *Review* lack substance. The absence of younger writers cannot be attributed to the editorial policies of one journal, or even several journals. Nevertheless, no periodical simply mirrors cultural currents, and a closer look at *The New York Review* reveals a deplorable record. It never nurtured or heeded younger American intellectuals. For a quarter century it withdrew from the cultural bank without making any investments. Today the operation must rely on imported intellectual capital, mainly from England. A delayed political consequence even surfaces. Conservative journals, such as *The New Criterion* and *Commentary*, assiduously, and wisely, cultivate younger writers. *The New York Review*, although it now has abandoned radicalism, never did; partly as a result fewer writers on the left had the same chance to acquire a public voice.

Yet the vagaries of *The New York Review* may signify little. Editors do not control the sluice gates of culture. Cause and effect inextricably mesh. While *The New York Review* has never welcomed younger writers, intellectual generations do not wait for hand-addressed invitations before emerging. The general absence of younger intellectuals, the particular absence of younger New York intellectuals, is due not to a lockout but to a shutdown of the old urban and cultural centers.

IV

TO IDENTIFY intellectuals with academics and their fate almost capitulates to the historical juggernaut; it implies that to be an intellectual requires a campus address. Others are barred. Why? Even apart from plumbers or carpenters who might be intellectuals, some professions would seem to possess at least the prerequisites, if not a claim, to join this group. For instance, of the 136,000 full-time librarians in the United States,[68] might not some or many be intellectuals? And what about booksellers and editors, lawyers and doctors, journalists and foundation managers? Are they forever excluded from the ranks of intellectuals simply for the lack of university letterhead?

Obviously not. Yet the decisive category here is not intellectuals, those who cherish thinking and ideas, but public intellectuals, those who contribute to open discussions. Evidently nothing or no one says that carpenters or librarians or brain surgeons cannot be public intellectuals; some are, but very few. The dearth points to the everyday work circumstances that encourage or discourage public interventions. Lawyers may often write, but unless they also teach, only judges and other lawyers will read, or want to read, their briefs. Librarians may love books but may be too exhausted to write any after eight hours of sifting through those already published.

One hundred years after Marx (perhaps a hundred years before), the first or second question we ask of someone is, what does he or she do? The question smacks of a repressive social order, where work is life. The query also means, what can he or she do for me? Anyone who finds himself at the "wrong" social gathering, where people are hustling—a carpenter among lawyers, a teacher among film people—receives a lesson in instrumentality. Interest dies when one's occupation comes up. "A high school teacher? . . . Very interesting . . . hmmmm . . . I think I need a refill. . . ." In a different social order, perhaps, the question might be, what does he or she think or dream or believe?

However, stripped of its crassness, the question is not malicious. The social order is repressive. If we know a person's work we know something about the individual. If people are interior decorators or leathergoods importers, we have a clue to their thoughts and concerns. We also assume, unless we are informed otherwise, that they are not writers or public intellectuals. The assumption may be wrong. People sometimes resent, with good reason, being identified with their work. The assumption, however, is not a moral judgment; it is simply a generalization based on experience that work infuses life. The museum administrator or dentist lacks the time or circumstances to write for the public.

Apart from the academics, the work situation of only one other group requires public writing: journalists. Outside the university, and partly against it, journalists keep alive a tradition of writing on public issues in a public language. Although professors write most nonfiction books, journalists weigh in with a considerable number of titles.[69] America's classic man of letters, Edmund Wilson, called himself a journalist. "When I speak of myself as a journalist, I do not of course mean that I have always dealt with current events. . . . I mean that I have made my living mainly by writing in periodicals."[70]

Increasingly, journalists have sustained—more in their books than in their daily writing—the general culture; society has responded, almost in gratitude, by mythologizing them. As academic life and writing have grown wan, journalism has expanded, appearing bigger than life: vigorous, committed, public. Journalists themselves have been romanticized in countless movies from *All the President's Men* to *The Killing Fields* and *Under Fire*. Journalists search for truth, for which they risk their lives or careers; they are unswervingly devoted to a public. They are everything professors are not.

The reality is somewhat different. "Journalists" is a catch-all term; it includes those working in television and radio and those in the "print" media, which further subdivide into staff (full-time) writers and part-timers or free-lancers. Television journalists of the major networks and opinion shows constitute their own breed; few in number, they command high salaries and sometimes much attention. Like everything about television, the sins (and virtues) of its journalists spread across the land.

The lecture circuit has discovered television journalists. James Fallows reports that nowadays even minor trade groups like to kick off their conventions with a speaker who will edify and amuse them about life in Washington. Liberally bankrolled by dues-paying members, these associations inevitably choose the journalists they see on television, who have perfected its talk-show style. Fallows reflects on the deleterious consequences. Conservative, combative, and showy individuals with a gift for "scholarly sounding epigrams" dominate the television opinion shows and the lecture circuit. "Not everyone behaves this way, but to young people the model of success is clear. Ten years ago the models were Woodward and Bernstein, twenty years ago Richard Rovere or Theodore H. White, thirty years ago James Reston or Walter Lippmann. Now the model is George Will. . . . This new model has helped make political debate more catty and dismissive than at some other times."[71]

Print journalists, lacking this clout, are a much larger group whose contributions partake of more traditional intellectual life.[72] Nevertheless, as the campus defines academics, the newspaper office defines journalists; they work under the constraints of assignments and deadlines. These restrictions inhere to all newspaper work, but they also reflect specific historical periods. Currently, the shrinking number of newspapers and the intensifying effort to attract affluent readers through "soft" and "lifestyle" coverage constrict journalists. While universities have physically expanded, newspapers, have declined. One grim study asks whether newspapers are surrendering their role as "transmitters of information, education, and culture."[73]

The reasons for this are much discussed. One cause is familiar: the same forces that gutted the city and shipped Americans out to the suburbs eviscerated the big city newspapers. As individuals abandoned, and were abandoned by, mass transit, they took to cars. To and from work they scanned the road, not the front page. "The decay of both central cities and mass transit meant that the metropolitan papers no longer had customers pouring out of downtown offices and factories looking for a newspaper to read on the bus or train ride home. New suburbs . . . and workers commuting by car have diminished the newspaper-reading habit of millions of families."[74]

A single example: the *Newark News*, easily the best newspaper in New Jersey, was a complete outfit with five editorial writers, a Washington correspondent, its own theater, arts, and book reviews, and a Sunday magazine; it was sometimes known as *"The New York Times* of New Jersey." It died in 1972. The reason? Its downtown delivery trucks mired in traffic did not reach the new population centers. "It was a big city newspaper that refused to follow its readers to the suburbs."[75]

Of course, this is not the whole story. Television viewing has also slashed readership, especially of afternoon papers. Corporate mergers diminish the number of dailies, or eliminate differences among them. The days of the small family-owned newspaper are numbered. "The daily newspapers of the United States are being put in chains, newspaper chains. Of thirty-five dailies sold in 1982, thirty-two were absorbed by newspaper groups. . . . At the current rate, there will be no single, family-owned dailies by the year 2000."[76]

Buy-outs, sell-outs, and closings have sharply cut the number of dailies. "In 1920 there were 700 cities with competing dailies," Ben H. Bagdikian notes. "In 1982, though the country's population had more than doubled, there were only 27 cities with competing dailies."[77] Not only the closings and mergers but the purchase of small dailies by large newspaper corporations usually restrict job openings. The big chains often cut staff and utilize more syndicated and canned features. Almost identical newspapers can be produced in far-flung parts of the country.

These economic facts have taken their toll on journalists.

Fewer big city newspapers mean fewer opportunities for work that broaches the large political, economic, or cultural issues; and even the big newspapers relentlessly expand "soft" news, spinning out sections on homes or leisure. A difficult employment situation does not make the life of a reporter or an editorial writer any better. The fight for assignments or for copy is always colored by the possibility of resigning and finding another job. But if that possibility dwindles, journalistic backbone softens. This may be a reason why in an era that cries out for articulate and critical journalistic voices, there are virtually none.

A larger group of part-time and free-lance writers dwarfs the number of staff writers; here the term "journalism" may mislead since free-lance writers include any and all those who may write professionally—children's books, cookbooks, how-to-lose-fifty-pounds-by-eating-more books. However, very few writers actually earn a living from writing; they are free-lance as much by necessity—they must have other jobs—as from choice. This means that the free-lance writing pool is perpetually in flux with many entering and leaving. For those who are successful, it generally requires specialization in genres where there are expanding markets—cooking, travel, sports, movies.

One of the few detailed studies discovered that in 1979 half of American authors earned less than $5000 from their writings. "The principal message conveyed by the data on hand is that authors do not earn much from writing. If writers had to depend on writing income, the majority would be in serious financial trouble. This is so even for many winners of the truly major awards such as the National Book Award and Pulitzer Prizes." These are average figures, and what these researchers label "committed full-time" writers earn more, especially if they plow the turf called "genre fiction," the most lucrative area. Nevertheless, career-long full-time writers constitute only 5 percent of authors. Most authors shuttle between full-time and part-time writing, depending on the economic situation.[78]

All this indicates that writing is a difficult occupation. As an exclusive means of economic support, free-lance writing easily drains an author. Proposing, researching, and completing projects that are economically viable—for which an editor will pay— allows little space for projects that might have less cash value. The free-lance writer is at the mercy of a market, which, as Mumford has noted, supports less and less serious and general prose. To suggest a piece on the hobbies or exercising regime of a celebrity might draw an editor's interest; to propose an article on the urban crisis would draw a blank.

The obsessive interest of free-lance writers in *The New Yorker* reflects this situation. For the unestablished *The New Yorker* is almost the only periodical that might support sustained, and serious, nonfiction (and fiction) with a living wage. *The New Yorker* to the free-lancer is not only the royal way but the only way; after rejection from *The New Yorker*—easily elicited—the next choice is proposing a hundred projects to twenty editors. That *The New Yorker* itself, amid reports of declining revenues, has recently been sold to a large media company suggests the vulnerability of the last outlets.[79]

It takes an immense amount of talent, devotion, or plain luck to overcome the usual lot of free-lance writers and contribute to the general culture. It can and is done. However, the oeuvre of free-lance writers is simply too variegated to allow for sensible generalizations; moreover, precisely because of their precarious economic situation, those writing one year are gone the next. They have either become staff writers with regular assignments and salaries or have moved on to something else. For these reasons an emphatic journalistic voice of younger writers is difficult to identify.

In the 1960s the emergence of "new journalism" and a revitalized muckraking promised to transform the face of American writing. New journalism arose on the fringes of the traditional press or in the new "underground press." By their subject matter or personal tone, the new journalists broke with the straitlaced neutrality of the traditional press. New journalism, wrote Morris Dickstein, was marked by "atmosphere, personal feeling, intepretation, advocacy and opinion, novelist characterization and description, touches of obscenity, concern with fashion and cultural change, and political savvy."[80]

Tom Wolfe's manifesto and anthology, *The New Journalism*, proposed a different justification and cast of characters. The new journalists had nothing to do with an underground press or a personal voice; they were younger members of the regular press, who preferred the "third-person point of view." The new journalists discovered the "joys of detailed realism and its strange powers," frightening the old men of letters and morals.[81]

These descriptions hardly tally; both contain some truth, overstated in the heat of the moment, as the whole truth. Like most "new" movements, "new" journalism was also old, a remembrance and a retrieval. The classic of the genre, James Agee and Walker Evans's extraordinary *Let Us Now Praise Famous Men*, a study of southern tenant farmers in the Depression, looms over the new journalism; their book contained equal measures of pure fact and raw passion. Based on articles commissioned and rejected by *Fortune* magazine, it was published in 1941 and ignored until its reissue in 1960.

"It is intended that this record and analysis be exhaustive, with no detail, however trivial it may seem, left untouched," stated Agee. This "record" included poems, photographs, curtain calls, speeches, relentless descriptions of shoes and overalls, lyrical writing, cries from the heart—all in the service of undermining traditional journalism. "It seems to me curious," stated Agee in an opening rush of words,

> not to say obscene and thoroughly terrifying, that it could occur to an association of human beings drawn together through need and chance and for profit into a company, an organ of journalism, to pry intimately into the lives of an undefended and appallingly damaged group of human beings, an ignorant and helpless rural family, for the purpose of parading the nakedness, disadvantage and humiliation of these lives before another group of human beings, in the name of science, of "honest journalism" (whatever that paradox may mean), of humanity, of social fearlessness, for money, and for a reputation for crusading and for unbias which, when skillfully enough qualified, is exchangeable at any bank for money. . . .[82]

Today new journalism, not as a body of writing but as a generational presence, hardly exists. The writers Wolfe anthologized have generally stayed with the craft but do not, and probably never did, represent a coherent movement.[83] A recent survey identified a new species, "the literary journalists," graduates of the new journalism but, like the times themselves, quieter and more professional. "Now there has appeared a younger generation of writers who don't necessarily think of themselves as New Journalists, but do find immersion, voice, accuracy and symbolism to be the hallmarks of their work."[84] "The literary journalists" encompass some fine writers—among others, John McPhee, Joan Didion, Jane Kramer, Tracy Kidder, Sara Davidson—but it hardly adds up to either a new species of writing or a cultural presence.

The left version of new journalism, which was more political *and* more personal also underwent dispersal and loss of identity. At its height every small city, every sizable college, boasted an "underground" newspaper. Liberation News Service, a clearing house for the underground press, had six hundred subscribers who regularly received packets of information. A small army of journalists staffed these newspapers. What happened? The press vanished; the most successful publications transformed themselves into entertainment guides.

Of course, this is unfair. Like the sixties as a whole, success was part of the undoing. The traditional press incorporated elements of the underground press. A more personal feature writing made its appearance in the established dailies; the coverage of sexuality, drugs, and, for a moment, a left critique of official America was allowed. Until *The New York Times* decided to risk it, Daniel Ellsberg planned to publish the Pentagon Papers in the underground press.[85]

The underground journalists themselves disbanded for a thousand destinations. Devoted and talented people stayed, but no clear dominant voice or voices emerged. Abe Peck, in his account of the "underground press," closes with a survey of the current whereabouts of its main figures. His own trajectory is not representative, but familiar. "From 1967 to 1971 . . . I wrote, edited, typed, swept up, sold papers, and was arrested at the *Seed*, Chicago's best-known underground press." He later free-lanced, became a music columnist for the Associated Press, and subsequently joined the staff at the Chicago *Daily News* and *Sun-Times* "In 1980 I applied for a leave from the *Sun-Times* that became a resignation. . . . I felt caught up in the feed-the-machine nature of too much daily journalism." Today he is a professor of journalism at Northwestern University.[86]

Peck reports on the whereabouts of seventy-five other participants. Those still writing include David Harris (*Dreams Die Hard*); Greil Marcus, rock critic; Adam Hochschild, a founder/contributor of *Mother Jones*; Harvey Wasserman (*Harvey Wasserman's History of the United States*); Dave Marsh (*Rock and Roll Confidential*); and a number of others, some active in television news (Danny Schechter, Lowell Bergman).[87] Peck's complete list implies a conclusion by virtue of no conclusion. Where once there was hope and a chance of a distinct generational voice, there are now a number of writers.

The 1960s revitalized muckraking, the return to power-structure research, and scathing attacks on official lies and cover-ups.[88] For a while, during the period of Watergate, muckraking journalists were cultural heroes. The revival has ebbed, if only because the political atmosphere has changed. *Ramparts*, most closely associated with left-wing muckraking, folded; one successor (*Seven Days*) never got off the ground; another (*Mother Jones*) teeters—and is considering abandoning its name, that of the great coalminer agitator, as too brash.[89]

For several reasons the ante has been raised; muckraking or investigative reporting is expensive; it requires gobs of time, often with no results. To research property ownership in downtown slums or American corporations in the Third World is a protracted commitment that requires either a hefty publisher's advance or a clear audience; the first is very rare, the second questionable. Moreover, the increasing use of litigation can stop a free-lancer in his or her tracks. "Without the money and lawyers" available to major newspapers, comments a study of the "new" muckrakers, "free-lancers can be wiped out by the expense of fighting a libel suit."[90] The major newspapers that do hire investigative reporters, of course, do not give them free reign; they examine subjects that editors and management deem proper.[91]

"I am," wrote I. F. Stone in 1963, "an anachronism. . . . In an age when young men, setting out on a career of journalism, must find their niche in some huge newspaper or magazine combine, I am a wholly independent newspaperman, standing alone, without organizational or party backing. . . ."[92] I. F. Stone

(1907–) exemplifies a last generation muckraker who seems to have no successors. Stone, always a journalist, worked for a series of left-wing newspapers, the last of which, the New York *Daily Compass*, expired during the darker days of the early fifties. Without employment, Stone devised a plan to launch a four-page weekly newsletter using the mailing lists of the defunct radical press. In 1953, Stone published the first *I. F. Stone's Weekly* with some five thousand subscribers.

For nineteen years he lived for and from his *Weekly*, a one-man operation, which eventually reached a circulation of seventy thousand. Deliberately severe in appearance, it tirelessly exposed lies and contradictions of government and press, becoming an indispensable source for radicals. " 'Intellectual' may sound like an incongruous word to describe a man who has devoted a working life of half a century to daily and weekly journalism," wrote Robert Sklar in an introduction to a collection of Stone's pieces; but "it is precisely because he is an intellectual that Stone's old articles seem to grow in value. He is a historian, a philosopher, a man of letters. . . ."[93]

Stone's retirement in 1971 left a hole difficult to plug; there are numerous muckrakers and critics of government and press but none with the persistence and scope of Stone. Many are professors, with other obligations, who weigh in only occasionally; some are journalists who do not have the forum or means to engage in full-time scrutiny of official malfeasance. The cultural trajectory is familiar: where once there were few, now there are many, but the many seem quieter.[94]

"Where are our intellectuals?" As a slogan of the sixties had it (referring to revolutionaries): we are everywhere. When Harold Rosenberg alluded to Berkeley as a refutation of reports of vanishing bohemias and rootless intellectuals, he was not all wrong.

There is a lesson here: to apprehend the present as history is risky, perhaps impossible; it is easy to confuse the gasps of the past and future. For conservatives it is sobering, for radicals, encouraging to realize that the sixties arrived almost unannounced.

Nevertheless, the temptation to view history in cycles should be resisted. The long view suggests that intellectual work has been recast; and this means intellectuals have been recast in the way they live and function. It is too simple to draw a direct line connecting life and thought, matching professors who are preoccupied with research or conference papers and their cultural contribution; it would also be foolish to deny a relationship. The history of philosophy is also the history of philosophers. The history of journalism is also the history of journalists.

The transformation of the traditional intellectual habitat is not instantaneous; it parallels the decay of the cities, the growth of the suburbs, and the expansion of the universities. There is no need to announce the collapse of civilization when fast food outlets nudge out greasy spoons, vending machines replace newspaper stands, or green campuses supplant vandalized city parks; but there is little reason to ignore its impact on the rhythm of cultural life. It matters whether people grow up on city streets or in suburban malls; whether intellectuals obsess about a single editor who judges their work or three "referees," ten colleagues, several committees, and various deans.

Universities encourage a definite intellectual form. They do not shoot, they simply do not hire those who are unable or unwilling to fit in. Even Henry Luce of the *Time* magazine empire, often denounced as a master propagandist, employed and even liked mavericks and dissenters. Universities, on the other hand, hire by committees: one needs degrees, references, the proper deference, a pleasant demeanor. To win over a committee that recommends to a department which counsels a chairman who advises a dean who suggests to a college president takes a talent very different from gaining the assent of a single individual. It is almost ludicrous to imagine "Professor Edmund Wilson" or "Professor H. L. Mencken."

It is even possible to chart a cultural shift in the unlikely quarter of book acknowledgments and dedications. Early Elizabethan books were usually graced by flowery prefaces dedicated to a patron who supported the writer and who, it was hoped, would be instructed and edified by the work. In the course of the seventeenth and eighteenth centuries, the reading and book-buying public replaced the patron; and books frequently were dedicated and directed to the gentle and interested reader. "The reading group was no longer confined to court and gentry," explains a study of Elizabethan prefaces, and "writers could safely appeal to a circle of readers of all classes." "To the Gentlemen Readers" or "To the Courteous and Courtly Ladies of England" or "To the right honorable citizens of the citie of London" ran some typical dedications.[95]

To jump to the present, opening serious nonfiction books is like skimming personal telephone books; often a dense list of colleagues, friends, institutions, and foundations precedes the text. The anonymous reader has become named, addressed, saluted. This is a change in style, but it is more; it is the imprimatur of a democratic age. It suggests that the author or book passed the test, gaining the approval of a specific network, which filtered out the unkempt and unacceptable. It is a notice of a serious and reputable work. It serves to reassure as well as intimidate readers and reviewers. Even with the requisite qualifier—the opinions and mistakes are strictly the author's—who wants to challenge a book inspected by scores of scholars, published by a major university, and supported by several foundations?

These are tendencies, not laws of nature. The country is too vast, the culture too contradictory, to neatly categorize. Nevertheless, this undeniable truth easily degenerates into apologetics, as if no generalization could be true and everything is possible. Everything may be possible, but not probable. Intellectuals may be everywhere, but almost everywhere they face similar and limited options: the young especially are vulnerable, precisely because they emerge in a situation of dwindling intellectual choices. Hence the historical witticism: intellectuals of the irrational, far-out, hang-loose sixties matured into a more buttoned-up, professional, and invisible group than did preceding intellectual generations. One thousand radical sociologists, but no Mills; three hundred critical literary theorists but no Wilson; scads of Marxist economists but no Sweezy or Braverman; urban critics galore but no Mumford or Jacobs.

Private and public, invisible and visible, professional and amateur, these are loaded, difficult terms. They are not simply opposites. What is quiet and professional today may be open and public tomorrow. Younger intellectuals, if they mainly teach and write for each other, have little immediate impact; but they have students who pass through and on to other things. Everyone has had influential teachers, unknown to a wider world, but decisive in one's own development; these teachers inspired, cajoled, taught. Isn't it possible that the entire transmission belt of culture has shifted? That it is no longer public in the way it once was but now takes place invisibly in university classrooms and reading assignments?

This is the conservatives' nightmare: while radicals and liberals have been chased from public and visible posts, they actually staff the educational system, corroding the Republic from within. Conservatives frequently complain bitterly that they send their children to elite universities, and during Chistmas vacation, discover them studying Marxism. Of course, "studying Marxism"

means one professor in a department of forty teaches Marxism—
one professor too many. Like Buckley, their faith in truth is limited; they believe that conservative ideas are more convincing
when others have been excluded.

Yet it is only their nightmare; at least there seems little reason
to posit an emerging gap between a university and a public culture, the former subversive, the latter apologetic. Studies of undergraduates generally show them to be more conservative than
in the past, more concerned with careers and money, and less
interested in what some graying New Left professors might
think. This too encourages a professionalization, a turning in
toward more receptive colleagues. Nevertheless, today as in the
past, universities preserve a cultural breathing space where people do study Marx—and Adam Smith. This should not be dismissed nor mythologized as if left-wing literary critics threaten
anyone but each other.

"Public intellectual" is a category even more fraught with
difficulties. "Publicist," if it once connotated an engagement
with the state and law, is almost obsolete, victimized by Hollywood and "public relations": it now signifies someone who han-
dles and manipulates the media, an advance or front man (or
woman). A public intellectual or old-style publicist is something
else, perhaps the opposite, an incorrigibly independent soul answering to no one. Yet, this does not suffice; the definition must
include a commitment not simply to a professional or private
domain but to a public world—and a public language, the
vernacular.

The elaboration of national and vernacular languages, the
voice of new urban classes, in the face of an ossifying Latin, the
idiom of a scholastic elite, characterizes modern culture since
the Renaissance. "All over Europe," explains Erich Auerbach,
while Latin turned brittle, "first in Italy, then in the Iberian pen-

insula, France, and England, an educated public with a *Hochsprache* of its own now made its appearance."[96] The adoption of the vernacular was not always simple or peaceful, for it meant that groups once excluded from religious and scientific controversy could now enter the fray.

The "crime" of Galileo, for instance, was less what he discovered or said but how and where he said it. He renounced Latin to write in fluid Italian for a new public. As the Florentine ambassador reported after a meeting of papal authorities with Galileo, "If he wanted to hold this Copernican opinion, he was told, let him hold it quietly and not spend so much effort in trying to have others share it."[97] This is precisely what Galileo rejected. He had decided, states a modern account, "to by-pass the universities and address himself in the vernacular to the intelligent public at large. This involved no doubt a sacrifice of the international value of Latin, but Galileo did not care to mark himself as an exclusive member of the light-shy and scattered republic of scholars. . . . He felt right at ease in the street, in the square. . . ."[98]

It would be unfair and overdramatic to charge younger intellectuals with sabotaging this historical project—the commitment to a wider educated world—which in any event hardly rides on the shoulders of a single generation. Yet the danger of yielding to a new Latin, a new scholasticism insulated from larger public life, tints the future gray on gray. While professional and arcane languages can be a refuge, and a necessity, they can also be an excuse and a flight.

Is there a choice? Any study that is both historical and critical engenders a fundamental antinomy: it sketches major and minor tendencies that might have shaped a world—and it protests against them. There is no doubt that the demise of public intellectuals reflects the recomposition of the public itself; it coincides with the wild success of television, the expansion of the suburbs, the corrosion of the cities, the fattening of the universities. The eclipse of the big general magazines, such as *Look* and *Life*, itself registers a parcellation of a once more homogeneous public; they have been replaced by "special interest" magazines—tennis, computer, travel, sports. In view of these developments, the disappearance of general intellectuals into professions seems completely understandable, inevitable, and perhaps desirable.

And yet if this or any study were only to ratify what has been and must be, it would be pointless. Younger intellectuals have responded to their times, as they must; they have also surrendered to them, as they need not. Humanity does not make history just as it pleases, but it does make history. By the back door choice enters the historical edifice.

NOTES

Preface

1. Harold Stearns, "Where Are Our Intellectuals?" in his *America and the Young Intellectual* (New York: George H. Doran, 1921), pp. 46–51.

2. Even successful novelists must supplement their earnings from writings; see "For a Young Novelist Success but No Riches," *New York Times*, January 2, 1986, p. C19.

3. Michael Anania, "Of Living Belfry and Rampart: On American Literary Magazines Since 1950," in *The Little Magazine in America: A Modern Documentary History*, ed. E. Anderson and M. Kinzie (Yonkers, N.Y.: Pushcart, 1978), pp. 12–13. This is a superb compendium on the state and fate of little magazines.

4. David M. Ricci, *The Tragedy of Political Science: Politics, Scholarship and Democracy* (New Haven: Yale University Press, 1984); Donald N. McCloskey, *The Rhetoric of Economics* (Madison: University of Wisconsin Press, 1985); Robert A. McCaughey, *International Studies and Academic Enterprise: A Chapter in the Enclosure of American Learning* (New York: Columbia University Press, 1984); Paul A. Attewell, *Radical Political Economy Since the Sixties: A Sociology of Knowledge Analysis* (New Brunswick, N.J.: Rutgers University Press, 1984).

5. Robert L. Jacobson, "Nearly 40 Pct. of Faculty Members Said to Consider Leaving Academe," *Chronicle of Higher Education*, October 23, 1985, p. 1.

Chapter 1 / Missing Intellectuals?

1. James Atlas, "The Changing World of New York Intellectuals," *New York Times Magazine*, August 25, 1985, and replies; Alexander Cockburn, "Beat the Devil," *The Nation*, September 7, 1985, and Ellen Willis, "Atlas Shrugged," *Village Voice*, October 1, 1985.

2. See John Keane, *Public Life and Late Capitalism* (Cambridge: Cambridge University Press, 1984).

3. See Neil Postman, *Amusing Ourselves to Death: Public Discourse in the Age of Show Business* (New York: Viking, 1985), pp. 44–63.

4. Cited in James Gilbert, *Writers and Partisans* (New York: John Wiley, 1968), p. 36. For a discussion of *The Seven Arts*, see Arthur Frank Wertheim, *The New York Little Renaissance* (New York: New York University Press, 1976), pp. 176–83.

5. Charles Kadushin, *The American Intellectual Elite* (Boston: Little, Brown, 1974).

6. Robert Silvers, editor of *The New York Review of Books*, is the odd name on this list; in conventional terms he is not a leading intellectual, although perhaps a leading editor.

7. Kadushin, *American Intellectual Elite*, pp. 26, 32.

8. Daniel Bell, "The 'Intelligentsia" in American Society" (1976), in his *The Winding Passage* (New York: Basic Books, 1980), pp. 127–29.

9. Might the absence of younger intellectuals at *The New York Review* also be due to a lack of welcome for them? I discuss this further in chapter 7.

10. Harold Stearns, *America and the Young Intellectual* (New York: George H. Doran, 1921), p. 47.

11. Bell, *Winding Passage*, p. xiii.

12. Schwartz to Karl Shapiro, September 13, 1954, *Letters of Delmore Schwartz*, ed. Robert Phillips (Princeton: Ontario Review Press, 1984), p. 291. However, for his unhappy search for an academic post, see James Atlas, *Delmore Schwartz* (New York: Avon, 1978).

13. Edmund Wilson, "Paul Rosenfeld," in *Paul Rosenfeld*, ed. J. Mellquist and L. Wiese (New York: Creative Age Press, 1948), p. 16.

14. Joseph Dorfman, *Thorstein Veblen and His America* (New York: Viking, 1934), p. 353.

15. Thorstein Veblen, *Higher Learning in America* (New York: Huebsch, 1918), p. 222.

16. Stearns, *America and the Young Intellectual*, p. 46.

17. See Peter Loewenberg, *Decoding the Past* (New York: Knopf, 1983), pp. 48–80.

18. Lionel Trilling, "Some Notes for an Autobiographical Lecture," in Trilling, *The Last Decade: Essays and Reviews, 1965–75*, ed. D. Trilling (New York: Harcourt Brace, 1979), p. 239.

19. Cited in Alexander Bloom, *Prodigal Sons: The New York Intellectuals and Their World* (New York: Oxford University Press, 1986), p. 430.

Notes

20. Michael Harrington, *Fragments of the Century* (New York: Dutton, 1973), pp. 38, 50.

21. H. L. Mencken, *Prejudices: Second Series* (1920; reprint, New York: Octagon Books, 1977), pp. 26–28.

22. Jerrold Seigel, *Bohemian Paris* (New York: Viking, 1986), p. 396.

23. Russell Jacoby, "Los Angeles Times Book Review," *LA Weekly*, January 15–21, 1982. See the *Los Angeles Times*'s own candid survey and self-criticism: "Choosing the Best of the Book Reviews," *Los Angeles Times*, December 13, 1985.

24. Lionel Trilling, *The Liberal Imagination* (1950; reprint, Garden City, N.Y.: Doubleday Anchor, n.d.), p. 1.

25. Mark Krupnick, *Lionel Trilling and the Fate of Cultural Criticism* (Evanston, Ill.: Northwestern University Press, 1986), pp. 155–72.

Chapter 2 / The Decline of Bohemia

1. See Jerrold Seigel, *Bohemian Paris* (New York: Viking, 1986), pp. 31–58.

2. Robert Michels, "On the Sociology of Bohemia and Its Connection to the Intellectual Proletariat" (1932), in *Catalyst* 15 (1983): 14, 22–23.

3. As an occasional "surplus" intellectual, Michels knew these realities; see Arthur Mitzman, *Sociology and Estrangement: Three Sociologists of Imperial Germany* (New York: Knopf, 1973), pp. 267–89.

4. See the survey focusing on painters, Michael Jacobs, *The Good and Simple Life: Artist Colonies in Europe and America* (Oxford: Phaidon Press, 1985).

5. Alfred Polgar, "Theorie des Cafe Central," in his *Auswahlband* (Berlin: Ernst Rowohlt, 1930), pp. 60–65.

6. Albert Salomon, *The Tyranny of Progress* (New York: Noonday Press, 1955), pp. 28–29.

7. See the vast compendium, Helmut Kreuzer, *Die Boheme. Beitraege zur ihrer Beschreibung* (Stuttgart: Metzlersche Verlag, 1968).

8. Cited in William M. Johnston, *The Austrian Mind: An Intellectual and Social History 1848–1938* (Berkeley: University of California Press, 1983), p. 119. Ironically Salomon attributes the same remark to the socialist Rudolf Hilferding; see Salomon, *Tyranny of Progress*, p. 29.

9. Benedikt Livshits, *The One and a Half-Eyed Archer*, trans. John E. Bowlt (Newtonville, Mass.: Oriental Research Partners, 1977), p. 214.

10. Walter Benjamin, *Charles Baudelaire: A Lyric Poet in the Era of High Capitalism* (London: NLB, 1973), pp. 28–37.

11. Walter Benjamin, "A Berlin Chronicle," *One-Way Street and Other Writings* (London: NLB, 1979), pp. 310–11.

12. For instance, see Ernst Blass, "The Old Cafe des Westens," in *The Era of German Expressionism*, ed. Paul Raabe (London: John Calder, 1980), pp. 27–33.

13. Henry Pachter, *Weimar Etudes* (New York: Columbia University Press, 1982), p. 338.

14. Milton Klonsky, "Greenwich Village: Decline and Fall," in *Commentary*, 6 (November 1948) 5: 459.

15. Ibid., p. 457.

16. Ibid., pp. 458–59, 461.

17. Albert Parry, "Greenwich Village Revisited: 1948," in *Garrets and Pretenders: A History of Bohemianism in America*, rev. ed. (New York: Dover, 1960), pp. 367, 374–75.

18. Michael Harrington, *Fragments of the Century* (New York: Dutton, 1973), pp. 38–39.

19. John Gruen, *The Party's Over Now* (New York: Viking, 1972).

20. Joyce Johnson, *Minor Characters: The Romantic Odyssey of a Woman in the Beat Generation* (New York: Washington Square Press, 1984), pp. 27–34.

21. Floyd Dell, *Homecoming: An Autobiography* (New York: Farrar and Rinehart, 1933), pp. 324–25.

22. Floyd Dell, *Love in Greenwich Village* (New York: George H. Doran, 1926), pp. 16–17.

23. Ibid., p. 321.

24. *New York Times*, July 26, 1963, p. 30.

25. Quoted by G. William Domhoff, *The Bohemian Grove and Other Retreats* (New York: Harper and Row, 1974), p. 54.

26. John van der Zee, *The Greatest Men's Party on Earth: Inside the Bohemian Grove* (New York: Harcourt Brace, 1974), pp. 22–23.

27. "Early Bohemia," cited in Domhoff, *The Bohemian Grove*, p. 55.

28. Cited in van der Zee, *The Greatest Men's Party*, p. 28.

29. Kevin Starr, *Americans and the California Dream 1850–1915* (Santa Barbara: Peregrine Smith, 1981), p. 270.

30. For a memoir of Sterling, Bierce, and others, see Elsie Whitaker Martinez, *San Francisco Bay Area Writers and Artists* (Berkeley: University of California Press, Bancroft Library, Regional Oral History, 1969), and Gelett Bur-

Notes

gess, *Bayside Bohemia: Fin de Siècle San Francisco and Its Little Magazines* (San Francisco: Book Club of California, 1954).

31. See Manuel Castells, *The City and the Grassroots* (Berkeley: University of California Press, 1983), pp. 140–42.

32. See the lovely survey co-authored by a founder of City Lights, Lawrence Ferlinghetti, with Nancy J. Peters, *Literary San Francisco* (San Francisco: City Lights and Harper and Row, 1980).

33. See Alter F. Landesman, *Brownsville: The Birth, Development and Passing of a Jewish Community in New York* (New York: Bloch Publishing, 1969).

34. Malcolm Cowley, *And I Worked at the Writer's Trade* (New York: Viking, 1978), pp. 1, 9.

35. Malcolm Cowley, *Exile's Return* (1951; reprint, New York: Penguin, 1976), pp. 48, 59.

36. In a neat bit of symmetry, after he was sacked in 1920 by Johns Hopkins University for sexual improprieties, John B. Watson, the founder of American behaviorism, joined the advertising industry, where he became quite successful; see David Cohen, *J. B. Watson: The Founder of Behaviorism* (London: Routledge and Kegan Paul, 1979), pp. 145–94.

37. Cited in and see Stuart Ewen, *Captains of Consciousness* (New York: McGraw-Hill, 1976), pp. 159–61.

38. Cowley, *Exile's Return*, pp. 64–65.

39. Kenneth S. Lynn, *The Air-Line to Seattle* (Chicago: University of Chicago Press, 1983), p. 79. To be sure, Lynn is trying desparately to counter liberal myths about bohemian Greenwich Village—with not much success.

40. Daniel Horowitz, *The Morality of Spending: Attitudes Toward the Consumer Society, 1875–1940* (Baltimore: Johns Hopkins University Press, 1985), p. 118; T. J. Jackson Lears, "From Salvation to Self-Realization," in *The Culture of Consumption*, ed. R. W. Fox and T. J. J. Lears (New York: Pantheon, 1983), p. 4.

41. Harrington, *Fragments of the Century*, p. 50.

42. Ronald Sukenick, "Up from the Garret: Success Then and Now," *New York Times Book Review*, January 27, 1985, p. 30.

43. David R. Goldfield and Blaine A. Brownell, *Urban America: From Downtown to No Town* (Boston: Houghton, Mifflin, 1979).

44. See Douglas T. Miller, Marion Nowak, *The Fifties: The Way We Really Were* (Garden City, N.Y.: Doubleday, 1977), pp. 133–34.

45. See Lewis Mumford, *The City in History* (New York: Harcourt Brace, 1961), pp. 482–524.

46. Harlan Paul Douglas, *The Suburban Trend* (1925; reprint, New York: Johnson, 1970), p. 327.

47. Quoted by Scott Donaldson, *The Suburban Myth* (New York: Columbia University Press, 1969), p. 28.

48. Delos F. Wilcox, *The American City: Problem in Democracy* (New York: Macmillan, 1904), p. 28.

49. See John H. Mollenkopf, *The Contested City* (Princeton: Princeton University Press, 1983), which discusses the federal role in suburbanization, its subsidizing of suburban factories and home building; Gary A. Tobin, "Suburbanization and the Development of Motor Transportation," in *The Changing Face of the Suburbs*, ed. Barry Schwartz (Chicago: University of Chicago Press, 1976), pp. 95–111. For a neo-Marxist account, see Richard A. Walker, "A Theory of Suburbanization," in *Urbanization and Urban Planning in Capitalist Society*, ed. Michael Dear and Allen J. Scott (London: Methuen, 1981), pp. 383–429.

50. Kenneth T. Jackson, *Crabgrass Frontier: The Suburbanization of the United States* (New York: Oxford University Press, 1985), pp. 233, 238, 244.

51. Ibid., pp. 249–50.

52. See Stanley Mallach, "The Origins of the Decline of Urban Mass Transportation in the United States, 1890–1930," in *Urbanism Past and Present* 8 (1979): 1–17.

53. Lewis Mumford, "The Highway and the City" (1958), in *The Urban Prospects* (New York: Harcourt Brace, 1968), p. 105.

54. Michael C. D. Macdonald, *America's Cities* (New York: Simon and Schuster, 1984), p. 360.

55. Herman Wouk, *Marjorie Morningstar* (Garden City, N.Y.: Doubleday, 1955), pp. 530, 547, 557.

56. Cited by Robert Caro, *The Power Broker: Robert Moses and the Fall of New York* (New York: Vintage Books, 1975), p. 12.

57. Quoted by Caro, *The Power Broker*, p. 952.

58. William S. Kowinski, *The Malling of America* (New York: William Morrow, 1985), p. 50.

59. John B. Rae, *The Road and the Car in American Life* (Cambridge, Mass.: MIT Press, 1971), pp. 230–31. This is a classic celebration of highway culture as providing freedom of choice; according to Rae, loyalty to Soviet subways motivates the critics of suburbia (pp. 246–48).

60. Victor Gruen and Larry Smith, *Shopping Towns USA* (New York: Reinhold, 1960), pp. 147, 24.

61. Victor Gruen, *Centers for the Urban Environment* (New York: Van

Notes

Nostrand Reinhold, 1973); p. 6. This volume is the best overview of Gruen's thought.

62. Victor Gruen, *The Heart of Our Cities: The Urban Crisis* (New York: Simon and Schuster, 1964), pp. 72, 337–39.

63. See Victor Gruen, *Ist Fortschritt ein Verbrechen? Umweltplannung statt Weltuntergang* (Vienna: Europa Verlag, 1975).

64. See Dennis E. Gale, "Middle-Class Settlement in Older Urban Neighborhoods," in *Neighborhood Policy and Planning*, ed. Phillip L. Clay and Robert M. Hollister (Lexington, Mass.: Lexington Books, 1983), pp. 21–33.

65. See Roman C. Cybriwsky, "Revitalization Trends in Downtown Area Neighborhoods," in *American Metropolitan System*, ed. Stanley D. Brunn and James O. Wheeler (New York: John Wiley, 1980), pp. 21–36.

66. Michael H. Lang, *Gentrification Amid Urban Decline* (Cambridge, Mass.: Ballinger, 1982), p. 33. Will this change as the baby boom generation finally starts reproducing? Yes, according to *Newsweek* in an article entitled "A Return to the Suburbs: Boomers Are Behaving like Their Parents." "By and large . . . Yuppies are leaving the cities for the same reasons as their parents did: a better life for their children or, in some cases, for their dogs" (*Newsweek*, July 21, 1986, pp. 52–54).

67. This is stressed in Damaris Rose, "Rethinking Gentrification," *Environment and Planning: Society and Space*, 5 (1984) 1: 47–74.

68. See Sharon Zukin, *Loft Living: Culture and Capital in Urban Change* (Baltimore: Johns Hopkins University Press, 1982), pp. 19, 60.

69. Jane Jacobs, *The Death and Life of Great American Cities* (New York: Vintage Books, 1961), p. 249.

70. "As New Shops Replace the Old in Brooklyn Heights, Bookseller Fights Back," *New York Times*, January 8, 1985, p. B1.

71. Lionel Abel, *The Intellectual Follies: A Memoir of the Literary Venture in New York* (New York: Norton, 1984), p. 17.

72. William Phillips, in "Our Country and Our Culture," in *Partisan Review* 19 (1952): 586.

73. Irving Howe, *World of Our Fathers* (New York: Simon and Schuster, 1983), p. 501.

74. For instance, see "An Artists' Colony Is Emerging in Newark," *New York Times*, February 26, 1985, p. 1.

75. Zukin, *Loft Living*, p. 16.

76. Craig Owens, *Art in America* (Summer, 1984): 162–63.

77. See the article by Erika Munk, "New York to the Arts: Drop Dead," *Village Voice*, May 13, 1986, and "Real-Estate Boom Cited as Peril to Arts in City," *New York Times*, April 15, 1986, p. C13.

78. Morton White and Lucia White, *The Intellectuals Against the City* (Toronto: Mentor Books, 1964).

79. "Rural Homesteaders Seek Self-Sufficiency and Cherish Solitude," *New York Times*, January 28, 1985, p. B1.

Chapter 3 / On the Road to Suburbia: Urbanists and Beats

1. Helen L. Horowitz, "The 1960s and the Transformation of Campus Culture," *History of Education Quarterly*, 26 (1986) 1: 10.

2. For a brief survey of left urban studies, see David Harvey and Neil Smith, "Geography: From Capitals to Capital," in *The Left Academy*, vol. 2, ed. B. Ollman and E. Vernoff (New York: Praeger, 1984), pp. 99–121.

3. David Harvey, *The Urbanization of Capital* (Oxford: Basil Blackwell, 1985), pp. x, 226. With some minor changes he uses the same preface in the other volume, *Consciousness and the Urban Experience* (Oxford: Basil Blackwell, 1985), p. xi.

4. Ibid., p. 190.

5. I discuss Richard Sennett's *The Fall of Public Man* and Marshall Berman's *All That Is Solid Melts into Air* in the final chapter.

6. This appeared first in 1947, but only its much revised second edition of 1960 obtained a wide audience. See the comments by Percival Goodman in his "Architect from New York," in *Creators and Disturbers: Reminiscences by Jewish Intellectuals of New York*, ed. Bernard Rosenberg and Ernest Goldstein (New York: Columbia University Press, 1982), p. 317.

7. This was published in book form only in 1974 (New York: Harper and Row), but large sections had appeared in 1960 in the periodical *Contemporary Issues*.

8. Of course, these writers did not uphold a single position; see, for instance, Lewis Mumford's sharp critique of Jane Jacobs, "Home Remedies for Urban Cancer," published originally in *The New Yorker* (1962), in his *The Urban Prospects* (New York: Harcourt Brace, 1968), pp. 182–207.

9. Jane Jacobs, *The Death and Life of Great American Cities* (New York: Vintage Books, 1961).

10. Ibid., p. 55.

11. Ibid., p. 442.

12. Ibid., pp. 445–48.

13. Lewis Mumford, "The Highway and the City" (1958), reprinted in *Urban Prospect* (New York: Harcourt Brace, 1968), pp. 92–107.

Notes

14. William H. Whyte, *The Organization Man* (New York: Simon and Schuster, 1956), p. 10.

15. *The Exploding Metropolis*, ed. William H. Whyte and editors of *Fortune* (New York: Doubleday, 1958), pp. 1, 2.

16. See the report on his lecture by Charlotte Curtis, "Fighting the Nation's Fortresses," *New York Times*, March 11, 1986, p. C13.

17. Edward Engberg, "The Organization Man Today," in *The Wall Street Journal Magazine* (June 1981), p. 29.

18. William H. Whyte, *The Social Life of Small Urban Spaces* (Washington, D.C.: Conservation Foundation, 1980), pp. 85–86.

19. Whyte, *Organization Man*, p. 68.

20. Malcolm Cowley, *The Literary Situation* (New York: Viking, 1954), pp. 157, 166.

21. Ludwig Marcuse, "The Oldest Younger Generation," in *Partisan Review*, 19 (1952): 211–16.

22. Caroline Bird, "Born 1930: The Unlost Generation," in *Harper's Bazaar*, February 1957, pp. 104–5.

23. Otto Butz, ed., *The Unsilent Generation: An Anonymous Symposium in Which Eleven College Seniors Look at Themselves and Their World* (New York: Rinehart, 1958), pp. 7, 12.

24. Robert Gutman, review of Butz, *The Unsilent Generation* in *Commentary* 27 (April 1959): 366.

25. At least, according to James P. O'Brien, "The New Left's Early Years," *Radical America*, 2 (1968), 3: 4.

26. Benjamin Fine, *1,000,000 Delinquents* (New York: World Publishing, 1955), pp. 27–28.

27. See Marty Jezer, *The Dark Ages: Life in the United States 1945–1960* (Boston: South End Press, 1982), pp. 237–46; and for a survey, see Mark T. McGee and R. J. Robertson, *The J. D. Films* (Jefferson, N.C.: McFarland, 1982).

28. Peter Biskind, *Seeing Is Believing: How Hollywood Taught Us to Stop Worrying and Love the Fifties* (New York: Pantheon, 1983), pp. 197–99.

29. Robert Lindner, *Must You Conform?* (1956; reprint, New York: Grove Press, 1961), p. 25.

30. James Gilbert, A *Cycle of Outrage: America's Reaction to the Juvenile Delinquent in the 1950s* (New York: Oxford University Press, 1986), p. 66. Daniel Bell, "The Myth of the Crime Waves" in his *The End of Ideology* (New York: Free Press, 1962) had already argued that the increase in juvenile (and adult) crime was largely illusory.

31. Bell, *End of Ideology*, pp. 157–58.

32. Senator Robert C. Hendrickson, cited by Gilbert, *Cycle of Outrage*, p. 75.

33. Cowley, *Literary Situation*, p. 241; see Adam Gussow, "Bohemia Revisited: Malcolm Cowley, Jack Kerouac and *On the Road*," in *Georgia Review*, 38 (1984): 291–311.

34. John Clellon Holmes, *Go* (New York: New American Library, 1980), p. 36.

35. Paul O'Neil, "The Only Rebellion Around," published originally in *Life Magazine* (1959), reprinted in *A Casebook on the Beat*, ed. Thomas Parkinson (New York: Crowell, 1961), pp. 232, 235.

36. On Lipton, see the entry by his wife in *Dictionary of Literary Biography*, vol. 16, *The Beats: Literary Bohemians in Postwar America* pt. 1, ed. Ann Charters (Detroit: Gale Research, 1983), pp. 352–56.

37. Lawrence Lipton, *The Holy Barbarians* (1959; reprint, New York: Grove Press, 1962), p. 7.

38. Kenneth Rexroth, "The World Is Full of Strangers," in *New Directions 16* (New York: New Directions Books, 1957), pp. 181, 199.

39. Lipton, *Holy Barbarians*, pp. 272–83.

40. Elias Wilentz, "Introduction," in *Beat Scene* (New York: Corinth Books, 1960), p. 9.

41. For a good discussion of this and related matters, see Bruce Cook, *The Beat Generation* (New York: Charles Scribner's, 1971).

42. "An Interview with John Clellon Holmes," in *The Beat Journey*, ed. Arthur and Kit Knight (California, Pa.: n.p., 1978), pp. 162–63.

43. Jack Kerouac, *On the Road* (New York: Signet, 1957), p. 37.

44. Ibid., p. 149.

45. Ibid., p. 11.

46. Norman Podhoretz, "The Know-Nothing Bohemians" (1958), in his *Doings and Undoings* (New York: Noonday Press, 1964), pp. 157, 147, 156.

47. Ibid., p. 157.

48. Paul Goodman, review; reprinted in appendices in his *Growing Up Absurd* (New York: Vintage Books, 1962), p. 279.

49. Gary Snyder, cited in Ann Charters, *Kerouac* (San Francisco: Straight Arrow Books, 1973), pp. 286–87.

50. Landon Y. Jones, *Great Expectations: America and the Baby Boom Generation* (New York: Coward, McCann, 1980), pp. 83–84.

51. Sean Wilentz, "Beat Streets," in *Voice Literary Supplement*, February 1985, p. 10.

Notes

Chapter 4 / New York, Jewish, and Other Intellectuals

1. H. Stuart Hughes, "Is the Intellectual Obsolete?" in *Commentary*, 22 (1956): 313–19.

2. See John P. Diggins, "The New Republic and Its Times," in *The New Republic*, December 10, 1984, p. 58. Some professional journals added their thoughts; for instance, see Martin Cronin, "The American Intellectual," in *AAUP Bulletin*, 44 (1958): 403–15.

3. Arthur M. Schlesinger, Jr., "The Highbrow in American Politics," (1953), in *The Scene Before You*, ed. Chandler Brossard (New York: Rinehart, 1955), p. 263.

4. John W. Aldridge, *In Search of Heresy: American Literature in the Age of Conformity* (1956; reprint, Port Washington, N.Y.: Kennikat Press, 1967), p. 5.

5. Merle King, "The Intellectual: Will He Wither Away?" in *New Republic*, April 8, 1957, pp. 14–15.

6. Newton Arvin, "Report from the Academy: The Professor as Manager," in *Partisan Review* 12 (1945): 275, 277.

7. J. F. Wolpert, "Notes on the American Intelligentsia," published originally in *Partisan Review* (1947), reprinted in Brossard, *The Scene Before You*, pp. 241–43.

8. With a certain amount of satisfaction, Lewis Coser charts this development; see his *Men of Ideas* (New York: Free Press, 1970), pp. 263–74.

9. Alfred Kazin, *New York Jew* (New York: Vintage Books, 1979), p. 7.

10. Malcolm Cowley, "Limousines on Grub Street" (1946), in his *The Flower and the Leaf*, ed. D. W. Faulkner (New York: Viking, 1985), pp. 95–96.

11. See Kenneth C. Davis, *Two-Bit Culture: The Paperbacking of America* (Boston: Houghton Mifflin, 1984), pp. 190–202.

12. Isaac Rosenfeld, "On the Role of the Writer and the Little Magazine" (1956), in *Chicago Review Anthology*, ed. David Ray (Chicago: University of Chicago Press, 1959), pp. 6, 4.

13. Lionel Trilling, "The Situation of the American Intellectual at the Present Time," in *Perspectives USA*, 3 (Spring 1953): 29.

14. Ibid., p. 32.

15. Editorial Statement, "Our Country and Our Culture," in *Partisan Review*, 19 (1952): 283–84.

16. Philip Rahv, in "Our Country and Our Culture," 306.

17. David Riesman, in "Our Country and Our Culture," 311–12.

18. Max Lerner in "Our Country and Our Culture," 582.

19. Richard Chase, "Neo-Conservatism and American Literature," in *Commentary*, 23 (1957): 254. "It is hardly news that on the university campus, a new outlook and a new tone have become established," explained one observer in 1955 of the "new conservatism"; see Gaylord C. Leroy, "The New Conservatism," in *AAUP Bulletin*, 41 (1955): 270.

20. This is emphasized in David K. Moore, "Liberalism and Liberal Education at Columbia University: The Columbia Careers of Jacques Barzun, Lionel Trilling, Richard Hofstadter, Daniel Bell, and C. Wright Mills" (Ph.D. diss., University of Maryland, 1978), pp. 147–78.

21. C. Wright Mills, "On Knowledge and Power" (1955), in his *Power, Politics and People*, ed. Irving L. Horowitz (New York: Ballantine Books, 1963), p. 603.

22. Trilling, as cited by Irving L. Horowitz, *C. Wright Mills: An American Utopian* (New York: Free Press, 1983), p. 86.

23. Mills, as cited by Horowitz, *C. Wright Mills*, pp. 85–86.

24. C. Wright Mills, "The Powerless People" (1944), reprinted as "The Social Role of the Intellectual," in *Power, Politics and People*, ed. I. L. Horowitz (New York: Ballantine, 1963), p. 292.

25. C. Wright Mills, *White Collar* (New York: Oxford University Press, 1956), pp. 130–31, 158–59.

26. Cited in Horowitz, *C. Wright Mills*, p. 251.

27. Richard Hofstadter, *The Progressive Historians* (New York: Knopf, 1968), p. xv.

28. Kazin, *New York Jew*, p. 22.

29. See Daniel Joseph Singal, "Beyond Consensus: Richard Hofstadter and American Historiography," in *American Historial Review*, 89 (1984): 979–80. For a study of Hofstadter's relationship to Marxism and the Communist party, see Susan Stout Baker, *Radical Beginnings: Richard Hofstadter and the 1930s* (Westport, Conn.: Greenwood Press, 1985).

30. Richard Hofstadter, *Anti-Intellectualism in American Life* (New York: Vintage Books, 1963), p. 5.

31. Ibid., pp. 416–17.

32. Irving Howe, "This Age of Conformity," in *Partisan Review*, 21 (1954): 10, 13.

33. Ibid., 14.

34. Irving Howe, *Margin of Hope* (San Diego: Harcourt Brace, 1982), pp. 181–83.

35. In looking back, Howe himself retracts some of his harsh words about

Notes

academization. "There were New York voices, mine among them, that indulged in gloomy forebodings" (*Margin of Hope*, p. 171).

36. Hofstadter, *Anti-Intellectualism*, p. 419.

37. Ibid., pp. 429, 432.

38. R. Hofstadter, "The Idea of the Power Elite," cited in Moore, "Liberalism," pp. 213–14.

39. Christopher Lasch, Foreword, to Richard Hofstadter, *The American Political Tradition* (New York: Knopf, 1982), p. xix.

40. Cited in Horowitz, C. *Wright Mills*, p. 84.

41. Kazin, *New York Jew*, p. 21. See also Richard Gillam, "Richard Hofstadter, C. Wright Mills and the Critical Ideal," in *American Scholar*, 47 (1977–78): 69–85.

42. Norman Podhoretz, "The Young Generation" (1957), in his *Doings and Undoings* (New York: Farrar, Straus and Giroux, 1964), p. 108.

43. Ibid., p. 109.

44. Podhoretz declaims that "the antiwar movement bears a certain measure of responsibility for the horrors that have overtaken the people of Vietnam" (*Why We Were In Vietnam* [New York: Simon and Schuster, 1982], p. 205). Podhoretz, who regularly tells all, tells nothing of his own opposition to the war. Theodore Draper, who pointed this out, concludes, "As history, Podhoretz's version of the Vietnam war cannot be taken seriously. Its significance must be sought in the present rather than in the past. It represents a selective moralistic zealotry. . . . It opens the door to a viciously dangerous stab-in-the-back legend by inferentially blaming the horrors of the war on those who opposed it rather than on those who waged it" (Draper, *Present History* [New York: Random House, 1983], p. 360).

45. Norman Podhoretz, *Breaking Ranks* (New York: Harper and Row, 1979), pp. 362–63.

46. Arthur Liebman, *Jews and the Left* (New York: John Wiley, 1979), p. 1.

47. For a fairly complete summary of the literature, with their own theory of Jewish radicalism, see Stanley Rothman and S. Robert Lichter, *Roots of Radicalism: Jews, Christians and the New Left* (New York: Oxford University Press, 1982), pp. 80–145.

48. George H. Nash, *The Conservative Intellectual Movement in America Since 1945* (New York: Basic Books, 1979), pp. 330–31.

49. Irving Howe, *World of Our Fathers* (New York: Simon and Schuster, 1976), pp. 604–5.

50. For a good discussion of Jewish links to the left and their weakening in the postwar period, see Arthur Liebman, "The Ties That Bind: The Jewish

Support for the Left in the United States," *American Jewish Historical Quarterly*, 66 (1976): 285–321.

51. Lewis S. Feuer, *The Conflict of Generations: The Character and Significance of Student Movements* (New York: Basic Books, 1969), esp. pp. 476–82.

52. Cited in Jack Newfield, *A Prophetic Minority* (1966; reprint, New York: Signet, 1970), p. 136.

53. Sidney Hook, "The Academic Ethic in Abeyance: Recollections of *Walpurgisnacht* at New York University," *Minerva*, 22 (1984): 303–4.

54. Stephen J. Whitfield, *A Critical American: The Politics of Dwight Macdonald* (Hamden, Conn.: Archon Books, 1984), pp. 123–24.

55. Irving Howe, "The Range of the New York Intellectual," in *Creators and Disturbers: Reminiscences by Jewish Intellectuals of New York*, ed. Bernard Rosenberg and Ernest Goldstein (New York: Columbia University Press, 1982), p. 274.

56. Seymour Martin Lipset and Everett C. Ladd, Jr., "Jewish Academics in the United States," in *The Jew in American Society*, ed. Marshall Sklare (New York: Behrman, 1974), pp. 273–74.

57. I am side-stepping one issue: angst over Israel that drives Jewish intellectuals to the right as they identify with and support its supporters, mainly the United States. This must be weighed; however, it can be easily overemphasized. Initially the neoconservative Jewish intellectuals expressed little concern for Israel, or even endangered Jews in Europe. They were anticommunists and conservatives before they were preoccupied with Israel; see Earl Shorris, *Jews Without Mercy: A Lament* (New York: Doubleday, 1982).

58. Diana Trilling, "Lionel Trilling, A Jew at Columbia," *Commentary*, 67 (March 1979) 3: 44.

59. Mark Krupnick, "Lionel Trilling, Freud and the Fifties," *Humanities in Society*, 3 (Summer 1980) 3: 280.

60. Alfred Kazin, *New York Jew*, p. 70.

61. John Kenneth Galbraith, *Made to Last* (London: Hamish Hamilton, 1964).

62. Kenneth Rexroth, *An Autobiographical Novel* (Weybridge, Surrey, England: Whittet Books, 1977), p. ix.

63. Ibid., p. vi.

64. Gore Vidal, in *Three Honest Men: Edmund Wilson, F. R. Leavis, Lionel Trilling*, ed. Philip French (Manchester: Carcanet New Press, 1980), p. 34.

65. Edmund Wilson, *Upstate: Records and Recollections of Northern New York State* (New York: Farrar, Straus and Giroux, 1971), p. 45.

Notes

66. Edmund Wilson, *Apologies to the Iroquois* (New York: Vintage Books, 1960), pp. 285–86.

67. William Cowper Brann, *The Iconoclast: A Collection of the Writings of W. C. Brann*, with a biography by J. D. Shaw (Waco, Tex.: Herz Brothers, 1898), 2: 201–2. It should be noted that Brann was an iconoclast on many things; he was also a rabid racist.

68. For appreciations of Brann, see Donna Dickerson, "William Cowper Brann," in *Journalism History* 5 (1978) 2: 42–45, and Charles Carver, *Brann and the Iconoclast* (Austin: University of Texas Press, 1957).

69. Cited in Richard Gillam, "*White Collar* from Start to Finish: C. Wright Mills in Transition," in *Theory and Society*, 10 (January 1981): 27.

70. Dan Wakefield, "Taking It Big: A Memoir of C. Wright Mills," in *Atlantic*, 228 (September 1971): 71.

71. C. Wright Mills, *The New Men of Power* (New York: Harcourt Brace, 1948).

72. Wakefield, "Taking It Big," p. 64.

73. See Lewis Mumford, "Thorstein Veblen," in *The New Republic*, August 5, 1931, pp. 314–16.

74. C. Wright Mills, Introduction in Thorstein Veblen, *The Theory of the Leisure Class* (New York: New American Library, 1953), pp. viii–ix.

75. Cited in Horowitz, *C. Wright Mills*, p. 77.

76. C. Wright Mills, Introduction in Veblen, pp. viii–ix.

77. The abbreviated life of Isaac Rosenfeld (1918–56), novelist and essayist, is peripheral to this story. He followed the almost prescribed path for young New York intellectuals: ensconced in his Greenwich Village apartment at a youthful twenty-four, he was writing reviews and articles for *The New Republic*, *Partisan Review*, and *Commentary*. Minor successes, however, did not ease his way; he remained devoted to the badge of alienation that his friends began packing away as a souvenir. "In the 1940s," explains Mark Shechner, Rosenfeld shared with other Jewish intellectuals an "exclusion from and disdain for" American life. "In the 1950s, when universities, fellowships, and publishing opportunities opened up" most of his friends settled their accounts with prosperity, but Rosenfeld kept apart, a practitioner of "perverse monasticism." Eventually, he was drawn to a mystical or cultural version of Wilhelm Reich. "Unlike other Jewish intellectuals of his generation," states Shechner, "he never made his peace with the American dream." Mark Shechner, "Isaac Rosenfeld," in his *After the Revolution: Studies in Contemporary Jewish-American Imagination* (Bloomington: Indiana University Press, forthcoming). see also Shechner, "Isaac Rosenfeld's World," in *Partisan Review*, 43 (1976): 524–56.

78. Cited in, and see "Introduction to the Colophon Edition," *Our Synthetic Environment* (New York: Harper and Row, 1974), pp. xiii, 244.

79. Murray Bookchin, "Listen, Marxist!" reprinted in his *Post-Scarcity Anarchism* (Berkeley: Ramparts Press, 1971), p. 173.

80. Murray Bookchin, *Towards an Ecological Society* (Montreal: Black Rose Books, 1980), pp. 11–12.

81. Bookchin, letter to author, June 21, 1986.

82. Bookchin, *Ecological Society*, p. 22.

83. See my *Dialectic of Defeat: Contours of Western Marxism* (Cambridge, Cambridge University Press, 1981), pp. 11–36.

84. Daniel Bell, "The 'Intelligentsia' in American Society," (1976) in his *The Winding Passage* (New York: Basic Books, 1980), p. 131.

85. For a critical evaluation of Bell, see Nathan Liebowitz, *Daniel Bell and the Agony of Modern Liberalism* (Westport, Conn.: Greenwood Press, 1985); and Howard Brick, *Daniel Bell and the Decline of Intellectual Radicalism* (Madison: University of Wisconsin Press, 1986).

86. So far only fragments of Hook's memoirs have appeared; his piece, "The Radical Comedians: Inside *Partisan Review*" (in *American Scholar*, 54 [1984–85], 1:45), is described as "an excerpt from his autobiography."

87. Thorstein Veblen, "The Intellectual Pre-eminence of Jews in Modern Europe," in *Essays in Our Changing Order* (New York: Viking, 1934), pp. 219–31.

88. Of course, "New York intellectuals" is a cultural, not precisely an empirical category; both Mills and Jacobs lived in New York, though neither was from New York nor part of a New York intellectual scene. For instance, the encyclopedic study of New York intellectuals, Alexander Bloom's *Prodigal Sons: The New York Intellectuals and Their World* (New York: Oxford University Press, 1986), contains only a passing reference to Mills and Jacobs.

89. Trilling comments briefly on Brown in *Sincerity and Authenticity* (Cambridge, Mass.: Harvard University Press, 1972), pp. 162, 169.

90. Steven Marcus, "Lionel Trilling, 1905–1975" in *Art, Politics and Will: Essays in Honor of Lionel Trilling*, ed. Quentin Anderson (New York: Basic Books, 1977), p. 268.

91. Bell, *The End of Ideology* (1962; reprint, New York: Free Press, 1965), p. 409.

92. Kristol, "Life with Sidney," in *Sidney Hook: Philosopher of Democracy and Humanism*, ed. Paul Kurtz (Buffalo: Prometheus Books, 1983), p. 31.

93. See Bloom, *Prodigal Sons*, pp. 102–4.

94. See Paul Berman, "The Last True Marxist Is a Neoconservative," *Voice Literary Supplement*, March 1984, p. 10.

Notes

95. Sidney Hook, *Education and the Taming of Power* (n. p.: Alcove Press, 1974).

96. Sidney Hook, *Marxism and Beyond* (Totowa, N.J.: Rowman and Littlefield, 1983), p. 150.

97. His book-length work, apart from that on Marxism, is extremely limited; it includes discussions of Dewey and modern education, such as *Education for Modern Man* (New York: Dial Press, 1946)—not exactly a memorable work—and a small book, *The Hero in History* (London: Secker and Warburg, 1945), on historical choice and determinism, much of which, inevitably, is about Marxism and totalitarianism.

98. See "A Complete Bibliography of Sidney Hook" in *Sidney Hook*, pp. 311–47.

99. Kurtz, Preface, in *Sidney Hook*, p. x.

100. Hook, *Education and the Taming of Power*, pp. 1, 15.

101. Sidney Hook, "A Dictionary?" in *Encounter*, 66 (January 1986) 1: 71–72. The *Dictionary of Marxist Thought*, ed. Tom Bottomore (Cambridge, Mass.; Harvard University Press; Oxford: Basil Blackwell, 1983), is vulnerable to some serious criticisms, but its failure to cite Hook may not be one of them. When Hook adds that the *Dictionary* also does not cite other notable American contributors, such as Max Eastman and Louis Boudin, he reveals the problem—like his own contributions, theirs play no role in current Marxism.

102. Cited and discussed in Bloom, *Prodigal Sons*, pp. 138–39.

103. Ferdinand Brunetière, cited by Victor Brombert, *The Intellectual Hero: Studies in the French Novel, 1880–1955* (New York: Lippincott, 1961), p. 23. Cf. F. Brunetière, "Après le procès," in *Revue des deux Mondes*, 146 (1898): 442–46. For additional references to intellectuals and Dreyfus, see Jean Denis Bredin, *L'affaire* (Paris: Julliard, 1983), pp. 257–65.

104. For a recent discussion, see Timonthy E. O'Connor, *The Politics of Soviet Culture* (Ann Arbor: UMI Research, 1983), pp. 29–32.

105. Pyotr Struve, "The Intelligentsia and Revolution," in *Landmarks: A Collection of Essays on the Russian Intelligentsia—1909*, ed. Boris Shragin and Albert Todd (New York: Karz Howard, 1977), p. 141.

106. See Robert J. Brym, *Intellectuals and Politics* (London: Allen and Unwin, 1980).

107. H. Stuart Hughes, *Consciousness and Society* (New York: Vintage Books, 1958).

108. Alvin Gouldner, *The Future of Intellectuals and the Rise of the New Class* (New York: Continuum, 1979), p. 83.

109. Irving Kristol, *Two Cheers for Capitalism* (New York: New American Library, 1979), p. 25.

110. Robert L. Bartley, "Business and the New Class," in *The New Class?* ed. B. Bruce-Briggs (New York: McGraw-Hill, 1981), p. 61

111. Daniel Bell, "The New Class: A Muddled Concept," in his *The Winding Passage* (New York: Basic Books, 1980), pp. 158–59.

112. Lewis, *Men of Ideas*, (New York: Free Press, 1970), p. 267.

113. For a good discussion of Machajski, see Anthony D'Agostino, *Marxism and the Russian Anarchists* (San Francisco: Germinal Press, 1977), esp. pp. 110–55; also see Paul Avrich, *The Russian Anarchists* (Princeton: Princeton University Press, 1967), pp. 102–6. And for an appreciation of Nomad, see Edmund Wilson's introduction to Max Nomad's *Aspects of Revolt* (New York: Noonday, 1961), pp. vii–xx.

114. Mary McCarthy, *The Groves of Academe* (New York: Avon, 1981), p. 33.

115. For a full historical survey, see John O. Lyons, *The College Novel in America* (Carbondale, Ill.: Southern Illinois University Press, 1962).

116. Don DeLillo, *White Noise* (New York: Penguin Books, 1986), pp. 11–12.

117. Roger Rosenblatt, review of David Lodge's, *Small World*, in *New Republic*, April 15, 1985, p. 30.

118. Harold Rosenberg, "The Vanishing Intellectual," published originally in *The New Yorker* (1965), reprinted as "The Intellectual and His Future," in his *Discovering the Present* (Chicago: University of Chicago Press, 1973), p. 195.

Chapter 5 / The New Left on Campus I:
The Freedom to Be Academic

1. Jack Newfield, *A Prophetic Minority* (1966; reprint, New York: Signet, 1970), p. 154.

2. Joseph Epstein, "It's Only Culture," in *Commentary*, November 1983, p. 61.

3. Hilton Kramer, "A Note on *The New Criterion*," *New Criterion*, 1 (1982) 1: 2.

4. Sandy Vogelgesang, *The Long Dark Night of the Soul: The American Intellectual Left and the Vietnam War* (New York: Harper and Row, 1974), p. 73.

5. See Steven Unger, "Deutscher and the New Left in America," in *Isaac*

Notes

Deutscher: The Man and his Work, ed. D. Horowitz (London: Macdonald, 1971), pp. 211–25.

6. C. Wright Mills, "The Decline of the New Left" (1959) in *Power, Politics and People: Collected Essays of C. Wright Mills*, ed. I. L. Horowitz (New York: Ballantine Books, 1963), pp. 221–35.

7. Mills, "Letter to the New Left" (1967), reprinted as "The New Left" in *Power, Politics and People*, pp. 247–59.

8. See the critique of Mills by Freddy Perlman, *The Incoherence of the Intellectual* (Detroit: Black and Red, 1970).

9. From a manuscript, "New Left," cited by Irving L. Horowitz, *C. Wright Mills* (New York: Free Press, 1983), p. 314.

10. C. Wright Mills, "The Social Role of the Intellectual," in *Power, Politics and People*, p. 296.

11. C. Wright Mills, *White Collar* (New York: Oxford University Press, 1956), p. 156.

12. Mills, "On Knowledge and Power" (1955) in *Power, Politics and People*, p. 611.

13. Mills, *The Causes of World War Three* (New York: Simon and Schuster, 1958), p. 135.

14. Irving L. Horowitz, *C. Wright Mills: An American Utopian* (New York: Free Press, 1983), pp. 282–302.

15. Kirkpatrick Sale, *SDS* (New York: Vintage Books, 1974), p. 49. An excerpt of the Port Huron Statement can be found in *The New Left: A Documentary History*, ed. Massimo Teodori (New York: Bobbs-Merrill, 1969), pp. 163–172. On Mills and the New Left see James Miller, "C. Wright Mills Reconsidered," *Salmagundi*, 70–71 (1986): esp. 95–97.

16. The volume contains twenty-eight essays; the younger Americans who wrote the first ten are: Irving Louis Horowitz, Robert B. Notestein, Douglas F. Dowd, Rose K. Goldsen, Anatol Rapoport, Kenneth Winetrout, Fred H. Blum, Sidney M. Wilhelm, Abraham Edel, Marvin B. Scott. *The New Sociology: Essays in Social Science and Social Theory in Honor of C. Wright Mills*, ed. Irving L. Horowitz (New York: Oxford University Press, 1964).

17. See James Weinstein and David W. Eakens, "Introduction," in *For A New America: Essays in History and Politics from "Studies on the Left," 1959–1967* (New York: Random House, 1970).

18. Editors, "The Radicalism of Disclosure," in *Studies on the Left*, 1 (1959) 1: 3.

19. For a discussion of Robert S. Lynd, see Richard W. Fox, "Epitaph for Middletown," in *The Culture of Consumption*, ed. R. F. Fox and T. J. Jackson Lears (New York: Pantheon, 1983), pp. 103–41.

20. Staughton Lynd, "Nonviolent Alternatives to American Violence," in *Teach-Ins: U.S.A.*, ed. L. Menashe and R. Radosh (New York: Praeger, 1967), p. 54.

21. Staughton Lynd, in *Visions of History by MARHO—The Radical Historians Organization*, ed. Henry Abelove (New York: Pantheon Books, 1983), p. 151.

22. Staughton Lynd, *The Fight Against Shutdowns* (San Pedro, Cal.: Singlejack Books, 1982), p. 11.

23. Paul Breines, "Germans, Journals and Jews/Madison, Men, Marxism and Mosse, " in *New German Critique*, no. 20 (1980), p. 83.

24. Stanley Aronowitz, "When the New Left Was New," in *60s Without Apology*, ed. Sohnya Sayres, et al. (Minneapolis: University of Minnesota Press, 1984), pp. 12–13.

25. Stanley Aronowitz, *False Promises* (New York: McGraw-Hill, 1973), pp. 337–91.

26. Stanley Aronowitz, *The Crisis in Historical Materialism* (New York: Praeger, 1981), p. 301.

27. Aronowitz, *Working Class Hero*, (New York: Pilgrim Press, 1983).

28. For a consideration of Aronowitz's last two books, see Jeremy Brecher's review in *Our Generation*, 17 (1985–86): 197–218.

29. For Nearing's own account, see his *The Making of a Radical* (New York: Harper and Row, 1972), pp. 83–96.

30. William L. O'Neill, *The Last Romantic: A Life of Max Eastman* (New York: Oxford University Press, 1978), pp. 19–31.

31. Ellen Schrecker, "The Missing Generation: Academics and the Communist Party from the Depression to the Cold War," in *Humanities and Society*, 6 (1983) 2–3: 155.

32. Of course, some did again, and some prospered. One example: M. I. Finley, who had been associated with the Frankfurt School (as Moses I. Finkelstein), was fired by Rutgers University in 1952 for invoking the Fifth Amendment before the Senate Subcommittee on Internal Security. He moved to England and eventually received showers of academic honors and positions, including election to the British Academy and Master of Darwin College, Cambridge; he was knighted in 1979. See Ellen Schrecker, "Academic Freedom," in *Regulating the Intellectuals*, ed. C. Kaplan and E. Schrecker (New York: Praeger, 1983), pp. 36–37; Martin Jay, *The Dialectical Imagination* (Boston: Little, Brown, 1973), pp. 284–285; and his obituary, *New York Times*, July 11, 1986.

33. Jane Sanders, *Cold War on the Campus: Academic Freedom at the University of Washington, 1946–1964* (Seattle: University of Washington Press,

Notes

1979), pp. 96–97; see Melvin Rader's own account, *False Witness* (Seattle: University of Washington Press, 1969).

34. Ellen W. Schrecker, *No Ivory Tower: McCarthyism and the Universities* (New York: Oxford University Press, 1986), p. 340.

35. H. L. Mencken, *Prejudices: Third Series* (New York: Knopf, 1922), p. 283. William L. O'Neill will say. He writes that it shows "recklessness" to suggest that all professors at the University of Washington were threatened when "only six members of a large faculty had been investigated—and three dismissed—as if to insecure individuals it makes a difference whether two or a dozen were investigated." One wonders at what point Professor O'Neill might grow concerned if the large faculty of Rutgers University, where O'Neill teaches, were investigated for neoconservatism. After eight neoconservatives were investigated and four dismissed? Twelve? (*A Better World* [New York: Simon and Schuster, 1982], p. 331).

36. Cited in Merle Curti and Vernon Carstensen, *University of Wisconsin 1848–1925* vol. 1 (Madison: University of Wisconsin, 1949), p. 525.

37. Benjamin G. Rader, *The Academic Mind and Reform: The Influence of Richard T. Ely in American Life* (n.p.: University of Kentucky Press, 1966), p. 154. For a discussion of the retreat of socialist professors, see Dorothy Ross, "Socialism and American Liberalism: Academic Social Thought in the 1880's," in *Perspectives in American History*, 11 (1977–78): 5–79.

38. Cited in Richard Hofstadter and Walter P. Metzger, *The Development of Academic Freedom in the United States* (New York: Columbia University Press, 1955), pp. 427–28.

39. Ibid., p. 434.

40. Cited by Rader, *The Academic Mind*, p. 154.

41. Hofstadter and Metzger, *Development of Academic Freedom*, pp. 434–35.

42. See generally, Carol S. Gruber, *Mars and Minerva: World War I and the Uses of Higher Learning* (Baton Rouge: Louisiana State University Press, 1975).

43. J. McKeen Catell, *University Control* (New York: Science Press, 1913), pp. 61–62.

44. See Hofstadter and Metzer, *Development of Academic Freedom*, pp. 472–73, 497–502.

45. See Joseph Dorfman, *Thorstein Veblen and His America*, pp. 449–50.

46. Peter M. Rutkoff and William B. Scott, *New School: A History of the New School for Social Research* (New York: Free Press, 1986), pp. 16–17.

47. See Alvin Johnson's autobiography, *Pioneer's Progress* (New York: Viking Press, 1952), esp. pp. 271–88.

48. Luther V. Hendricks, *James Harvey Robinson: Teacher of History* (New York: King's Crown Press, 1946), pp. 23–24.

49. Cited in Ellen Nore, *Charles A. Beard: An Intellectual Biography* (Carbondale, Ill.: Southern Illinois University Press, 1983), p. 90.

50. See the chapter on the New School in Lewis A. Coser, *Refugee Scholars in America* (New Haven: Yale University Press, 1984), pp. 102–9; and my review in *Voice Literary Supplement*, January 15, 1985, p. 47.

51. Irving Louis Horowitz and William H. Friedland, *The Knowledge Factory: Student Power and Academic Politics in America* (Chicago: Adline, 1970), p. 130.

52. Richard C. Mandell, *The Professor Game* (Garden City, N.Y.: Doubleday, 1977), p. 58.

53. Ibid., p. 1.

54. See Christopher Jencks and David Riesman, *Academic Revolution* (Garden City, N.Y.: Doubleday, 1968), p. 95; *American Universities and Colleges*, 12th ed. (New York: Walter de Gruyer, 1983), pp. 5, 20; *Statistical History of the United States*, intro. B. J. Wattenberg (New York: Basic Books, 1976), p. 382.

55. See the discussion in Wini Breines, *Community and Organization in the New Left: 1962–1968* (New York: Praeger, 1982), pp. 96–122.

56. Dick Howard, "Preface" to Serge Mallet, in *Essays on the New Working Class* (St. Louis: Telos Press, 1973), p. 13.

57. Todd Gitlin, in *Harvard Class of 1963: 5th Anniversary Report*, p. 105.

58. Maurice Isserman, *If I Had a Hammer* . . . (New York: Basic Books, 1987), p. 116.

59. *The New Radicals* (New York: Vintage Books, 1966) pp. 90–91.

60. George Fischer, "Preface," in *The Revival of American Socialism: Selected Papers of the Socialist Scholars Conference*, ed. G. Fischer (New York: Oxford University Press, 1971), pp. viii–ix.

61. David Brock, "Combatting Those Campus Marxists," in *The Wall Street Journal*, December 12, 1985, p. 30.

62. See *American Radicals*, ed. Harvey Goldberg (New York: Monthly Review Press, 1957). This collection of essays on past American radicals, written mainly by academics, attempted to rally the spirits. "Now especially . . . dissenters are confronted with the need to survive, to analyse, and to function" ("Introduction," p. 12). Of the contributors, perhaps William A. Williams became the most prominent.

63. Bertell Ollman and Edward Vernoff, "Introduction" in *The Left Academy: Marxist Scholarship on American Campuses* (New York: McGraw-Hill,

Notes

1982), p. 1; see their *The Left Academy*, vol. 2 (New York: Praeger, 1984). The third volume appeared too late for me to consult.

64. Ewa M. Thompson, "Dialectical Methodologies in the American Academy," in *Modern Age*, 28 (Winter 1984). Thompson believes that these dialectical literary critics are not actually in the pay of the KGB but that they "perform effectively the same job which in the Soviet Union is assigned to Party propagandists." (15).

65. All information and quotes from "Tenure Denial of Noted Sociologist Stirs Troubling Queries at Harvard," *New York Times*, April 21, 1985, p. 42.

66. See David F. Noble, "Slander in Academia" (letter), in *The Nation*, May 25, 1985, p. 610. Christine Stansell and Sean Wilentz write, "If the stakes had been smaller, if Abraham had been up for tenure at a small liberal arts college, for example, we doubt that Turner and Feldman would have embarked on their crusade to oust him from the profession" ("The Sins of David Abraham," in *Radical History Review*, 32 [1985]: 87).

67. See Laurence Parker, "Henry Giroux's Tenure Decision," *Psychology and Social Theory*, 4 (1984): 68–70. John Silber's efforts to force out numerous Boston University faculty members have generally not received national attention; see, however, Stephen Arons, "The Teachers and the Tyrant," *Saturday Review*, March 15, 1980, pp. 16–19. For some comments on Silber's political machinations, see Alexander Cockburn, "Beat the Devil," *The Nation*, March 21, 1987, pp. 350–51.

68. All quotes and citations from materials accompanying "An Open Letter to Chancellor William H. Danforth," February 12, 1979 (privately printed).

69. Letter to Chancellor Danforth.

70. Ibid.

71. See Charles R. Monroe, *Profile of the Community College* (San Francisco: Jossey-Bass, 1972), pp. 256–58.

72. See Emily K. Abel, *Terminal Degrees: The Job Crisis in Higher Education* (New York: Praeger, 1984); and *The Hidden Professoriate: Credentialism, Professionalism and the Tenure Crisis*, ed. Arthur S. Wilke (Westport, Conn.: Greenwood Press, 1979).

73. Philip G. Altbach, "The Crisis of the Professoriate," *Annals*, 448 (March 1980): 9.

74. Edward E. Ericson, Jr., *Radicals in the University* (Stanford: Hoover Institution Press, 1975), p. 142.

75. Mark Lilla, "Among the Philosophers," *New Criterion*, 1 (February 1983) 6: 89.

Chapter 6 / The New Left on Campus II:
The Long March Through the Institutions

1. Cited in Bruce Kuklick, *The Rise of American Philosophy* (New Haven: Yale University Press, 1977), p. 433.

2. Max Weber, "Science as a Vocation," in *From Max Weber*, ed. H. Gerth and C. W. Mills (New York: Oxford University Press, 1958), p. 134.

3. Upton Sinclair, *The Goose-Step* (Pasadena, Cal.: Upton Sinclair, 1923), p. 13.

4. Thorstein Veblen, *The Higher Learning in America* (New York: Huebsch, 1918), p. 186.

5. H. L. Mencken, *Prejudices: Second Series* (1920; reprint, New York: Octagon Books, 1977), pp. 82–84.

6. C. Wright Mills, "The Powerless People" (1944), reprinted as "The Social Role of the Intellectual," in his *Power, Politics and People*, ed. by Irving L. Horowitz (New York: Ballantine Books, 1963), p. 297.

7. Martin Finkelstein, *The American Academic Profession: A Synthesis of Social Scientific Inquiry Since World War II* (Columbus: Ohio State University Press, 1984), pp. 52–53, 222–23.

8. Lionel S. Lewis, *Scaling the Ivory Tower: Merits and Its Limits in Academic Careers* (Baltimore: Johns Hopkins University Press, 1975), p. 116.

9. Ibid., pp. 65–66, 190.

10. Jon Wiener, "The Footnote Fetish," in *Telos*, 31 (1977): 174–75. See also Robert B. Archibald and David H. Finifter, "Biases in Citations-based Ranking of Journals," *Scholarly Publishing*, 18 (1987): 131–38.

11. C. Wright Mills, *Sociology and Pragmatism: The Higher Learning in America* (New.York: Oxford University Press, 1966), pp. 348–51.

12. Ibid., p. 442.

13. John Dewey, "The Scholastic and the Speculator" (1891–92), in his *Early Works*, vol. 3 (Carbondale, Ill.: Southern Illinois University Press, 1975), pp. 150–51.

14. John Dewey, *Reconstruction in Philosophy* (Boston: Beacon Press, 1957), pp. vi, v, xxiii.

15. The "newspaper" never appeared; for details see Neil Coughlan, *Young John Dewey* (Chicago: University of Chicago Press, 1975), pp. 93–112.

16. See George Dykhuizen, *The Life and Mind of John Dewey* (Carbondale, Ill.: Southern Illinois University Press, 1973), pp. 280–84.

17. Bruce Kuklick, *The Rise of American Philosophy* (New Haven: Yale University Press, 1977), pp. 568–72. For a larger look at contemporary philoso-

Notes

phy, see Albert William Levi, *Philosophy as Social Expression* (Chicago: University of Chicago Press, 1974), esp. the chapter "Contemporary Philosophy: The Age of the Professional," pp. 231–300.

18. William M. Sullivan, *Reconstructing Public Philosophy* (Berkeley: University of California Press, 1982), p. 97. He does not consider major political philosophers (John Rawls, Robert Nozick) as successfully breaking with technical philosophy.

19. Ibid., p. 10.

20. John E. Smith, *The Spirit of American Philosophy*, rev. ed. (Albany: State University of New York Press, 1983), pp. vi, 221, 227, 222.

21. Richard J. Bernstein, "Dewey, Democracy: The Task Ahead of Us," in *Post-Analytic Philosophy*, ed. R. Rajchman and C. West (New York: Columbia University Press, 1985), p. 58.

22. A flat statistical study of the philosophical profession showed that in comparison to other teachers philosophers ranked worst in a number of indices, such as unemployment. This report closed commenting on "the recent exodus of philosophers from philosophy and academe," apparently due to frustration and discouragement (Peter D. Suber, "The Place of Philosophy in the Humanities: A Statistical Profile," in *American Philosophy Association: Proceedings and Addresses*, 55 [1981–82]: 420, 423). Of course, the economic woes—or prosperity—of any discipline do not reflect its intellectual viability.

23. Editorial statement, *Telos* 1 (1968): 2 (inside cover).

24. John Fekete, "Telos at 50," in *Telos* 50 (1981–82): 164.

25. Robert A. McCaughey, *International Studies and Academic Enterprise: A Chapter in the Enclosure of American Learning* (New York: Columbia University Press, 1984), p. xiv.

26. Ibid., pp. 227, 254.

27. Ibid., pp. 232–33.

28. Marshall Windmiller, "The New American Mandarins," in *The Dissenting Academy*, ed. T. Roszak (New York: Vintage Books, 1968), pp. 112–13. There is a related matter to ponder: the role of the large private foundations both in virtually creating outfits, such as the Harvard Center for International Affairs, the MIT Center for International Studies, and the Center for Strategic Studies at Georgetown University, and in promoting select scholars and theories. See Edward H. Berman, *The Influence of the Carneigie, Ford and Rockefeller Foundations on American Foreign Policy: The Ideology of Philanthropy* (Albany: State University of New York Press, 1983), pp. 107, 121. Even the dominance of a "behavioral" approach to political conflict was decisively helped by funds from the Ford Foundation: in the early 1950s its Behavioral Science Division restructured the field by giving $23 million to select graduate depart-

ments, individual scholars and research institutes. See Peter J. Seybold, "The Ford Foundation and the Triumph of Behavioralism in American Political Science," in *Philanthropy and Cultural Imperialism: The Foundations at Home and Abroad*, ed. Robert F. Arnove (Boston: G. K. Hall, 1980), pp. 269–303. This volume contains a fascinating collection of essays on the impact of foundations.

29. David Halberstam, *The Best and the Brightest* (New York: Random House, 1972), pp. 390–91. See generally E. J. Kahn, Jr., in *The China Hands: America's Foreign Service Officers and What Befell Them* (New York: Viking, 1975). Owen Latimore commented in his autobiography:

> Looking back, I recall that my own thinking was not formed by any kind of theoretical dogma. The combination of an American family background, education in England, and the maturing effect of early business experience and independent travel . . . had given me a taste for observing and comparing facts . . . But I belonged to the last generation of Americans who could expect to train themselves by such easy, casual methods . . . Our future experts on these regions will have to work more in books and less in the field . . .

Owen Lattimore, *Ordeal by Slander* (Boston: Little, Brown, 1950), pp. 217–18. See also John King Fairbank, *Chinabound: A Fifty-Year Memoir* (New York: Harper and Row, 1982), p. 350.

30. David M. Ricci, *The Tragedy of Political Science: Politics, Scholarship and Democracy* (New Haven: Yale University Press, 1984), pp. ix–x.

31. Raymond Seidelman, with Edward J. Harpham, *Disenchanted Realists: Political Science and the American Crisis, 1884–1984* (Albany: State University of New York Press, 1985), p. 190.

32. Ricci, *Tragedy*, pp. 65, 224.

33. Ibid., pp. 221–222.

34. Ibid., pp. 196–197, 232–236.

35. Alvin Gouldner, *The Coming Crisis of Western Sociology* (New York: Avon, 1971), p. 286.

36. Ibid., pp. 57–58, 200–201.

37. Ibid., pp. 200–201.

38. With some hoopla, a Harvard graduate—and student of Parson's students—recently launched a four-volume set to redeem the theorist. Of course, Jeffrey Alexander's *Theoretical Logic in Sociology* may not return Parsons to his sociological throne. "Reviews of these four volumes have been almost unanimously negative," summarizes a reviewer, and their impact on the profession is "likely to be nil." This reviewer concludes that the issue is not the intellectual

Notes

merit of these books, which he considers not much above a standard textbook, but "academic warlordism—the pursuit of acclamation, vassals and the honours of fellowships and awards" (Stephen P. Turner, review of J. Alexander, *Theoretical Logic in Sociology*, vol. 4, in *Philosophy of the Social Sciences*, 15 [1985]: 521–22). Turner also reviewed the other three volumes in the same journal, 15: 77–82, 211–16, 365–68. See Alan Sica's brilliantly scathing discussion, "Parsons, Jr.," in *American Journal of Sociology*, 89 (1983): 200–19.

39. Patricia Wilner, "The Main Drift of Sociology Between 1936 and 1982," in *History of Sociology*, (Spring 1985) 2: 1–20.

40. Ricci, *Tragedy*, pp. 308–9.

41. Seidelman and Harpham, *Disenchanted Realists*, p. 226.

42. Robert Kuttner, "The Poverty of Economics," in *Atlantic Monthly*, February 1985, pp. 74–84.

43. Wassily Leontief, "Theoretical Assumptions and Nonobserved Facts," in his *Essays in Economics* (New Brunswick, N.J.: Transaction Books, 1985), pp. 272–82.

44. Leontief, "Introduction to the Transaction Edition: Academic Economics," in *Essays*, pp. xi–xii.

45. Kuttner, "The Poverty of Economics," p. 78.

46. Ibid., p. 84.

47. Donald M. McCloskey, *The Rhetoric of Economics* (Madison: University of Wisconsin Press, 1985), p. 7.

48. Ibid., pp. 4–5.

49. Ibid., p. 114.

50. Ibid., pp. 114, 121, 123.

51. Robert W. Fogel and G. R. Elton, *Which Road to the Past? Two Views of History* (New Haven: Yale University Press, 1983), pp. 64–65.

52. Ibid., pp. 62, 37.

53. Herbert G. Gutman, *Slavery and the Numbers Game: A Critique of "Time on the Cross"* (Urbana, Ill.: University of Illinois Press, 1975).

54. Robert W. Fogel and Stanley L. Engerman, *Time on the Cross: The Economics of American Negro Slavery* (Boston: Little, Brown, 1974), p. 145.

55. Gutman, *Slavery and the Numbers Game*, pp. 17–41. For another perspective, see Elizabeth Fox-Genovese and Eugene D. Genovese, "The Debate over *Time on the Cross*," in their *Fruits of Merchant Capital* (New York: Oxford University Press, 1983), pp. 136–71.

56. See Gregory S. Kealey, "Herbert G. Gutman, 1928–1985," in *Monthly Review*, 38 (May 1986): 22–30; Sean Wilentz, "Herbert Gutman 1928–1985," in *History Workshop* 22 (1986): 222–25; and Paul Buhle,

"Memories of Madison in the Fifties," in *Radical History Review*, 36 (1986): 101–9 (this includes interviews with Gutman and Warren Susman).

57. Herbert G. Gutman, *The Black Family in Slavery and Freedom, 1750–1925* (New York: Vintage Books, 1976), p. xvii.

58. See Lee Rainwater and William L. Yancey, *The Moynihan Report and the Politics of Controversy* (Cambridge, Mass.: MIT Press, 1967).

59. Herbert G. Gutman, *Work, Culture and Society* (New York: Vintage Books, 1977), p. xii.

60. For a discussion of its films and slide shows, see Jesse Lemisch, "I Dreamed I Saw MTV Last Night," in *The Nation*, October 18, 1986, p. 361.

61. Christopher Lasch, "Foreword," in Richard Hofstadter, *The American Political Tradition* (New York: Knopf, 1982), p. xix.

62. Susan P. Benson, Stephen Brier, and Roy Rosenzweig, "Introduction," in *Presenting the Past: Essays on History and the Public* (Philadelphia: Temple University Press, 1986), p. xvi. This collection is dedicated to Gutman.

63. Casey Blake, "Where Are the Young Left Historians?" in *Radical History Review*, 28–30 (1984): 115, 116.

64. Martin Jay, *Marxism and Totality* (Berkeley: University of California Press, 1984). To be sure, Jay lists over fifty Americans, whom he even calls a "distinct generation." It is clear, however, that they do not merit extended treatment; nor would they be acknowledged or known to any but other specialists; the list runs, alphabetically from Walter Adamson and Frank Adler to Jack Zipes and Sharon Zukin (p. 19).

65. Michael Clark, "Introduction," in "The Jameson Issue," in *New Orleans Review*, 11 (1984): 7.

66. Several journals have devoted entire issues to Jameson; see *New Orleans Review*, cited above, and *Diacritics* (Fall, 1982).

67. William C. Dowling, *Jameson, Althusser, Marx: An Introduction to "The Political Unconscious"* (Ithaca: Cornell University Press, 1984), pp. 94, 85.

68. Ibid., p. 10.

69. Fredric Jameson, "Postmodernism, or the Cultural Logic of Late Capitalism," in *New Left Review*, 146 (July–August 1984): 54–55.

70. Marco Dezzi-Bardeschi, "The Big Void," in *Domus* (Italy), 606 (1980): 16.

71. Jameson, "Postmodernism," 80.

72. Ibid., 81.

73. Ibid., 81.

74. Ibid., 82.

Notes

75. Michael F. Ross, "A Star for Tinseltown," in *Progressive Architecture*, February 1978, p. 52.

76. Paul Goldberger, *On The Rise: Architecture and Design in a Postmodern Age* (New York: Times Books, 1983), p. 88.

77. Ross, "A Star for Tinseltown," p. 53.

78. Ibid., p. 54.

79. Frank Lentricchia, *After the New Criticism* (Chicago: University of Chicago Press, 1980), pp. 170, 161.

80. Gerald Graff, *Literature Against Itself* (Chicago: University of Chicago Press, 1979), pp. 96–97.

81. Charles Newman, "The Post-Modern Aura: The Age of Fiction in an Age of Inflation," in *Salmagundi*, 63–64 (Spring/Summer 1984): 14.

82. Sinclair, *The Goose-Step*, p. 436.

83. Economics Education Project of the Union for Radical Political Economics (New York: Monthly Review Press, n.d. [1982?]), p. 7.

84. Samuel Bowles and Herbert Gintis, *Democracy and Capitalism: Property, Community and the Contradictions of Modern Social Thought* (New York: Basic Books, 1986), p. 215.

85. See also Josef Steindl, "Reflections on the Present State of Economics," in *Monthly Review*, 36 (February 1985) 9: 35–48.

86. Paul A. Attewell, *Radical Political Economy Since the Sixties: A Sociology of Knowledge Analysis* (New Brunswick, N.J.: Rutgers University Press, 1984), pp. 24, 27, 92.

87. As foreign-born and foreign-educated, he should be excluded by the terms I set out in the preface; however, since he closely collaborated with Sweezy and their *Monopoly Capital* is perhaps the key work of the *Monthly Review* group, Baran needs some discussion.

88. John Kenneth Galbraith, *A Life in Our Times* (Boston: Houghton Mifflin, 1981), pp. 219–20.

89. Paul M. Sweezy, "Paul Alexander Baran: A Personal Memoir," in *Paul A. Baran (1910–1964): A Collective Portrait*, ed. Paul M. Sweezy and Leo Huberman (New York: Monthly Review Press, 1965), p. 40.

90. Baran letter, June 30, 1961, cited in Sweezy, "Baran: A Personal Memoir, p. 57.

91. Michael Hillard, "Harry Magdoff and Paul Sweezy: Biographical Notes," in *Rethinking Marxism: Essays for Harry Magdoff and Paul Sweezy*, ed. S. Resnick and R. Wolff (New York: Autonomedia, 1985), p. 402.

92. See my review of Braverman in *Telos*, 29 (1976): 343–48.

93. Paul Baran, "The Commitment of the Intellectual," in *The Longer View*, ed. J. O'Neill (New York: Monthly Review Press, 1969), p. 14.

94. Sweezy, Huberman, eds., *Paul A. Baran (1910–1964)*.

95. Some of these remarks are taken from my "Graying of the Intellectuals," in *Dissent* (Spring 1983): 236.

96. Resnick and Wolff, eds., *Rethinking Marxism*.

97. All citations from Richard Peet, "Radical Geography in the United States: A Personal Account," in *Antipode*, 17 (1985): 3–4.

98. Ibid., 4.

99. See Noam Chomsky, "The Responsibility of Intellectuals," in his *American Power and the New Mandarins* (New York: Vintage Books, 1969) p. 323.

100. See the comparison of Macdonald and Chomsky in Stephen J. Whitfield, *A Critical American: The Politics of Dwight Macdonald* (Hamden, Conn.: Archon Books, 1984), pp. 113–16.

101. Chomsky, *American Power*, p. 30.

102. Noam Chomsky, *Problems of Knowledge and Freedom* (New York: Vintage, 1971), p. 75.

103. See Christopher Lasch, "Politics as Social Control" in his *New Radicalism in America 1889–1963* (New York: Knopf, 1965), pp. 141–80.

104. Alvin Gouldner, who sketched a theory of intellectuals as possible reformers, was much closer to the mainstream than he imagined. See his *The Future of Intellectuals and the Rise of the New Class* (New York: Continuum, 1979).

105. See Bernie Fels, "The Academy and Its Discontents," in *Telos*, 40 (1979): 173–77.

106. Cited by Richard Hofstadter, *Anti-Intellectualism in American Life* (New York: Vintage Books, 1963), pp. 200–201.

107. Seidelman and Harpham, *Disenchanted Realists*, pp. 198–200.

108. Theda Skocpol, "Sociology's Historical Imagination," in *Vision and Method in Historical Sociology*, ed. T. Skocpol (Cambridge: Cambridge University Press, 1984), p. 8. She goes on to argue, however, that this academic success actually masks the marginal status of historical sociologists. Perhaps.

109. Skocpol offers a "map" of historical sociology situating various figures, including herself. See "Emerging Agendas and Recurrent Strategies in Historical Sociology," in *Vision and Method in Historical Sociology*, ed. T. Skocpol, p. 363.

110. See Carl Boggs, *The Two Revolutions: Gramsci and the Dilemmas of Western Marxism* (Boston: South End Press, 1984).

111. See my remarks in *Dialectic of Defeat: Contours of Western Marxism* (Cambridge: Cambridge University Press, 1981), pp. 1–36.

112. William Buxton comments that the critics of Parsonian sociology have substituted one reductionist scheme for another. See W. Buxton, *Talcott Par-*

Notes

sons and the Capitalist Nation-State: Political Sociology as a Strategic Vocation (Toronto: University of Toronto Press, 1985), pp. 260, 296.

113. Carl Boggs, "The Intellectuals and Social Movements: Some Reflections on Academic Marxism," in Humanities in Society, 6 (1983): 228.

114. Erik Olin Wright, Class, Crisis and the State (London: NLB, 1978), pp. 9–10.

115. Ibid., p. 11.

116. Ibid., p. 25.

117. Ibid., p. 108.

118. Immanuel Wallerstein, "Radical Intellectuals in a Liberal Society," in The University Crisis Reader, ed. I. Wallerstein and P. Starr, vol. 2 (New York: Random House, 1971), pp. 475–76.

119. Immanuel Wallerstein, The Politics of the World-Economy (Cambridge: Cambridge University Press, 1984), pp. 183–84.

120. See generally Charles Ragin and Daniel Chirot, "The World System of Immanuel Wallerstein," in Vision and Method in Historical Sociology, ed. T. Skocpol, pp. 276–312.

Chapter 7 / After the Last Intellectuals

1. Lewis Mumford, Sketches from Life (New York: Dial Press, 1982), pp. 125–26, 213–14, 220–21.

2. The Lewis Mumford-David Liebovitz Letters 1923–1968, ed. B. L. Knapp (Troy, N.Y.: Whitston, 1983), p. 188.

3. Mumford, Sketches, p. 190.

4. See Thomas S. W. Lewis, "Mumford and the Academy," Salmagundi, 49 (Summer 1980): 99–111.

5. Letters of Lewis Mumford and Frederic J. Osborn, ed. M. R. Hughes (Bath: Adams and Dart, 1971), p. 431.

6. Lewis Mumford, "Emerson's Journals" (1968), reprinted in his Interpretations and Forecasts: 1922–1972 (New York, Harcourt Brace, 1973), pp. 107–8.

7. Ibid., p. 108.

8. Alfred Kazin, New York Jew (New York: Vintage Books, 1979), p. 374.

9. Edmund Wilson, "Thoughts on Being Bibiliographed" (1944), in The Portable Edmund Wilson, ed. Lewis M. Dabney (New York: Viking Penguin, 1983), pp. 112–13.

10. Edmund Wilson, "The Fruits of the MLA" (1968), in his The Devils

and Canon Barham (New York: Farrar, Straus and Giroux, 1973), pp. 154–202.

11. Gordon N. Ray, *Professional Standards and American Editions: A Response to Edmund Wilson* (New York: Modern Language Association, 1969), p. i.

12. See John Gross, *The Rise and Fall of the Man-of-Letters* (New York: Macmillan, 1969).

13. Cited in Richard Hofstadter, *Anti-Intellectualism in American Life* (New York: Vintage Books, 1963), pp. 147–49.

14. Robert Nisbet, *The Degradation of the Academic Dogma* (New York: Basic Books, 1971), pp. 71–72.

15. Ibid., pp. 82, 86, 72–73.

16. Frederick Crews, "Criticism Without Constraint," in *Commentary*, 73 (January 1982): 65–71.

17. Robert Alter, "The Decline and Fall of Literary Criticism," in *Commentary*, 77 (March 1984): 51.

18. See the exemplary study by Peter Steinfels, *The Neoconservatives* (New York: Simon and Schuster, 1980), esp., pp. 188–213.

19. Will Herberg, "The New Estate," published originally in *National Review* (1965), reprinted in *Teach-Ins: U.S.A.*, ed. L. Menashe and R. Radosh (New York: Praeger, 1967), p. 102.

20. Noam Chomsky, *Language and Responsibility*, trans. John Viertel (New York: Pantheon, 1979), pp. 6–7, 8.

21. Joseph Epstein, "Reviewing and Being Reviewed," *New Criterion*, 1 (1982): 40.

22. Alfred Kazin, "Saving My Soul at the Plaza," in *New York Review of Books*, March 31, 1983, p. 38.

23. Stephen H. Balch, "Radical Delusions," in *Society*, 23 (March–April 1986): 3. This is part of a symposium, "The Politicization of Scholarship."

24. Stanley Rothman, "Academics on the Left," in *Society*, 23 (March–April 1986): 4–8.

25. Edward Shils, "Lewis Mumford," in *New Criterion*, 1 (1983), 9: 38, 43.

26. William F. Buckley, Jr., *God and Man at Yale: The Superstitions of 'Academic Freedom'* (Chicago: Henry Regnery, 1951), p. 172.

27. Ibid., pp. 169–70.

28. Russell Kirk, *Decadence and Renewal in the Higher Learning* (South Bend, Ind.: Gateway, 1978), pp. 18–19.

29. Russell Kirk, *Academic Freedom* (Chicago: Henry Regnery, 1955), pp.

Notes

136, 158, 165; see also his "Ethics of Censorship," in *Beyond the Dreams of Avarice* (Chicago: Henry Regnery, 1956), pp. 101–32.

30. See William L. O'Neill, *A Better World* (New York: Simon and Schuster, 1982) p. 333.

31. Sidney Hook, *Heresy, Yes. Conspiracy, No* (New York: John Day, 1953), p. 208.

32. Ibid., p. 209.

33. See Sidney Hook, *Academic Freedom and Academic Anarchy* (New York: Cowles, 1970).

34. Sidney Hook, *Pragmatism and the Tragic Sense of Life* (New York: Basic Books, 1974), p. 93. This is not the obsolete voice of a cranky conservative. Recent writings by conservatives regularly call to limit academic freedom. Conservatives hate the state and love the state police. Joseph Epstein believes too much political claptrap is being taught in universities. In fact one of his colleagues serves up all kinds of nonsense. "Twenty or so years ago he would have been told to knock off the politics and teach the books. Today even senior professors are fearful of interfering with what they wrongly construe to be his academic freedom . . ." (Joseph Epstein, "Anti-Americanism and Other Cliches," in *Commentary*, April 1983, p. 63). Exactly what "senior professors" knew about academic freedom "twenty or so years ago" is unclear.

35. According to Hans Haacke, as cited by Connie Samaras, "Sponsorship or Censorship?" in *New Art Examiner*, November 1985, p. 24:

> Hilton Kramer's journal is generously subsidized by three wealthy right-wing foundations. For the years 1982 and 1983 alone he got about three quarters of a million dollars. Anyone familiar with publishing knows that this is an awful lot of money for putting out a journal that doesn't carry illustrations other than advertising. . . . One of the three, the John M. Olin Foundation in New York, is the "philanthropic" arm of the Olin Corporation, a company which produces ammunition and other war material. . . . In the '70s the Olin Corporation was found guilty by a federal judge of having illegally supplied its arms and bullets to South Africa. Also, in other respects it has a noteworthy record. It includes the illegal dumping of mercury, price fixing, strike breaking, and questionable payments to foreign government officials. . . . The foundation's president was recently listed by the *New York Times* among the individuals who are collecting money to bankroll the Contras. . . .

Presumably this economic support does not affect the political orientation of Kramer's journal; this would be a case of "politicizing" culture, a left-wing disease.

270

36. He provided over $2 million to General William Westmoreland—more than 70 percent of the costs—for his suit against CBS's documentary, "The Uncounted Enemy: A Vietnam Deception." See Walter and Miriam Schneir, "The Right's Attack on the Press," in *The Nation*, March 30, 1985, pp. 361–67.

37. Michael Useem, "The Rise of Corporate Politics and the Decline of Academic Freedom," in *Regulating the Intellectuals*, ed. C. Kaplan and E. Schrecker (New York: Praeger, 1983), p. 110.

38. *Public Interest*, 81 (Fall 1985).

39. Buckley, *God and Man*, pp. 186–89.

40. Joseph Epstein, *Ambition* (New York: Penguin Books, 1982), pp. 274–75.

41. Kenneth S. Lynn, *The Air-Line to Seattle* (Chicago: University of Chicago Press, 1983), p. 32. If Lynn knew something about Marxism, he might have had a better time with Marx, who was often supported by a capitalist and factory owner—Engels.

42. H. L. Mencken, "The Dismal Science," in *Prejudices: Third Series* (New York: Knopf, 1922), pp. 280, 282–83.

43. Ibid., p. 283.

44. Ibid., p. 288.

45. Richard Sennett, *Uses of Disorder: Personal Identity and City Life* (New York: Vintage Books, 1970), p. vii.

46. Marshall Berman, *All That is Solid Melts Into Air* (New York: Simon and Schuster, 1982), pp. 146–47.

47. Sheldon Wolin, review of *The Fall of Public Man*, in *New York Review of Books*, April 14, 1977, p. 19.

48. Richard Sennett, *Authority* (New York: Vintage Books, 1981), p. 10.

49. Ibid., p. 168.

50. Berman, *All That Is Solid*, pp. 120–21.

51. Ibid., pp. 315, 324.

52. Ibid., pp. 295–96, 309.

53. Ibid., p. 171.

54. Sennett, *Authority*, p. 187.

55. Berman, *All That Is Solid*, p. 36.

56. Ibid., p. 340.

57. Ibid., pp. 342–43.

58. Ibid., p. 343.

59. Ibid., p. 345.

60. Richard Sennett, *The Fall of Public Man* (New York: Vintage Books, 1978), p. 282.

Notes

61. Norman Podhoretz, "Book Reviewing and Everyone I Know" (1963), in his *Doings and Undoings* (New York: Noonday, 1964), p. 260.

62. Renata Adler, "Polemic and the New Reviewers," published originally in *The New Yorker*, (1964), reprinted in her *Toward a Radical Middle* (New York: Random House, 1974), pp. 102–3.

63. Adler, "Polemic," p. 117.

64. Philip Nobile, *Intellectual Skywriting: Literary Politics and the New York Review of Books* (New York: Charterhouse, 1974), pp. 189–90.

65. Almost any issue reveals this orientation. For instance, the February 14, 1985, edition has twelve major reviews, seven by Americans, including two by old independent contributors, Mary McCarthy and Theodore Draper; five are heavily weighted toward Ivy League and titled professors, Sterling Professor History Emertius at Yale, Edgar Pierde Professor of Philosophy at Harvard, and professors at MIT and Columbia: The other five are by English academics and writers, Chichel Professor of Modern History at Oxford, Fellow of Merton College, Oxford, Warburg Institute, and so on.

66. For instance, see *The Young American Writers*, ed. Richard Kostelanetz (New York: Funk and Wagnalls, 1967).

67. See Richard Kostelanetz, *The End of Intelligent Writing: Literary Politics in America* (New York: Sheed and Ward, 1974).

68. See Nancy K. Rodery, "The Library Labor Market," in *Bowker Annual of Library and Book Trade Information* (New York: Bowker, 1984), pp. 283–90.

69. See Lewis A. Coser, Charles Kadushin, and Walter W. Powell, *Books: The Culture and Commerce of Publishing* (New York: Basic Books, 1982), pp. 232–33.

70. Wilson, "Thoughts on Being Bibliographed, p. 109.

71. James Fallows, "The New Celebrities of Washington," in *New York Review of Books*, June 12, 1986, p. 47.

72. Some estimates in John W. C. Johnstone, Edward M. Slawski, and William W. Bowman, *The News People* (Urbana, Ill.: University of Illinois Press, 1976), pp. 18–19.

73. William A. Tillinghast, "Declining Newspaper Readership," in *Journalism Quarterly*, 58 (1981): 14. For statistics and discussion of the impact of the concentration of the media on an individual's "freedom of expression" see Bruce M. Owen, *Economics and the Freedom of Expression* (Cambridge, Mass.: Ballinger, 1975), esp. pp. 33–85. For a more positive view of the role of newspapers, especially in relationship to television, see Philip Weiss and Laurence Zuckerman, "The Shadow of a Medium," *Columbia Journalism Review* 25 (1987): 33–39.

74. Ben H. Bagdikian, *The Media Monopoly* (Boston: Beacon Press, 1983), p. 198.

75. David Sachsman, Warren Sloat, *The Press and the Suburbs: The Daily Newspapers of New Jersey* (New Brunswick, N.J.: State University of New Jersey, 1985), pp. 28–32.

76. Loren Ghiglione, "Introduction," in *The Buying and Selling of America's Newspapers*, ed. L. Ghiglione (Indianapolis: R. J. Berg, 1984), p. xi. Of course, as this collection is at pains to show, sometimes the buy-out improves a mediocre local product.

77. Bagdikian, *Media*, p. 126.

78. See generally Paul W. Kingston and Jonathan R. Cole, "Summary of Findings of the Columbia University Economic Survey of American Authors," in *Art and the Law*, 6 (1981) 4: 83–95.

79. See "Newhouse Ties into New Yorker," in *Advertising Age*, November 19, 1984, p. 97; "New Yorker Takes a Turn," in *Advertising Age*, March 11, 1985, p. 1.

80. Morris Dickstein, *Gates of Eden: American Culture in the Sixties* (New York: Basic Books, 1977), pp. 132–33.

81. Tom Wolfe, "The New Journalism," in *The New Journalism*, ed. T. Wolfe and E. W. Johnson (New York: Harper and Row, 1973), pp. 28, 32.

82. James Agee and Walker Evans, *Let Us Now Praise Famous Men* (New York: Ballantine Books, 1966), pp. xiv, 7.

83. The first selections to Wolfe's anthology were by Rex Reed, Gay Talese, Richard Goldstein, Michael Herr, Truman Capote, Joe Eszterhas, and Terry Southern.

84. Norman Sims, "The Literary Journalists," in *The Literary Journalists*, ed. N. Sims (New York: Ballantine Books, 1984), p. 4.

85. Abe Peck, *Uncovering the Sixties: The Life and Times of the Underground Press* (New York: Pantheon, 1985), p. 270.

86. Ibid., pp. xvi, 298.

87. Ibid., pp. 299–325.

88. See Michael Schudson, *Discovering the News* (New York: Basic Books, 1978), pp. 187–92.

89. Joan Walsh, "The Mother Jones Story," in *In These Times*, September 24–30, 1986, pp. 8–9.

90. Leonard Downie, Jr., *The New Muckrakers* (Washington, D.C.: New Republic Books, 1976), p. 230.

91. Insofar as the large newspapers themselves are controlled by even larger corporations, the commitment, or at least the scope, of staff investigative report-

Notes

ing will probably be limited. See Peter Dreier, Steve Weinberg, "Interlocking Directorates," in *Columbia Journalism Review* 18 (1979): 51–68.

92. I. F. Stone, *The Haunted Fifties* (1963; reprint, New York: Vintage Books, 1969), p. xv.

93. Robert Sklar, "Introduction," in I. F. Stone, *The Truman Era* (New York: Random House, 1972), pp. xi–xii.

94. Is it an accident that several of the very few socialist free-lance writers who write trenchantly and think boldly are not American by birth or education but English? Is an English dissenting tradition less vulnerable to the pressures of profession and bureaucracy?

95. Clara Gebert, "Introduction," in *An Anthology of Elizabethan Dedications and Prefaces*, ed. C. Gebert (New York: Russell and Russell, 1966), p. 25.

96. Erich Auerbach, *Literary Language and Its Public* (New York: Bollingen, 1965), p. 334.

97. Guicciardini, as cited by Giorgio de Santillana, *The Crime of Galileo* (Chicago: University of Chicago Press, 1959), p. 119.

98. Santillana, *Crime of Galileo*, p. 15.

INDEX

Abel, Lionel (1910–   ), 50, 100

Abraham, David (1946–   ), 136, 260n66

Academic Freedom and Academic Anarchy (Hook), 104

Academic intellectuals, 6, 7, 14–19, 73–74; criteria for success of, 144–46; criticism of, 141–44; Marxist, 4, 166–90; and New Left, 118–19, 130–39; professionalization and, 147–66; radicalism and, 124–30

Adler, Renata (1938–   ), 217–18

Advertisements for Myself (Mailer), 101

Affluent Society, The (Galbraith), 9

Agee, James (1909–55), 227–28

"Age of Conformity, The" (Howe), 82

Age of Imperialism, The (Magdoff), 179

Age of Reform, The (Hofstadter), 80

Air-Line to Seattle, The (Lynn), 207

Aldridge, John W. (1922–   ), 72–73

Alexander, Jeffrey, 263n38

All That Is Solid Melts into Air (Berman), 210, 211, 216

All the President's Men (film), 222

Althusser, Louis, 187

Ambition (Epstein), 207

America and the Young Intellectual (Stearns), *ix*

American Economic Review, The, 160

American Mercury, The, 192

American Philosophical Association, 139

American Political Science Association, 155

American Political Science Review, 157

American Radicals (Goldberg), 259n62

American Scholar, 134, 196, 200, 201

American Social History Project, 165

American Social Hygiene Association, 204

American Sociological Association, 185

American Sociological Review, 158

American Tobacco Company, 38

Anarchism, 96–100, 180, 182–83, 199

Anticommunism, 77

Anti-Federalism in Dutchess County, New York (Lynd), 121

Anti-Intellectualism in American Life (Hofstadter), 80, 81, 111

Antipode, 134, 181, 182

Architectural Forum, 58

Architecture, postmodern, 169–72

Aronowitz, Stanley (1933–   ), 120, 122–24, 210

Art in America, 51

Arvin, Newton, Jr. (1900–1963), 73, 109

Associated Press, 229

Association of American Geographers, 181

275

Index

Index

Index

Index

Index

Modernism, 212–16

Modern Language Association (MLA), 139, 193–95

Modern World-System, The (Wallerstein), 189

Mollenkopf, John H., 243n49

Monopoly Capital (Baran and Sweezy), 176, 178–80, 266n87

Monthly Review, 176, 178–80, 266n87

Moscow Trials, 97

Moses, Robert, 42–44, 47, 213

Mother Jones, 229, 230

Motherwell, Robert, 33

Moynihan, Daniel P., 165

Muckraking, 142, 227, 230–31

Mumford, Lewis (1895–   ), 9, 17, 25, 47, 55, 57, 74, 176, 179, 191–94, 226; conservative attack on, 203; critique of Jacobs by, 245n8; on mass transportation, 41, 59; on Moses, 42; as public intellectual, 167, 168; on Veblen, 95

Murger, Henry, 27

Must You Conform? (Lindner), 63

Myth of the Machine, The, 91

Nabokov, Vladimir, 109

Nation, The, 24, 96

National Book Award, 225

National Guard, 114

National Review, 87

Nazism, 31, 97, 106

Nearing, Scott (1883–1983), 125, 126, 209

Negro Family in America, The (Moynihan), 165

Neoconservatism, 77; rise of, 4

New American Library, 75

Newark News, 224

"New class," 108–9

New Criterion, The, 113–14, 196, 198, 200, 201, 206, 220

New Deal, 178

Newfield, Jack (1938–   ), 112–13

New German Critique, 122

New Journalism, The (Wolfe), 227

New Left, 87, 99, 100, 112–90; and academic intellectuals, 130–39, 166–90, 235; and Aronowitz, 122–24; and Lynd, 120–22; and Mills, 115–19

Newman, Charles, 173

New Men of Power, The (Mills), 94

New Political Science, 134

New Radicals, The (Landau and Jacobs), 133

New Republic, The, 15, 73, 149, 252n77

New School for Social Research, 128–30

New Sociology, The (Horowitz), 118

Newsweek, 244n66

New Voices, 74–75

New World Writing, 75

New Writers, 75

New York, State University of: at Albany, 131; at Binghamton, 189; at Buffalo, 151, 152

New York Daily Compass, 231

New Yorker, The, 9, 15, 22, 24, 74, 110–11, 217, 226

New York intellectuals, 78, 81, 100–103, 210–20, 253n88; and cult of science, 161; *see also* Jewish intellectuals

New York Jew (Kazin), 84, 101

New York Public Library, 74

New York Review of Books, The, 9, 11, 12, 24, 217–20, 239nn6, 9

Index

Index

Sica, Alan, 264n38

Silber, John, 137, 260n67

Silent Spring (Carson), 98

Silvers, Robert (1929–), 10, 11, 239n6

Sinclair, Upton (1878–1968), 15, 174

Sklar, Martin (1935–), 120

Sklar, Robert, 231

Skocpol, Theda, 185, 189, 267nn108, 109

Slavery and the Numbers Game (Gutman), 163

Slesinger, Tess, 100

Smith, Adam, 235

Smith, John E. (1921–), 150

Smith College, 202

Smith Kline Corporation, 206

Snyder, Gary, 70

Socialist Geography Specialty Group, 181

Socialist Scholars Conference, 133

Social Justice and the City (Harvey), 56

Social Life of Small Urban Spaces, The (Whyte), 60

Social Science Citation Index, The, 146

Social Text, 122, 198

Social Transformation of American Medicine, The (Starr), 136

Sociology: historical, 185; Marxist, 187–89; professionalization of, 157–58

SoHo, 51, 52

Solotaroff, Theodore (1928–), 11

Sontag, Susan (1933–), 10, 11, 24, 219

Southern, Terry, 273n83

Southwestern Oklahoma State University, 137

Soviet Union: charges against Trotsky by, 149; disenchantment with, 81; pact with Nazis, 97

Spanish Anarchists (Bookchin), 98

Spillane, Mickey, 75

Spirit of American Philosophy, The (Smith), 150

Sputnik, 130

Stalin, Josef, 106

Stalinism, 176

Stanford University, 177

Stansell, Christine, 260n66

Starr, Paul (1949–), 136, 188

Stearns, Harold (1891–1943), *ix,* 12, 16

Sterling, George (1869–1926), 35–36

Stevenson, Adlai, 81

Stone, I. F. (1907–), 178, 230–31

Story of Utopias, The (Mumford), 191

Structure of Social Action, The (Parson), 157

Student movement, *see* New Left

Student Non-Violent Coordinating Committee (SNCC), 114

Student Peace Union (SPU), 114

Students for a Democratic Society (SDS), 114, 132; Port Huron Statement of, 117

Studies on the Left, 119–20, 122–24, 131, 133

Suber, Peter D., 262n22

Suburbs: boredom of, 44–45; growth of, 40–44; shopping malls in, 45–47; trend away from, 47–48; urbanists on, 59

Sukenick, Ronald (1932–), 39

Index